Middle East Conflict

Biographies

SECOND EDITION

Middle East Conflict

Biographies

SECOND EDITION

Carol Brennan
Sonia G. Benson, Contributing Writer
Jennifer Stock, Project Editor

U·X·L
A part of Gale, Cengage Learning

GALE
CENGAGE Learning·

Detroit • New York • San Francisco • New Haven, Conn • Waterville, Maine • London

GALE
CENGAGE Learning

Middle East Conflict: Biographies, 2nd Edition
Carol Brennan, Sonia G. Benson

Project Editor: Jennifer Stock

Rights Acquisition and Management: Christine Myaskvoksy

Composition: Evi Abou-El-Seoud

Manufacturing: Wendy Blurton

Imaging: John Watkins

Product Design: Kristine Julien

For product information and technology assistance, contact us at **Gale Customer Support, 1-800-877-4253.**
For permission to use material from this text or product, submit all requests online at **www.cengage.com/permissions.**
Further permissions questions can be emailed to **permissionrequest@cengage.com**

Cover photographs reproduced by permission of Bettmann/Corbis (Ayatollah Khomeini greeting followers in Tehran, Iran, after returning from exile in 1979), Peter Horree/Alamy (Mustafa Kemal Atatürk), and Manahem Kahana/AFP/Getty Image (Benjamin Netanyahu). Cover art reproduced by permission of Shutterstock.com (border image and arabic classical ornament).

While every effort has been made to ensure the reliability of the information presented in this publication, Gale, a part of Cengage Learning, does not guarantee the accuracy of the data contained herein. Gale accepts no payment for listing; and inclusion in the publication of any organization, agency, institution, publication, service, or individual does not imply endorsement of the editors or publisher. Errors brought to the attention of the publisher and verified to the satisfaction of the publisher will be corrected in future editions.

Library of Congress Cataloging-in-Publication Data

Middle East conflict reference library / [Jennifer Stock, project editor]. -- 2nd ed.
    v. cm.
    "U-X-L Reference Library".
    Includes bibliographical references and index.
    Contents: 1. Almanac / Sonia Benson -- 2. Biographies / Carol Brennan -- 3. Primary sources / Terri Schell.
    ISBN 978-1-4144-8607-9 (set) -- ISBN 978-1-4144-8608-6 (almanac) -- ISBN 978-1-4144-8609-3 (biographies) -- ISBN 978-1-4144-8610-9 (primary sources)
    1. Arab-Israeli conflict--Sources--Juvenile literature. 2. Arab-Israeli conflict--Juvenile literature. 3. Middle East--History--Juvenile literature. I. Stock, Jennifer York, 1974- II. Benson, Sonia. Almanac. III. Brennan, Carol, 1966- Biographies. IV. Schell, Terri, 1968- Primary sources.
    DS119.7.M4713 2012
    956.04--dc23   2011050994

Gale
27500 Drake Rd.
Farmington Hills, MI, 48331-3535

ISBN-13: 978-1-4144-8607-9 (set)
ISBN-13: 978-1-4144-8608-6 (Almanac)
ISBN-13: 978-1-4144-8609-3 (Biographies)
ISBN-13: 978-1-4144-8610-9 (Primary Sources)
ISBN-13: 978-1-4144-8612-3 (Cumulative Index)

ISBN-10: 1-4144-8607-3 (set)
ISBN-10: 1-4144-8608-1 (Almanac)
ISBN-10: 1-4144-8609-X (Biographies)
ISBN-10: 1-4144-8610-3 (Primary Sources)
ISBN-10: 1-4144-8612-X (Cumulative Index)

This title is also available as an e-book.
ISBN-13: 978-1-4144-9087-8 ISBN-10: 1-4144-9087-9
Contact your Gale, a part of Cengage Learning sales representative for ordering information.

Printed in China
1 2 3 4 5 6 7 16 15 14 13 12

Table of Contents

Reader's Guide

From the early twentieth century to present times, no region in the world has been so badly torn by conflict as the Middle East and North Africa. What is most striking about the many conflicts that have occurred in the Middle East is their complexity. For many years differences over religion, cultural identity, and political philosophy have combined with tribal and ethnic biases to fan the flames of conflict. Western imperialism and influence, as well as the struggle between modernization and traditionalism, have also played important roles in Middle East conflict. Untangling these numerous and overlapping elements presents a challenge to even the most experienced scholars and diplomats.

Even the term "Middle East" is somewhat complicated. Because the region is not strictly defined by geography, culture, or language, its definition has never been precise. The term was originally coined by Europeans (for whom Asia lies to the east). In the nineteenth century Europeans used the term "Near East" to distinguish areas of western Asia that were closer to Europe than the "Far East," the area that includes Southeast Asia, China, Japan, and Korea. In the twentieth century, the newer term "Middle East" came to replace "Near East," denoting the same basic area of Western Asia.

The nations that are most often included as part of the Middle East in the twenty-first century are: Saudi Arabia, Yemen, Oman, Qatar, Kuwait, Bahrain, the United Arab Emirates, Israel, the Palestinian territories, Jordan, Lebanon, Syria, Iraq, and Iran. Turkey, which is located in western Asia and also in Europe, is considered part of the Middle East due to its location and its many cultural and historical connections to the region. Egypt, although geographically part of North Africa, is also considered a Middle Eastern nation. Other North African states, notably

Libya, Algeria, Tunisia, Morocco, and sometimes Sudan, are included as part of the Middle East by many authorities.

To understand the conflicts that have shaped the Middle East, one must keep in mind a variety of important forces that have shaped the region. The oldest and most enduring force is that of religion. The Middle East is home to three of the world's great monotheistic (belief in one god) religions—Judaism, Christianity, and Islam. Each of these religions has deep roots in the Middle East and places great importance on religious shrines and temples that continue to exist in the region, especially in the fiercely contested city of Jerusalem, in present-day Israel. Religious differences, both those between the religions and those that arise among sects (groups) within the same religion, such as followers of the Sunni and Shiite branches of Islam, continue to play an important role in the Middle East.

Other sources of conflict are based in the Middle East's long political history. The region's ancient cultures were shaped and influenced by the rule of the Islamic empires, whose great caliphs were the spiritual, political, and military leaders of the world's Muslims from the seventh to the thirteenth century, and then by the Ottoman Empire, whose sultans ruled over an area encompassing most of the Middle East and North Africa and a large part of southeastern Europe for six hundred years, from 1299 to 1923. After the relatively stable rule of these great Muslim empires, many Middle East countries came under the rule of Western governments in the early twentieth century. Foreigners divided the Middle East into separate countries without regard to the cultures and politics of the inhabitants. The internal politics of the new nations often arose in opposition to foreign rule. After gaining independence from Western rule, many of the countries of the Middle East fell under the power of authoritarian leaders with powerful security forces.

In addition to the enduring influence of religion and Western power, other hostilities have contributed to conflict in the Middle East. Ethnic differences have often resulted in wars among groups such as the Arabs, Persians, and Turks, to name a few. Armenians and Kurds (a non-Arab ethnic group) struggled to establish self-rule over their own territories. The Armenians have been successful, but the Kurds remain the largest ethnic group in the world without a country of their own.

The flashpoint for much of the conflict in the Middle East has been the area of present-day Israel and the Palestinian territories. This region, known historically as Palestine, was home to the ancient Jewish kingdom. The Jews were expelled from Palestine as other ancient empires took control of the region, especially the Romans. As the centuries passed they faced anti-Semitism (prejudice against Jews) throughout the world. Then, in the nineteenth century, the Zionist movement arose calling for the creation of an independent Jewish state in Palestine. By this time Palestine had been home to Arabs for hundreds of years, and both groups pressed their claim to this land. The Jews were better organized, both politically and militarily, and in 1948 they declared the creation of the state of Israel. In the mid–twentieth century, Arabs fought against the Jewish state of Israel in a series of Arab-Israeli Wars. Arab Palestinians continue to claim the land that they believe was stolen from them, and they have sought various means—ranging from terrorism to political negotiation—to express their political will.

One of the driving forces of the conflicts in the Middle East since the mid–twentieth century has been oil. Oil has dramatically increased the wealth of those countries that produce it—especially Iran, Iraq, Kuwait, and Saudi Arabia—but it has not brought those countries peace, democracy, or political stability. In each of these countries, oil wealth has been controlled by a select few who hold power in the government. Foreign powers have worked aggressively to ensure that the oil-producing countries behave in ways that do not threaten foreign access to oil. Tensions created between various parties vying for control of oil in these countries causes ongoing conflict.

In 2011, the nature of Middle East conflict took a sudden, unexpected, and far-reaching turn when a series of prodemocracy uprisings rapidly spread throughout countries of the Middle East and North Africa that had long been suppressed by authoritarian rulers. Through their courageous efforts, the people of several Middle Eastern countries have overthrown their authoritarian leaders and worked create democratic governments. The place in history that this powerful prodemocracy movement, known as the Arab Spring, will take may be better understood in future times, but it has provided enormous insight into the causes and consequences of Middle East conflicts in modern times.

Coverage and features

Middle East Conflict: Biographies, 2nd Edition profiles thirty-five of the most influential figures from throughout the Middle East and North Africa. The volume profiles kings, presidents, and other political leaders, as well as activists and militants. Included are Iranian president

Mahmoud Ahmadinejad, Lebanese politician Pierre Gemayel, Jewish author and activist Theodor Herzl, Libyan leader Mu'ammar al-Qaddafi, Israeli prime minister Benjamin Netanyahu, and Egyptian president Anwar Sadat. Also included are prominent female leaders Golda Meir and Tzipporah Livni of Israel and Palestinian activist Hanan Ashrawi. The volume includes more than ninety photographs and illustrations, a timeline, sources for further reading, and an index.

Middle East Conflict Reference Library, 2nd Edition

Middle East Conflict: Almanac, 2nd Edition examines the historical events that have contributed to conflicts in the in the Middle East and North Africa and traces developments to the present day. The volume's sixteen chapters cover the ancient Middle East, the rise and fall of the Ottoman Empire, the creation of Israel, the Palestinian Authority, the rise of Hezbollah in Lebanon, the Gulf Wars, terrorism, the Arab Spring uprisings, and more. Each chapter features informative sidebar boxes highlighting glossary terms and issues discussed in the text. Also included are more than one hundred photographs and illustrations, a timeline, a glossary, a list of research and activity ideas, sources for further reading, and an index providing easy access to subjects discussed throughout the volume.

Middle East Conflict: Primary Sources, 2nd Edition presents twenty-nine full or excerpted written works, poems, proclamations, or other documents relating to conflict in the Middle East and North Africa, divided into eight thematically organized chapters. Among the historic documents included are the Peel Commission Report of 1937, which recommended the division of Palestine into Arab and Jewish states; the 1948 declaration establishing the nation of Israel; and the 1968 Palestinian National Charter, which stated the goals of the Palestinian people. The volume also features personal accounts and artistic works, including an account by journalist Terry Anderson describing his time as a hostage in Lebanon and excerpts from the graphic novels *Palestine* and *Persepolis*. Also included are documents relating to the Arab Spring uprisings. More than eighty photographs and illustrations, a timeline, sources for further reading, and an index supplement the volume.

A cumulative index of all three volumes in *Middle East Conflict Reference Library, 2nd Edition* is also available.

Acknowledgements

The editors would like to thank the advisor for *Middle East Conflict Reference Library, 2nd Edition*, Michael R. Fischbach, PhD. Dr. Fischbach is a Professor of History at Randolph-Macon College, in Ashland, Virginia. He specializes in the history of the modern Middle East, especially Palestine, Israel, Jordan, and the Arab-Israeli conflict.

The editors also would like to acknowledge Tom and Sara Pendergast, authors of the first edition of *Middle East Conflict Reference Library*.

Comments and suggestions

We welcome your comments on *Middle East Conflict: Biographies, 2nd Edition* and suggestions for other topics to consider. Please write: Editors, *Middle East Conflict: Biographies, 2nd Edition*, Gale Cengage Learning, 27500 Drake Road, Farmington Hills, Michigan 48331-3535; call toll free: 1-800-877-4253; fax to 248-699-8097; or send e-mail via http://www.gale.cengage.com.

Timeline of Events

7000 BCE: The first-known human civilizations begin to form in Mesopotamia, the site of present-day Iraq and parts of Syria, Turkey, and Iran.

2700 BCE: Egyptian society has developed into a sophisticated civilization.

c. 1030 BCE: Israelites, descendants of the Hebrew patriarch Abraham and ancestors of the Jews, take control of Canaan and call their kingdom Eretz Yisrael.

970–931 BCE: The First Temple of Solomon, which will become the center of the Jewish faith, is built in Jerusalem.

587–518 BCE: The First Temple of Solomon is destroyed by Babylonians and a second temple is built on the site.

146 BCE–476 CE: Most of the Mediterranean region comes under the control of the Roman Empire.

66–73 CE: In the Great Revolt, the Jews rise up against Roman rule; the Romans, in return, destroy the Second Temple.

c. 312: Constantine I, emperor of the Eastern Roman (later Byzantine) Empire, embraces Christianity and proclaims it the official religion of the empire.

632: The Muslim prophet Muhammad dies.

635–750: Muslims create the caliphate, the entire community of Muslims under the leadership of the caliph. The Islamic Empire spreads to Damascus, Syria, Mesopotamia, Palestine, and Egypt, and then on to North Africa, across Persia toward India and China, and westward beyond present-day Turkey, toward Italy, and Spain.

750–1050: The Islamic empire experiences a golden age in the arts and sciences.

1095–1291: The Crusades begin when the pope urges thousands of Roman Catholic men to join military campaigns to take control of the Holy Land from Muslims.

1204: The crusaders conquer the Christian Byzantine capital city of Constantinople, sharpening divisions between the Eastern Orthodox Church and the Roman Catholic Church.

1243: Mongol armies led by Genghis Khan conquer much of central Asia and the Middle East, including Anatolia.

1299: Turkish leader Osman I begins to conquer new territories around Anatolia, establishing the Ottoman Empire.

1453: Constantinople is conquered by the Ottoman Empire, which has grown to include the Balkan Peninsula, as well as Albania, Greece, and Hungary.

1500s: Under Ottoman sultans Selim I and his son Süleyman I, the Ottoman Empire attains worldwide supremacy, expanding from its base in Anatolia and Europe to include Syria, Egypt, and the western Arabian Peninsula, as well as North Africa.

1744: Wahhabi religious leader Muhammad ibn Abd al-Wahhab allies with Arab leader Mohammad ibn Saud and together they take power in the southern Arabian Peninsula. Though eventually forced to retreat by the Ottomans, Ibn Saud and his family maintain control in the desert regions of Arabia.

1768–1774: The Russo-Ottoman War results in Russia gaining control of the Crimea and other Ottoman territory.

1785: The Qahar dynasty begins in Iran.

1798–1801: The French invade and occupy Egypt.

1805–1848: Reign of Muhammad Ali in Egypt.

1839: A series of reforms known as Tanzimat, based mainly on the European style of government, are instituted in the Ottoman Empire.

1858–1860: Civil unrest in Lebanon and Syria leads to European intervention.

1869: Construction is completed on Egypt's Suez Canal, linking the Mediterranean Sea to the Red Sea.

1878: European powers convene the Congress of Berlin to settle territorial questions of the weakening Ottoman Empire; they grant independence to several Balkan countries, humiliating the fiercely proud Ottomans.

1881: France declares Tunisia a protectorate.

1881–1884: A vicious series of pogroms directed against Jews sweeps through Russia.

1882–1922: Great Britain invades and occupies Egypt.

1896: Theodor Herzl publishes *The Jewish State*, drawing attention to the ideas of Zionism, and promoting the immigration of Jews to Palestine. By the twentieth century, thousands of Jews had moved to the region.

1908–1909: The Young Turks overthrow the Ottoman sultan, announcing their intentions to separate government from religion and to make the Turkish language the official language of the empire.

1912: Italy begins its rule of Libya. Most of Morocco becomes a French protectorate, while a small part goes to Spain.

1914–1918: World War I; the Ottoman Empire joins the Central Powers of Germany and Austria-Hungary against the Allies: Great Britain, France, Russia, and the United States. Defeated, the Ottoman Empire collapses at war's end.

1914: At the outbreak of World War I, Great Britain declares Egypt to be a protectorate of the British Empire.

1915–1923: The Turkish leaders of the Ottoman Empire order the mass killing and displacement of the Armenians living in the empire; between 600,000 and 1.5 million Armenians die.

1916–1918: Arabs revolt against the Ottomans under an agreement with the British, hoping for Arab independence after World War I.

1917: The Balfour Declaration is approved by the British war cabinet, promising British support for the Zionist cause in Palestine.

1919: Iran becomes a British protectorate when it signs the Anglo-Persian Agreement of 1919.

1919–1922: Under several international treaties, a large portion of former Ottoman lands are divided up into mandates, to be administered by European nations under the supervision of the League of Nations. France receives control of Syria and Lebanon, and Great Britain receives control of Palestine and Iraq.

1922: British diplomate **Herbert Louis Samuel** is appointed high commissioner of Palestine.

1922: **Amin al-Husayni** becomes the Mufti (Islamic religious leader) of Jerusalem, the most important religious and political leader of Muslims in Palestine.

1922: Great Britain declares Egypt a constitutional monarchy.

1923: The independent Republic of Turkey is recognized by the international community. **Mustafa Kemal Atatürk**, the new nation's first president, begins a sweeping program of reform and modernization.

1925: Reza Khan establishes the Pahlavi dynasty in Iran.

1928: The Muslim Brotherhood, an Islamist group that seeks to promote Islam and rid Egypt of foreign influence, is established in Egypt.

1931: Zionists in the mandate of Palestine form one of the first contemporary terrorist groups in the Middle East: Irgun Zvai Leumi, better known as Irgun, which attacks Arab civilians and British authorities.

1932: Iraq gains independence from Great Britain.

1932: Ibn Saud unites large portions of the Arabian Peninsula under his rule and calls his kingdom Saudi Arabia.

1935: The German government under the Nazis passes the Nuremberg Laws, which take away the civil rights of German Jews.

1935–1939: Thousands of Zionist immigrants pour into Palestine.

1936: **Pierre Gemayel** founds the Phalange Party (also known as the Kataeb Party) with the goal of uniting Maronite Christians in Lebanon in an effort to protect them from domination by foreign or religious rivals.

1936–1939: The Arab Revolt in Palestine is organized to protest British rule and Jewish immigration.

1938: Vast quantities of oil are discovered in Saudi Arabia.

1939–1945: During World War II, the German Nazis initiate the systematic murder of Jewish people and several other groups, an act of genocide that will become known as the Holocaust.

1943: **Menachem Begin** reorganizes the Jewish underground militia called Irgun Zvai Leumi, or simply Irgun.

1943: As France withdraws from Lebanon, it frames the National Pact, a sectarian system of government that calls for a ratio of six Christians to every five Muslims in the Lebanese government.

1945: The leaders of Egypt, Iraq, Lebanon, Transjordan, Saudi Arabia, Syria, and Yemen join to form the Arab League to promote cooperation within the Arab world. In the initial agreement, members pledge to preserve the rights of the Palestinians.

1946: France withdraws from its mandatory rule of Syria after decades of bitter resistance to its rule. With France gone, Syria faces many internal divisions.

1947: The United Nations Special Committee on Palestine (UNSCOP) calls for the partition of Palestine into two separate states, a Jewish one and an Arab one. The Palestinians reject this plan.

1947: The Ba'ath Party is founded with the objective of bringing about a rebirth of Arab power. It is popular in Syria and Iraq.

1947–1948: Civil war breaks out between the Palestinians and the Jews in the British Mandate of Palestine.

May 14, 1948: Jewish leader **David Ben-Gurion** announces the establishment of the independent state of Israel.

May 15, 1948: The armies of Egypt, Iraq, Lebanon, Syria, and Transjordan invade the former mandate of Palestine in an attempt to stop the creation of the new state of Israel, beginning the 1948 Arab-Israeli War.

August 1948: The 1948 Arab-Israeli War concludes with the defeat of the Arab forces. Israeli forces significantly expand their territory and ensure Israeli independence. An estimated 750,000 Palestinians are either forced to, or willingly, leave their homes and become refugees. Arabs refer to the events of 1948 as *al-Nakba* ("the catastrophe").

1949: As deputy to the Israeli minister of defense, **Shimon Peres** is among the first officials to represent the new country of Israel abroad. He travels to New York to procure weapons for the newly formed Israeli army.

1952–1953: The Free Officers launch a military coup that overthrows the Egyptian monarchy.

1954: The United States helps Iranians stage a coup to return the ousted **Mohammad Reza Pahlavi** to power as shah of Iran.

1954–1962: In the eight-year Algerian war for independence from France nearly one million people are killed. Algeria declares its independence in 1962.

1956: Gamal Abdel Nasser becomes president of Egypt; he soon announces the nationalization of the Suez Canal, resulting in the Suez Crisis, a brief armed conflict with Great Britain, France, and Israel.

1956: France grants Tunisia independence.

1958–1961: In an attempt at creating a pan-Arab state, Gamal Abdel Nasser organizes the United Arab Republic (UAR), initially a political union between Egypt and Syria. Problems arise immediately, and a military coup in 1961 restores Syria's independence and disbands the UAR.

1959: Fatah, a Palestinian militant group dedicated to the establishment of an independent Palestinian state, is founded.

1960: Palestinian poet **Mahmoud Darwish** publishes his first collection of poetry, *Asafir bila ajnihah* (*Sparrows without Wings*) and is promptly jailed by the Israeli police.

1964: King **Faisal ibn Abd al Aziz ibn Saud** of Saudi Arabia assumes the throne.

1964: The Palestine Liberation Organization (PLO) is founded.

1964: Ayatollah Ruhollah Khomeini is exiled after speaking out against the shah of Iran.

1967: Meir Kahane founds the Jewish Defense League to support Zionism from its headquarters in New York.

1967: The 1967 Arab-Israeli War begins when Israel, fearing an attack from the Arab countries, attacks first, striking Egypt, Syria, and Jordan decisively. Israel nearly triples its size by taking the Golan Heights, the West Bank, the Gaza Strip, and the Sinai Peninsula. Israel establishes military rule in the captured regions, which come to be known as the occupied territories.

1968: The Popular Front for the Liberation of Palestine (PFLP) hijacks an Israeli jetliner and diverts it to Algeria. The international attention gained by the hijacking encourages the PFLP and similar groups to continue to stage terrorist acts.

1969: **Yasser Arafat** becomes the chairman of the PLO, which has grown increasingly radical and violent. Palestinian militants launch constant guerrilla attacks against Israel in order to retake Palestinian land and return refugees to their homes.

1969: A group of military officers headed by Colonel **Mu'ammar al-Qaddafi** overthrows the Libyan king; al-Qaddafi establishes the Libyan Arab Republic and becomes its leader.

1969: **Golda Meir** becomes the first female prime minister of Israel.

1970: The King **Hussein I** of Jordan expels the PLO from his country in a bloody event known as Black September, in which three thousand Palestinians are killed. PLO leadership, forced out of the country, relocates to southern Lebanon.

1970: Syria's Ba'athist Party places **Hafez Assad** in power.

1972: At the Olympic Games in Munich, Germany, eight armed members of a Palestinian group calling itself Black September storm the apartments of the Israeli Olympic team, killing two team members and taking nine others hostage. During a rescue attempt, Black September murders the hostages.

1973: The brief 1973 Arab-Israeli War is launched by Egypt and Syria-led Arab forces against Israel. Arabs experience some initial success, although Israel successfully defends itself.

1973: **Yitzhak Rabin** becomes Israel's first native-born prime minister.

1973: Arabs and Arab members of the Organization of Petroleum Exporting Countries (OPEC), furious at U.S. interference in the 1973 Arab-Israel War, organize an embargo of oil shipments to the United States, effectively cutting off the majority of the U.S. oil supply.

1974: **Abu Nidal** attempts to assassinate fellow Palestinian rebel Yasser Arafat and is kicked out of Fatah; Abu Nidal and his terrorist organization target both Palestinians and Israelis over the coming years.

1975: The fifteen-year Civil War in Lebanon begins.

1975: The Iraqi government tries to evict the Kurds from the country, forcing residents out of eight hundred Kurdish villages near the Iran-Iraq border.

1976: The Arab League grants Syria permission to station forty thousand Syrian troops in Lebanon as part of a peace agreement.

1978: The Camp David Accords are signed by Egyptian President **Anwar Sadat** and Israeli Prime Minister Menachem Begin at Camp David, setting the framework for Egypt to become the first Arab nation to recognize Israel as a state. Sadat and Begin are awarded Nobel Peace Prizes for their contributions to peace in the Middle East.

1978: Fatah members hijack an Israeli tourist bus, resulting in the deaths of thirty-eight Israelis. Outraged Israeli leaders launch Operation Litani, sending more than twenty thousand troops into southern Lebanon in an attempt to destroy the PLO.

1979: The Iranian Revolution (also known as the Islamic Revolution) transforms Iran from a secular (nonreligious) country into an Islamic country, in which the social, political, and economic institutions of the country are based on Islamic holy law.

1979: **Saddam Hussein** becomes president of Iraq and begins immediately to use his power to destroy opponents and establish an authoritarian government.

1979: The U.S. embassy in Iran is overtaken by a group of Iranian students. Fifty-two Americans are held hostage for 444 days.

September 1980: Iraq invades Iran, beginning the brutal, eight-year Iran-Iraq War.

1981: Egyptian president Anwar Sadat is assassinated; the militant group Egyptian Islamic Jihad is responsible.

1982: Israel launches an attack on Lebanon called Operation Peace for Galilee to push the PLO in southern Lebanon back from the Israeli borders. With international intervention, the fighting is stopped; the PLO leadership moves to Tunisia.

1982: The Phalangists militia enter the Sabra and Shatila Palestinian refugee camps outside Beirut and massacre approximately one thousand Palestinian men, women, and children. During the massacre, Israeli troops surround the camps, doing little to stop the massacre.

1982: Syrian president Hafez Assad orders a brutal attack on the city of Hama, where the Muslim Brotherhood is headquartered. His forces kill more than ten thousand innocent inhabitants of the city.

1983: Small, militant Shiite Lebanese groups protesting the 1982 Israeli invasion of Lebanon launch a deadly series of suicide bombings: the first at the Beirut airport, which kills 241 U.S. Marines; a second that kills 58 French paratroopers; and a third that strikes an Israeli headquarters in southern Lebanon, killing 29 Israeli troops.

1985: Lebanese Shiite militant groups merge into a new Islamist group called Hezbollah. Hezbollah's immediate purpose is to drive Israeli forces, and all Western influences, out of Lebanon.

1987: The Palestinians in the West Bank and the Gaza Strip launch the First Intifada, an extended protest against Israeli occupation.

1988: Yasser Arafat promises to recognize Israel and to renounce terrorism.

1988: Palestinian **Hanan Ashrawi's** eloquent, televised argument in support of the Palestinian cause wins international attention and respect.

1988: Iraq launches Anfal, an operation designed to destroy the Kurdish population in Iraq that includes bombing Kurdish villages, destroying Kurdish homes and farmlands, and forcing tens of thousands of Kurds to flee. One of the Anfal attacks is on the Kurdish town of Halabja, and it makes use of poison gases, such as sarin and mustard gas, killing and wounding thousands of Kurds.

1988: A terrorist bomb blows up Pan Am Flight 103 from London to New York over Lockerbie, Scotland, killing 243 passengers and 16 crew members. Libya's leader al-Qaddafi is suspected of being responsible.

1989: **Osama bin Laden** establishes al-Qaeda headquarters in Sudan and begins to train warriors to carry out terrorist acts.

1989: Islamic Jihad, a militant Palestinian group, claims responsibility for the first known suicide bombing of the Israeli-Palestinian conflict.

1989: Lebanese lawmakers convene in Taif, Saudi Arabia, to restructure Lebanon's sectarian government, allowing for better representation for Muslims.

1989: **Ayatollah Ali Khamenei** becomes Supreme Leader of Iran.

1990: The Lebanese Civil War ends, but Syria's forces remain in Lebanon. The Lebanese government grants Syria control of Lebanon's internal affairs and management of its foreign policy and security issues.

1990: North Yemen and South Yemen unify, becoming the Republic of Yemen.

1990–1991: The Persian Gulf War begins with Iraq's invasion of Kuwait. A U.S.-led coalition of more than thirty countries challenges and defeats Iraq but leaves Saddam Hussein in power. International sanctions on trade with Iraq cause great suffering in the country in the decade after the war.

1992: Lebanon holds its first parliamentary elections since 1972 and elects Rafiq Hariri as prime minister.

1992: Hassan Nasrallah becomes secretary-general of Hezbollah, a militant group that has struggled against Israel and developed great military and political power in Lebanon.

1993: The Oslo Accords, a set of agreements between the Israelis and the Palestinians, outlines a process in which Palestinians can achieve self-rule under an elected body called the Palestinian Authority (PA).

1993: Four radical Islamist conspirators explode a powerful bomb in the underground parking garage in one of the towers of New York City's World Trade Center, killing six and injuring more than one thousand people.

1996: Benjamin Netanyahu begins his first term as prime minister of Israel.

1997: Egyptian diplomat **Mohamed ElBaradei** becomes director general of the International Atomic Energy Agency (IAEA), an intergovernmental body affiliated with the United Nations.

1998: Osama bin Laden publicly declares that it is the duty of all Muslims to kill Americans, both military and civilian.

2000: Yasser Arafat and Israeli Prime Minister Ehud Barak meet at Camp David to prepare for a Palestinian state, but the negotiations fail.

2000: The Second Intifada begins in the occupied Palestinian territories, with more violence than the first.

2000: The eighteen-year Israeli occupation of Lebanon ends with the withdrawal of Israeli soldiers, a huge victory for Hezbollah.

2001: Following the death of president Hafez Assad in 2000, a period called Damascus Spring begins in Syria. Assad's son, Bashar Assad, promises reforms and eventual democracy, but quickly breaks his word and crushes democratic movements.

September 11, 2001: Al-Qaeda terrorists use passenger jets to destroy the World Trade Center towers in New York and damage the Pentagon building in Virginia. Nearly three thousand people are killed in the attack. The United States declares a war on terror.

2002: Turkish politician **Recep Tayyip Erdoğan** founds the Justice and Development Party.

2002: Israel launches Operation Defensive Shield, a military offensive against several West Bank cities. Yasser Arafat's compound in Ramallah is surrounded and the city is devastated.

2002: The United States claims that Iraq is secretly manufacturing weapons of mass destruction.

March 2003: A U.S.-led coalition makes air strikes on Baghdad, Iraq, starting the Iraq War.

2004: Photos are released to the public showing Iraqi prisoners being beaten and sexually humiliated by U.S. soldiers at Abu Ghraib, a prison in Baghdad where the United States is holding its detainees.

2004: Yasser Arafat dies.

2005: Fatah leader **Mahmoud Abbas** is elected president of the Palestinian Authority.

2005: Israeli Prime Minister **Ariel Sharon** orders the evacuation all of Israel's twenty-one settlements in the Gaza Strip and four in the West Bank.

2005: Former Lebanese prime minister Rafiq Hariri is assassinated in Beirut. Blaming Syria for the murder, an estimated one million Lebanese people demonstrate against Syria's oppressive presence in their country. Syria is forced to end its twenty-nine-year occupation of Lebanon.

2006: The Palestinian Authority holds its first national legislative elections to choose members of the Palestinian Legislative Council. Hamas, a militant Islamist group wins the majority of the seats in the council.

2006: **Mahmoud Ahmadinejad** is elected president of Iran.

2006: War erupts between Israel and Hezbollah in Lebanon. Thirty-three days of fighting devastate Lebanon but the war also harms Israel.

2006: A group of al-Qaeda in Iraq and Sunni extremists bomb the Askariya Mosque in Samarra, Iraq. Outraged Shiites blamed the Sunnis and form militias that sweep into Sunni neighborhoods, beating and killing Sunnis. Sunnis bomb and attack Shiites in revenge. An estimated one thousand deaths ensue, and hundreds of thousands of Iraqis flee their homes as the sectarian violence escalates.

December 2006: Iraqi President Saddam Hussein is executed for crimes against humanity.

2007: Fighting breaks out between Hamas and Fatah. After a violent split, Hamas serves as the sole ruler of the Gaza Strip and Fatah rules in the West Bank for the next four years. Under Hamas, the Gaza Strip continues to be a site for launching rockets into Israel.

2007: Israel labels the Gaza Strip a hostile entity and establishes a blockade of the territory that causes great suffering among the Gaza Strip's inhabitants.

2007: Mahmoud Abbas declares a state of emergency in the Palestinian Authority and creates a new government with moderate economist Salam Fayyad as prime minister.

2008: In response to attacks from Hamas, Israel launches Operation Cast Lead, a strike against the Gaza Strip that leaves thirteen hundred people dead and causes massive destruction.

2008: Hezbollah achieves a majority in the Lebanese government.

2009: In large numbers, Iranians protest what appear to be rigged elections, demanding the resignation of the president and democratic reforms. A government crackdown ends the demonstrations that come to be known as the Green Movement.

2009: Tzipporah Livni becomes head of the opposition party in the Israeli Knesset (legislature).

August 19, 2010: U.S. president Barack Obama declares the U.S. combat mission in Iraq over. All troops are scheduled to leave Iraq by the end of 2011.

December 17, 2010: In Sidi Bouzid, Tunisia, Mohamed Bouazizi sets himself on fire to protest poor treatment at the hands of officials, igniting a revolt against the authoritarian government in Tunisia. The revolt quickly leads to the Arab Spring, a series of prodemocracy uprisings throughout the Middle East.

2011: Fatah and Hamas reach a reconciliation agreement under which they agree to form a coalition government for the Palestinian Authority and then hold new elections in the Gaza Strip and the West Bank.

2011: The United Nation's Special Tribunal for Lebanon officially indicts four Hezbollah members in the assassination of Rafik Hariri; Hezbollah will not allow them to be arrested.

January 25, 2011: Tens of thousands of protesters position themselves in Tahrir Square in Cairo, Egypt, denouncing police brutality and demanding an end to president **Hosni Mubarak's** rule.

May 2, 2011: Osama bin Laden is killed by a U.S. Navy SEAL team in Pakistan.

October 20, 2011: Mu'ammar al-Qaddafi is killed by rebel forces while fleeing. The Libyan civil war is over.

March 18, 2011: Syrian security forces arrest, beat, and torture fifteen teenagers for painting graffiti on a school wall in Dara'a, setting off a protest that soon spreads to other cities. Within weeks, the Syrian government launches a violent crackdown.

Words to Know

Alawis: Also spelled Alawites; followers of a sect of Shia Islam that live in Syria. Their belief system and practices vary from Shiites in several ways, particularly in the belief that Ali, the son-in-law of the prophet Muhammad, was the human form of Allah (the Arabic word for God).

aliyah: The immigration of Jews to the historic Eretz Yisrael (Land of Israel).

anti-Semitism: Prejudice against Jews.

Arab League: A regional political alliance of Arab nations formed in 1945 to promote political, military, and economic cooperation within the Arab world.

Arabs: People of the Middle East and North Africa who speak the Arabic language or who live in countries in which Arabic is the dominant language.

Arab Spring: A series of prodemocracy uprisings in the Middle East and North Africa.

authoritarianism: A type of leadership in which power is consolidated under one strong leader, or a small group of elite leaders, who do not answer to the will of the people.

ayatollah: A high-ranking Shiite religious leader.

Ba'ath Party: A secular (nonreligious) political party founded in the 1940s with the goal of uniting the Arab world and creating one powerful Arab state.

Byzantine Empire: The eastern part of the Roman Empire, which thrived for one thousand years after the collapse of Rome in 476.

caliph: The spiritual, political, and military leader of the world's Muslims from the death of Muhammad in 632 until the caliphate was abolished in 1924.

caliphate: The entire community of Muslims under the leadership of the caliph.

chemical weapons: Toxic chemical substances used during armed conflict to kill, injure, or incapacitate an enemy.

Christianity: A religion based on the teachings of Jesus Christ.

cleric: An ordained religious official.

Cold War: A period of intense political and economic rivalry between the United States and the Soviet Union that lasted from 1945 to 1991.

Communism: A system of government in which the state plans and controls the economy and a single political party holds power.

Crusades: A series of military campaigns ordered by the Roman Catholic Church between 1095 and 1291 with the main goal of taking the Holy Land from the Muslims.

crucifixion: A form of execution in which a person is nailed or bound to a cross and left to die.

D

Druze: Members of a small sect of Islam who believe that the ninth-century caliph Tariq al-Hakim was God.

dynasty: A series of rulers from the same family.

E

Eretz Yisrael: "Land of Israel" in Hebrew; the ancient kingdom of the Jews.

emir: A ruler, chief, or commander in some Islamic countries.

ethnicity: Groupings of people in a society according to their common racial, national, tribal, religious, language, or cultural backgrounds.

evangelist: A Christian follower dedicated to converting others to Christianity.

excommunication: The official exclusion of a person from membership in the church.

Fatah: A Palestinian militant group and political party dedicated to the establishment of an independent Palestinian state.

fatwa: A statement of religious law issued by Islamic clerics.

fedayeen: An Arabic term meaning one who sacrifices for a cause; used to describe several distinct militant groups that have formed in the Arab world at different times. Opponents of the fedayeen use the term to describe members of Arab terrorist groups.

fundamentalism: A movement stressing adherence to a strict or literal interpretation of religious principles.

G

Gaza Strip: A narrow strip of land along the eastern shore of the Mediterranean Sea, west of Israel and bordering Egypt in the southwest. The region was occupied by Israel after the 1967 Arab-Israeli War.

Geneva Conventions: A series of international agreements that establish how prisoners of war and civilians in wartime are to be treated.

genocide: The deliberate and systematic destruction of a group of people based on religion, ethnicity, or nationality.

Golan Heights: A mountainous region located on the border of Syria and Israel, northwest of the Sea of Galilee. The region was occupied by Israel after the 1967 Arab-Israeli War and annexed in 1981.

guerilla warfare: Combat tactics used by a smaller, less equipped fighting force against a more powerful foe.

H

Haganah: The underground defense force of Zionists in Palestine from 1920 to 1948. It became the basis for the Israeli army.

hajj: The annual Muslim pilgrimage to Mecca that takes place in the last month of the year, which every Muslim is expected to perform at least once during their lifetime if they are able.

Hamas: A Palestinian Islamic fundamentalist group and political party operating primarily in the West Bank and the Gaza Strip with the goal of establishing a Palestinian state and opposing the existence of Israel. It has been labeled a terrorist organization by several countries.

Hebrew: The ancient language of the Jewish people and the official language of present-day Israel.

Hejaz: A coastal region on the western Arabian Peninsula that includes the Muslim holy cities of Mecca and Medina.

heretic: Someone whose opinions or beliefs oppose official church doctrine.

heresy: Opinions or beliefs that oppose official church doctrine.

Hezbollah: A Shiite militant group and political party based in Lebanon.

Holocaust: The mass murder of European Jews and other groups by the Nazis during World War II.

Holy Land: Roughly the present-day territory of Israel, the Palestinian territories, and parts of Jordan and Lebanon. This area includes sacred sites for Jews, Christians, and Muslims.

I

insurgency: An uprising, or rebellion, against a political authority.

Intifada: The Palestinian uprising against Israeli occupation in the West Bank and the Gaza Strip.

Irgun Zvai Leumi: A militant underground group founded in 1931 that worked to secure Israeli independence by staging violent attacks on British and Arab targets. Also known simply as Irgun.

Islam: The religious faith followed by Muslims based on a belief in Allah as the sole god and in Muhammad as his prophet.

Islamism: A fundamentalist movement characterized by the belief that Islam should provide the basis for political, social, and cultural life in Muslim nations.

J

jihad: An armed struggle against unbelievers, in defense of Islam; often interpreted to mean holy war. The term also refers to the spiritual struggle of Muslims against sin.

Jews: People who practice the religion of Judaism.

Judaism: The religion of the Jewish people based on the belief in one god and the teachings the Talmud.

K

kibbutz: A Jewish communal farming settlement in Israel, where settlers share all property and work collaboratively together. Plural is kibbutzim.

Koran: Also spelled Qur'an or Quran; the holy book of Islam.

Kurds: A non-Arab ethnic group who live mainly in present-day Turkey, Iraq, and Iran.

L

League of Nations: An international organization of sovereign countries established after World War I to promote peace.

M

mandate: A commission granting one country the authority to administer the affairs of another country. Also describes the territory entrusted to foreign administration.

mandate system: The system established after World War I to administer former territories of Germany and the Ottoman Empire.

Maronites: Members of an Arabic-speaking group of Christians, living mainly in Lebanon, who are in communion (share essential doctrines) with the Roman Catholic Church.

martyr: A person who dies for his or her religion.

militia: Armed civilian military forces.

millet: A community for non-Muslims in the Ottoman Empire, organized by religious group and headed by a religious leader.

Muslim Brotherhood: An Islamic fundamentalist group organized in opposition to Western influence and in support of Islamic principles.

Muslims: People who practice the religion of Islam.

mosque: A Muslim place of worship.

N

nationalism: The belief that a people with shared ethnic, cultural, and/ or religious identities have the right to form their own nation. In established nations nationalism is devotion and loyalty to the nation and its culture.

nationalization: The practice of bringing private industry under the ownership and control of the government.

North Atlantic Treaty Organization (NATO): An international organization created in 1949 for purposes of collective security.

O

occupation: The physical and political control of an area seized by a foreign military force.

occupied territories: The lands under the political and military control of Israel, especially the West Bank and the Gaza Strip.

Organization of Petroleum Exporting Countries (OPEC): An organization formed in 1960 by the world's major oil-producing nations to coordinate policies and ensure stable oil prices in world markets.

Ottoman Empire: The vast empire of the Ottoman Turks which included southwest Asia, northeast Africa, and southeast Europe, and lasted from the thirteenth century to the early twentieth century.

P

Palestine: A historical region in the Middle East on the eastern shore of the Mediterranean Sea, comprising parts of present-day Israel and Jordan.

Palestine Liberation Organization (PLO): A political and military organization formed to unite various Palestinian Arab groups with the goal of establishing an independent Palestinian state.

Palestinian Authority (PA): The recognized governing institution for Palestinians in the West Bank and the Gaza Strip, established in 1993. Also known as the Palestinian National Authority.

Palestinians: An Arab people whose ancestors lived in the historical region of Palestine and who continue to lay claim to that land.

Pan-Arabism: A movement for the unification of Arab peoples and the political alliance of Arab states.

Pan-Islamism: A movement for the unification of Muslims under a single Islamic state where Islam provides the basis for political, social, and cultural life.

pasha: A provincial governor or powerful official of the Ottoman Empire.

pilgrim: A person who travels to a sacred place for religious reasons.

pilgrimage: A journey to a sacred place for religious reasons.

pogrom: A racially-motivated riot in which mobs, usually organized and sanctioned by the state, attack a minority group, most often Jews.

R

rabbi: A Jewish scholar, teacher, and religious leader.

refugees: People who flee their country to escape violence or persecution.

right of return: The right, claimed by a dispossessed people, to return to their historic homeland.

S

sanctions: Punitive measures adopted by the international community against a nation that has violated international law, usually in the form of diplomatic, economic, or social restrictions.

sect: A social unit within a society that is defined by its distinct beliefs or customs.

sectarian government: A government that distributes political and institutional power among its various religious sects and ethnic communities on a proportional basis.

settlements: Communities established and inhabited in order to claim land.

sharia: A system of Islamic law based on the Koran and other sacred writings. Sharia attempts to create the perfect social order, based on God's will and justice, and covers a wide range of human activities, including acts of religious worship, the law of contracts and obligations, personal status law, and public law.

sharif: A nobleman and political leader chosen from among descendants of the Muslim prophet Muhammad.

sheikh: An Arab tribal leader.

Shiites: Followers of the Shia branch of Islam. Shiites believe that only direct descendants of the prophet Muhammad are qualified to lead the Islamic faith.

socialism: A system in which the government owns the means of production and controls the distribution of goods and services.

Suez Canal: A shipping canal that connects the Mediterranean Sea with the Red Sea.

suicide bombing: An attack intended to kill others and cause widespread damage, carried about by someone who does not hope to survive the attack.

sultan: A ruler of a Muslim state, especially the Ottoman Empire.

Sunnis: Followers of the Sunni branch of Islam. Sunnis believe that elected officials, regardless of their heritage, are qualified to lead the Islamic faith.

synagogue: A Jewish place of worship.

T

Taliban: An Islamic militant and political group that controlled Afghanistan from 1996 to 2001.

Talmud: The authoritative, ancient body of Jewish teachings and tradition.

Tanakh: The Jewish Bible.

Temple Mount: A contested religious site in Jerusalem. It is the holiest site in Judaism, the third holiest site in Islam, and also important to the Christian faith.

Torah: A Hebrew word meaning teaching or instruction, it literally refers to the first five books of the Jewish Bible. The term is often used to refer to the body of wisdom held in Jewish scriptures and sacred literature.

tribute: Payment from one ruler of a state to another, usually for protection or to acknowledge submission.

U

United Nations: An international organization of countries founded in 1945 to promote international peace, security, and cooperation.

W

weapons of mass destruction: Any nuclear, chemical, or biological weapons capable of killing or injuring large numbers of people.

West Bank: An area between Israel and Jordan on the west bank of the Jordan River, populated largely by Palestinians. The region was occupied by Israel after the 1967 Arab-Israeli War.

World War I: 1914–18; a global war between the Allies (Great Britain, France, and Russia, joined later by the United States) and the Central Powers (Germany, Austria-Hungary, and their allies).

World War II: 1939–45; a war in which the Allies (Great Britain, France, the Soviet Union, the United States, and China) defeated the Axis Powers (Germany, Italy, and Japan).

Z

Zionism: An international political movement originating in the late nineteenth century that called for the creation of an independent Jewish state in Palestine.

Zionists: Supporters of an international political movement that called for the creation of an independent Jewish state in Palestine.

Text Credits

The following is a list of the copyright holders who have granted us permission to reproduce excerpts from primary source documents in *Middle East Conflict: Biographies, 2nd Edition*. Every effort has been made to trace copyright; if omissions have been made, please contact us.

Copyrighted excerpts reproduced from the following sources:

- 'The Balfour Declaration', November 2, 1917. Letter by Arthur James Lord Balfour to Lord Rothschild, www.mfa.gov.il/MFA/Peace Process/Guide to the Peace Process/The Balfour Declaration.

Mahmoud Abbas

BORN: March 26, 1935 • Zefat, Palestine

Palestinian president

"The choice is not between Palestinian unity or peace with Israel; it is between a two-state solution or settlement-colonies."

Mahmoud Abbas is the first elected president of the Palestinian Authority (PA), the recognized governing institution for some 2.5 million Palestinians in the West Bank and the Gaza Strip, Arab (Arabic-speaking) regions occupied by Israel after the 1967 Arab-Israeli War. (Palestinians are an Arab people whose ancestors lived in the historical region of Palestine, comprising parts of present-day Israel and Jordan, and who continue to lay claim to that land.) He also serves as chair of the Palestine Liberation Organization (PLO), a political and military organization formed to unite various Palestinian Arab groups with the goal of establishing an independent Palestinian state. The PLO represents nearly 4 million Palestinians around the world. In both roles he succeeded PLO founder **Yasser Arafat** (1929–2004; see entry), with whom he had worked closely for decades. For most of that period Abbas was largely unknown, working as Arafat's chief negotiator. He took over the PLO after Arafat's death in 2004 and was elected president of the Palestinian Authority in

Mahmoud Abbas. © ALI JAREKJ/REUTERS/CORBIS.

1

January 2005. "The Arafat style was one of bluff, drama, flattery, purposeful contradiction, mystery, fog," writes David Remnick in the *New Yorker* magazine. "Abbas is a logician [logical thinker], stern, arid [dry]."

Flees Palestine

Abbas was born on March 26, 1935, in the village of Zefat in Palestine. The British had been granted a mandate over Palestine after World War I (1914–18). (A mandate is a commission granting one country the authority to administer the affairs of another country.) The British permitted the continuing immigration of Jews from Europe and elsewhere into the region. The Jews had long been facing anti-Semitism (prejudice against Jews) and many came to Palestine, the site of the ancient Jewish kingdom, hoping to establish a Jewish homeland where they would be safe from the discrimination and violence they had faced elsewhere. Their presence caused friction with the predominantly Muslim, Arabic-speaking people who had lived in Palestine for hundreds of years. The two groups were engaging in violent skirmishes by the time of Abbas's birth. The events of World War II (1939–45) increased tensions in the area, with the arrival of thousands of new Jewish settlers fleeing persecution from the genocidal policies of Nazi Germany, which controlled much of Europe before its defeat in the spring of 1945. (Genocide is the deliberate and systematic destruction of a group of people based on religion, ethnicity, or nationality.)

In 1947 the United Nations (an international organization of countries founded in 1945 to promote international peace, security, and cooperation) sponsored a plan that would allow for the creation of a sovereign (self-governing) Jewish state, called Israel, in part of Palestine. The Arab Palestinians and the surrounding Arab nations vehemently protested the plan. In 1948 the British exited the area, and Jews declared the establishment of the state of Israel. Neighboring Arab nations attacked Israel, and the 1948 Arab-Israeli War resulted in a victory for Israel. Thousands of Arab Palestinians were forced from their homes by the fighting. The refugees (people who flee their country to escape violence or persecution) moved to neighboring Arab nations, and most lived in refugee camps. Abbas's family was among the many refugees who settled in Syria.

Just thirteen years old at the start of the 1948 Arab-Israeli War, Abbas first lived in a tent with his family, but they were able to settle into more

Abbas's Dissertation

Material from Abbas's doctoral dissertation (a paper required to earn a PhD degree), *The Other Side: The Secret Relationship between Nazism and Zionism*, which he wrote in 1982 and published 1984, has been used by his critics to cast doubt on his credentials as a political figure. In the dissertation he discusses possible links between Germany under the Nazi Party and the Zionists (supporters of an international political movement that called for the creation of an independent Jewish state in Palestine) during World War II (1939–45). Among these ties were the controversial Haavara Agreement of 1933, between the newly installed Nazi regime, a federation of German Zionists, and the Anglo-Palestine Bank. The agreement was arranged with the hope of encouraging emigration of German Jews to British-controlled Palestine.

Also controversial are the questions the dissertation raises over the number of Jews killed in the Holocaust, the mass murder of European Jews and other groups by the Nazis during World War II. Abbas cites the total number of World War II casualties at forty million. "But after the war it was publicized that six million Jews were among the victims, and that the war of annihilation had been aimed first of all against the Jews, and only then against the rest of the peoples of Europe," Abbas writes, as quoted in the *New Yorker*. "The truth of the matter is that no one can verify this number. Or completely deny it." He goes on to state that the Nazis' genocidal policies were an "atrocity" and "the killing of a human being—any human being—is a crime the civilized world cannot accept and humanity cannot comprehend." (Genocide is the deliberate and systematic destruction of a group of people based on religion, ethnicity, or nationality.) He also notes that "It seems that the interest of the Zionist movement was to inflate the number of murdered in the war so as to insure greater gains." Those "gains," according to Abbas, were public and international support for the creation of a Jewish national homeland.

Abbas publicly distanced himself from the negative interpretations of his work, which some Jewish academics and supporters of Israel classified under the spurious field of scholarship known as 'Holocaust denial.' In 2003 he gave an interview to the Israeli newspaper *Haaretz* in which he defended his work, characterizing it as an assessment of long-running scholarly debate. "I quoted an argument between historians in which various numbers of casualties were mentioned. One wrote there were 12 million victims and another wrote there were 800,000," he told *Haaretz*. "I have no desire to argue with the figures. The Holocaust was a terrible, unforgiveable crime against the Jewish nation, a crime against humanity that cannot be accepted by humankind. The Holocaust was a terrible thing and nobody can claim I denied it."

REMNICK, DAVID. "CHECKPOINT." *NEW YORKER* (FEBRUARY 7, 2005): 52.

ELDAR, AKIVA. "'U.S. TOLD US TO IGNORE ISRAELI MAP RESERVATIONS.'" *HAARETZ* (MAY 28, 2003). HTTP:// WWW.HAARETZ.COM/PRINT-EDITION/ NEWS/U-S-TOLD-US-TO-IGNORE-ISRA ELI-MAP-RESERVATIONS-1.8840 (ACCESSED ON NOVEMBER 30, 2011).

permanent quarters in Syria. After completing high school, he laid floor tiles for a time before becoming a teacher at an elementary school. He earned a bachelor's degree from the University of Damascus in Damascus, Syria, then traveled to Egypt to study law. He then studied at the People's Friendship University, in Moscow, in the Soviet Union. This university had been established in 1960 to provide higher-education opportunities to young students from developing nations. Abbas earned his PhD in 1982. Later in his political career the title and topic of his doctoral dissertation (a paper required to earn PhD degree) would stir controversy and debate.

Joins PLO

Like many educated Palestinians of his generation seeking a professional career, Abbas settled in one of the oil-rich countries located along the Persian Gulf. He chose Qatar and worked as a director of personnel in the civil administration of that country in the mid–1950s. The late 1950s and early 1960s were an important time for Palestinians. The more fortunate Palestinians who fled during the 1948 Arab-Israeli War were those who had the resources to settle elsewhere, as Abbas's family did in Syria, and were able to obtain an education and citizenship in their newly adopted homelands. Less fortunate Palestinians held refugee status in Arab countries, meaning that they were granted governmental protection, but not citizenship. Their refugee status often restricted their civil, political, and economic rights and opportunities.

In 1959 Arafat created Fatah, a Palestinian militant group and (later) political party dedicated to the establishment of an independent Palestinian state. Fatah quickly became the leading voice for the Palestinians. At its founding, Fatah was dedicated to the destruction of Israel as a nation in order to reclaim Palestine for Palestinians. Abbas first met Arafat when Arafat came to Qatar on a fund-raising trip in 1961. Abbas joined Fatah soon afterward.

In 1964 the PLO was created by the Arab League, a regional political alliance of Arab nations formed in 1945 to promote political, military, and economic cooperation within the Arab world. The PLO served as an umbrella organization, bringing together many smaller organizations with similar goals in order to share their skills and resources, and Fatah soon became the lead group in the PLO. Arafat became the organization's most visible figure. Abbas became a full-time member of the organization, traveling with Arafat and the PLO leadership for the next three decades. He lived in Jordan, Lebanon, Syria, and Tunisia during these years and went by the name Abu Mazen.

The PLO often used violence to further its cause, launching attacks against Israel from across the borders of various neighboring Arab states. However, in the early 1970s, the PLO began to use negotiation and compromise along with armed struggle as tools to gain political advantage. This prompted the breakaway of a longtime PLO member known as **Abu Nidal** (also known as Sabri al-Banna; 1937–2002; see entry), who believed that violent action was the only way for Palestinians to achieve their goal. Abu Nidal and his group, called the Abu Nidal Organization (ANO), carried out scores of attacks against Israeli, Western, and even Palestinian targets. One such operation was an assassination attempt on Abbas and Arafat in Damascus that was foiled with the help of the Syrian intelligence services. A PLO panel tried Abu Nidal in absentia (in the absence of the person concerned) for the plot and issued a death sentence. Nidal remained an active, disruptive force in the peace process until the late 1980s, when he disappeared into Iraq.

The Oslo Accords

In the early 1970s Abbas served as PLO treasurer, and in 1980 he became the head of the Department of National and International Relations. Eventually he became secretary-general of the PLO executive committee, the organization's most powerful group. By 1988 he was serving as the PLO's national security adviser and foreign relations minister.

Over the years Abbas earned a reputation as an intellectual and extremely practical man. He thought through the long-term implications of PLO positions and urged its leadership to take approaches that would bring about positive results, but he admitted years later that he and Arafat had at times disagreed strongly on vital issues. Abbas is thought to have been behind secret talks with political groups inside Israel that led to more widespread sympathy for the Palestinian call for an independent country. Abbas always believed that Palestinians could not overcome Israeli opposition through military force, simply because Israel's military power was vastly superior. Abbas, as quoted by an article on the *CNN* Web site, believed "the only way [to solve the Arab-Israeli conflict] is the choice of peace. It is impossible to liberate Palestinians with the use of weapons because the balance of power is not with us."

By the 1990s Abbas had a solid reputation and a wide network of contacts on both sides of the conflict. This made him the ideal person to participate in secret talks between the PLO and the Israelis in Oslo, Norway, in 1993. Neither the United States, which arranged the talks, nor Israel wanted to negotiate directly with Arafat, because they had long considered him to be a terrorist for his violent actions aimed at the destruction of Israel. Arriving on separate airplanes and meeting in secluded locations, Abbas's team and Israeli negotiators met to work out a peace deal. Under the deal, known as the Oslo Accords, Israel and the PLO recognized each other's existence, Israel agreed to allow Palestinians to rule themselves in the Gaza Strip and the West Bank, and the PLO agreed that Israel could protect its settlers in those areas. Abbas was the PLO representative who signed the agreement at the White House in Washington, D.C., on September 13, 1993, with Israeli foreign minister **Shimon Peres** (1923–; see entry).

The Oslo Accords did not solve all the problems between Israel and the PLO, but it marked a major turning point in the Arab-Israeli conflict. The accords also amplified tensions inside Israel, with conservative political elements bitterly opposed to it. Israeli prime minister **Yitzhak Rabin** (1922–1995; see entry) was assassinated in 1995 because of his participation in the Oslo Accords, and in the 1996 elections his Labor Party lost several seats in the Knesset, Israel's parliament, to the Likud Party.

Becomes prime minister

The Oslo Accords established the Palestinian Authority (PA) to act as the governing body for Palestinians in the West Bank and the Gaza Strip. Arafat, as PLO leader, became the first president of the PA. While Arafat had been effective as the fiery leader of the PLO, he was less effective in his administrative duties as PA president. In the years after 1993, Arafat proved unable to control Palestinian militant groups that had refused to end the violence against Israel. He also proved unable to bring effective administration of health, education, and other services to Palestinians. In 2000 Palestinians in the occupied territories (the lands under the political and military control of Israel, especially the West Bank and the Gaza Strip) began what became known as the Second Intifada, or uprising. Unlike the First Intifada (1987–91), which was strictly an uprising against Israeli occupation in the West Bank and the Gaza Strip, demonstrators used violence. Militant groups launched rocket attacks against Israel and used suicide bombers. (A suicide bombing is an attack intended to kill others and cause widespread damage, carried about by someone who does not hope to survive the attack.) In 2001, as the uprising continued, Israeli forces placed Arafat under house arrest in his compound in the West Bank city of Ramallah.

In 2002 Abbas agreed to a new peace plan proposed by the United States, the United Nations, Russia, and the European Union (EU; an economic and political association of European countries) called the Road Map for Peace. Israel objected to the plan, as did militant groups like Hamas (a Palestinian Islamic fundamentalist group and political party operating primarily in the West Bank and the Gaza Strip with the goal of establishing a Palestinian state and opposing the existence of Israel), which continued their attacks on Israeli targets. Facing the collapse of the PA, Arafat finally agreed to one of the main points of the new peace plan, which was to appoint Abbas as prime minister of the PA, which he did in March 2003. Middle East political analysts commended the choice, for Abbas had long been known to Israeli leaders and others across the Arab world as a trusted, level-headed negotiator.

In 2003 Abbas was named the first Palestinian prime minister, a position that required him to work closely with Palestinian president Yasser Arafat.
© REUTERS/CORBIS.

However, Abbas's authority as prime minister was limited. Abbas lobbied the PA parliament to grant him more authority to negotiate on its behalf and to improve the delivery of services within the occupied territories. He also sought to rein in militant groups, who were stepping up their attacks on Israeli targets. Arafat, meanwhile, had failed to follow through on some of the goals for achieving Palestinian sovereignty. "With national liberation as his goal, Arafat was able to [ignore] such niceties of nation-building as creating an independent court system," explained journalist James Bennet in the *New York Times* in 2005. "For many Palestinians, building a state before they have one puts the cart before the horse."

Abbas made little progress as prime minister throughout the spring and summer of 2003. Publicly claiming that he was unwilling to govern while Arafat was undermining his power, Abbas resigned as prime minister on September 6, 2003, delivering his notice of resignation in a private meeting with the PA leadership.

Elected president

The friction between Abbas and Arafat ended permanently on November 11, 2004, when Arafat died in a Paris, France, hospital after a brief illness. The two had been estranged, not for the first time, for more than a year, but Abbas told Bennet in 2005 that the onset of Arafat's sudden illness in late October 2004 had prompted a reconciliation. "I went to him," he recalled to Bennet. "I talked to him, and I followed him to Paris. He is my brother, but the brothers also have their own differences."

Arafat's death, widely mourned throughout the Arab world, immediately resulted in a power vacuum in the leadership of the PA. Abbas emerged as a possible presidential candidate, even though he had never before run for public office. Not surprisingly, there were several rivals for this position. Yet Abbas was the only candidate who offered a reasonable negotiating stance and a plan for ending corruption and bringing efficient government to the occupied territories. On January 9, 2005, Abbas received over 60 percent of the vote. "In the name of God, this victory is for the soul of [Yasser] Arafat," Abbas told supporters on the night of his victory, according to Remnick. "It's also a gift for the Palestinian people from [the cities of] Rafah to Jenin. Also for the souls of the martyrs and wounded and the eleven thousand prisoners in Israeli jails! They are all celebrating this victory with you now!"

Abbas's election was hailed as a positive sign for peace in the Middle East. He even recieved a congratulatory phone call from Israeli prime minister **Ariel Sharon** (1928–; see entry). As a candidate, Abbas had spoken bluntly about the situation in the West Bank and the Gaza Strip and his outline for an end to the violence. "I told them everything openly—that I'm against the armed intifada, I'm against the rockets," he recalled in his 2005 interview with Bennet a few weeks after his victory. "It was in the interest of our people. So I told them the truth, and for that . . . they elected me."

Internal divisions

Abbas faced grave challenges as the elected president of the PA, however, because the job gave him much more control over the PA than did his former position of prime minister. In early February he and Sharon met in the Egyptian Red Sea resort town of Sharm el Sheik for the first diplomatic talks since the start of the Second Intifada. The pair agreed to a truce, which Hamas pledged to honor. Sharon, meanwhile, carried out a controversial program, called the disengagement plan, to remove Israeli settlements from the Gaza Strip and parts of the West Bank. In the spring, Abbas announced that Hamas had met the requirements for participation in the upcoming parliamentary elections, scheduled for January 2006. Hamas candidates won a majority of seats. This stirred outrage in Israel and the West, and the victory placed "Abbas in an awkward situation, in control of the country's foreign policy and security forces, but with Hamas in charge of virtually everything else," noted the *New York Times* in "Times Topics: Mahmoud Abbas." "The strains were [made worse] by Israel's move to cut off tax revenues that paid for the bulk of government salaries, and by the decision of the United States and the European Union to suspend most of its aid in protest of Hamas's refusal to recognize Israel or renounce violence."

Tensions increased in the late spring and early summer of 2006 as Abbas tried to find support for a proposed referendum (a direct public vote on a single proposal) on a two-state solution, in which an independent Palestinian state would exist alongside Israel. Deadly attacks continued in the border areas, with militants of Hamas, Hezbollah (a militant group and political party based in Lebanon), and the al-Aqsa Martyrs' Brigade carrying out raids on and kidnappings of Israeli forces. This led to the outbreak of war once again, with the Israel Defense Forces launching a major assault on the Gaza Strip in June and on neighboring Lebanon in July. The conflict dragged on for months, with significant civilian casualties.

Meanwhile, internal divisions continued to plague the PA. In 2007 Abbas and representatives of Hamas agreed to form a unity government. Despite this cooperation, however, fighting broke out between Hamas and Fatah, with the worst of the violence occurring in June. Finally Abbas dissolved the unity government. Abbas and Fatah took control of the West Bank, forming an interim (temporary) government, and Hamas took control of the Gaza Strip. The PA was divided in two.

Seeks UN recognition

Abbas's term as president expired in January 2009, but he extended it for one year under the terms of PA Basic Law. Hamas voiced its objection to this move and considered its political leader in the PA legislature, Speaker of the Palestinian Legislative Council Aziz Duwaik (c. 1950–), the acting president. Abbas attempted to schedule new parliamentary elections for a date in early 2010, but with the PA effectively divided in two, the contestable legitimacy of the ballot would render any results legally invalid.

Abbas has been praised for his effective management and meeting of the goals necessary for the creation of a sovereign Palestinian state, including the overhaul of its internal security services. He has been critical of Israel regarding its settlements in the West Bank and planned to make his case for the PA to be admitted as a full member of the United Nations. In an article he wrote for the *New York Times* in May 2011, Abbas argues that the United Nations had long ago voted to divide Palestine into two countries, then it formally recognized Israel as a sovereign member of the United Nations a few months later. "The State of Palestine intends to be a peace-loving nation, committed to human rights, democracy, the rule of law and the principles of the United Nations Charter. Once admitted to the United Nations, our state stands ready to negotiate all core issues of the conflict with Israel," he writes. "Palestine would be negotiating from the position of one United Nations member whose territory is militarily occupied by another, however, and not as a vanquished people ready to accept whatever terms are put in front of us."

However, Abbas knew that only a united Palestine could press for UN recognition. Abbas met with representatives of Hamas in March 2011 and proposed the formation of a temporary government. Hamas unexpectedly agreed. In September 2011 Abbas appeared before the United Nations

Security Council to request recognition of a Palestinian state. One month later, the United Nations Educational, Scientific and Cultural Organization (UNESCO) voted in favor of granting Palestinian membership to that organization. However, the appeal for UN membership stalled in November 2011 when the Security Council committee reviewing the application failed to reach an agreement.

For More Information

BOOKS

Abbas, Mahmoud. *Through Secret Channels: The Road to Oslo.* Ithaca, NY: Garnet, 1995.

PERIODICALS

Abbas, Mahmoud. "The Long Overdue Palestinian State." *New York Times* (May 16, 2011). Available online at http://www.nytimes.com/2011/05/17/opinion/17abbas.html?scp=4&sq=%22mahmoud+abbas%22&st=nyt (accessed on November 30, 2011).

Bennet, James. "Abbas Steps Down, Dealing Big Blow to U.S. Peace Plan." *New York Times* (September 7, 2003). Available online at http://www.nytimes.com/2003/09/07/world/mideast-turmoil-leadership-abbas-steps-down-dealing-big-blow-us-peace-plan.html?scp=441&sq=%22mahmoud+abbas%22&st=nyt&pagewanted=all (accessed on November 30, 2011).

Bennet, James. "The Interregnum." *New York Times* (March 13, 2005). Available online at http://www.nytimes.com/2005/03/13/magazine/13PALESTINIANS.html?sq=&st=nyt%22mahmoud%20abbas=%22=&scp-62&pagewanted=all&position= (accessed on November 30, 2011).

Remnick, David. "Checkpoint." *New Yorker* (February 7, 2005): 52.

WEB SITES

Eldar, Akiva. "'U.S. Told Us to Ignore Israeli Map Reservations.'" *Haaretz* (May 28, 2003). http://www.haaretz.com/print-edition/news/u-s-told-us-to-ignore-israeli-map-reservations-1.8840 (accessed on November 30, 2011).

"Profile: Mahmoud Abbas." *BBC News* (November 5, 2009). http://news.bbc.co.uk/2/hi/middle_east/1933453.stm (accessed on November 30, 2011).

"Times Topics: Mahmoud Abbas." *New York Times* (May 5, 2011). http://topics.nytimes.com/top/reference/timestopics/people/a/mahmoud_abbas/index.html (accessed on November 30, 2011).

"Who Is Mahmoud Abbas?" *CNN.com* (January 7, 2005). http://www.cnn.com/2005/WORLD/meast/01/07/who.is.abbas/ (accessed on November 30, 2011).

Abu Nidal

BORN: May 1937 • Jaffa, Palestine

DIED: August 16, 2002 • Baghdad, Iraq

Palestinian militant

Abu Nidal. © REUTERS
NEWMEDIA INC./CORBIS.

"I am Abu Nidal—the answer to all Arab suffering and misfortunes."

Abu Nidal was a Palestinian militant who operated an organization that carried out bomb attacks, assassinations, and abductions in the Middle East and Europe to promote independence for Palestinians and to support pro-Muslim causes. (Palestinians are an Arab people whose ancestors lived in the historical region of Palestine, comprising parts of present-day Israel and Jordan, and who continue to lay claim to that land.) Like many of his allies in Arab (Arabic-speaking) nations, Abu Nidal was convinced that the only way to establish a safe homeland for Palestinians was to destroy Israel. At times his actions tested the authority of the Palestine Liberation Organization (PLO), a political and military organization formed to unite various Palestinian Arab groups with the goal of establishing an independent Palestinian state. As head of the Abu Nidal Organization, Abu Nidal is estimated to have masterminded the murder or wounding of more than nine hundred people in twenty countries from the 1970s to the 1990s.

The name Abu Nidal, which is Arabic for "father of the struggle," is a fictitious name. Despite the fact that the name Abu Nidal was known throughout the Middle East and was the target of intense manhunts undertaken by the security agencies of Israel, the United States, and other Western countries, relatively little is known about the man himself and few photos of him exist. Yossi Melman, an Israeli journalist and the author of the biography *The Master Terrorist: The True Story behind Abu Nidal*, writes that Abu Nidal was "cautious to the point of paranoia," never speaking on the phone, traveling frequently, and keeping few close friends or confidantes. A high-ranking PLO officer once said, as quoted by Melman, "Abu Nidal is so distrustful that he even suspects his wife of being an agent of the C.I.A. [the Central Intelligence Agency of the United States]." Abu Nidal even boasted in one interview that his own daughter did not know who he was.

Raised in comfort, then chaos

Despite Abu Nidal's carefully constructed anonymity, some elements of the secretive militant leader's early life are known. He was born Sabri al-Banna in May 1937, in the town of Jaffa, Palestine. Abu Nidal's father, Khalil al-Banna, owned vast orange orchards in the area and profited handsomely by exporting some of his crop to Europe. The family lived in a large, three-story house with a swimming pool. Khalil al-Banna was also wealthy enough to own homes in France and Turkey, and had several wives. He died when Abu Nidal was around eight years old. Abu Nidal briefly attended a French-run school in Jaffa before moving to a private Muslim elementary school in Jerusalem, Palestine, in second grade.

During Abu Nidal's childhood, Zionism (an international political movement originating in the late nineteenth century that called for the creation of an independent Jewish state in Palestine) was gaining support. Increasing numbers of Jews immigrated to Palestine. Tensions between Arabs and Jews in the region escalated. In November 1947, following a resolution by the United Nations that called for the creation of two states, one Arab and one Jewish, in Palestine, Jews and Arabs began to fight over who would control which areas of land. (The United Nations is an international organization of countries founded in 1945 to promote international peace, security, and cooperation.) Both sides had militias, and the fighting intensified in areas with mixed Arab and Jewish populations, such as Jaffa. The al-Banna family fled the fighting, and in April

1948 Jewish forces overtook and occupied their town. The entire al-Banna family, like many Arabs living in Palestine, was forced to move into a refugee camp. Palestinian leaders, meanwhile, rejected the United Nations plan to divide Palestine. The British, who had administered Palestine after World War I (1914–18), withdrew from Palestine in May 1948. Israel declared itself an independent nation, the world's first Jewish state. Arab nations attempted—and failed—to reclaim Arab land in the 1948 Arab-Israeli War and large numbers of Palestinians fled the violence and became refugees.

Melman describes the conditions that the al-Bannas and others faced in the refugee camps:

> Instead of unlimited wealth, [Abu Nidal] was suddenly forced into abject poverty. Rather than having large houses and rooms filled with toys, he had to adjust to nothing more than a tent. Instead of having servants at his beck and call, he saw how his mother and brothers had to make their way to the UNRWA (United Nations Relief and Welfare Agency) office to receive their weekly food allowance—oil, rice, and potatoes.

The stark contrast between Abu Nidal's earlier life of comfort and safety to one of want and insecurity resulting from conflict with Jews played a pivotal role in his psychological development.

Troubling path

The more fortunate Palestinians were able to leave the refugee camps, the al-Bannas among them. By 1949 the family had moved to Nablus, a town on the west bank of the Jordan River, in territory then controlled by Transjordan (present-day Jordan). The family were fruit-growers and merchants, and young Abu Nidal attended public school. He graduated from high school in 1955 and then attended Cairo University in Egypt to study engineering. Later he would claim to have an engineering degree, but the university's records indicate that he did not graduate. In 1960 he joined his brother in Saudi Arabia, where he worked as an electrician's assistant at Aramco, a Saudi oil company. In 1962 he met and married a young woman from Nablus, and the pair eventually had three children, daughters Bisan and Naifa, and son Abu Nidal. It was during these years in the early 1960s that Abu Nidal became committed to the political struggle of the Palestinians and began attending secret meetings and recruiting others. While working for Aramco, his political organizing activities were discovered by the Saudi internal police, which placed tight restrictions on all political activities in the kingdom, and he spent time in jail before being expelled from Saudi Arabia.

Abu Nidal had similarities with the young men of his generation who went on to build pro-Palestinian militant groups. Fatah was one such group, founded in 1959 by **Yasser Arafat** (1929–2004; see entry) as an organization dedicated to the establishment of an independent Palestinian state. These men came from Arab families that had been forced out of Palestine. They were generally well educated and had settled in the countries along the Persian Gulf; in Cairo; or in Beirut, Lebanon. A turning point in the Arab-Israeli conflict came with the 1967 Arab-Israeli War. In a surprise offensive, Israel captured significant portions of Arab land, including the West Bank, an area between Israel and Jordan on the west bank of the Jordan River. Israel lost a significant amount of international goodwill with this move, and the Palestinian liberation movement materialized into a full-fledged assault after this, with scores of competing factions carrying out attacks against Israeli targets.

The Israelis' seizure of the West Bank, which included his former home of Nablus, is thought to have prompted Abu Nidal to commit himself to Fatah (a Palestinian militant group and political party dedicated to the establishment of an independent Palestinian state) in earnest. One of his first acts upon becoming a Fatah fighter was the adoption of the name Abu Nidal. After taking this moniker, Abu Nidal became difficult to track. As a member of Fatah, Abu Nidal was a target for attack by Israeli armed forces and intelligence operations. He moved frequently, spending time in Jordan, and then leading Fatah operations in Sudan after 1969, where his recruiting efforts were so aggressive that he was asked to leave the country's government. He was eventually sent to Baghdad, Iraq, to act as the PLO's link to the Iraqi government around 1970. (The PLO was founded in 1964 to unite various Palestinian Arab groups, such as Fatah.)

In Iraq Abu Nidal grew even more convinced that the only way for Palestinians to make gains against Israel was through violent action. At the same time, the PLO began to use negotiation and compromise along with armed struggle as tools to gain political advantage. Abu Nidal attended military training camps in North Korea and China, where he learned how to use explosives. Against the orders of the PLO, he began to recruit Palestinians to strike against Israel, thus forming his own small wing of radical militants. In 1974 leaders of Fatah believed him responsible for the hijacking of an airplane in Iraq, which occurred against PLO wishes. In March of that same year Fatah spread the word that Abu Nidal no longer acted as a representative of their group. But by then Abu Nidal was more than ready to operate on his own. This period also coincided with a breakthrough for the PLO; Arafat traveled to the United States to address the United Nations in November 1974. Abu Nidal and the more radical members of the Palestinian movement criticized Arafat for betraying the cause by agreeing to negotiate with Israel and its allies.

Abu Nidal's goals and targets

Abu Nidal was a staunch pan-Arabist and anti-Zionist, holding firm that the elimination of Israel was mandatory. (Pan-Arabism is a movement for the unification of Arab peoples and the political alliance of Arab states.) In one interview, he stated some of the key elements of his program, as quoted by Melman: "Total destruction of the Zionist entity [Israel]. Participation in Arab unity. The path of Pan-Arabism. Building a democratic people's regime in which Palestine is a homeland. In other words, our struggle is for the liberation of Palestine, in which we wish to establish a secular [nonreligious] democratic state." These ideas became the basis for Abu Nidal's acts of international terrorism in the 1970s and 1980s.

One of Abu Nidal's targets was Israel itself, which he viewed as an oppressive force depriving Palestinians of their rights to self-determination. Abu Nidal could not attack within Israel itself, because Israeli security was too tight. It was easier to attack representatives of the Israeli government while they were in other countries. Abu Nidal and his followers executed numerous attacks against ambassadors and other diplomats over the years, including an unsuccessful but high-profile strike against the Israeli ambassador to Great Britain in 1982. Non-government representatives were also targets. Abu Nidal's organization carried out almost simultaneous attacks at the ticket counters of El Al, the Israeli national airline, at airports in Vienna, Austria, and Rome, Italy, in December 1985. Eighteen people were killed and more than one hundred were wounded.

Abu Nidal did not, however, limit his group's deadly attacks to Israel and its representatives. He also targeted any country he saw as supporting Israeli policies. The attacks on El Al airline passengers in Vienna and Rome, for example, were not just targeting Jewish passengers; they were also meant to send a message to the governments of Austria and Italy that it was dangerous to be friendly to Israel. On behalf of Libyan leader **Mu'ammar**

al-Qaddafi (also spelled Moammar al-Gaddafi; 1942–; see entry), Abu Nidal was suspected of carrying out attacks on U.S. targets, including the kidnapping and murder of foreigners in Beirut, according to intelligence sources. The bombing of a café in Paris, France, that left forty wounded was also linked to his shadowy cell of militants. These attacks were designed to send a clear message to France and other nations that their support for Israel was an affront to the Palestinian cause.

Perhaps Abu Nidal's most surprising and frequent targets turned out to be his fellow Arabs, especially members of the PLO. After the 1973 Arab-Israeli War, the PLO and other Arab nations began, in various ways, to negotiate with Israel. Abu Nidal and other militants were strongly opposed to any compromise with Israel; they felt that the only way to make progress against this enemy was through warfare. Therefore, Abu Nidal began to target the PLO and other Arab representatives who indicated a willingness to resolve the conflict with Israel through other means.

The attacks against fellow Arabs began in 1973 with the storming of Saudi Arabia's embassy in Paris; Iraq, which enjoyed cordial relations with the West at the time, was also drawn into the fray. "The attack on the embassy was apparently intended by Abu Nidal to embarrass Mr. Arafat and by the Iraqis to intimidate Saudi Arabia," wrote Thomas L. Friedman in a 1986 *New York Times* article. "Credit for the attack was taken by a group called Al Aqab (Punishment), which was one of the names used by Abu Nidal." Next was an aborted attempt to assassinate Arafat in October 1974. After Arafat learned of the plans, the PLO tried Abu Nidal in absentia (in the absence of the person concerned) and sentenced him to death. Abu Nidal then initiated multiple strikes against the PLO, assassinating that group's representatives in Kuwait City, Kuwait; London, England; Paris, France; and other cities in the late 1970s and early 1980s, and bombing the car of the PLO military chief in 1980. Abu Nidal's group also struck at editors of Arab newspapers they considered too soft on Israel and at countries, such as Egypt and Jordan, that were willing to negotiate separate peace treaties with Israel. In one of its most deadly attacks, Abu Nidal's group blew up a Gulf Air flight originating out of Karachi International Airport in Pakistan in 1986. The plane exploded over the United Arab Emirates, killing all 122 passengers, most of them Pakistanis returning to their jobs in countries along the Persian Gulf.

Abu Nidal's Most Notorious Attacks

According to Ariel Merari, an Israeli terrorism expert at the Center of Strategic Studies at Tel Aviv University in Israel, the Abu Nidal Organization was responsible for seventy-two attacks between 1973 and 1984. These attacks, conducted in twenty countries, killed more than three hundred people and wounded another six hundred. Abu Nidal "definitely holds all the records" for suspected terrorist attacks on Western targets, said Merari, as quoted by Thomas L. Friedman in the *New York Times*. Abu Nidal is best known, however, for two attacks, one that started a war and another that resulted in the placement of military personnel as security forces at European airports.

In 1982 Israeli and Palestine Liberation Organization (PLO) forces stationed in Lebanon, just north of the Israeli border, stood poised on the brink of war, a fragile cease-fire barely keeping the peace. Hoping to push the two sides into war, Abu Nidal ordered the assassination of Israel's ambassador to Great Britain, Shlomo Argov (1929–2003). In London, England, Abu Nidal's supporters shot Argov as he left a dinner, and he was left permanently paralyzed from his injuries. A justifiably outraged Israel blamed the Palestinians. The PLO insisted that Abu Nidal was not under their control, but Israeli defense minister **Ariel Sharon** (1928–; see entry) was skeptical, declaring that "they [Palestinian militants] are all PLO," according to Zeev Maoz in *Defending the Holy Land: A Critical Analysis of Israel's Security & Foreign Policy*. Sharon ordered Israeli forces to invade Lebanon, where the PLO was based at the time. Abu Nidal's action had thus pushed

Israel into the 1982 Lebanon War, which subsequently damaged its reputation around the world.

On December 27, 1985, passengers waiting at the counter of El Al, an Israeli airline, in Leonardo da Vinci Airport in Rome, Italy, were stunned when several well-dressed Arab men tossed hand grenades toward a snack bar, then pulled AK-47 rifles from beneath their jackets and began firing at the passengers. Within minutes, fifteen people were dead, including three of the Arab attackers. At the same time, at Vienna International Airport in Austria, three men opened fire on travelers waiting to board an El Al flight to Tel Aviv, Israel. Three people were killed, including one attacker. In both locations, dozens were wounded. The attackers left a note, written in Arabic and directed toward Israel. It read, as quoted by Ed Magnuson in *Time* "As you have violated our land, our honor, our people, we in exchange will violate everything, even your children, to make you feel the sadness of our children. The tears we have shed will be exchanged for blood. The war started from this moment." The Abu Nidal Organization soon came forward to claim credit for the attacks.

FRIEDMAN, THOMAS L. "ABU NIDAL: LIFE OF A P.L.O. RENEGADE." *NEW YORK TIMES* (JANUARY 1, 1986).

MAGNUSON, ED. "TEN MINUTES OF HORROR: IN WELL-TIMED ATTACKS, GUNMEN BRING CARNAGE TO ROME AND VIENNA AIRPORTS." *TIME* (JANUARY 6, 1986): 74.

MAOZ, ZEEV. *DEFENDING THE HOLY LAND: A CRITICAL ANALYSIS OF ISRAEL'S SECURITY & FOREIGN POLICY.* ANN ARBOR: UNIVERSITY OF MICHIGAN PRESS, 2009: 189.

The Abu Nidal Organization

After being evicted from Fatah in 1974 and forming his own armed-militant organization, initially called the Fatah Revolutionary Council, Abu Nidal largely disappeared from public view. Thereafter, all that was known of him were rumors and reported sightings, but intelligence officers and investigative reporters pieced together a picture of the organization he formed, known as the Abu Nidal Organization (ANO). Both Iraqi leader **Saddam Hussein** (1937–2006; see entry) and Syrian president **Hafez Assad** (also spelled al-Assad; 1930–2000; see entry) permitted him to use their countries for training bases and weaponry shipment points.

At any given time the ANO consisted of between two hundred and five hundred operatives. These members were mostly Palestinians, and they were often recruited from among the brightest young students attending universities in the Middle East and around the world. ANO members

Abu Nidal and his organization set up numerous training camps and cells that taught followers how to use violence and terror to reach their objectives. © ALAIN NOGUES/SYGMA/CORBIS.

were extremely secretive. They organized themselves into small cells, or groups, of between three and five members, and only the cell leader was ever exposed to other members of the organization. Because individual members seldom knew each other, they could not name other members if they were captured and interrogated. ANO cells were created in many countries, with operatives living normal lives as they awaited orders. At various times, the ANO had cells operating in Great Britain, India, Pakistan, Egypt, Libya, Syria, Iraq, Kuwait, Saudi Arabia, and the United Arab Emirates, as well as other countries.

Another method the ANO used to protect itself was the creation of multiple names, like the Arab Revolutionary Brigades and the Revolutionary Organization of Socialist Muslims. This made it harder for security agencies to track the ANO. Furthermore, the group often took credit for actions in which it had no involvement, such as attacks carried out by other groups.

The end of the Abu Nidal

As early as 1984, rumors began to circulate that Abu Nidal was dead, after he reportedly had heart surgery in East Germany. Over the years, such reports continued, only to be quashed when Abu Nidal granted a rare interview or claimed responsibility for an attack in ways that confirmed his identity. After the mid–1980s, his attacks became less frequent and were not directed at any specific enemy. He initiated attacks on behalf of Iraq, Libya, and Syria, and sometimes carried out retaliatory strikes for one group against another with which he had previously worked.

The Abu Nidal Organization remained active through the 1980s. In 1984 Abu Nidal or members of his group assassinated the ambassador of the United Arab Emirates in Paris, and in the late 1980s he killed several enemies of al-Qaddafi. In 1988 his group killed nine people and injured nearly one hundred more when they attacked a Greek passenger ferry, the *City of Poros*, as it was sailing to Athens. By the 1990s, however, Abu Nidal had largely faded from view in the Middle East. Reports indicated that he was expelled from Iraq in the early 1990s and then from Libya in 1998. At some point he returned to Baghdad, Iraq.

In early September 2002 reports emerged from Baghdad's official news agency that Abu Nidal had committed suicide by shooting himself in the head. Other reports soon contradicted death by suicide, noting that his body had multiple gunshot wounds. Some reports suggested that he had been assassinated by Mossad, Israel's intelligence agency. Most intelligence-community sources believed his murder was carried out by fellow Palestinians. There were also rumors that he had been killed by operatives of Saddam Hussein, either because Abu Nidal had plotted to kill Saddam or because he refused Saddam's requests to reactivate his network of militant operatives abroad on Iraq's behalf.

For More Information

BOOKS

Andrew, Christopher M. *Defend the Realm: The Authorized History of MI5*. New York: Knopf, 2009.

Maoz, Zeev. *Defending the Holy Land: A Critical Analysis of Israel's Security & Foreign Policy*. Ann Arbor: University of Michigan Press, 2009: 189.

Melman, Yossi. *The Master Terrorist: The True Story behind Abu Nidal*. New York: Avon Books (reprint), 1987.

Seale, Patrick. *Abu Nidal: A Gun for Hire*. New York: Random House, 1992.

PERIODICALS

Fisk, Robert. "Abu Nidal, Notorious Palestinian Mercenary, 'Was a US Spy.'" *Independent* (London, England; October 25, 2008). Available online at http://www. independent.co.uk/news/world/middle-east/abu-nidal-notorious-palestinian-mercenary-was-a-us-spy-972812.html (accessed on November 30, 2011).

Friedman, Thomas L. "Abu Nidal: Life of a P.L.O. Renegade." *New York Times* (January 1, 1986). Available online at http://www.nytimes.com/1986/01/01/world/abu-nidal-life-of-a-plo-renegade.html?scp=5&sq=%22abu+nidal%22&st=nyt (accessed on November 30, 2011).

Magnuson, Ed. "Ten Minutes of Horror: In Well-Timed Attacks, Gunmen Bring Carnage to Rome and Vienna Airports." *Time* (January 6, 1986): 74.

Moubayed, Sami. "The Death of Abu Nidal: 'Nationalist Turned Psychopath.'" *Washington Report on Middle East Affairs* (November 2002): 48.

Ripley, Amanda. "Assisted Suicide? In Baghdad, Notorious Extremist Abu Nidal Meets a Violent, Mysterious End—One Worthy of His Life." *Time* (September 2, 2002): 35.

Russell, George. "Master of Mystery and Murder: For the Shadowy Abu Nidal, Terror Is a Way of Life." *Time* (January 13, 1986): 31.

WEB SITES

"Abu Nidal 'Found Dead.'" *BBC News* (August 19, 2002). http://news.bbc.co.uk/2/hi/middle_east/2203004.stm (accessed on November 30, 2011).

"Abu Nidal Organization (ANO), aka Fatah Revolutionary Council, the Arab Revolutionary Brigades, or the Revolutionary Organization of Socialist Muslims." *Council on Foreign Relations* (May 29, 2009). http://www.cfr.org/israel/abu-nidal-organization-ano-aka-fatah-revolutionary-council-arab-revolutionary-brigades-revolutionary-organization-socialist-muslims/p9153 (accessed on November 30, 2011).

Mahmoud Ahmadinejad

BORN: October 28, 1956 • Aradan, Iran

Iranian president

"Some European countries insist on saying that during World War II, [German leader Adolf] Hitler burned millions of Jews and put them in concentration camps.... Let's assume what the Europeans say is true.... Let's give some land to the Zionists in Europe or in Germany or Austria. They faced injustice in Europe, so why do the repercussions fall on the Palestinians?"

Mahmoud (mah-MOOD) Ahmadinejad (ah-mah-dih-nee-JAHD) became the sixth president of the Islamic Republic of Iran in 2005, and in 2009 he began serving his second term. The son of a blacksmith, Ahmadinejad won the political support of Iran's large working-class population because of his simple image as a friend to the poor. He is also a defender of the most traditional values of Islam, which gained him invaluable political support from Iran's powerful Supreme Leader, **Ayatollah Ali Khamenei** (also spelled Khāmen'i; 1939–; see entry). Ahmadinejad was initially popular with the people of Iran, but he frequently outraged Western nations with his anti-Israel positions and his defiance of international calls to restrict Iran's nuclear development programs. By his second term Ahmadinejad faced widespread discontent within Iran as well as from the international community.

Humble beginnings

Ahmadinejad was born on October 28, 1956, in Aradan, Iran, a small desert town 65 miles (105 kilometers) southeast of Iran's capital, Tehran. He was the fourth son among seven children of a poor family. His original surname was Saborjhian, which means "thread painter," referring to a humble job in the carpet-weaving industry. When Ahmadinejad was a year old, he and his family moved to Tehran where his father found work as a blacksmith. To avoid discrimination against their humble social status, the family took the name of Ahmadinejad, which roughly means "race of Muhammad." (Muhammad [c. 570–632] was the greatest prophet of the religion of Islam.)

As a child, Ahmadinejad was very close to his mother, who was devoutly religious and carefully observed Muslim traditions regarding women's clothing and the separation of men from women. While young, Ahmadinejad spent much of his time studying the Koran (also spelled Qur'an or Quran), the holy book of Islam. He was well behaved, a devout Muslim, and a good student. In 1975 his hard work in high school paid off. When he took the university entrance exams, he finished 130th of all students in Iran. He enrolled in the University of Science and Technology in Tehran as a civil engineering student in 1976. To pay for school and living expenses, he worked in a shop.

A time of political activism

Ahmadinejad grew up in an uneasy political environment. During Ahmadinejad's childhood, Iran was ruled by **Mohammad Reza Pahlavi** (1919–1980; see entry), an authoritarian, pro-Western leader. The Shah of Iran, as he was known, modernized and secularized (separated religion from political matters) Iran, but in doing so angered the Iranian people. The country's conservative Islamic clerics, or ordained religious officials, and their many followers disliked the Western-influenced lifestyle the shah and his elite circle of followers brought to Iran. The country's poor, who were barely able to eke out a living, resented the lavish wealth of the elite. Advocates of democracy condemned the shah's harsh repression of those who disagreed with him.

When Ahmadinejad started college, resentment against the shah's regime had reached a high point. Ahmadinejad soon entered the world of political activism, joining the masses of university students who were rising up in opposition. With help from like-minded students, he began secretly printing and distributing leaflets denouncing the shah. In 1978 public discontent became so strong that the shah's regime began to collapse. The longtime leader fled the country in January 1979.

The Iranian Revolution

Two weeks later, in February 1979, the renowned and highly charismatic Muslim religious leader **Ayatollah Ruhollah Khomeini** (1900–1989; see entry) returned to Iran. The shah had expelled Khomeini from Iran in 1964 because he had persistently criticized the regime. In his fifteen years of exile in Iraq and later France, the ayatollah continued his outspoken opposition of the shah from afar. Khomeini was traditional in his religious values, strongly anti-Western, and a charismatic leader. Upon his arrival in Iran, millions of Iranians, unhappy with the shah's rule, took to the streets to joyously greet him as the leader of the revolution.

Khomeini and his followers created a new constitution for Iran. The constitution was formed in keeping with the belief that government must be based on the law of Islam and maintained by clerics. But many Iranians also wanted democracy. After several unsuccessful attempts to draft a constitution that would suit everyone, a compromise was found. The ayatollah would rule as the Supreme Leader of the Islamic Republic, a position involving almost full control of the country, but the country would also have an elected president and legislative assembly. The president and the legislative assembly, however, were restricted in their powers by the Supreme Leader and a powerful Guardian Council, composed of six clerics and six experts in Islamic law. The six clerics were appointed by the ayatollah and the other six were nominated by the leaders of the court system and then approved by parliament. The Guardian Council, which has since that time been made up of conservative Islamists, is empowered to approve bills passed by parliament or veto them if they are not in accordance with Islamic law or the constitution. It also supervises elections and has the power to bar candidates from running in them.

The people of Iran were allowed to vote on whether or not to adopt the ayatollah's constitution. The result was an overwhelming 99 percent approval, and at that point, the 1979 Iranian Revolution (also known as the Islamic Revolution) was over. Once in office as the Supreme Leader of the Islamic Republic of Iran, Khomeini immediately imposed new laws, such as mandating that women wear head scarves and banning Western movies. He also closed down the universities for three years to rid them of non-Islamic influences. Books with a Western slant were burned and teaching practices were revised to adhere with Khomeini's rigid sense of Islamic values. Opponents of the ayatollah were punished with long prison sentences and even death.

Ahmadinejad enthusiastically dedicated himself to the ayatollah's vision of an Islamic republic. He joined a student group called the Office for Strengthening Unity between Universities and Theological Seminaries, which supported Khomeini. During the revolution, this group was involved in the takeover of the U.S. embassy in Tehran in 1979, during which fifty-two Americans were taken hostage and held for more than a year. Years later, after Ahmadinejad's election as president in 2005, some of the former hostages identified him as one of the hostage takers, but most experts do not believe he took part in the kidnapping.

The road to political leadership

In 1980 the eight-year Iran-Iraq War (1980–88) began, and Ahmadinejad volunteered to fight. Little is known about his activities during the war. Some reports say he served as a member of Iran's Revolutionary Guard, an elite wing of the Iranian military formed after the revolution, but other reports cast doubt on this. Whatever his role, Ahmadinejad was greatly influenced by the war, as was most of his generation. By some estimates, Iran suffered five hundred thousand deaths during the Iran-Iraq War. And when the weary young men who fought in the war returned home, they were shocked to find that the spirit of the revolution had been replaced by greed and corruption in most local and regional governments.

In 1986 Ahmadinejad enrolled in a master's degree program in engineering at the University of Science and Technology. At that time he also married a university professor, with whom he would have two sons and a daughter. In 1989 he joined the university's civil engineering faculty and taught there for four years.

In the meantime, Khomeini died in 1989 and was succeeded as Supreme Leader by Ayatollah Ali Khamenei. The new ayatollah's ministers recognized Ahmadinejad's loyalty to the revolution and traditional Islam. They appointed him to be adviser for cultural affairs to the minister of culture and higher education in 1993. Later that year, he was appointed governor of a new province in northern Iran.

In his first years as Supreme Leader, Khamenei faced resistance due to a popular reformist movement that sought more democracy and freedom of speech. In 1997 moderate scholar and politician Mohammad Khatami (1943–) was elected president of Iran. His administration removed hard-liners, including Ahmadinejad, from government positions to clear the way for planned reforms. Thus, in 1997, Ahmadinejad's budding political career temporarily came to an abrupt halt. He returned to teaching and at the same time obtained a Ph.D. in transportation engineering.

In 2003 Ahmadinejad was appointed mayor of Tehran by the city's conservative council. As mayor, Ahmadinejad modernized Tehran's roads and traffic system. He strove to uphold the principles of the 1979 revolution by banning Western influences, which he considered decadent. He fought corruption of all kinds and encouraged devout adherence to Islam. His acts as mayor included closing down Western-style fast-food restaurants; creating prayer halls; and separating men and women in elevators and other public places. Many of Tehran's city officers lived in luxury, but Ahmadinejad kept to a simple lifestyle.

At first, Ahmadinejad's working-class roots were apparent in his unsophisticated manner of speech and in his lack of experience. Some of Tehran's elite citizens scoffed at him, but he quickly won the devotion of the city's working-class citizens, who viewed him as one of their own and trusted him to avoid the corrupt practices that had plagued the city. The vast majority of the working poor were very religious and admired his conservative religious views.

The presidential candidate

Despite being relatively unknown in Iran, Ahmadinejad entered the race for the presidency in 2005. Another candidate, Ali Akbar Hashemi Rafsanjani (1934–), a cleric and former president known for his moderate views, was expected to win the election. In the campaign, Ahmadinejad positioned himself as a humble and pious man of the people. He promised to reduce unemployment, institute social programs that would help the poor, and defend Iran's position in the world.

Mahmoud Ahmadinejad speaks during a campaign event in 2005. MAJID/ GETTY IMAGES.

Ahmadinejad promoted traditional Islam as the key to the spiritual improvement of Iranians. He pledged to create a model government in Iran, based on the principles of the Islamic revolution. Like most Iranians, Ahmadinejad belonged to the majority Shiite group, the Twelver

Shiites. Twelver Shia is based on the belief that there have been twelve imams (leaders of the Islam community), each one of whom was a male descendant of Ali, the first imam acknowledged by Shiites. Twelvers believe that the twelfth imam, the Mahdi, who disappeared or went into hiding in the ninth century, was the messiah and that he would return to create a perfect Muslim society one day. Ahmadinejad declared that his purpose as president would be to help bring back the Mahdi.

Ahmadinejad is said to have spent no money on his presidential campaign, but he won the crucial backing of the Supreme Leader and his powerful clerics, as well as the Revolutionary Guards. He won a surprising, but significant, victory over Rafsanjani in the runoff election, garnering 62 percent of the vote. (A runoff is a second election that takes place when an earlier election did not produce a clear winner).

In office

Upon taking office, Ahmadinejad lived up to many of his campaign promises, particularly that of being a defender of the working poor. He established numerous aid programs, increased workers' pensions, undertook major construction projects, and increased the minimum wage. He also cleared his government of many corrupt or potentially disloyal politicians, replacing them with known allies, mainly from the Revolutionary Guards or Iran's intelligence agencies.

On the international front, Ahmadinejad took an exceptionally confrontational stance toward the West and Israel, and was outspoken in his views that Israel had stolen the land of the Palestinians when it established itself as a state in the 1948 Arab-Israeli War and expanded its borders in the 1967 Arab-Israeli War. In October 2005, while quoting Khamenei's position on Israel, he created international shock waves. Ahmadinejad said that Israel should be "wiped off the map," as quoted in the media at the time, including Nazila Fathi's *New York Times* article. He later said the translation exaggerated his meaning, but his anti-Israel rhetoric continued. A year later Iran hosted the International Conference to Review the Global Vision of the Holocaust. The participants, including members of the American white supremacy group the Ku Klux Klan and Nazi sympathizers, questioned whether the Holocaust (the mass murder of European Jews and other groups by the Nazis during World War II [1939–45]) actually happened. Ahmadinejad was one of the conference's speakers. Observers throughout the world strongly objected to his participation in this platform of Holocaust denial, which many view as a gross distortion of history as well as highly disrespectful to Jewish survivors and their descendants. Others objected to the statements Ahmadinjad made at the conference in favor of eliminating the state of Israel.

These positions gravely concerned the United States and other Western nations, particularly in light of suspicions about Iran's nuclear development. Iran's leaders admitted only to trying to develop nuclear power as a needed source of energy, but many feared the country was also developing nuclear weapons. A nuclear-armed Iran could pose a grave threat, particularly to Israel. U.S. president George W. Bush (1946–) demanded that Iran halt its civilian nuclear power program, and the United Nations (an international organization of countries founded in 1945 to promote international peace, security, and cooperation) took steps to slow the program down. Ahmadinejad defied the international community, saying that he would focus on a nuclear energy program regardless of international concerns. The vast majority of the Iranian public viewed nuclear energy as essential to the nation's economic needs and stood behind their president on this issue. The United States, the United Nations, and the European Union, however, decided to place trade restrictions on Iran which prohibited trade in products that could be used in the nuclear program and its finance.

Iran drew the disfavor of Western nations in other ways, as well. In 2007 the United States, then engaged in the Iraq War (2003–11), claimed that Iran was supplying Iraq's Shiite insurgents with weapons, such as the roadside bombs and mortars they used to kill U.S. troops. That same year, Iranian forces captured British patrol vessels, seizing fifteen Royal Navy personnel and holding them for nearly two weeks. Ahmadinejad claimed the British vessels had crossed into Iranian waters, but the British reported that they had been in Iraqi waters.

Iranians, for the most part, supported their president regarding this event, since most citizens were strongly opposed to the U.S. military intervention in Iraq. However, by the end of his first term Ahmadinejad had lost the support of most of the middle and upper classes of Iran, who were inclining toward a more modern government with increased freedom of speech and personal liberty.

Although Ahmadinejad's attitudes were highly provocative, many political analysts speculated that the president actually had little power. According to this theory, the Supreme Leader had been tightening his grip over Iran for years and by Ahmadinejad's time in office,

Khamenei may have been the actual leader of the country. The truth about the power structures within the Iranian government may never be known, but it appeared that Ahmadinejad and Khamenei worked well together in Ahmadinejad's first term.

The 2009 election and the Green Movement

Ahmadinejad ran for reelection in 2009, waging a heated campaign against the reform-minded Mir Hossein Mousavi (1942–). Shortly after the Iranian people voted on June 12, Iran's interior minister announced that Ahmadinejad had won 62 percent of the vote. Mousavi's supporters and many others claimed that the vote had been rigged and asked for a new vote. Khamenei then ruled that the vote was secure. Ahmadinejad was president for another term.

Protestors at a rally in Tehran demonstrate in response to the allegedly fraudulent presidential election of 2009 in which Mahmoud Ahmadinejad was reelected. SIPA VIA AP IMAGES.

On hearing the news of an allegedly fraudulent election, hundreds of thousands of Iranians poured into the streets demanding Ahmadinejad's resignation and major reforms to their government. Because the demonstrators waved green flags, their protest became known as the Green Movement. The government quickly sent out its militias to forcibly end the protests. Thousands of protesters were arrested, and by some estimates, as many as one hundred protesters were killed. The government banned foreign journalists and shut down Internet connections in its efforts to stifle the protest.

For several weeks, the protesters used cell phones and cameras to document beatings and other acts of police violence, posting photos and videos on the Internet. On June 20 a young woman named Neda Agha-Soltan was watching the protests when a government guard shot and killed her. Her death was videotaped and immediately posted on the Internet. It quickly went viral (spread rapidly by being shared by Internet users worldwide). The gruesome video of an unnecessary death, even though it was only one among many such incidents, became an emotional turning point for the movement. Eventually government militias regained control of the streets, and the protesters went home. The demonstrations continued intermittently in the years that followed.

Ahmadinejad's second term

During Ahmadinejad's second term in office, his popularity eroded on other fronts. Many questioned his handling of Iran's economy. Although he proclaimed in public speeches that the nation was thriving even in the face of international sanctions that restricted Iran's ability to trade in certain products, Iran was actually beset by increasing unemployment and inflation (rising prices). (Sanctions are punitive measures adopted by the international community against a nation that has violated international law, usually in the form of diplomatic, economic, or social restrictions.) Costs of essential goods, such as bread and gasoline, skyrocketed. The deteriorating economy devastated Iran's working classes, who had been the base of Ahmadinejad's support in previous years. Two years into his second term, Ahmadinejad gave a speech in a poor industrial town where he once had been very popular. According to lecturer Darius Zahedi and journalist Hamed Aleaziz reporting for NPR, this time Ahmadinejad "found the mood rather cold. A sign held up above the crowd read, 'We the workers of Parsilon [a factory] are hungry.' Another sign in the crowd read, 'Swear to God, we've come to a breaking point from all the discrimination and injustice.'"

Ahmadinejad Addresses the United Nations

On September 23, 2010, Mamoud Ahmadinejad spoke before the United Nations General Assembly in New York City. He talked about his religious beliefs and offered his perspectives on a range of subjects, including the conflict over land between Palestinians and Israelis; the world dominance of the United States; and the failure of capitalism. He also presented his thoughts on the September 11, 2001, terrorist attacks on the United States:

> Almost all governments and known figures strongly condemned this incident.
>
> But then a propaganda machine came into full force; it was implied that the whole world was exposed to a huge danger, namely terrorism, and that the only way to save the world would be to deploy forces into Afghanistan. . . .
>
> Eventually Afghanistan, and shortly thereafter Iraq were occupied.
>
> *Please take note:*
>
> It was said that some three thousand people were killed on the 11 September for which we are all very saddened. Yet, up until now, in Afghanistan and Iraq hundreds of thousands of people have been killed, millions wounded and displaced and the conflict is still going on and expanding.

> In identifying those responsible for the attack, there were three viewpoints:
>
> 1- That a very powerful and complex terrorist group, able to successfully cross all layers of the American intelligence and security, carried out the attack.
>
> This is the main viewpoint advocated by American statesmen.
>
> 2- That some segments within the U.S. government orchestrated the attack to reverse the declining American economy and its grips on the Middle East in order also to save the Zionist regime [the government of Israel].
>
> The majority of American people as well as other nations and politicians agree with this view.
>
> 3 It was carried out by a terrorist group but the American government supported and took advantage of the situation. Apparently this view has fewer proponents.

The U.S. delegation walked out in protest while Ahmadinjad was speaking.

ADDRESS BY H.E. DR. AHMADINEJAD PRESIDENT OF THE ISLAMIC REPUBLIC OF IRAN BEFORE THE 65TH SESSION OF THE UNITED NATIONS GENERAL ASSEMBLY (SEPTEMBER 23, 2010).

Ahmadinejad continued to find ways to infuriate Western nations. In several instances, his forces arrested foreign journalists and U.S. citizens in Iran and held them as spies. International attention was once again drawn to Iran with the July 2009 arrest of three young Americans, who said they had mistakenly crossed an unclearly marked border into Iran while hiking in northern Iraq. One of the hikers, the only female, was released after being held for more than a year, but the other two were charged with espionage (spying) and illegal entry into the country. In September 2011 they were sentenced to eight years in Iranian prison. That same month, diplomatic efforts were successful and the two hikers were released.

In May 2011 there were widespread reports of a rift between the ayatollah and the president. Their disagreement surfaced when Ahmadinejad fired an intelligence minister in April. The ayatollah quickly overrode his decision and reinstated the minister. At the same time the clerics serving Khamenei ordered investigations of several members of Ahmadinejad's inner circle. One was accused of sorcery. Presidents in Iran can only serve two, four-year terms, and many political analysts believe that Ahmadinejad angered the Supreme Leader by trying to place close associates in powerful positions in order to maintain his own power even after the expiration of his second term. Although the ayatollah has expressed his continued support for the president, political analysts worldwide note that Ahmadinejad has probably overstepped the limited role the ayatollah had intended for the presidency.

For More Information

BOOKS

Broyles, Matthew. *Mahmoud Ahmadinejad*. Sydney, Australia: ReadHowYouWant, 2009.

Wright, Robin. *Dreams and Shadows: The Future of the Middle East*. New York: Penguin, 2006.

PERIODICALS

Anderson, Jon Lee. "Can Iran Change? High Stakes in Mahmoud Ahmadinejad's Reelection Campaign." *New Yorker* (April 13, 2009). Available online at http://www.newyorker.com/reporting/2009/04/13/090413fa_fact_anderson?currentPage=all (accessed on November 30, 2011).

Fathi, Nazila. "Wipe Israel 'Off the Map' Iranian Says," *New York Times*, (October 27, 2005). Available online at http://www.nytimes.com/2005/10/26/world/africa/26iht-iran.html (accessed on November 30, 2011).

Hassan, Hussein D. "Iran: Profile of President Mahmoud Ahmadinejad." *CRS Report for Congress* (July 9, 2008). Available online at http://www.fas.org/sgp/crs/mideast/RS22569.pdf (accessed on November 30, 2011).

Milani, Abbas. "Pious Populist: Understanding the Rise of Iran's President." *Boston Review* (November/December 2007). Available online at http://bostonreview.net/BR32.6/milani.php (accessed on November 30, 2011).

Slackman, Michael. "Behind Ahmadinejad, a Powerful Cleric," *New York Times* (September 8, 2006). Available online at http://www.iranvajahan.net/cgi-bin/news.pl?l=en&y=2006&m=09&d=09&a=1 (accessed on November 30, 2011).

Tait, Robert. "A Humble Beginning Helped to Form Iran's Hard Man," *The Guardian* (July 2, 2005). Available online at http://www.guardian.co.uk/world/2005/jul/02/iran.roberttait (accessed November 30, 2011).

WEB SITES

Cole, Juan. "Iran Primer: Iran and Islam." *Frontline* (October 19, 2010). http://www.pbs.org/wgbh/pages/frontline/tehranbureau/2010/10/iran-primer-iran-and-islam.html (accessed on November 30, 2011).

"Mahmoud Ahmadinejad." *Global Security.org.* http://www.globalsecurity.org/military/world/iran/ahmadinejad.htm (accessed on November 30, 2011).

"Profile: Mahmoud Ahmadinejad." *BBC News Middle East* (August 4, 2010). http://www.bbc.co.uk/news/world-middle-east-10866448 (accessed on November 30, 2011).

Zahedi, Dariush, and Hamed Aleaziz. "Foreign Policy: Iran's Green Movement Could Go Blue." *NPR* (April 8, 2011). http://www.npr.org/2011/04/08/135235930/foreign-policy-irans-green-movement-could-go-blue (accessed on November 30, 2011).

OTHER SOURCES

Address by H.E. Dr. Ahmadinejad President of the Islamic Republic of Iran Before the 65th Session of the United Nations General Assembly (September 23, 2010). Available online at http://www.un.org/en/ga/65/meetings/generaldebate/Portals/1/statements/634208557381562500IR_en.pdf (accessed on November 30, 2011)

Yasser Arafat

BORN: August 24, 1929 • Cairo, Egypt

DIED: November 11, 2004 • Paris, France

Palestinian political leader

"Those who call us terrorists wish to prevent world public opinion from discovering the truth about us and from seeing the justice on our faces."

Yasser Arafat. © PETER TURNLEY/CORBIS.

Yasser Arafat, the leader of the Palestinian people from 1969 until his death in 2004, dedicated his life to the establishment of an independent Palestinian state in the territories occupied by Israel after 1967. Over the years, he tried many different ways of attaining recognition and self-rule for the Palestinian people, ranging from unconventional warfare to statesmanship. (Palestinians are an Arab people whose ancestors lived in the historical region of Palestine, comprising parts of present-day Israel and Jordan, and who continue to lay claim to that land.) During the 1970s and 1980s, Arafat was considered a terrorist by the Israelis and a menace by most of the international community. But to achieve his goal of a Palestinian state, in 1988 he renounced violence and recognized Israel's right to exist as a nation, and he won the Nobel Peace Prize in 1994 for his part in historic peace negotiations with Israel. Although

Arafat was unable to achieve his dream of a Palestinian state, many Palestinian people remember him as the groundbreaking leader who strove, both as a freedom fighter and a peace negotiator, to pave the way for Palestinian self-government.

The radicalization of an unhappy boy

Yasser Arafat was born on August 24, 1929, into a privileged Palestinian family living in Cairo, the capital of Egypt. His mother, Zahwa Arafat, came from the Husseini family, which had prominent members in the Sunni Muslim community in Jerusalem. (Sunni Muslims are followers of the Sunni branch of Islam.) His father, Adber Rauf Arafat, was a food and spice merchant, who made a good living selling his wares around the Middle East. Arafat's parents had lived in the then-British-controlled territory of Palestine before moving to Cairo two years before his birth. Arafat's mother died when he was four years old, and his father sent him, along with his six brothers and sisters, to Jerusalem (then the capital of Palestine) to live with their uncle. In Jerusalem he lived in a house located near the Al-Aqsa Mosque and the Western Wall (also known as the Wailing Wall, a remnant of an ancient Jewish temple), two of the holiest sites in Palestine. His early experiences in Jerusalem shaped the rest of his life.

At the time Arafat lived in Jerusalem as a child, the region known as Palestine was ruled by Great Britain. After World War I (1914–18) the League of Nations established the British Mandate of Palestine, a commission that granted Great Britain the authority to administer the affairs of Palestine. (The League of Nations was an international organization of sovereign countries established after World War I to promote peace.) The British Mandate of Palestine was roughly made up of the areas known in the early twenty-first century as Israel, the West Bank, the Gaza Strip, and part of Jordan. During Arafat's youth, the region became increasingly unstable. The Zionist movement, which supported the formation of an independent state in Palestine for Jews, was encouraging Jews to immigrate to Palestine from America and Europe. Arafat's family, like most Arabs in Palestine (called Palestinians), was alarmed by the rapid expansion of Jewish settlements. Across the dinner table they had many politically charged debates, so as a young boy, Arafat received his first taste of Palestinian discontent and anger over the uncertain future of

Palestine. His quick and active mind soon focused on the unrest, instead of on schoolwork or worries at home.

In 1937 Arafat returned to Cairo to live with his father. By this time, his father had remarried. Afaraft's step-mother, as noted by biographer Alan Hart in *Arafat: A Political Biography* was "cruel to the Arafat children" and brought discontent to the family home with constant arguing. Arafat's relationship with his father deteriorated, and he and his brothers and sisters went to live with the eldest sister, Inam.

Arafat's attendance at school was poor but by the time he was about ten years old people around him began to notice that he had talents as a natural leader, although not always a kind one. He was often found giving orders to groups of his fellow schoolchildren. According to Hart, he "carried a stick and he used to beat those who did not obey his commands."

By 1946, as Jewish claims to Palestine were intensifying and causing more violence, Arafat had become a bossy, idealistic, and political teenager. He believed the only way to save Palestine from Jewish occupation was for Palestinians to arm themselves with weapons and fight the Jews. To this end, he joined a group of men smuggling weapons from Egypt into Palestine. But he was shocked when he witnessed Egyptian soldiers disarming these men. Hart quotes Arafat as saying, "The Arab regimes of the day put on a show to pretend they supported our cause. But really their intention was to neutralize us. . . . They were corrupt and they were under the hand of Britain and other big powers." This event strengthened Arafat's belief that only the Palestinians could save themselves from Jewish occupation.

The Jewish state is created

In 1947 the British were looking for ways to withdraw from their commitment in Palestine. In February, Great Britain requested the United Nations (UN; a world organization formed in 1945 to promote peace and cooperation between nations) provide assistance with Palestine. The UN voted to split Palestine between the Jews and the Palestinians. Under this plan, the Jews would receive about 56 percent of Palestine and the Arabs would receive about 44 percent. This would give the Jews, who only owned about 7 percent of Palestinian land at the time, a great deal of land and power over hundreds of thousands of Arabs living on the lands they acquired. The Palestinians rejected this plan and it was never put into effect. War between the Jews and the Palestinians began when Jewish troops moved into some of the lands they would have received under the UN proposal. On May 14, 1948, **David Ben-Gurion** (1886–1973; see entry), who would become the first prime minister of Israel, proclaimed the existence of the new state of Israel roughly within the borders defined by the United Nations partition plan. On that same day British forces departed from Palestine; the mandate was finished. The next day, the armies of Egypt, Iraq, Lebanon, Syria, and Transjordan (present-day Jordan) invaded Israel to retake the land. The 1948 Arab-Israeli War, which erupted between the Arab and Israeli armies, lasted for months. By the time the Arabs were defeated, an estimated 750,000 Palestinians fled or were forcibly removed from their homes and became refugees (people who flee their country to escape violence or persecution).

In 1948 the newly created nation of Israel occupied 78 percent of the former territory of Palestine. For Arafat it was the beginning of a lifelong struggle against the occupation. He devoted all his energy to preparing the Palestinians to fight the Israelis. In 1951, while studying engineering at Cairo University, he established the Union of Palestinian Students, an organization that provided students with an opportunity to discuss the plight of the Palestinian people and share their ideas. Arafat also started to wear a *keffiyeh* (ka-FEE-yah), a black-and-white-checked head scarf that became the symbol of the Palestinian cause as more and more Palestinian fighters wore them into battle.

The Palestinian movement forms

Armed with an engineering degree and a highly political mind, Arafat traveled to Kuwait in 1957, where he began to publish a magazine called *Our Palestine.* The publication called for armed struggle against the occupying Jews and the right of return for the Palestinians (that is, the right of Arabs to return to the homes they had in Palestine before the 1948 war), demands that remained at the center of his politics throughout his life. Together with five friends, and still in Kuwait, in 1959 he formed Fatah, a political and military organization dedicated to the creation of a Palestinian state. Lacking money and experience, the group initially posed little threat to the Israelis. In the early 1960s, Arafat received some training in armed resistance in Algeria and Syria. Meanwhile, Fatah's growing popularity among Palestinians had begun to turn it into an internationally recognized organization.

In 1967 Arab armies once again gathered on Israel's borders, determined to carry out a full-scale war in the hope of regaining their land. When Israeli leaders learned of the buildup at their borders, they decided to attack first. Despite the small numbers of Israeli troops, they were triumphant, capturing the Sinai Peninsula, the Gaza Strip, the West Bank, and the Golan Heights within just six days. Israel set up a military occupation, in which it exercised control over the Arabs who lived in the West Bank, the Gaza Strip, and the Golan Heights. The outcome of this war, known as the 1967 Arab-Israeli War, was a devastating and humiliating blow to the Arab armies. At this point Arafat, furious and intent on revenge, decided that the war against Israel must be fought in an unconventional way.

Fatah's unsuccessful attempts at fighting the Israelis drew widespread attention from other Palestinian factions, which soon joined Fatah in the recently formed Palestine Liberation Organization (PLO), a political and military organization formed to unite various Palestinian Arab groups with the goal of establishing an independent Palestinian state. The PLO was established by Egyptian president **Gamal Abdel Nasser** (1918–1970; see entry) in 1964. The PLO was a Palestinian nationalist umbrella organization. (An umbrella organization brings together many smaller organizations with similar goals, so that they can share their skills and resources.) The organizations that joined the PLO agreed that the PLO would serve as the representatives of the Palestinians, who, as refugees, had no other form of government. One of Nasser's motivations was to keep an eye on young men, such as Arafat, who were politically active. He was afraid that their actions could lead to another full-scale war with Israel, which he did not believe the Arab armies could win.

From terrorism to negotiation

In February 1969 Arafat was elected chairman of the PLO's Executive Committee. Under his leadership throughout the 1970s and most of the 1980s, the PLO conducted a series of terrorist attacks, including airplane hijackings and the murder of Israeli athletes at the 1972 Olympics in Munich, Germany. The PLO hoped that its actions would draw the world's attention to its plight. Outraged by the attacks, the Israeli government responded by tracking down the terrorists and either arresting or killing them. It was therefore necessary for the PLO to operate from bases in neighboring countries.

At the end of the 1960s, Arafat and his Palestinian fighters were based in Amman, Jordan, the country just east of Israel. The Fatah movement had grown rapidly and violently. Its politically charged speeches and radical activities began to worry Jordan's **King Hussein I** (1939–199-; see entry), who, like Nasser, did not want trouble in his country or trouble with Israel. In September 1970, after learning of several violent PLO terrorist acts, King Hussein ordered his soldiers to drive the PLO out of Jordan. Arafat fled to Lebanon, where he reassembled his Fatah forces, aided by financial support from wealthy Arabs and governments throughout the Middle East.

In October 1973, on Yom Kippur, the holiest day on the Jewish calendar, Egyptian and Syrian troops launched a series of surprise attacks on Israel in which Arab troops caught the Israelis by surprise and managed to cross the borders to enter the occupied territories of the Gaza Strip and the West Bank. Several days later, the Israelis counterattacked and drove the Egyptians and Syrians back well within their own borders. (This action is known as the 1973 Arab-Israeli War.) In Syria, Israeli forces advanced so far that they were able to bomb the capital, Damascus; in Egypt, they captured the Suez Canal and threatened to penetrate further into Egypt. Soon pressure from countries outside of the Middle East forced the end of the war and, eventually, Israel agreed to return to the borders determined by the 1967 Arab-Israeli War. Still, the Arab nations felt they had a won a victory, because in the first few days of the war Israel had seemed weak and vulnerable for the first time.

Feeling empowered, Arafat temporarily embraced the idea of a peaceful solution to the Palestinian struggle. In 1974 he stood before the United Nations General Assembly during that organization's first full debate on the Palestinian situation. He was the first nongovernment leader to speak before the General Assembly, which officially recognized him as the sole representative of the Palestinian people. Arafat offered peace but warned that, if necessary, he would fight for his people's right to their land. Arafat said, as quoted by the *Al-bab* web site, "Today I have come bearing an olive branch and a freedom fighter's gun. Do not let the olive branch fall from my hand. I repeat: do not let the olive branch fall from my hand."

Uprising and bloodshed

The peace after the 1973 Arab-Israeli War did not last long. In 1982 the Israelis, angered by a series of small-scale attacks by PLO forces based in neighboring Lebanon, invaded that country in an attempt to crush the

Yasser Arafat delivers his historic speech before the United Nations General Assembly on November 13, 1974. AP PHOTO.

PLO. During a three-month attack on the Lebanese capital of Beirut, orders were given by the Israeli government to hunt down and kill Arafat. Israeli planes dropped bombs on buildings in which Arafat was believed to be staying, causing hundreds of deaths. The PLO, using worn-out old tanks and rocket launchers, fought a long, drawn-out, and bloody war with the better-armed Israelis in Lebanon. The Israelis were swift to arrest PLO fighters, and Arafat was forced to flee to Tunis, Tunisia, where the PLO had its headquarters. The Israelis did not give up. They tried to bomb Arafat's headquarters in Tunis, but he eluded the bomb. Arafat became renowned in the Middle East for being difficult to kill. He survived multiple attempts on his life as well as a plane crash and several car accidents.

With Arafat and the PLO in Tunis, the Palestinians in the West Bank and the Gaza Strip (territories occupied by Israel), became increasingly frustrated. Although many of them were loyal to Arafat, his distant leadership was not enough to help them. At home, they suffered from a lack of

The Intifada

In December 1987 the Palestinian people in the West Bank and the Gaza Strip rose up against the Israeli occupation of their land in a demonstration that later came to be known as the First Intifada. ("Intifada" is an Arabic word meaning "shaking off.") This protest demonstration differed from the many that had come before it in that it continued for several years. The Palestinian demonstrators consisted of men, women, and children, who participated due to anger and frustration. For the most part, the First Intifada was nonviolent. The Palestinians staged regular strikes, boycotted Israeli goods, mounted huge demonstrations, and refused to pay their taxes. But there were violent actions, too. Young boys regularly threw stones at Israeli soldiers, and some threw Molotov cocktails (bottles filled with flammable fluids that are lit and thrown at targets).

Israel responded swiftly and with brutal force. Between 1987 and 1992 more than one thousand Palestinians were killed, and many of the First Intifada's leaders were arrested and thrown into Israeli jails. A lack of leadership led to the decline of the uprising, but the First Intifada brought international attention to the Palestinians' plight.

In 2000 the Second Intifada, much bloodier than the first, also drew the attention of the world. The demonstration was due to Palestinian frustrations over still not having a state and over the poor living conditions and repression of the Palestinians in the West Bank and the Gaza Strip. The uprising began on September 28, 2000, after **Ariel Sharon** (1928–; see entry), a hard-line Israeli politician and former military leader, visited the Al-Aqsa Mosque, the third holiest shrine of Islam on Temple Mount in Jerusalem, accompanied by one thousand riot police. Sharon's presence at the holy site provoked rage among Palestinians that escalated further the next day when Israeli police killed 6 and injured 220 rock-throwing (but otherwise unarmed) Palestinian demonstrators.

At the outset of the Second Intifada, Palestinians used nonviolent methods, but after many Palestinians were killed by Israeli forces, incidents of violence increased. Islamist groups, such as Hamas and Islamic Jihad, and the new Fatah

democratic institutions and infrastructure (roads, schools, and other social systems). In December 1987 the Palestinians took matters into their own hands. A large majority of the population in the West Bank and the Gaza Strip started a mass uprising against the Israeli occupation. This uprising became known as the Intifada.

The Intifada showed Arafat that his control over Palestinians was limited and that a new approach was necessary. In 1988, while the Intifada still raged, Arafat, as PLO leader, decided to officially condemn any acts of terrorism. In an amazing turn of policy, he also recognized Israel's right to exist. The PLO eventually supported their leader on this

group called Al-Aqsa Martyr's Brigade, staged a campaign of suicide bombings. Fighting continued between Israel and the Palestinians for years. There was never a true end to the Second Intifada, but historians usually cite 2004 or 2005 as an end date. During the Intifada, thousands of Palestinians were killed or wounded, the Palestinian economy was severely damaged, and parts of the Gaza Strip and the West Bank were reduced to rubble.

Palestinian children hold a portrait of Palestine Liberation Organization (PLO) leader Yasser Arafat during a 1989 demonstration marking the third year of the Intifada. JOSEPH HEDDADIN/AFP/GETTY IMAGES.

astonishing change of heart. He was ready to give the official channels of negotiation a try.

Extending an olive branch

In 1991 Arafat attended a peace conference with Israeli representatives in Madrid, Spain, to discuss the rights of the Palestinian people. It was the first time that the two sides had come together. However, the Israelis still considered Arafat a terrorist who had orchestrated attacks on their people. They spoke with other representatives of the Palestinians, but refused to negotiate with him, and the talks collapsed. The stalemate came to an end when the Israeli people elected a new government in 1992 with Prime

Minister **Yitzhak Rabin** (1922–1995; see entry) at the helm, a man who was elected by the Israeli people because he promised to make peace between Israel and the Palestinians. Arafat stunned the world when he attended a series of peace talks in Oslo, Norway, with Rabin. His colleagues were shocked and many accused him of being a traitor to his cause, but the Oslo Accords that came out of these meetings were a milestone in the peace process.

In an event orchestrated by U.S. president Bill Clinton (1946–) to honor the progress made in the Oslo peace talks, Arafat stood on the White House lawn in front of news cameras from around the world on September 13, 1993. The man many had called a terrorist shook hands with Rabin. The images of these two adversaries shaking hands remain some of the most famous of the twentieth century. The following year both men, along with Israeli foreign minister **Shimon Peres** (1923–; see entry) were awarded the Nobel Peace Prize.

Arafat and Israeli prime minister Yitzhak Rabin shake hands after signing the Israeli-PLO peace accords at the White House in Washington, D.C. This was the first peace settlement between the Arabs and the Jews since the creation of Israel. © REUTERS/CORBIS.

Arafat thought he had put the Palestinians on the road to statehood, and nine months later he returned to live in the West Bank. The Oslo Accords created the Palestinian Authority (PA), a body of self-government for the West Bank and the Gaza Strip that allowed Palestinians to form their own police forces and city governments. In 1996 Arafat won the PA's first election and became its president. But despite all the media attention and all the praise, the Oslo Accords failed to lead to full Palestinian statehood. Israel still occupied the Palestinian terrorities, leaving the Palestinian people frustrated. Some of the more radical groups continued to fight.

By the late 1990s frustration among the Palestinians was again mounting. Within the West Bank and the Gaza Strip, corruption was widespread, and unemployment and poverty were everywhere. This deplorable situation became one of Arafat's greatest failures. Despite provisions for a democratic PA government, Arafat had led the Palestinians as an authoritarian leader; that is, a ruler under whom power is consolidated and who does not answer to the will of the people. He did not go forward with elections. Instead he placed his close associates in positions of power, and members of his government were accused of dishonestly taking money that belonged to the people. Hopes were high in 2000 when Arafat and Israeli prime minister Ehud Barak (1942–) entered negotiations organized by President Clinton for a lasting peace, but these negotiations failed. After that, Arafat lost popularity among his own people.

Palestinian frustration culminated in the eruption of the Second Intifada in 2000. This time it was a massive uprising, and one that involved a great deal more violence than the first. Young confident men, similar to Arafat in his youth, marched in the streets. Other groups joined in, including Hamas and Islamic Jihad, which were Islamist groups (groups that believe Islam should provide the basis for political, social, and cultural life in Muslim nations). Violence spilled over the border into Israel. The images of angry Palestinian men, women, and children inspired fear within Israel, resulting in the election of one of the country's most conservative governments under Prime Minister **Ariel Sharon** (1928–; see entry). Sharon's goal was to crush the Second Intifada and get rid of Arafat. This prime minister had no intention of negotiating.

Cooperation with the West and decline of power

In the early twenty-first century, Arafat and the PLO were increasingly isolated. His attempts at negotiations were rejected by Sharon and U.S. president George W. Bush (1946–). While he attempted to negotiate with Israel, however, Palestinian militant groups, some of which were clearly attached to Fatah, began to carry out suicide bombings and other terrorist acts in Israel. Arafat condemned their actions, even though the groups professed their loyalty to him.

In December 2001 Israeli tanks pulled up in front of Arafat's compound in the city of Ramallah in the West Bank. The Palestinian leader invited television reporters to join him at the compound, which was surrounded by Israeli tanks, and then he read a speech in which he called for a halt to all attacks on Israel. Although the attacks stopped for a time, the tanks never left Arafat's compound, and he was unable to leave for the next two and a half years. While under this house arrest, Arafat had limited access to visitors and basic amenities and endured frequent Israeli harassment. His health deteriorated. In November 2004 he was flown to a hospital in Paris, France, where he slipped into a coma and died a few days later of an unknown illness. Arafat's body was flown to Egypt, where he received a military funeral. Heads of state, prime ministers, and foreign ministers from around the world attended. After the service, Arafat's body was flown to Ramallah in the West Bank and laid to rest.

For More Information

BOOKS

Abu Sharif, Bassam. *Arafat and the Dream of Palestine: An Insider's Account.* Palgrave Macmillan, 2009.

Ferber, Elizabeth. *Yasir Arafat: A Life of War and Peace.* Brookfield, CT: Millbrook Press, 1995.

Hart, Alan. *Arafat: A Political Biography.* Bloomington: Indiana University Press, 1989, pp. 69, 70.

Myre, Greg, and Jennifer Griffen. *This Burning Land: Lessons from the Front Lines of the Transformed Israeli-Palestinian Conflict.* Hoboken, NJ: Wiley. 2010.

Rubinstein, Danny. *The Mystery of Arafat.* South Royalton, VT: Steerforth Press, 1995.

Shlaim, Avi. *Israel and Palestine: Reappraisals, Revisions, Refutations.* London: Verso, 2009.

Stefoff, Rebecca. *Yasir Arafat.* New York: Chelsea House, 1988.

Walker, Tony, and Andrew Gowers. *Arafat, the Biography.* London: Virgin, 2003.

PERIODICALS

Morris, Harvey. "Palestinians Swift to Create Arafat Legend." *Financial Times* (November 12, 2004).

Ross, Dennis R. "Think Again: Yasir Arafat." *Foreign Policy* (July–August, 2002). Available online at http://www.foreignpolicy.com/articles/2002/07/01/think_again_yasir_arafat (accessed on November 30, 2011).

WEB SITES

"Speech by Yasser Arafat to the UN General Assembly in New York, 13 November, 1974." *Al-bab.* http://www.al-bab.com/arab/docs/pal/arafat_gun_and_olive_branch.htm (accessed on November 30, 2011).

"Yasser Arafat—Biography." *Nobelprize.org.* http://nobelprize.org/peace/laureates/1994/arafat-bio.html (accessed on November 30, 2011).

Hanan Ashrawi

BORN: October 8, 1946 • Nablus, Palestine

Palestinian political activist, author, educator

"Palestinians are called upon to be docile, to stop the 'violence,' to end the 'siege' of Israel—as though the strongest army in the region is being 'threatened' by the unarmed people's rejection of its occupation and brutality."

Hanan Ashrawi is one of the most important and respected female figures in the Middle East in the early twenty-first century. The Palestinian professor of English shot to international fame in the late 1980s after she eloquently defended the rights of the Palestinian people. (Palestinians are an Arab people whose ancestors lived in the historical region of Palestine, comprising parts of present-day Israel and Jordan, and who continue to lay claim to that land.) She spread her message around the world and made the Palestinian cause well-known. She was also a prominent spokesperson for the Palestinian delegation during peace talks between Palestinians and Israelis. She chaired a group focusing on the violation of human rights in the West Bank and the Gaza Strip and served in the Palestinian Authority legislature. (The West Bank and the Gaza Strip are Arab regions occupied by Israel after the 1967

Hanan Ashrawi. AP PHOTO/
JEROME DELAY.

51

Arab-Israeli War.) Ashrawi, who is Christian and keenly intellectual, defies all stereotypes as she struggles for her people.

A supportive upbringing

Ashrawi was born Hanan Mikhail in Nablus, Palestine, on October 8, 1946. The city of Nablus, built over forty-five hundred years ago, is one of the oldest cities in the world and was the economic capital of the region then known as Palestine. Ashrawi was the youngest of five children, all of them female, born to a Christian family. Her mother was a nurse, and her father was a surgeon.

In 1948, when Ashrawi was less than two years old, **David Ben-Gurion** (1886–1973; see entry), the first prime minister of Israel, declared Israeli independence, making Israel an independent Jewish state on Palestinian land. War erupted between the Palestinian and Israeli armies and lasted for months. This was the 1948 Arab-Israeli War. An estimated 750,000 Palestinians fled or were forcibly removed from their homes and became refugees during the war. (Refugees are people who flee their country to escape violence or persecution.) Ashrawi's family was lucky, for they had the resources to move to Amman, the capital of neighboring Jordan. Ashrawi's father took a well-paid job as a health inspector for the Jordanian government.

Ashrawi grew up in a happy and relaxed household. Her father, Daoud Mikhail, was an intelligent, kind, enlightened, and progressive man. He was also politically active, and his membership in the Arab Socialist Party landed him in a Jordanian prison for a short time. Jordan was ruled by a monarchy that felt threatened by socialist groups calling for democratic rule. (Socialism is a system in which the government owns the means of production and controls the distribution of goods and services.) Mikhail came out of prison unscathed.

Mikhail trusted his daughters and believed they should take responsibility for their own lives. He had lost his own father when he was a young boy and was raised by women. He learned to respect their position in society and thought they should play a more important role in the Arab world. These beliefs were contrary to the views widely held by Arab society at the time. Ashrawi's father had a profound impact on her belief system and she grew up believing that she could do anything she wanted and that being a woman would never be an obstacle to her.

Palestinian Christians

When Hanan Ashrawi was a child living in the West Bank, there were many more Palestinian Christians there than there are today. The Christian presence in Palestine dates back more than two thousand years. Palestine is the cradle of Christianity, where Jesus Christ (c. 6 BCE–30 CE) lived and died. During the Byzantine rule of Palestine, from 330 to 640 CE, Christianity was the official religion of the land. (The Byzantine Empire was the eastern part of the Roman Empire, which thrived for one thousand years after the collapse of Rome in 476.)

By some estimates, the Christian population of the area of present-day Israel, the West Bank, and the Gaza Strip was about 10 percent of the total population when Ashrawi was born in 1946. But by 2010, the estimated 51,710 Palestinian Christians in the region made up only about 2 percent of the population of the region. Islam made up about 75 percent of the population in the West Bank, the Gaza Strip, and Jerusalem.

Although Christians have become a very small minority community, the Christian population remains fairly concentrated in certain locations. Bethlehem in the West Bank is the site of one of the largest Palestinian Christian communities with about 43.4 percent Christians. Ramallah, also in the West Bank, is 24.7 percent Christian, and Jerusalem is 17.9 percent Christian.

Christians have been represented in the Palestinian Authority government, and they have had freedom to practice their religion. Many identify themselves primarily as Palestinian or Arab. However, Palestinian Christians have been moving away from the region at a high rate for decades. One of the reported reasons for this emigration is the displacement of Palestinian Christians (as well as Muslims) by the founding of Israel in 1948 and the subsequent wars and conflicts. Another reason for the declining numbers is reported discrimination against Christians by Muslim neighbors.

Not long after their move to Amman, the Mikhails began to miss their home in Palestine, as well as other members of their large family who had stayed behind when the Israelis declared independence. The family decided to move to Ramallah, a city just 10 miles (16 kilometers) from Jerusalem, in 1950. Ramallah is in a region known as the West Bank, which during the 1950s and early 1960s was part of Jordan. Ashrawi attended a Quaker school for girls in Ramallah. (Quakers are members of the Religious Society of Friends, a Christian group opposed to war, oath-taking, and rituals.) She had a quick mind and earned a place at the American University in Beirut, Lebanon.

Exile after the 1967 Arab-Israeli War

In 1967, while Ashrawi was at the American University, the armies of several Arab nations gathered on Israel's borders, determined to carry out a full-scale war in the hope of reclaiming land they felt belonged to

Palestinians. Despite being outnumbered, the Israeli troops triumphed, capturing the Sinai Peninsula, the Gaza Strip, the West Bank (including Ramallah), and the Golan Heights in just six days. These territories represented the remaining 22 percent of Palestine not claimed by Israel during the 1948 Arab-Israeli War. The outcome of this war, known as the 1967 Arab-Israeli War, was a devastating and humiliating blow to the Arab armies.

When Ramallah was taken over by Israel, Ashrawi was still in school in Lebanon. Israel declared her an absentee, and prohibited her from returning to her home in the West Bank. In this period of exile, Ashrawi made good use of her time. An activist like her father, she joined the General Union of Palestinian Students and rose quickly in the ranks to become head of the organization. She also ventured into the Palestinian refugee camps (places where Palestinians fleeing Israel found shelter) in southern Lebanon and taught classes to uneducated refugees about basic political concepts, in order to make them aware of their rights. By 1970 she had earned a bachelor's degree and a master's degree. When her studies were completed in Lebanon, she traveled to the United States, where she continued as a graduate student at the University of Virginia. She completed a Ph.D. in English and comparative literature in the early 1970s.

While Ashrawi was studying in the United States, Palestinian activists were forming the Palestine Liberation Organization (PLO), a political and military organization formed to unite various Palestinian Arab groups with the goal of establishing an independent Palestinian state. Ashrawi's father quickly became an important figure in the PLO. Another activist was **Yasser Arafat** (1929–2004; see entry). He was a founding member of Fatah, a militant and political group dedicated to the establishment of an independent Palestinian state. Fatah was one of the key groups in the PLO. Ashrawi met Arafat in 1969, the year he became chairman of the PLO. She soon became an active member of Fatah.

Return to the West Bank

In 1973 Ashrawi returned to the West Bank for the first time since 1967, after the Israeli Knesset (legislature) passed a family reunification act allowing Palestinians to be reunited with their families inside the territories Israel had occupied since the 1967 Arab-Israeli War. She was shocked at the poor and unsanitary conditions her fellow Palestinians were living in, and she set about forming women's rights groups. She knew that trying to fight the Israeli occupation would end in failure, so she spoke out about the possibility of a two-state solution to the Palestinian-Israeli conflict, where Arabs and Jews could live side by side. She also believed in the right of return of the Palestinian refugees, which is the right of the refugees to claim their former homes and be citizens in the new state of Israel. The right of return is a key issue in the Arab-Israeli conflict.

Ashrawi's life was not all about politics. In 1973 she accepted a job as a professor in the English Department at Birzeit University in the West Bank, and in 1975 she married Emile Ashrawi, an artist, filmmaker, and photographer based in Jerusalem who worked for the United Nations refugee relief group. (The United Nations is an international organization of countries founded in 1945 to promote international peace, security, and cooperation.) The couple had two children. Over the next decade, Ashrawi worked at the university, allying herself with student groups that protested conditions faced by Palestinians and speaking out for the rights of Arab women. Over time she also accepted a number of positions of responsibility at the university, acting as chair of the English Department from 1973 to 1978 and 1981 to 1984 and as dean of the university from 1986 to 1990.

Becoming a Palestinian spokesperson

Ashrawi's shift from being a prominent regional activist to being an international figure came in April 1988, when she agreed to appear on American television, on the ABC program *Nightline*, airing from Jerusalem. The show featured a debate over the Palestinian situation between Ashrawi and an Israeli spokesperson. Ashrawi stunned and intrigued the world with her rational and reasonable arguments. Following her appearance on the show, she began to receive invitations to speak all over the world. Her eloquent position on Palestine had commanded attention everywhere, including at the U.S. State Department and within the Israeli government. The Palestinian question was on every international policy maker's agenda at the time. Only five months earlier, in December 1987, a large majority of the Palestinian population in the West Bank and the Gaza Strip had started a mass uprising against the Israeli occupation known as the First Intifada, drawing the world's attention to the Palestinians' plight.

The years between 1991 and 2000 were marked by a series of peace conferences between the Arabs and Israelis. In 1991 Arafat attended the Madrid, Spain, peace conference to discuss the rights of the Palestinian people. It was the first time that the two sides had come together. But the Israelis considered Arafat a terrorist who had orchestrated attacks on their people. Though they were willing to talk to other Palestinian representatives, they refused to negotiate with Arafat, and the talks collapsed. The stalemate came to an end when the Israeli people elected a Labor Party government in 1992 with Prime Minister **Yitzhak Rabin** (1922–1995; see entry) at the helm. Rabin was interested in peace between the two peoples.

Ashrawi was thrown into the messy and treacherous world of global politics. Described by many journalists as one of the most eloquent women ever to speak for the Palestinian cause, Ashrawi captured world attention with her articulate defense of the Palestinian position during the various peace talks of the 1990s. As an educated and highly intelligent woman, she was one of the most important members of the Palestinian negotiating team. She was invited to attend talks on the Palestinian-Israeli conflict chaired by U.S. secretary of state James Baker (1930–), which culminated in the Madrid peace talks. But because Ashrawi lived in the Arab quarter of Jerusalem, which is known as East Jerusalem, Israel would not allow her to participate.

Israel, in its military occupation of East Jerusalem, the West Bank, and Gaza, greatly restricted the travel of Arabs living there. Thus, when Ashrawi did travel, she was subject to humiliating strip searches by Israeli soldiers. In 1992 she refused to fill out the security form allowing her to travel into Jordan. The Israelis would not let her pass, and she filed a complaint with the U.S. State Department and threatened to boycott peace talks being held in Washington, D.C. The next day she was allowed entry into Jordan, an act that proved Israel had finally recognized her diplomatic status. She continued to fight with the Israeli authorities and was arrested twice but was released shortly afterward.

Dissatisfied with the Palestinian Authority

Being so visible meant that Ashrawi attracted criticism from all sides of the conflict. She was criticized by her fellow Palestinians for being, among other things, too moderate and too friendly with the Americans. In 1993 Ashrawi was initially one of the Palestinian negotiators in the peace talks that took place in Oslo, Norway. At the conference, the negotiators agreed to mutual recognition; Israel recognized that the PLO was the representative of the Palestinian people, and the PLO formally agreed to Arafat's 1988 promise to recognize Israel and renounce terrorism. In a document known as the Declaration of Principles on Palestinian Self-Rule, they agreed to a gradual process by which Israeli troops would withdraw from the West Bank and Gaza. Palestinians would be granted limited, administrative self-rule under a temporary elected body called the Palestinian Authority (PA). But Ashrawi had become disenchanted with the leadership of the PLO and particularly with Arafat, whose methods she found dishonest. She resigned as a Palestinian negotiator in Oslo. When Arafat formed the Palestinian Authority, Ashrawi was asked to be chairwoman. She declined and decided instead to turn her attention to one of the groups she had founded, the Palestinian Independent Commission for Citizens' Rights, which investigated both Israeli and Palestinian human rights violations.

Ashrawi decided to run for the Palestinian Legislative Council during the first elections of the Palestinian Authority in 1996 and won a seat. Although disagreements between Arafat and Ashrawi had become profound, he named her to his cabinet as minister of higher education. As a member of the cabinet, Ashrawi was soon dissatisfied with the internal workings of the Palestinian Authority and spoke out against it as a corrupt organization that did little for the Palestinian people. Her outspoken character worried Arafat, and he changed her position in the government from minister of higher education to that of tourism minister in 1998, without informing her. She resigned immediately.

Despite problems with the PA leadership, Ashrawi remained deeply involved in Palestinian politics and in the politics of the larger world. In 1995 she published a book, *This Side of Peace*, which presents her perspective on the Arab-Israeli peace process. In August 1998 she founded the Palestinian Initiative for the Promotion of Global Dialogue and Democracy (MIFTAH) and since that time has served as its secretary-general and chair of the executive committee.

In September 2000 peace talks between the Israelis and the Palestinians collapsed. Israel closed the border with the West Bank and the Gaza Strip, hoping to stop attacks by Palestinian militants. Border closures meant that less food was allowed into the area, and those Palestinians who held jobs in Israel could not go to work. The Palestinians claimed that the border closures amounted to collective punishment. Palestinian frustration culminated in the eruption of the Second Intifada. This time it was a massive uprising, not only against Israeli occupation but also against Arafat and his officials. People had begun to realize that Israel would remain in the West Bank and the Gaza Strip for the foreseeable future, and they felt powerless to do anything about it. Young men marched in the streets. Other groups joined in, including the radical Islamist groups Hamas and Islamic Jihad. (Islamists believe that Islam should provide the basis for political, social, and cultural life in Muslim nations.) Violence erupted and Israel responded with military attacks. During this period of civil unrest, Ashrawi was injured by a stun grenade thrown by an Israeli soldier, giving her firsthand experience of the violence that occurs often in the region.

In July 2001 Ashrawi took over as head of media relations for the Arab League, a regional political alliance of Arab nations, and the PLO. As a legislator in the Palestinian Authority since 1996, she challenged Arafat's decisions up until his death in 2004.

Elections of 2006

One of Fatah's cofounders, **Mahmoud Abbas** (1935–; see entry), succeeded Arafat as leader of the PLO. He took over a desperate situation. The West Bank and the Gaza Strip had little security, a failing economy, and little hope for a resolution to the ongoing conflict with Israel. Despite the intensity of the problems, the PLO went ahead with plans to hold democratic elections. Abbas, as Fatah's candidate, was easily elected and preparations began for the 2006 legislative elections. Hamas, the Islamist organization that had long refused to recognize Israel or renounce violence against it, surprised almost all observers when it won an overwhelming majority of parliamentary seats, giving it the right to form the next cabinet under Abbas.

Ashrawi was at odds with Fatah but unhappy about having an Islamist party running the Palestinian Authority. In a 2006 interview with Jon Elmer for *Progressive* magazine, she expressed her concerns:

> Palestinian society has always been much more open, tolerant, pluralistic, not a religion-based society. Palestinians were religious in many ways, but they did not subscribe to political Islam, historically. . . . Now, suddenly we are seeing the election of a religious party with extreme political ideologies and with a social agenda that seems inconsistent with the cultural heritage of the Palestinian people.

Hanan Ashrawi arrives at Damascus Gate in Arab East Jerusalem to launch her campaign for the Palestinian legislature in January 2006.
AWAD AWAD/AFP/GETTY IMAGES.

Ashrawi became a member of a new independent party called the Third Way, formed by former Fatah minister Salam Fayyad (1952–), a highly respected moderate. Both Ashrawi and Fayyad won legislative seats in the 2006 election. However, less than a year after the 2006 election, fighting broke out between Hamas and Fatah, leading to a split in which Hamas took over the rule of the Gaza Strip and Fatah ruled in the West Bank. Abbas appointed Fayyad as prime minister of the Fatah emergency government in the West Bank. Ashrawi continued to serve in Abbas's government, and in 2009 she became the first woman on the eighteen-member PLO Executive Committee. In this position, she strongly protested new Jewish settlements in Palestinian territories (Jewish settlements are civilian communities established in the territories that were occupied by the Israeli army in the 1967 Arab-Israeli War.) Ashrawi sought international support in the efforts to stop them.

In 2011 at a conference in Cairo, Egypt, Fatah and Hamas agreed to at least temporarily unite, and to stage presidential and legislative elections within the year, despite warnings from Israel that it would not negotiate with a government that included Hamas. Ashrawi greeted the reconciliation enthusiastically. In a 2011 interview for *AsiaNews* she said, "The reconciliation pact between Fatah and Hamas opens the way to a long journey to rebuild a political system and become a vibrant, active and pluralistic democracy." When asked if Christians such as herself might suffer under a new, more Islamist government, she remarked, "Palestinian law is clear on tolerance. Christians are not a minority but an essential component of the Palestinian identity. Anyone who wants to turn Palestine into an Islamic state will not succeed." She strongly endorsed the united government's plan to seek recognition as a nation from the United Nations.

For More Information

BOOKS

Ashrawi, Hanan. *This Side of Peace: A Personal Account.* New York: Simon and Schuster, 1995.

Myre, Greg, and Jennifer Griffin. *This Burning Land: Lessons from the Front Lines of the Transformed Israeli-Palestinian Conflict.* Hoboken, NJ: Wiley, 2010.

Shlaim, Avi. *Israel and Palestine.* London: Verso, 2010.

Victor, Barbara. *A Voice of Reason: Hanan Ashrawi and Peace in the Middle East.* San Diego, CA: Harcourt Brace, 1994.

PERIODICALS

Amrani, Israel. "Mother Jones MA93: Hanan Ashrawi." *Mother Jones* (March–April 1993). Available online at http://www.motherjones.com/news/feature/1993/03/amrani.html (accessed on November 30, 2011).

Byker, Gaylen. "The Darkest Hour of the Soul." *Books and Culture* (March 2002): 17.

Elmer, John. "John Elmer: An Interview with Hanan Ashrawi." *The Progressive* (April 2006). Available online at http://www.progressive.org/mag_intv0406 (accessed on November 30, 2011).

Victor, Barbara. "A Voice of Reason: Hanan Ashrawi and Peace in the Middle East." *Foreign Affairs* (July–August 1995).

Nicolaou-Garcia, Silvia. "Christian-Muslim Relations in Palestine." *Middle East Monitor* (June 2010). Available online at http://www.middleeastmonitor. org.uk/resources/briefing-papers/1208-christian-muslim-relations-in-palestine (accessed on November 30, 2011).

WEB SITES

Ashrawi, Hanan. "Anatomy of Racism." *Palestinian American Council* (October, 18, 2000). http://www.pac-usa.org/hanan2.htm (accessed on November 30, 2011).

"Fatah-Hamas Deal Brings a Palestinian State Closer Says Hanan Ashrawi." *AsiaNews* (May 5, 2011). http://www.asianews.it/news-en/Fatah-Hamas-deal-brings-a-Palestinian-state-closer,-says-Hanan-Ashrawi-21481.html (accessed on November 30, 2011).

Kreisler, Harry. "A Palestinian Voice: Conversation with Hanan Ashrawi." *Conversations with History.* Institute of International Studies, UC Berkeley. http://globetrotter.berkeley.edu/conversations/Elberg/Ashrawi/ashrawi-con0.html (accessed on November 30, 2011).

Hafez Assad

BORN: October 6, 1930 • Qurdaha, Syria

DIED: June 10, 2000 • Damascus, Syria

Syrian president, military leader

"The Israelis should realize that their current policies towards the Arabs cannot bring security for them nor peace to the region."

Hafez Assad. © PETER TURNLEY/CORBIS.

Hafez Assad (also spelled al-Assad) was the president of Syria from 1971 until his death in 2000. He was one of the longest-serving leaders in modern Middle Eastern history. By the time Assad assumed the presidency, Syria had been suffering from political upheaval for many years, and under Assad, it became an independent and stable nation. He silenced critics of his policies by ruling effectively and forcefully and by suppressing any opposition. Although much of his time in office was spent struggling with issues surrounding the Israeli occupation of the former Palestinian territories, he became an important player in the Middle East, developing his country's infrastructure and presiding over the emergence of a Syrian middle class. Assad was a quiet man who lived simply in his personal life, rarely appearing in public or on the radio, but in his public role, he earned a reputation as a ruthless leader, because of his harsh suppression of those who disagreed with him.

Humble beginnings

Hafez Assad was born Abu Sulayman Wahish on October 6, 1930, in the small village of Qurdaha, located in a mountainous region in northwestern Syria. His family was typical of rural Syrian communities—large and very poor, but close-knit. Assad was the oldest of his five brothers and two sisters. His father, Ali, was a hardworking farmer who had strong political ideas. At that time Syria was ruled by the French. After World War I (1914–18) the League of Nations (an international organization of sovereign countries established after World War I to promote peace) established a French mandate over both Syria and Lebanon, a commission that granted France the authority to administer the affairs of both countries. Ali had demonstrated against the French, whose mandate over Syria lasted from 1920 until the country gained its independence in 1946.

Assad and his family were members of a minority religious group called the Alawis (also spelled Alawites), followers of a sect of Shia Islam that believed that the son-in-law of the Islamic prophet Muhammad (c. 570–632) was the human form of Allah (the Arabic word for God). Sunni Muslims (followers of the Sunni branch of Islam) made up about 75 percent of the Syrian population. In 1930 most Sunnis treated the Alawis as extremists and not as members of Islam. The Alawis, who represented about 15 percent of the Syrian population, were thus a very poor community living mainly in Syria's mountainous regions in order to escape persecution.

Growing up as a poor country boy had a major effect on Assad. His sisters were forced to leave the family in order to seek work with rich families in the country's capital, Damascus. Their jobs did not pay well and involved long hours. Assad was determined from a young age that his children would have a different life. His family's status as poor Alawis at the bottom of Syrian society also had an impact on Assad's social philosophy. He developed a hatred for wealthy landowners, and even when he became leader of Syria, he continued to be suspicious of those who did not share his humble origins.

Assad attended the local primary school in his village, but secondary education did not exist in the remote mountainous regions of Syria. Realizing that Assad was a very intelligent boy, his family decided to move closer to the coast when Assad turned fourteen so he could continue his education. At this time the family changed its name. They associated the Wahish name, which means "wild beast," with the harsh life they had been living. Hoping for a nobler future, they took the name Assad, Arabic for "lion." Abu Sulayman changed his first name to Hafez. Hafez Assad means "lion's guard" in Arabic.

After finishing his secondary education, Assad aspired to become a doctor, but his parents did not have enough money to send him to medical school. In 1951 Assad enrolled in the Homs Military Academy, in the hope that a military career would bring a decent wage that he could share with his family. He proved to be a quick-minded soldier and an excellent marksman. He graduated as an air force pilot with the rank of lieutenant in 1953 and was one of the first Alawites to achieve this status in the armed forces. In the military Assad distinguished himself as a dedicated, talented pilot, and by 1958 he was selected to travel to the Soviet Union for further flight training.

The Ba'ath Party and military advancement

When Assad was a teenager, he had joined the Ba'ath Party, a secular (nonreligious) political party founded in the 1940s with the goal of uniting the Arab world and creating one powerful Arab state. Many Alawis joined the Ba'ath Party, because it was open to all minority groups. Throughout the 1940s, Assad had joined political activities to help Syria win its independence from France. Syria achieved its independence in 1946. As he matured, Assad became ever more politically active and developed strong opinions about the future of Syria.

During the 1950s Egyptian president **Gamal Abdel Nasser** (1918–1970; see entry) began to strongly promote Pan-Arabism, a movement for the unification of Arab peoples and the political alliance of Arab states. In 1958 Syria agreed to unite with Egypt in a new Arab state called the United Arab Republic (UAR). The two countries pursued a merger of their economies and political systems. Although Syrians were initially in favor of the union, after they merged Syrians grew concerned that Nasser simply wanted to take over Syria. Popular resistance led to a military coup (overthrow of the government) in 1961 that restored independence to Syria. During the union with Egypt, however, leaders of the UAR had purged Syria of communists as well as many of the social and military elite. (Communists are advocates of communism, a system of government in which the state controls the economy and a single political party holds power.) These purges left top positions in the country open. Assad worked diligently and quickly rose from his post as captain to positions of increasing responsibility.

The 1960s were a time of political turmoil in Syria. The failure of the political union with Egypt enabled various military factions to form and fight with each other for control of Syria. In 1963 Assad took part in one such coup. By the end of 1964 he had risen to the rank of air force commander. In 1966 Assad took part in yet another military coup (the thirteenth in seventeen years in Syria). Within the new government Assad remained leader of the air force and also took the position of defense minister.

The 1967 Arab-Israeli War and the presidency

The turmoil and internal conflicts that occurred in Syria in the 1950s and 1960s were overshadowed by an even larger problem in the region. In 1948, Jewish forces in the British Mandate of Palestine had proclaimed the existence of the new state of Israel. The new state was located on portions of territory that had long been inhabited by Arab Palestinians, and the Palestinians battled with the more powerful Israeli forces, but without much effect. The British had grown weary of the conflict, and their forces departed from Palestine after the fighting began, ending their mandate. Almost immediately, the armies of Egypt, Iraq, Lebanon, Syria, and Transjordan (present-day Jordan) invaded Israel in support of their fellow Arabs, the Palestinians, thus beginning the 1948 Arab-Israeli War. The Arab countries were defeated and during the war, hundreds of thousands of Palestinians fled the lands that Israel had claimed, becoming refugees without a state of their own. (Refugees are people who flee their country to escape violence or persecution.) The conflict between Israel and the Arab countries of the Middle East would continue to plague the region for decades to come.

By 1967 Arab armies were determined to crush Israel by engaging in a full-scale war. However, despite their small numbers, the Israeli soldiers were victorious, capturing the Sinai Peninsula and the Gaza Strip from Egypt, the West Bank and East Jerusalem from Jordan, and the Golan Heights from Syria, within just six days. The conflict was a devastating and humiliating blow to the Arab armies. Syria lost many of its air force planes and one-seventh of its land to the Israelis. The Syrian people had to lay the blame for the defeat somewhere, and Assad, who was minister of defense, took the brunt of the criticism. Nevertheless, he used his innate political skill to deflect the responsibility for Syria's failures onto the Ba'ath Party as a whole, accusing of it of being disorganized and ill prepared for war. His political savvy saved his top military position and set him on a course that would result in his ascent to the presidency.

After the 1967 Arab-Israeli War, Assad pushed to rebuild the damaged Syrian air force. His close relationship with the military worried other members of the Ba'ath Party, because it gave him enormous power, and friction ultimately developed between Assad and the party leader, Salah al-Jadid (c. 1926–1993). In 1970 the Syrian congress voted to remove Assad from his government post, but Assad quickly rallied his supporters and staged a coup of his own, taking control of the Ba'ath Party and government offices. In 1971 he ran unopposed for the presidency.

The Ba'ath Party at the time promoted a form of socialism in which most Syrian businesses and industries were nationalized, or placed under the control of the government, and farm land was distributed in a somewhat equal fashion among rural workers. (Socialism is an economic system in which the means of production and distribution is owned collectively by all the workers and there is no private property or social class structure.) Assad changed some of the Ba'ath fundamentals. He moved away from the party's foreign policy that had so isolated the country from its Arab and Turkish neighbors. He also expanded the private sector (the part of a nation's economy that is not controlled by the government), creating an economy that was composed of both large state enterprises and small private businesses. He relaxed rules on domestic and international trade.

The first to benefit from Assad's rise to power were his fellow Alawis. Even though the Alawis only represented 12 percent of the population, Assad poured money into regenerating their poor, rural areas. He built schools and hospitals and created jobs.

Assad knew that in order to stay in power, he needed the unbending support of the military, the Ba'ath Party, and the Alawis. He placed his family members, including brothers, cousins, and uncles, in senior positions. He promoted Alawis to leading positions, paid his military generously, and developed a system of security checks to make sure that his fellow Ba'ath Party members remained loyal to him.

Hafez Assad speaking in 1971, during the first year of his presidency. AP PHOTO

Various groups did form and plot to overthrow Assad. To protect himself, Assad organized a rigorous security system, which saved him from several assassination attempts over the years. Nevertheless, Assad still had enemies. They were unhappy with the minority Alawi rule, and they believed the government to be corrupt and incapable of fixing the economy, which had stagnated under large military expenditures.

Brutal repression of opponents

Civil unrest over corruption, the bad economy, and authoritarian rule spilled into the streets off and on between 1972 and 1982, and Assad used his police to brutally break up the riots. He was faced with a growing Sunni Muslim challenge to his rule. To show that he meant to remain in power, Assad sent troops into the northern Syrian towns of Aleppo and Hama, where Sunni groups, including the Muslim Brotherhood (an Islamic fundamentalist group organized in opposition to Western influence and in support of Islamic principles), had launched an armed rebellion against Assad's regime. Under Assad's orders, the Syrian military first bombed the city of Hama, then sent thousands of military troops and tanks into the city. Many of the city's buildings were destroyed. Military troops searched the city for Muslim Brotherhood members and other insurgents. When they found anyone who seemed suspicious or sympathetic to the rebels, they performed torture and mass executions. In the end, the Hama massacre is thought to have killed an estimated ten to twenty thousand Syrians, most of them civilians. Assad's decisive but bloody actions caught the attention of his fellow Arab leaders, who recognized him as an important regional leader, commanding both respect and fear. The destruction of the town and people of Hama ranks as one of the more brutal acts of suppression in the modern Middle East's history.

As a leader among Arabs, Assad was a zealous supporter of Arab nationalism (a political philosophy that celebrates Arab culture and identity and calls for Arabs worldwide to unite), war with Israel, and Palestinian statehood. He rarely made a speech without referring to the necessity of a military solution to end the Arab-Israeli conflict. He called for the Arab world to build up its armies to fight the Israelis and collaborated with Egypt in the 1973 Arab-Israeli War. This conflict ended in a basic stalemate, but Syria viewed it as a victory. In the aftermath of the 1967 and 1973 Arab-Israeli Wars, Syria had remained hostile toward Israel. Assad fiercely opposed direct negotiations with Israel. He was therefore shocked in the early 1970s when Egyptian president **Anwar Sadat** (also spelled al-Sadat; 1918–1981; see entry)

Bashar Assad

When Hafez Assad died in 2000, his son Bashar Assad (also spelled al-Assad; 1965–) took his place as president of Syria. Bashar was not the original choice for successor. His more outgoing, older brother Basil was expected to assume the presidency and had been groomed to lead the country. Basil, however, was killed in a car crash in 1994. Bashar, who had studied to become an eye doctor, was training in that profession in London, England, when Basil died, and he was called home. Now heir to his father's rule, Bashar joined the Syrian military and took on more responsibility in the government itself, leading task forces against corruption and being an avid spokesperson for technology within Syria. Many had feared that Basil would become a harsh and authoritarian leader like his father. Bashar, on the other hand, seemed more soft-spoken.

When Bashar became president, he promised reform. He released hundreds of political prisoners as a gesture of goodwill to the international community. He also allowed the first nongovernment newspaper in thirty years to be printed and opened Internet cafés to allow information to flow freely in and out of Syria. As another gesture to the international community, he began to allow groups with democratic ideals to hold public meetings. He also made sweeping economic reforms, making plans to allow private banks to operate within Syrian borders and to open up more trade with Eastern and Western European countries. Syrians, feeling uplifted by the promise of new political freedoms, called this time the Damascus Spring.

Many of the changes that Bashar made early on, however, did not seem to last. The independence of the press was soon restricted by the government, and many of the groups supporting democratic ideas found it hard to get licenses for public speaking. Web site access was limited. And hundreds of political prisoners remained in Syrian jails. With a strong secret police force and control over

made peace with Israel in 1978. Assad felt that Egypt's compromise undermined the goals of the Arab nations of the Middle East.

Lebanon as a battleground with the West

Syria's involvement with its closest neighbor, Lebanon, is complex. In 1920 the French, under their mandate, had split the area known as Greater Syria into the two countries of Lebanon and Syria. Syria's leaders had never wholly accepted Lebanon's status as a separate state. Assad wished to pursue a more active leadership role among Arab nations. One way to do that was to form an international alliance of Arab states, with Syria as leader. He wanted Lebanon as his first follower.

the country's military, Bashar's government was able to crush his opponents effectively and brutally, using many of the same methods as his father, including imprisonment without trial, torture, and death for dissidents.

In March 2011, after the onset of the Arab Spring (a series of prodemocracy uprisings in the Middle East and North Africa) protesters took to the streets in Syria, protesting Assad's repressive measures and demanding democratic reform. The Assad regime at first responded with promises of reform but later launched a fierce military crackdown on dissenters. Despite drawing harsh criticism from governments around the world, including some of Syria's closest allies in the Middle East, Assad continued his crackdown on all opposition. In July, he followed in the footsteps of his father with an attack on the city of Hama, where his forces employed bombs, snipers, and other combat weapons against their fellow citizens. By December 2011, the United Nations estimated that more than five thousand people had been killed since the uprising began. The UN initiated an investigation into Syria's human rights abuses.

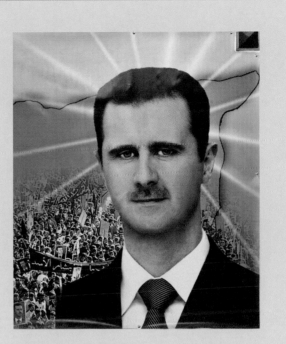

A propaganda poster of Bashar Assad. © JENS BENNINGHOFEN/ALAMY.

Lebanon erupted in a civil war in 1975, complicated greatly by the large number of Palestinian refugees living within its borders. Most problematic was that the Palestine Liberation Organization (PLO; a political and military organization formed to unite various Palestinian Arab groups with the goal of establishing an independent Palestinian state) had set up its headquarters in Lebanon and was conducting attacks on Israel from within Lebanon's borders. After a year of intense fighting between the different Lebanese groups, in 1976 the Arab League negotiated peace in Lebanon with the Riyadh Accords. Under these accords, Syria was authorized to station forty thousand troops in Lebanon to maintain peace.

Lebanon's civil war was still going on in 1982, when Israel invaded Lebanon in a campaign to push the PLO far enough away from Israeli borders so that their rockets could not reach Israeli settlements. To this end, Israel attacked Beirut, where thousands of PLO troops were assembled in fortified areas. The fighting was vicious, but by August that year, the United States negotiated a plan to evacuate Israeli, PLO, and Syrian troops from Beirut, with the help of U.S. Marines aided by French and Italian troops. These international forces soon arrived, but even their presence did not stop the fighting in Lebanon, and Syria repeatedly refused to remove its troops from the country. After several terrorist attacks on American, French, and Israeli troops in Lebanon, those forces had all withdrawn by 1983.

Assad helped Syria emerge as a powerful regional force. Even though he was suspicious of U.S. intentions in the Middle East and especially of its military and economic support of Israel, Assad joined the U.S.-led coalition against Iraq to free Kuwait from Iraqi invaders in the Persian Gulf War (1990–91). For this contribution to the Persian Gulf War, Syria received nearly two billion dollars in foreign aid.

Personal life and final years

Assad was an accomplished soldier, but he hardly ever wore his military uniform, and he rarely appeared in public. He was a family man at heart, who spent much of his time with his wife and children. He lived humbly and was not interested in money and riches. He created a secure state by using his intelligence and political skill, and by harshly suppressing those who opposed him. But he suffered from cancer and kidney problems for a long period, and died of apparent heart failure on June 10, 2000.

Assad's three decades as president of Syria made him the longest-serving leader in the country's history. Shortly after his death, the Syrian congress nominated Assad's thirty-four-year-old son, Bashar, to be the country's next president.

For More Information
BOOKS
Gordon, Matthew S. *Hafez Al-Assad*. New York: Chelsea House, 1989.

Lawson, Fred H. *Demystifying Syria*. London: Saqi Books, 2010.

Leverett, Flynt. *Inheriting Syria: Bashar's Trial By Fire*. Washington DC: The Brookings Institution, 2005.

Seale, Patrick. *Assad of Syria: Struggle*. Berkeley: University of California, 1992.

PERIODICALS

Ackerman, Gary L. "Portrait of a Despot: Hafez al-Assad" *New York Times* (May 1, 2011).

Friedman, Thomas L. "The New Hama Rules." *New York Times* (August 2, 2011).

MacFarquhar, Neil. "Hafez al-Assad, Who Turned Syria Into a Power in the Middle East, Dies at 69." *New York Times* (June 10, 2000).

WEB SITES

Assad, Hafez. Speech at the People's Assembly, Damascus, Syria. March 11, 1999. *Presidentassad.net.* http://www.presidentassad.net/HAFEZ_AL_ASSAD/President_Hafez_Al_Assad_CV.htm (accessed on November 30, 2011).

"Profile: Syria's Bashar al-Assad." *BBC News* (March 25, 2005). http://news.bbc.co.uk/2/hi/middle_east/2579331.stm (accessed on November 30, 2011).

Mustafa Kemal Atatürk

BORN: 1881 • Salonika, Ottoman Empire

DIED: November 10, 1938 • Istanbul, Turkey

Turkish president, military leader

"We shall raise our country to the level of the most prosperous and civilized nations of the world. We shall endow our nation with the broadest means and sources of welfare."

Mustafa Kemal Atatürk.
© PETER HORREE/ALAMY.

Mustafa Kemal Atatürk is widely hailed as the founder of modern Turkey, a nation that emerged in 1923 out of the wreckage of the Ottoman Empire. (The Ottoman Empire was vast empire of the Ottoman Turks which included southwest Asia, northeast Africa, and southeast Europe, and lasted from the thirteenth century to the early twentieth century.) Atatürk led the heroic fight for Turkey's independence in the early 1920s. Once independence was won, he was renowned for restoring the Turks' pride in their culture while at the same time enacting some remarkable changes. Atatürk established secular (nonreligious) rule in his predominantly Muslim nation and paved the way for democracy and the protection of individual rights, although Turkey would not become a true democracy until after his death.

Raised in a dying empire

Atatürk grew up in humble conditions. He was born sometime in 1881 to Ali Riza Efendi and Zübeyde Hanim ("Hanim" is the Turkish equivalent of "Mrs."), lower-middle-class Muslims living in the city of Salonika (present-day Thessalonika, Greece). His parents gave him the single name Mustafa. (Surnames, or family names, were not always given to children in Turkey prior to 1934.) When his father's business failed, the family fell into poverty. Then Atatürk's father died, and he was raised by his mother until he was about twelve years old. In 1893 Atatürk rejected the idea of going to a religious school and instead entered a military school in Salonika, where he soon became a star pupil. His skills were so strong in mathematics that his teacher is said to have nicknamed him Kemal, which means "perfection." For many years thereafter, he was known as Mustafa Kemal. He would later be awarded the last name of Atatürk by the Turkish government.

Atatürk thrived in military school. In 1899 he joined the infantry class of the Military Academy in Istanbul, and graduated from the General Staff College as a captain in 1905. Even though he was a member of the military, he came to dislike the corrupt and inefficient regime that ruled his land. Atatürk grew up at a time when the Ottoman Empire was in a state of severe decline. At its peak in the 1500s, the Ottoman Empire had ruled over all of the Middle East, much of northern Africa, and parts of southeastern Europe. But by the early 1900s the Ottoman sultan (ruler) reigned over a Middle East in which lesser nobles, such as minor sheikhs, emirs, and tribal chieftains, exercised the real power, obtaining great personal wealth while ignoring the needs of the common people. The majority religion in the Ottoman Empire was Islam, but within the empire there were people of many different cultures and backgrounds, with local governments and institutions. Roughly 40 percent of the people spoke a Turkish language, 40 percent spoke Arabic, and the remainder spoke a variety of other languages. The Ottoman Empire was thus a loose affiliation of weak alliances, ruled by a caliph, the spiritual, political, and military leader of the world's Muslims from the death of Muhammad in 632 until the caliphate was abolished in 1924. (The caliphate is the entire community of Muslims under the leadership of the caliph.)

Atatürk was one of many bright young men of his time who saw the weaknesses in the Ottoman Empire. In 1907 he became a member of a group called the Young Turks, or officially, the Committee of Union and Progress (CUP), which called for a government that represented the people. By 1908 the Young Turks movement had grown so popular among the Turkish people that the Ottoman sultan was forced to declare a constitutional government. The constitution offered equal rights to everyone in the empire. Within a year the unpopular sultan was deposed and another, far weaker, sultan took his place. After a few years vying for power with other groups for control, in 1912 the Young Turks took over the Turkish government in a violent revolt. They were at first divided among themselves between those who sought democracy and those who favored a strong central state. After a power struggle, the latter group established military dictatorship (in which the ruler has unrestricted power) under the leadership of three men: Enver Pasha (1881–1922) Mehmet Talat Pasha (1874–1921), Ahmed Djemal Pasha (1872–1922), sometimes known as the "three pashas." (Pashas were high-ranking officials of the Ottoman Empire.) The three-man dictatorship ruled the Ottoman Empire in its last years, from 1913 to 1918.

Atatürk had played a small role in pressuring the sultan along with the other Young Turks, but he did not get along well with the three Pashas. During most of their rule he was fighting in wars, far from the politics in the empire's capital city of Istanbul. In 1912 and 1913, he led the Turks in the Balkan Wars, two brief wars in which Serbia, Greece, Bulgaria, and Montenegro fought against the Ottoman Empire for independence. He was a well respected commander by the time the Ottoman Empire entered into a world war.

Leads quest for independence

In 1914, as European nations rushed into World War I (1914–18; a global war between the Allies [Great Britain, France, and Russia, joined later by the United States] and the Central Powers [Germany, Austria-Hungary, and their allies]). Enver Pasha, the Empire's minister of war, decided to enter the war on the side of Germany. Atatürk disagreed with this decision, thinking that the Turks should remain neutral. Nevertheless he fought bravely in the war that ensued. In April 1915, when the Ottoman Empire faced an attack by French and English forces on Gallipoli (a narrow peninsula in present-day northwest Turkey), he led a determined resistance. An estimated 250,000 men were lost on each side in this bloody battle, but due in large part to the bravery of the Turkish army led by Atatürk, the allied forces were stopped. It was one of the Ottoman Empire's few triumphs in the war, and in the eyes of the Turks, Atatürk became a national hero at Gallipoli. He spent the rest of the war leading important Turkish missions.

A statue of Mustafa Kemal Atatürk commanding Turkish forces at Gallipoli in 1915.
© ALI KABAS/ALAMY.

The Middle East was in disarray at the end of World War I. Victorious allied leaders appointed Sultan Mehmed VI (1861–1926), brother of Mehmed V, as leader of the Ottoman Empire. In 1920 the Ottoman Empire signed a peace treaty with the Allies. The Treaty of Sèvres, allowed military forces from Great Britain and France to take charge of the newly formed nations of Syria, Lebanon, Iraq, Palestine, and Transjordan (present-day Jordan) under the mandate system established by the League of Nations, an international organization of sovereign countries established after World War I to promote peace. (The mandate system grants one country the authority to administer the affairs of another country.) The Treaty of Sèvres, which was signed by the Ottoman sultan, also included plans to divide the region that forms present-day Turkey among European allies. The largest western region, Anatolia, was granted to Greece and Italy. Separate parcels were divided up to be given to the Armenians (Christian Turks) in the northeast and the Kurds in the southeast. (The Kurds are a non-Arab ethnic group who live mainly in present-day Turkey, Iraq, and Iran).

Atatürk could not stand to see the the Turkish homeland fall under foreign control. He rallied support among the many contacts he had made during his military career. Many Turks agreed to fight rather than to let their country be cut up by Western powers. They joined together in a new spirit of Turkish nationalism, the belief that a people with shared ethnic, cultural, and/or religious identities have the right to form their own nation. On April 23, 1920, the Turks named Atatürk president of a new legislature called the Grand National Assembly. He gathered together a powerful army to fight against the Greeks, who were preparing to take control of Turkey. The Turkish army's ultimate goal was Turkish independence. By 1922, Atatürk had asked the Grand National Assembly for, and received, absolute authority. The Turkish forces, led by Atatürk, went on to defeat the Greeks and their allies.

In 1922 the Ottoman sultanate was abolished and replaced by a temporary government based on a democratic model. The temporary government, led by Atatürk, negotiated a new treaty with Grat Britain and France. The Treaty of Lausanne, signed on July 24, 1923, established the modern borders of Turkey, which included the lands designated for Greece, part of the Armenian land, and all of the Kurdish land. With the 1923 treaty, the Turkish homelands were confirmed as the Republic of Turkey, a new nation in the eyes of the world.

Secularized the state

In 1923, Atatürk had already taken his position as Turkey's leader and he was in position to shape the new Turkish government from scratch. He created Turkey in the basic form of a democracy, with elections, a president, prime minister, court system, and a legislature, called the Grand National Assembly. But Atatürk created only a single political party, which was under his control. With only one party, elections did not give the people of Turkey choices regarding their government. Atatürk remained solidly in control of the new nation.

Atatürk's main goal as the new country's president was to make Turkey a modern, Western-style nation. He admired Western nations, such as Great Britain, France, and the United States, because of the individual freedoms and opportunities they allow their citizens. And he opposed the Ottoman system, with its great divide between rich and poor and with Muslim clerics in charge of most governmental functions. Atatürk, who was from a Muslim family, though not a practicing Muslim, set about breaking the historic chains that linked church and state under the caliphate. According to Cengiz Candar, writing in an article for *Wilson Quarterly* magazine, Atatürk once said that "the evils which had sapped the nation's strength had all been wrought in the name of religion." Among his most dramatic and historic actions were those that ended religious involvement in governmental affairs: the secularization of the state.

In March 1924 Atatürk abolished what was left of the caliphate. In early times, the caliphs of the Islamic empires had been powerful leaders, who, at least in theory, ruled over one great nation of Islam. During the Ottoman era, however, as local governments gained strength, the title of caliph had lost much of its significance. Atatürk believed that religion should be separated from the political and legal world. He eliminated the former Turkish legal structure that had been based on sharia (Islamic religious law) and *waqf*, a system for setting aside land for Muslim religious purposes. He also ordered that all educational institutions operate under state control and abolished the religious courts. In 1928 he ordered that Turkish be the official language and that it be written in the Latin alphabet, as opposed to the Arabic alphabet. He then ordered that the Koran be translated from Arabic into Turkish so that common Turks could read it for themselves, rather than relying on the interpretations of clerics, or ordained religious officials. (This policy was similar to one adopted by Protestants in Europe hundreds of years earlier when the Bible was translated from Latin.) And in 1934 Atatürk pushed through a constitutional amendment that granted citizenship rights to women.

Mustafa Kemal Atatürk teaching the Latin alphabet in 1928. FOTOSEARCH/ GETTY IMAGES.

Hero Worship

During his lifetime, Atatürk was revered as a war hero and beloved ruler who saved Turkey from foreign control, formed it into an independent nation, and restored the Turks' pride in their homeland and culture. In modern times he continues to be idolized as the "father" of the country and is sometimes even viewed as a god-like figure. Thus, even in the early twenty-first century Atatürk's picture is prominently displayed in restaurants, schools, and public places throughout Turkey. It is illegal in Turkey to criticize Atatürk. Each year, on November 10 (the date of Atatürk's death) the people of Turkey honor him with a moment of silence. This much respect for a leader who died more than half a century ago is highly unusual, especially when one considers that Atatürk was authoritarian in his political powers and had many human foibles in his personal life. A few scholars and artists have publicly contested this unquestioning idealization of Atatürk as a distortion of history.

Not only did Atatürk abolish any official links between Islam and the Republic of Turkey, as the country is officially known, but he also dictated rules that ended many Muslim customs. He banned people from wearing religious dress except during ceremonial occasions and eliminated the requirement that women wear a hijab, the veil common in many Muslim societies. In 1925 he stopped wearing a fez, a traditional Muslim cap that allowed wearers to touch their foreheads to the ground in prayer, and urged all Turks to wear Western-style hats. Atatürk allowed Western music and the use of alcohol, both formerly prohibited. Finally, in 1934 he required that all Turks take a Turkish last name. It was this requirement that led to the Turkish legislature officially giving him the name Atatürk, which means "Father Turk." According to an article in *New Criterion* by David Fromkin, "it was a total cultural revolution, imposed by one man's iron will and by the force of an army."

Atatürk instilled great pride in the Turkish people. From the moment he took control, he was a great promoter of all things Turkish. In his speeches he extolled the noble spirit of the Turkish people, and he helped his people see the positive elements in their history. He placed posters of himself everywhere in the country and urged his people to identify with their nation. This pride continued into the twenty-first century, and Atatürk's likeness remained visible in public buildings and private homes throughout the country.

A powerful leader

Although Atatürk wanted his country to be democratic, he exerted nearly complete control. He banned any political parties that criticized his changes and harassed and even ordered the murder of political opponents. Despite the strength of his leadership style, however, Atatürk did not wish to be seen as a dictator, or to be compared to German leader Adolf Hitler (1889–1945) or Italian leader Benito Mussolini (1883–1945), his contemporaries. He resisted the efforts of others to call him president-for-life and insisted that all of his orders be approved by the Grand National Assembly. According to Ahmet Kuyas, writing in *Encyclopedia of the Modern Middle East and North Africa*, Atatürk "was trying to establish a democratic tradition in Turkey," and his "dictatorial rule was in effect an apprenticeship in democracy." This view, quite common among historians, holds that in a country as ill-prepared for democracy as Turkey was at the time, strong, even antidemocratic leadership is required to bring about the conditions needed for the realization of true democratic rule. This insight is controversial in the twenty-first century, when many Middle Eastern countries are struggling to rid themselves of authoritarian rulers who also insist that their repressive rule is for the long-term benefit of their people.

Atatürk served as president of Turkey from 1923 until his death in 1938, and enabled his country to make a great leap forward in its development. He created democratic institutions of government, improved the school and social service systems, developed modern industries, and began to develop Turkey's infrastructure (its system of roads and communication networks). While Atatürk had a number of personally undesirable traits, such as being a womanizer (despite being married with a family) and an alcoholic, whose excessive drinking led to his death, most Turks remember him for the immense national pride that he stirred among his people.

According to biographer Andrew Mango in *Atatürk*, "Atatürk's message is that East and West can meet on the ground of universal secular values and mutual respect, that nationalism is compatible with peace, that human reason is the only true guide in life." Turkey is widely considered to have realized this goal, for its democratic structures have withstood the tests of time, allowing for political and religious freedom, and because the nation has managed to maintain friendly relations with its neighbors both to the East and to the West.

For More Information

BOOKS

Ahmad, Feroz. *The Making of Modern Turkey*. London: Routledge, 1993.

Findley, Carter Vaughn. *Turkey, Islam, Nationalism, and Modernity*. New Haven, CT: Yale University Press, 2010.

Hanioglu, M. Sukru. *Atatürk: An Intellectual Biography*. Princeton, NJ: Princeton University Press, 2011.

Kuyas, Ahmet. "Atatürk, Mustafa Kemal." In *Encyclopedia of the Modern Middle East and North Africa*. Edited by Philip Mattar. New York: Macmillan Reference USA, 2004, p. 324.

Macfie, A.L. *Atatürk*. London: Longman, 1994.

Mango, Andrew. *Atatürk*. Woodstock, NY: Overlook Press, 2000.

Pettifer, James. *The Turkish Labyrinth: Atatürk and the New Islam*. London: Viking, 1997.

PERIODICALS

Candar, Cengiz. "Atatürk's Ambiguous Legacy." *Wilson Quarterly* 24, no. 4 (Autumn 2000): 88.

Cherry, Matt. "When a Muslim Nation Embraces Secularism." *The Humanist* 62, no. 3 (May–June 2002): 21.

Fromkin, David. "Atatürk's Creation." *New Criterion* 18, no. 8 (April 2000): 14.

WEB SITES

"Mustafa Kemal Atatürk." *Ataturk.com*. http://www.Ataturk.org/index2.html (accessed on November 30, 2011).

"Mustafa Kemal Atatürk." *Encyclopedia of the Middle East: MidEast Web*. http://www.mideastweb.org/Middle-East-Encyclopedia/kemal-ataturk.htm (accessed on November 30, 2011).

Menachem Begin

BORN: August 16, 1913 • Brest-Litovsk, Poland

DIED: March 9, 1992 • Tel Aviv, Israel

Israeli prime minister, political activist

"We must beware of compromise. Any compromise, any agreement by the Jewish people in Palestine to a limitation of the concept of rule, or the concept of the Land of Israel, is likely to result in the loss of the entire political objective."

Menachem Begin devoted his life to Israel's independence. From an early age he experienced the misery of being Jewish at a time when widespread anti-Semitism (prejudice against Jews) had made much of Europe a place in which Jews were not welcome and yet, lacking a homeland, they had no place else to go. Begin survived imprisonment in Russia during World War II (1939–45; a war in which the Allies [Great Britain, France, the Soviet Union, the United States, and China] defeated the Axis Powers [Germany, Italy, and Japan]), but lost his entire family except his sister to the German concentration camps. (Concentration camps are complexes built by the Germans for the confinement and extermination of political opponents and ethnic minorities, especially Jews.) A frail man with thick spectacles, Begin

Menachem Begin. KEYSTONE-FRANCE/GAMMA-KEYSTONE VIA GETTY IMAGES.

85

rose to assume the leadership of Irgun Zvai Leumi, a militant group that worked to secure Israeli independence. For the violent attacks he led on British and Arab targets, Begin earned the contradictory labels of "hero" and "terrorist." (Arab are people who speak the Arabic language or who live in countries in which Arabic is the dominant language.) After the state of Israel was established in 1948, Begin turned his attention from war to peace. As prime minister of Israel, Begin negotiated Israel's first peace treaty with an Arab state, securing an end to more than thirty years of tension with Egypt and winning the Nobel Peace Prize in 1978, which he shared with Egyptian president **Anwar Sadat** (also spelled al-Sadat; 1918–1981; see entry).

Discrimination in Poland

Menachem Wolfovitch Begin was born on August 16, 1913, in Brest-Litovsk, Poland. He was the youngest of Ze'ev Dov and Hassia Begin's three children. Begin's father worked as a traveling timber salesman, an occupation that brought him into contact with a wide variety of people. Ze'ev Dov hoped that Jews would someday establish their own nation, and in his travels he made contact with many people who carried the same hope. Ze'ev Dov therefore committed himself to Zionism, an international political movement originating in the late nineteenth century that called for the creation of an independent Jewish state in Palestine, a historical region in the Middle East on the eastern shore of the Mediterranean Sea, comprising parts of present-day Israel and Jordan.

As Begin grew up, his father determined that the young man needed a good education, something he himself lacked, in order to work effectively for Zionism. Begin possessed a sharp mind; he studied hard in school, learned many languages (including English), mastered the game of chess, and developed a natural gift for public speaking.

Begin spent his first eight years in Brest-Litovsk, a Polish city in the Pale of Settlement, a region of the Russian Empire in which Jews were permitted to live legally, but where they suffered poverty and the threat of pogroms. (A pogrom is a racially motivated riot in which mobs, usually organized and sanctioned by the state, attack a minority group, most often Jews.) They also suffered discrimination from the Poles, as the Polish people are known. For example, Jews were forced to take separate classes in schools, refused service in some restaurants, and prohibited from some movie theaters. Begin was inspired, however, by the Poles' struggle for independence from Russia, which they gained in 1921.

At age fifteen Begin joined Betar, a Zionist youth group. Betar's founder, Vladimir Ze'ev Jabotinsky (1880–1940), strongly influenced the young Begin as he developed his own thoughts about Zionism. Begin, as quoted by Virginia Brackett in *Menachem Begin*, came to think that the Jewish homeland could only be formed through "war . . . not begging." Jabotinsky's beliefs formed the foundation of Betar's policies. In Betar's advocacy of Zionism, it emphasized self-defense, and its members were taught about weaponry. Begin became a devoted Betar member and remained committed throughout his college years. In college he focused on studies he thought would help him further the Zionist movement. After earning a law degree from Warsaw University, Begin assumed the leadership of Betar's seventy thousand members in Poland in 1935.

In the meantime the Nazi Party had come to power in Germany under the leadership of Adolf Hitler (1889–1945). In 1939, the Nazis began their invasion of France, Poland, and other countries; World War II had begun. Hitler's anti-Semitic policies led to the imprisonment of Jews (along with other minorities and political opponents) in concentration camps. Over the course of the war, millions of people were murdered in the camps, including six million Jews. The mass murder of Jews and other groups during World War II became known as the Holocaust.

Begin married Aliza Arnold in May 1939. In September of that year, the Germans occupied Poland. As the Nazis approached Warsaw, the young couple fled. They moved to Vilna, Lithuania, which became a hub for transporting Jews out of Nazi-controlled areas. There Begin continued to work for Zionism through Betar.

While in Vilna, Begin became aware that his actions and his house were being watched by the secret police of the Soviet Union. Vilna had come under Soviet control during the war, and Zionist activities were illegal under Soviet law. In 1940 the secret police came to Begin's home and escorted him to jail, where he was interrogated at length but not accused of any wrongdoing. For more than a year Begin remained in detention, surviving on one meal a day. In April 1941 Begin was tried and sentenced to eight years in a Siberian labor camp as "an element dangerous to society," according to Richard Amdur, author of *Menachem Begin*. The camp, located north of the Arctic Circle, was cold, and the work building a railroad was difficult. According to Amdur, a Soviet soldier at the camp said to Begin: "You'll get used to it. If you don't, you'll die."

Late in 1941, however, an agreement between Russia and Poland set Begin and 1.5 million other Polish prisoners free. Upon his release from prison, Begin discovered that most of his family had died in Nazi concentration camps.

While Begin was first in prison, his wife, Aliza, had remained with friends in Vilna. After he was sent to Siberia, the friends persuaded Aliza to go with them to Palestine. While still in prison, Begin had received word from his wife that she had gone. After his release, Begin wanted to join her, but he needed money to travel to Palestine, so he joined the Polish army as an English interpreter. His work with the army took him first to Iran and then to Palestine in May 1942, where he found his wife waiting for him. Reunited, the couple started a family. Benjamin (also spelled Binyamin) Ze'ev was born in 1943, followed by two daughters, Hasia in 1946 and Leah in 1949. Begin's family would always remain the center of his life.

Fighting for an independent Israel

In the early 1940s Palestine was a British mandate (a territory entrusted to foreign administration) and contained both Arab and Jewish communities. When Begin arrived there, Great Britain had begun limiting the number of Jewish immigrants allowed into the country, even as the Holocaust was taking place. As other Zionists tried to negotiate with the British authorities for Jewish freedoms, Begin took more drastic measures. From Begin's point of view, war was the only way for Jews to claim their own nation. Begin left his army position in 1943 to reorganize an underground militia that had been formed many years earlier by Jabostinsky. The militia was called Irgun Zvai Leumi, or simply Irgun. Begin issued a declaration against Great Britain, which read, as quoted by Amdur, "There is no longer any armistice [truce] between the Jewish people and the British administration in Eretz Israel [Land of Israel] which hands our brothers over to Hitler. Our people are at war with this regime—war to the end." Irgun carried out attacks against both British and Arab targets.

Irgun's attacks angered those within the Jewish community who hoped to win independence through diplomacy. But when Hitler's atrocities against Jews became known to the world in 1945, Jews of all political persuasions banded together in an umbrella group called the Hebrew Resistance Movement to carry out attacks against the British. (An umbrella organization brings together many smaller organizations with similar goals, so that they can share their skills and resources.) The Hebrew Resistance Movement sank British police boats, bombed railroads, and attacked British military posts in Palestine. The most significant raid occurred on July 22, 1946. Begin orchestrated the bombing of the King David Hotel in Jerusalem, which served as the headquarters of British criminal investigators who were investigating Irgun. The bombing of the hotel killed or injured more than one hundred British, Jews, and Arabs. Britain issued a fifty-thousand-dollar reward for Begin's capture, but he eluded police and continued to lead Irgun attacks. The disruption caused by fighting prompted the British to ask the United Nations (an international organization of countries founded in 1945 to promote international peace, security, and cooperation) for help in 1947.

The United Nations proposed a plan to divide Palestine into separate Arab and Jewish states. Talk of creating a separate Jewish state enraged the surrounding Arab nations, which vowed to block any such measure. Irgun continued its fight against the area's Arabs. The violence escalated in 1948 when an Irgun attack on the Arab town of Deir Yassin. The number of Palestinians killed is uncertain; some sources estimate that two hundred fifty men, women, and children were killed while other sources place the number closer to one hundred. The attack on Deir Yassin remains one of the most-remembered attacks against Palestinian Arabs. As Jewish forces moved into the areas that the United Nations had designated for the new Jewish section of Palestine, they caused many Palestinian Arabs to leave their homes; some were physically pushed out by Irgun and others were simply reacting to their terror by fleeing. Israel declared its independence on May 14, 1948.

The establishment of the state of Israel did not create immediate unity among all Jews, especially about military tactics. The young country's first prime minister was **David Ben-Gurion** (1886–1973; see entry). Ben-Gurion recognized the importance of having a strong military but did not agree with all of Irgun's practices. Ben-Gurion formed the Israel Defense Forces (IDF) on May 28, 1948, which sparked a standoff between Irgun and the IDF in the Tel Aviv harbor. Irgun sailed a ship bearing arms into the harbor. Ben-Gurion ordered the IDF to fire upon it as a warning that the new Israeli government would hold its ground. Begin ordered the ship to stand down, averting a civil war. Irgun dissolved, but the incident remained a point of disagreement in Israeli politics for many years.

Troops inspect the wreckage after the bombing of the King David Hotel in Jerusalem. Menachem Begin, then head of the underground militia Irgun Zvai Leumi, orchestrated the bombing. HULTON ARCHIVE/ GETTY IMAGES.

Begin's leadership of Irgun branded him a terrorist in the eyes of some, but others considered his actions necessary for Jewish freedom. Begin considered himself a freedom fighter, an instrument necessary for

Israel's "glorious revolution," as quoted by Brackett. With Israel's independence won, Begin turned his attention to politics, forming a political party called Herut. ("Herut" means "freedom" in Hebrew.) The Herut Party aimed to increase Israeli power through military force. Begin was elected the leader of Herut and ran the party in an authoritative manner, retaining complete power over party decisions for decades.

Turning to politics

In the first election of representatives to the Knesset, Israel's 120-member legislative body, Begin's party won fourteen seats. Ben-Gurion's party, the Mapai, or Labor party, won forty-four seats and the right to lead the government. In the Knesset, Begin and Ben-Gurion began a difficult political relationship. The two had vastly different opinions, and criticized each other openly and often. Begin called Ben-Gurion a "fool" and an "idiot," according to Amdur. Ben-Gurion characterized Begin as a "bespectacled petty Polish solicitor [lawyer]" and a "clown," according to Brackett.

As leader of the Herut Party, Begin vied for more political power. In 1952 he incited a riot at the steps of the Knesset in protest of Israel's acceptance of money from Germany for the atrocities against Jews committed during World War II. Although Ben-Gurion's support within Israel was stronger in these earlier years, Begin continued voicing his dissenting opinions. Begin's opinions about militant defense soon became more acceptable to the Israeli public as Israel battled with surrounding nations, especially Egypt, in the 1950s, and as more and more Israelis completed their mandatory service in the IDF. His party's growing strength enabled Begin to form a coalition between Herut and the Liberal Party in 1966. The new coalition party, called Gahal, won twenty-six seats in the Knesset, a number high enough to wield significant political power. Begin's influence in government was growing.

The 1967 Arab-Israeli War

In May 1967 it appeared to Israel that several Arab countries, including Egypt, Syria, and Jordan, were planning to attack. Israel's leaders argued that if Israel wished to win the war ahead, it must be the first to attack, catching the Arab countries unprepared. With war on the horizon, Israel moved quickly to form a government of national unity in order to wage the war. Since 1948, Israel had been ruled by coalition governments led by the Labor party, but with a war imminent, in 1967 Israel's leaders decided to create a coalition government that included all of Israel's parties (except the Communist party) so that the war effort would have the broad base of support it would need. In early June 1967, Begin assumed the role of minister without portfolio, a position that gave him a voice in the highest levels of the new government, but no specific area of government to control.

On June 5, 1967, the Israeli government ordered the Israeli Air Force (IAF) to attack Egyptian airfields. The IAF attack succeeded in surprising Egypt, destroying nearly every Egyptian warplane before the Egyptians could get a plane off the ground to counterattack. Encouraged by the success of their first strike, Israeli ground forces began to cross the Sinai desert into Egyptian territory, defeating a large number of Egyptian forces and establishing control in the Gaza Strip (a narrow strip of land along the eastern shore of the Mediterranean Sea, west of Israel and bordering Egypt in the southwest) and the entire Sinai Peninsula within three days. Israel's battles against Syria and Jordan were equally decisive. On the evening of June 5, 1967, the Israeli Air Force destroyed two-thirds of Syria's air force. Unwilling to advance ground troops into Israel, Syria instead began bombing Israeli towns from mountain bases in the Golan Heights, which towered some 1,700 feet (518 meters) above the Israeli valley below. Despite the overwhelming difficulty of climbing the mountains through narrow roads, the Israelis used a combination of aerial bombing and ground assault to capture the Golan Heights over the next several days. By June 9, they had pushed the Syrians from their mountain bases and established a cease-fire line along a border that gave Israel control of the Golan Heights. Jordanian forces attacked Israel from the West Bank on June 5, 1967, but they were quickly pushed out of the West Bank and retreated across the Jordan River. (The West Bank is an area between Israel and Jordan on the west bank of the Jordan River.) By June 10, 1967, each of the Arab countries had accepted a cease-fire agreement and the war, known at its end as the 1967 Arab-Israeli War (known in Israel as the Six-Day War), was over. Hundreds of thousands of Arab Palestinians living in the the West Bank and the Gaza Strip fled their homes as the Israeli military moved in.

Many Israelis believed that Israel should return the land it captured in the 1967 war to the Arab countries. Over the next three years, though, Begin used his position in the national unity government to promote his firm belief that Israel needed to obtain a peace treaty with the Arab nations before returning any of the land captured during the war.

The Israeli government agreed and quickly established a military occupation of the captured territories.

Egypt, unwilling to accept defeat, continued to conduct smaller attacks on Israel after the 1967 Arab-Israeli War but was continually rebuffed by Israel's superior forces. When Egypt's president **Gamal Abdel Nasser** (1918–1970; see entry) died in 1970, his successor, Anwar Sadat, began working to regain the Sinai Peninsula by negotiating for a peace treaty with Israel. The frustrated peace process led to another war between Israel and Egypt in 1973. The 1973 Arab-Israeli War (known in Israel as the Yom Kippur War), launched by Egyptian and Syrian forces on the Jewish holy day of Yom Kippur, took Israel by surprise. Egypt quickly won back some land across the Suez Canal, and Israel began to take peace negotiations more seriously.

Making peace as prime minister

In 1973 Begin tried to consolidate more power within the Israeli government by forming a new coalition, the Likud Party, the second-most powerful political party in Israel. In 1974 Begin suffered a severe heart attack, but despite his brush with death, he remained committed to the buildup of his political power. In the elections of 1977 the Likud Party won forty-three seats to the Labor Party's thirty-two, and Begin became the Israeli prime minister. As prime minister, Begin announced that he would seek peace for Israel.

In November 1977 Begin invited Sadat to Israel as an overture for peace. Negotiations between Israel and Egypt continued for nearly a year. No progress was made until September 1978, when U.S. president Jimmy Carter (1924–) invited Begin and Sadat to the U.S. presidential retreat of Camp David in the state of Maryland. There, after what Carter described, according to Amdur, as "thirteen intense and discouraging days, with success in prospect only during the final hours," Begin and Sadat came to an agreement. The two were awarded the Nobel Peace Prize in 1978 for their efforts. The final peace treaty was signed on March 13, 1979, marking the end of nearly thirty years of wars between Israel and Egypt.

Over the next four years, Israel and Egypt carried out most of the provisions detailed in the peace treaty. By April 25, 1982, Israel had completely withdrawn its troops from the Sinai Peninsula but had not seriously addressed the status of the West Bank or the self-rule of the

Egyptian president Anwar Sadat, U.S. president Jimmy Carter, and Israeli Prime Minister Menachem Begin during ceremonies for the Camp David Accords in 1978. © WALLY MCNAMEE/CORBIS.

Palestinians. While the peace process did not endear the two countries to each other, they did settle into what came to be known as a "cold peace."

In beginning of the 1980s, with another Israeli election on the horizon, Begin struggled with his health and was challenged by his political allies. He had lost the support of many of his advisers and ministers, who resigned after disagreements with him. Then, on June 7, 1981, Israeli military forces successfully destroyed an Iraqi nuclear reactor under construction. Begin was criticized by the United Nations and many world leaders, who asserted that Iraq's nuclear project had not been built for military use. Many Israeli people, however, supported their government's strong steps to prevent the existence of a nuclear-armed neighbor in the Middle East. Their faith in Begin was renewed, and he won reelection as prime minister on June 30, 1981.

Begin's fall from power came nearly a year later. On June 6, 1982, Israel invaded Lebanon in an attempt to drive the Palestine Liberation

Cold Peace

The peace negotiations between Israel and Egypt in the late 1970s generated a great sense of optimism. Israel was finally being recognized by the Arab state whose leader, **Gamal Abdel Nasser** (1918–1970; see entry), had said of Israel in 1967, "A State? No. We cannot recognize that," according to Richard Amdur in *Menachem Begin*. More than ignoring Israel's statehood, Egypt had been the leader of a coalition of Arab states whose announced goal was to destroy Israel. But after nearly thirty years of conflict, Egypt was ready for peace.

Egypt and Israel have maintained peace with each other since 1979, but that peace has been described as a "cold peace" by both sides, because the relations between the countries have not improved over the years. The major point of contention between the people of Egypt and Israel is the plight of the Palestinians. In polls conducted in Egypt, the population overwhelmingly sympathizes with the Palestinians and feels that Israel has treated them unfairly. Egyptian president **Hosni Mubarak** (1928–; see entry), who succeeded **Anwar Sadat** (also spelled al-Sadat; 1918–1981; see entry) after his assassination in 1981, conducted no formal visits to Israel, except to attend the funeral of Prime Minister **Yitzhak Rabin** (1922–1995;

see entry). Nevertheless, he was careful to maintain the alliance with Israel.

In 2009 conservative **Benjamin Netanyahu** (1949–; see entry) became prime minister of Israel, and a strange friendship developed between Mubarak and Netanyahu based primarily on their mutual fear of Iran's growing power in the Middle East and the widespread popularity of Islamists (people who believe that that Islam should provide the basis for political, social, and cultural life in Muslim nations). Egypt collaborated with Israel in 2007 in imposing a harsh blockade on its border with the Gaza Strip, where militants were launching rockets into Israel on a regular basis. The blockade prevented many supplies from entering or leaving the territory and, according to many international organizations, caused great suffering among the people.

The cold peace between Israel and Egypt, was threatened by the popular uprising in Egypt that occurred in February 2011, resulting in the removal of Mubarak from office. Responding to public pressure, the temporary military regime that took over Egypt's government removed its blockade on the Gaza Strip. The cold peace that had reigned between the two countries for more than thirty years was, at least for the time being, upheld, but it was being carefully reviewed by the Egyptian people.

Organization (PLO) from Israel's borders. (The PLO is a political and military organization formed to unite various Palestinian Arab groups with the goal of establishing an independent Palestinian state.) The PLO had been using Lebanon as a base for launching attacks on Israel's northern border. The plan seemed simple: Destroy the PLO's organization within Lebanon. Defense Minister **Ariel Sharon** (1928–; see entry) announced that Operation Peace for Galilee would conclude within forty-eight hours. He was wrong. The Israeli military became caught up in a lengthy and bloody war in Lebanon. World opinion of Israel deteriorated and the government began to lose the support of the Israeli people. Begin and his government came under intense scrutiny.

Begin's wife, Aliza, died on November 13, 1982. Begin's mourning distracted him from his government duties. On August 28, 1983, he announced to his cabinet, according to Amdur, "I cannot go on." He left office in September when Yitzhak Shamir (1915–) was elected prime minister. Begin lived a quiet retirement until his death after a heart attack on March 9, 1992.

For More Information

BOOKS

Amdur, Richard. *Menachem Begin*. New York: Chelsea House, 1988.

Brackett, Virginia. *Menachem Begin*. Philadelphia, PA: Chelsea House, 2003.

Hurwitz, Harry, and Yisrael Medad. *Peace in the Making: The Menachem Begin-Anwar Sadat Personal Correspondence*. New York and Jerusalem: Gefen Publishing House, 2011.

Stein, Leslie. *The Making of Modern Israel: 1948–1967*. Cambridge, UK: Polity, 2011.

PERIODICALS

James, Larry. "Egypt Frees Businessman Accused of Spying for Israel." *Voice of America* (December 5, 2004). Available online at http://www.voanews.com/english/news/a-13-2004-12-05-voa4.html (accessed on November 30, 2011).

Lynfield, Ben, and Dan Murphy. "Egypt, Israel Seize Chance for Thaw." *Christian Science Monitor* (December 6, 2004). Available online at http://www.csmonitor.com/2004/1206/p01s03-wome.html (accessed on November 30, 2011).

WEB SITES

"Menachem Begin: Biography." *Menachem Begin Heritage Center*. http://www.begincenter.org.il/en/FAQ.aspx?CID=8070 (accessed November 30, 2011).

"Middle East Conflict: History in Maps." *BBC News* (January 6, 2009). http://news.bbc.co.uk/2/hi/middle_east/7380642.stm#next (accessed on November 30, 2011).

David Ben-Gurion

BORN: October 16, 1886 • Plonsk, Poland

DIED: December 1, 1973 • Tel Aviv, Israel

Israeli prime minister, political activist

"We do not seek an agreement with the Palestinian Arabs in order to secure the peace. Of course we regard peace as an essential thing. . . . But peace for us is a means, and not an end."

David Ben-Gurion. DAVID ELDAN/GPO VIA GETTY IMAGES.

Revered among Israeli leaders, David Ben-Gurion is often referred to as the "father of the nation." Ben-Gurion was one of the chief organizers of the Jewish community in Palestine in the early part of the twentieth century and one of the chief framers of the new state of Israel in 1948. (Palestine is a historical region in the Middle East on the eastern shore of the Mediterranean Sea, comprising parts of present-day Israel and Jordan.) He served as the country's first prime minister and led his nation through the 1948 Arab-Israeli War (known in Israel as the War for Independence) and other conflicts before his retirement in 1963. Commemorating Ben-Gurion after his death, former Israeli prime minister **Golda Meir** (1898–1978; see entry) called him "the nation's chosen one," who "led the Jewish people to independence," according to the *Jewish News Archive.*

Early life

David Ben-Gurion was born David Ben Gruen on October 16, 1886, in Plonsk, a poor town in Poland, which at the time was part of Russia. He received a very strict, traditional Jewish education that consisted of long days studying Jewish history and learning Hebrew, the ancient language of the Jewish people. His father, Avigdor Gruen, was a lawyer and a committed Zionist, a supporter of an international political movement that called for the creation of an independent Jewish state in Palestine. Ben-Gurion's father founded the Hebrew school that his son attended and also dedicated much of his time to a political movement called the Lovers of Zion. This group worked to mobilize Jews around the world to immigrate to Palestine.

During the late 1800s and early 1900s, a wave of pogroms occurred throughout Europe. (A pogrom is an a racially-motivated riot in which mobs, usually organized and sanctioned by the state, attack a minority group, most often Jews.) Mobs of people in Poland, Russia, and other parts of Europe rounded up Jews and beat them, smashed Jewish shop windows, and committed other acts of violence. Jews were also arrested for crimes they did not commit. Ben-Gurion grew up surrounded by this hostile European attitude toward Jews.

In this environment, the young Ben-Gurion came to share his father's dream of a Jewish homeland in Palestine, and he began to apply his budding leadership skills to Zionism at an early age. As a teen, he founded and led a Zionist youth group called Ezra, in which the young conservative members were allowed to speak only Hebrew among themselves. In school, Ben-Gurion's passion for learning pushed him to the top of his class. His teachers recognized his intellectual talents and helped him apply for entry to Warsaw University at the age of eighteen; attending a university was not common for the children in his town. At Warsaw University, Ben-Gurion joined a sophisticated group called Poalei Zion (Workers of Zion), a group that promoted the ideals of Zionism.

In 1906 Ben-Gurion, like many European Jews of his generation, immigrated to Palestine. At that time, Palestine was under the rule of the Ottoman Empire, which tolerated groups of various religions. (The Ottoman Empire was the vast empire of the Ottoman Turks, which included southwest Asia, northeast Africa, and southeast Europe, and lasted from the thirteenth century to the early twentieth century.) Ben-Gurion first worked as a farmhand in Palestine. The grueling work required long hours and offered little pay. Ben-Gurion often went hungry, and he contracted the infectious disease malaria, from which he suffered for the rest of his life.

Life in Palestine had a profound impact on Ben-Gurion's political thinking. He changed his last name to Ben-Gurion, the name of a defender of Jerusalem who died in 70 CE. He became more and more active with Zionist groups and was elected to the editorial board of the *Poalei Zion* newspaper in Jerusalem in 1910. He came to believe that Jews from all over the world had an obligation to move to Palestine and to settle the land in order to build their own country. He also advocated that Jews speak only Hebrew among themselves. If they did not, he said, their survival could not be ensured. Ben-Gurion wanted Jewish cultural institutions, including the Jewish faith, to thrive in a recognized Jewish state. He also believed that the Jewish state should be ruled by the principles of socialism, a system of social organization in which the major means of production and distribution are owned, managed, and controlled by the government or the community.

Political activism

Ben-Gurion's political fervor and Zionist activities worried the Ottoman authorities in Palestine. Although the Ottoman Empire was tolerant toward Jews, it did not want Zionists to create a political base from which they could challenge Ottoman authority. Ben-Gurion's regular Zionist meetings were drawing much attention. In 1915 the Ottoman authorities expelled him from the region, along with his friend Yitzhak Ben-Zvi (1884–1963), who would later become Israel's second president. The two developed a lifelong friendship and came to be known as "the two Bens." They traveled to New York City together, learned English and, not surprisingly, got involved with local Zionist groups.

Although Ben-Gurion was a committed socialist, historians believe that his time in the United States had a profound impact on his political thought. He was fascinated by American-style democracy and believed that it was a system under which people could flourish. Years later, as prime minister, Ben-Gurion was often asked to suspend democracy due to regional instability, but he always refused to do so. Historians attribute this to his experience in the United States.

While in the United States, Ben-Gurion also met a Russian girl named Paula Munweis. She was a trainee at the Brooklyn Jewish Nursing School. The two married in 1917 and would eventually have three children.

Palestine becomes a British mandate

In 1914 European powers became involved in World War I (1914–18; a global war between the Allies [Great Britain, France, and Russia, joined later by the United States] and the Central Powers [Germany, Austria-Hungary, and their allies]). British foreign secretary Lord Arthur Balfour (1848–1930) issued the Balfour Declaration in 1917, which committed Great Britain to supporting Jewish interests in Palestine but also pledged that such support would not come at a cost to the Arab communities that had existed in Palestine for hundreds and hundreds of years. Ben-Gurion reacted to the Balfour Declaration by calling on all Jews to take up arms to free Palestine from Ottoman rule. In 1918 he arrived in Egypt in military uniform with a regiment of volunteers ready to do battle against the empire. But he was too late; World War I had just ended, and the Ottoman Empire had collapsed. Palestine was freed from Ottoman rule.

The League of Nations, an international organization of sovereign countries established after World War I to promote peace, granted Great Britain the authority to administer the affairs of Palestine under what came to be known as the mandate system. The terms of the British mandate were similar to the Balfour Declaration in that they declared the area to be a future Jewish national homeland, which was to be shared with the Arab communities already there. In 1920 the League of Nations declared Palestine to be the national home for the Jewish people. But achieving nationhood was not easy and the state of Israel would not be founded until over thirty years later, in 1948.

Ben-Gurion traveled to Palestine, which was undergoing a period of intense political instability. During the 1920s and 1930s, thousands of Jews fled Europe due to the increasing anti-Semitism (prejudice against Jews) there and immigrated to Palestine. Jewish emigration from the United States was also increasing. The Zionist movement called for total control over the region, and the Palestinian Arabs were struggling with their own goals for statehood. Ben-Gurion was quick to see that the Arabs had a legitimate quarrel with the Jews over the land. He predicted that the two peoples would constantly be at odds over this issue, and he was right.

After World War I, Ben-Gurion advocated a form of socialism based on the cooperative principle of the kibbutz movement. (A kibbutz is a Jewish communal farming settlement in Israel, where settlers share all property and work collaboratively together. Plural is kibbutzim.) The first kibbutzim were founded in Palestine by Zionist immigrants from

Eastern Europe in 1909. These young pioneers wished to settle the land and to establish a new way of life in which small communities were formed on jointly owned farms. Members of these communities shared in the farm labor and its rewards, and lived under principles of cooperation and social justice. With these ideals in mind, Ben-Gurion founded a powerful organization of trade unions, the Histadrut, or Jewish Federation of Labor, in 1921, which looked after the interest of Jewish workers. Ben-Gurion would serve as its secretary general for fourteen years. In the early 1930s he became head of the Labor Party and later chairman of the Zionist and Jewish Agency Executives, a world Jewish body that strove to unite all Jews, Zionists and non-Zionists alike, to strengthen the Jewish community in Palestine.

Publicly Ben-Gurion accepted the 1937 British Royal Commission's (also known as the Peel Commission) proposal to divide Palestine between the Arab communities and the Jewish ones. Privately, though, he foresaw an unavoidable conflict between the Jewish nation and the Palestinian Arabs. He firmly believed that building an independent Jewish state with a strong military force was the only way to deal with the problem. In order to understand how to go about this, he joined the Jewish Legion of the British army and trained as a member of the 40th Royal Fusiliers.

World War II

In 1939, German troops invaded Poland, officially beginning what would become known as World War II (1939–45; a war in which the Allies [Great Britain, France, the Soviet Union, the United States, and China] defeated the Axis Powers [Germany, Italy, and Japan]). The cruelty of the Nazis toward Jews in Germany had prompted thousands to attempt to immigrate to Palestine. In 1939, however, the British Parliament approved the White Paper, which set a policy to abandon the earlier Peel Commission proposal of physically dividing Palestine and instead to create one Palestine to be governed by Arabs and Jews in proportion to their numbers in the population. At a critical time when Jews were fleeing desperate conditions in Germany, the White Paper limited the number of Jewish immigrants to 75,000 per year. It also set restrictions on the rights of Jews to buy land from Arabs. Ben-Gurion was torn. He wanted to fight the British policies in Palestine, but at the same time he wanted to help the British defeat the Germans. During the war he helped tens of thousands of Jews to illegally immigrate to Palestine. He

The Holocaust

The Holocaust was the systematic murder of approximately six million Jews in an attempt to deliberately destroy the European Jews as a people. It was carried out by the German Nazis and those who allied with them during World War II (1939–45). The Nazi Party was a German political party that rose to power in 1933, under the leadership of Adolf Hitler (1889–1945). Hitler and his followers believed that Germans were the master race, and sought to establish a new world order under their rule. They actively sought to eliminate people they viewed as inferior. In addition to Jews, they also targeted Gypsies, homosexuals, Catholics, the Slavic peoples, the disabled, and socialists.

As the Nazis invaded neighboring nations, they built concentration camps (complexes built for the confinement and extermination of political opponents and ethnic minorities) all over Europe. Many concentration camps had specially designed killing facilities, particularly gas chambers. Jews and others taken to these camps were forced into slave labor, starved, beaten, and killed.

The Nazis carried out their Final Solution, the policy of exterminating European Jews. In 1933 there were over nine million Jews in Europe, but by 1945 two out of every three had been murdered. The war ended with Germany's surrender, after which Allied troops liberated the concentration camps. The survivors of these camps told their stories to the world, and the immensity of the tragedy profoundly influenced the generations that followed.

also urged Jews to join the war against Germany. "We must fight Hitler as though there were no White Paper, and fight the White Paper as if there were no Hitler," Ben-Gurion remarked, as quoted by Paul Johnson in *A History of Jews.*

In 1942, with news of widespread atrocities against Jews in Germany, Ben-Gurion declared that the sole aim of the Zionist movement was to create a homeland for Jews in Palestine. British policy makers failed to change their limitations on Jewish immigration into Palestine despite the growing knowledge of the Holocaust, the mass murder of European Jews and other groups by the Nazis during World War II. Ben-Gurion was furious with Great Britain's lack of support and called on all Jews to stage an armed struggle against the British. He believed the British policies threatened to turn Palestine's Jewish community into a permanent minority.

Ben-Gurion set about preparing for armed struggle with the Palestinian Arabs, which he saw as inevitable. In 1947 he spoke before the United Nations (UN), an international organization of countries founded in 1945 to promote international peace, security, and cooperation. He used the Holocaust and the horrible images of brutality in the Nazi concentration camps to influence world opinion. (Concentration camps are complexes built by the Germans for the confinement and extermination of political opponents and ethnic minorities, especially Jews.) He was successful. Slowly the world grew more sympathetic to the idea of a Jewish nation. Later that year the UN voted to split Palestine in half: one half to be controlled by the Jews and the other half controlled by the Arabs. The Palestinian Arabs rejected the plan. Soon after the proposal was made, small Arab militias began to fight with the Jewish militias.

On May 14, 1948, Ben-Gurion proclaimed the independence of the state of Israel, in accordance with the 1947 UN resolution calling for a Jewish state. The proclamation did not specify the borders of the new state. He ignored pleas from Great Britain and the United States not to proclaim Israeli independence for fear of war between Arabs and Jews.

Within hours of Ben-Gurion's announcement, Arab armies had gathered on Israel's borders. Five Arab nations invaded Israel. The 1948 Arab-Israeli War had begun. This was a particularly bloody war in which 1 percent of the Jewish population died, along with thousands of Arab soldiers and civilians. By 1949 the state of Israel was victorious, and the new nation claimed 78 percent of the former Palestine as its homeland. As a result of the war, almost one million Arab Palestinians fled or were forcibly removed from their homes and became refugees, people who flee their country to escape violence or persecution.

Leader of his country

Ben-Gurion served his country as prime minister and minister of defense between 1948 and 1963, except for a short retirement from 1953 to 1955. His years in office were considered a great success, and his colleagues described him as a natural leader and statesman. He defended Israel against Palestinian and Arab invasion by establishing a well-equipped and well-trained Jewish army. He built a modern and democratic country with a parliament (legislature). During his service as prime minister, more than one million Jews from eighty countries, speaking many languages, came to live in their new homeland. The successful integration of immigrants and developments in housing, agricultural settlement, employment, and industry under Ben-Gurion's government were enormous accomplishments.

Ben-Gurion's last years as prime minister, from 1960 to 1963, were marred by the Lavon Affair scandal. Named for Israeli defense minister Pinhas Lavon (1904–1976), who was later found to not be involved, the Lavon Affair stemmed from an Israeli plan designed to damage relations between the United States and Israel's longtime adversary, Egypt. The plan involved the explosion of bombs in Egypt, including detonations around a U.S. diplomatic facility, with the intent to blame the Egyptians. When the ploy was publicized, Ben-Gurion resigned from office and retired to his desert retreat to write a history of Israel. However, he never abandoned politics and kept in touch with many of his colleagues. Although he had no formal power, he continued to exert extraordinary

David Ben-Gurion in his office in Tel-Aviv in 1949. Ben-Gurion was the first prime minister of Israel, an office he held from 1948 to 1953, and again from 1955 to 1963. GPO VIA GETTY IMAGES.

authority in Israel. He died in Tel Aviv on December 1, 1973, from a brain hemorrhage. His body was buried in the courtyard of the Knesset (parliament), in Jerusalem. Thousands of Israelis visited his grave and the nation's flags flew at half-staff for weeks in his memory.

For More Information

BOOKS

Ben-Gurion, David. *Israel: A Personal History.* New York: Funk & Wagnalls, 1971.

Edelman, Maurice. *David! The Story of Ben-Gurion.* New York: Putnam, 1965.

Gilbert, Martin. *The Story of Israel: From Theodor Herzl to the Roadmap for Peace.* New York: Sterling, 2008.

Johnson, Paul. *A History of the Jews.* New York: Harper and Row, 1987, p. 520.

Peres, Shimon. *Ben-Gurion: A Political Life.* New York: Schocken, 2011.

St. John, Robert. *Ben-Gurion: The Biography of an Extraordinary Man.* New York: Doubleday, 1959.

Teveth, Shabtai. *Ben-Gurion and the Palestinian Arabs: From Peace to War.* New York: Oxford University Press, 1985.

WEB SITES

"David Ben Gurion" *The Jewish Magazine.* http://jewishmag.co.il/43mag/bengurion/bengurion.htm (accessed on November 30, 2011).

"David Ben Gurion The First Prime Minister." *Prime Minister's Office.* http://www.pmo.gov.il/PMOEng/History/FormerPrimeMinister/bengur.htm (accessed on November 30, 2011).

"Golda Meir Euologizes David Ben-Gurion as "the Nation's Chosen One,'" *Jewish News Archive* (December 3, 1973). http://archive.jta.org/article/1973/12/03/2966903/golda-meir-eulogizes-david-ben-gurion-as-the-nations-chosen-one (accessed on November 30, 2011).

Osama bin Laden

BORN: March 10, 1957 • Riyadh, Saudi Arabia

DIED: May 2, 2011 • Abbottabad, Khyber
  Pakhtunkhwa Pakistan

Saudi Arabian militant

"Allah [God] ordered us in this religion [Islam] to purify Muslim land of all nonbelievers."

As the founder and longtime leader of the terrorist organization al-Qaeda, Osama bin Laden reached a level of international notoriety few others have ever attained. His loosely organized but extraordinarily capable multinational network of Islamic militants planned and executed attacks on Western targets as a form of protest against foreign interference in the Middle East. After al-Qaeda operatives attacked the United States on September 11, 2001, killing nearly three thousand people, bin Laden became the world's most hunted fugitive. His network across the Middle East was so secure, however, it took U.S. forces nearly a decade to locate and kill him.

Child of privilege

Osama bin Laden. © SYGMA/ CORBIS.

Osama bin Laden was born in 1957, in Riyadh, Saudi Arabia. His parents were Hamida al-Attas, who was born in Syria, and Muhammad bin Awad bin Laden, a wealthy businessman originally from Yemen. The elder bin

Laden was in his mid–fifties by the time Osama, whose name means "young lion," was born, and his marriage to Osama's mother was his tenth. He fathered more than fifty children. He had come to the Saudi kingdom as a young man to work as a porter for Muslims making their hajj, or pilgrimage, to the holy cities of Mecca and Medina. (A pilgrimage is a journey to a sacred place for religious reasons.) He eventually started a construction company and built a wheelchair ramp for the elderly King Abdul-Aziz Ibn Saud (1876–1953).

Because of Muhammad bin Awad bin Laden's relationship with the king, his company became the sole infrastructure-contracting firm for the government, building major highways in Saudi Arabia and renovating Mecca and Medina. The bin Ladens were said to be the wealthiest family of nonroyal descent in the kingdom, and Osama was raised in modest affluence in Jeddah, where he lived with his mother. In 1967 his father was killed in a plane crash, and Osama received a share of his father's fortune, estimated at several million dollars. His eldest half brother, Salem, became head of the family business. Salem, who had been educated at a boarding school in England, had a British wife and owned a vacation home in Orlando, Florida, near Disney World. Several of bin Laden's half brothers and sisters eagerly moved away from Saudi Arabia as young adults, and a few of his nieces and nephews even had U.S. citizenship, because they were born when their parents were attending college in the United States. (Anyone who is born in the United States is granted citizenship, even if their parents are citizens of another country.)

Bin Laden attended the Al-Thaghr Model School, an elite high school in Jeddah, from 1968 to 1976, and became an increasingly devout Muslim in his teens. His family was Sunni Muslim (followers of the Sunni branch of Islam). Saudi society was guided by the principles of a particularly strict branch of Islam known as Wahhabism. Al-Thaghr was staffed by young teachers, some of whom were exiled from Egypt and Syria for their radical political activities. At the school they organized informal Islamic study groups and recruited students they thought might be receptive to more extremist views of Islam, and bin Laden was among them. The members learned about the late Egyptian cleric (ordained religious leader) Sayyid Qutb (1906–1966), who had spent time in the United States and became an ardent critic of the influence of Western culture in the Islamic world. One of Qutb's followers was a Palestinian cleric named Abdullah Yusuf Azzam (1941–1989), who taught at Jeddah's

King Abdul Aziz University, which bin Laden attended in the late 1970s. Azzam was an ardent supporter of jihad, or armed struggle against unbeleivers, and he became bin Laden's mentor.

Aids fighters in Afghanistan

At King Abdul Aziz University bin Laden studied engineering and management in preparation for following his brothers into the senior management ranks of the family's business, as was expected of him. His tenure in corporate management was short-lived. Instead bin Laden found his calling after a chain of pivotal events disrupted the Middle East when he was in his early twenties. In 1978 Egypt became the first Arab nation to openly acknowledge the Jewish state of Israel in the Camp David Peace Accords, a historic peace agreement that was nevertheless widely criticized by supporters of the Palestinians. (Palestinians are an Arab people whose ancestors lived in the historical region of Palestine, comprising parts of present-day Israel and Jordan, and who continue to lay claim to that land.) In early 1979 the shah of Iran, **Mohammad Reza Pahlavi** (1919–1980; see entry) was ousted by Islamists, people who believe that Islam should provide the basis for political, social, and cultural life in Muslim nations. And in December 1979 the Soviet Union invaded Afghanistan to aid Afghan Communists in seizing power. (Communists are supporters of Communism, a system of government in which the state plans and controls the economy and a single political party holds power.) A common link in all three of these events was the United States, which had helped arrange the Camp David Accords, had given the shah of Iran millions of dollars in foreign aid, and had started funding anti-Communist fighters in Afghanistan even before the Soviet invasion.

Several other nations also provided aid to each side in the Afghan Civil War (1979–2001), which would last more than two decades. The Saudi government considered sending one of its young princes to the Afghanistan-Pakistan border, to serve as a sort of informal emissary, but none of the princes were interested in this task. Bin Laden volunteered for the job and spent the next two years traveling back and forth between Saudi Arabia and Pakistan. Afghanistan was a Muslim nation, and the Soviet invasion had prompted widespread outrage across the Arab world. Bin Laden raised funds for an army of fighters, called mujahideen, and recruited volunteers for the cause in Saudi Arabia. He also brought in vital construction equipment that helped the anti-Soviet guerrilla fighters in the remote Khyber Pass region. (Guerrilla fighters are a smaller, less equipped fighting force that faces a more powerful foe.)

One of bin Laden's university professors, Azzam, was a prominent Islamic theologian who had issued a call for recruits to aid Muslims in Afghanistan at the onset of the war. Azzam moved to Pakistan and settled in Peshawar, a major city in the northwestern province of Khyber Pakhtunkhwa, where he and bin Laden are believed to have created the Maktab al-Khadamat (MAK) in 1984, to more formally aid the mujahideen. The MAK began as a resource for tracking the unofficial army of multinational Muslim fighters who fought in Afghanistan, communicating and providing aid to their families. It also operated guesthouses in Peshawar and paid airfare for new recruits to be trained for the fight.

It is unclear if bin Laden ever participated in any actual combat operations. Those close to him say he was caught once near Jaji, a border outpost, when members of a construction crew digging mujahideen cave hideouts were targeted in a Soviet assault. He nevertheless styled himself as one of the famed veterans of a war in which jihadists aiding an impoverished Muslim nation tenaciously battled a world superpower for a decade and won. He dressed in a standard guerrilla combat-fatigues uniform and was often photographed with an AK–47 automatic weapon he claimed to have taken from a freshly killed Soviet soldier.

The Soviets withdrew from Afghanistan in 1989, and bin Laden returned to Saudi Arabia a hero. He urged young men in the Middle East to heed the call of the jihad and hoped for a major role in a new conflict emerging in the nation of Kuwait on the Persian Gulf. In 1990 Iraqi leader **Saddam Hussein** (1937–2006; see entry) invaded Kuwait. The act of aggression prompted international condemnation, and bin Laden approached the Saudi leadership with an offer to mobilize his fighters to drive the Iraqi army out of Kuwait. He was stunned to hear that the Saudis planned to allow coalition forces led by the United States to gather on Saudi soil in preparation of liberating Kuwait. The Persian Gulf War (1990–91) was over by March 1991, although the United States did not achieve its goal of removing Saddam from power in Iraq.

Expelled from Saudi Arabia

In the Middle East, Saudi Arabia's cooperation with the West was controversial. Conservative Muslims in the kingdom were aghast that their leaders had permitted an army of nonbelievers to mobilize on Saudi territory in preparation for an attack on Muslims. Bin Laden openly criticized the regime for this and was even among those who refused to use the term *Saudi Arabia*, calling his birthplace "the land of the two Holy Mosques" instead, a reference to the holy sites of Mecca and Medina. Rarely tolerant of opposition, the Saudi government moved to silence bin Laden, at first barring him from leaving Jeddah, then exiling him from the country in 1991. He was welcomed in the African nation of Sudan.

Bin Laden ran several companies in Sudan that provided money to training camps he established with the blessing of the Sudanese government. The Sudanese also issued new passports to exiled militants and provided other forms of aid to the emerging group that called itself al-Qaeda, Arabic for "the base." Its origins, Western intelligence sources believe, date back to a 1988 meeting between bin Laden, Azzam, and other fundamentalist leaders. Azzam died in 1989, and bin Laden emerged as the shadowy head of the network. Al-Qaeda sent trained personnel to support Muslim groups in Tajikistan, Chechnya, and Bosnia in the early 1990s.

Targets Americans

Between 1993 and 1995 al-Qaeda was linked to attacks against Americans, including one that targeted the World Trade Center in New York City on February 26, 1993. That explosion killed six people and injured more than one thousand. A Kuwaiti national trained by al-Qaeda, Ramzi Yousef (1967–), was eventually convicted for that attack. Yousef had ties to another Kuwaiti member of al-Qaeda, Khalid Shaikh Mohammed (c. 1964–), who plotted to blow up a dozen airliners over the Pacific Ocean in 1995, an operation foiled by police in the Philippines. Bin Laden also claimed credit for the deaths of eighteen U.S. soldiers in Mogadishu, Somalia, in October 1993.

In 1994 Saudi Arabia revoked bin Laden's citizenship and froze his assets, meaning that bin Laden would not be able to gain access to his money in Saudi Arabian banks. However, he still wielded control over a large network of multinational companies with bank accounts on several continents that funded Islamic jihadist groups. The Saudis suspect him of involvement in a November 1995 truck bombing at the training center for the Saudi National Guard in Riyadh, where Saudis were trained by American military personnel. In May 1996 two men were publicly beheaded by the Saudi government for the attack after reading aloud statements asserting their link to bin Laden. On June 25, 1996, a massive

A group of Taliban fighters firing a missile. The Taliban sheltered Osama bin Laden in the 1990s.
© REUTERS/CORBIS.

explosion occurred in the eastern Saudi port city of Dhahran, a major center of operations for Saudi Arabia's state-run oil company, Saudi Aramco. The truck bomb targeted the Khobar Towers, which were being used as a U.S. Air Force housing complex. Nineteen U.S. soldiers died.

Saudi Arabia and the United States pressured the Sudanese government to exile bin Laden, and it complied. In the spring of 1996 bin

Laden moved with his four wives and several children to Afghanistan. At the time, an Islamic fundamentalist group known as the Taliban was moving to seize control of Afghanistan, an objective they achieved in September of that year. Bin Laden had ties to the Taliban leader and cleric, Mullah Mohammed Omar (1959–), who had lost an eye in the Soviet-Afghanistan war. One of bin Laden's daughters was married to Omar.

One of bin Laden's first actions in Afghanistan was to release a *fatwa* (a statement of religious law issued by an Islamic cleric and intended to instruct devout Muslims) titled "Declaration of War Against the Americans Who Occupy the Land of the Two Holy Mosques" in August 1996 to the London-based Arabic newspaper *Al-Quds al-Arabi*. "Muslims burn with anger at America," it read, as quoted by *PBS Newshour*. The fatwa also asserted that the continued presence of U.S. military personnel in the countries along the Persian Gulf "will provoke the people of the country and induces aggression on their religion, feelings, and prides and pushes them to take up armed struggle against the invaders occupying the land."

Establishes Al-Qaeda bases in Afghanistan

Al-Qaeda, still a little-known organization at the time, established new bases inside Afghanistan, including training camps in its ideally remote, impenetrable mountain ranges. Bin Laden also used his personal fortune to build a state-of-the-art satellite communications network. Al-Qaeda operatives communicated with one another via e-mail, disposable cell phones, and prepaid calling cards; they were so cautious about being spied on that one method of communication involved writing e-mails and then not sending them, leaving them unsent in the e-mail accounts, where they were read, then deleted, by visitors who signed in to the accounts from Internet cafés, business establishments that provide internet access to the public, usually for a fee.

In 1998 a group calling itself the World Islamic Front had issued a fatwa against the United States. It first appeared in *Al-Quds al-Arabi* and was signed by bin Laden and several other leaders of Islamic fundamentalist groups, including Ayman al-Zawahiri (1951–), the leader of the Egyptian Islamic Jihad (EIJ), which would merge into al-Qaeda in 2001. It read, in part, "The ruling to kill the Americans and their allies, civilians and military is an individual duty for every Muslim who can do it in any country in which it is possible to do it." According to Alia Brahimi, this fatwa was a turning point for Islamic fundamentalists and the Middle

East. "Historically, the idea behind jihad as an individual duty was for Muslim rulers in neighbouring provinces to come to the aid of their co-religionists in other parts of the empire," she writes in a July 2011 article on the *Al Jazeera* Web site. "The assumption was always that all jihads, including defensive ones, would be led by established Muslim leaders within clearly defined communities. In a move that subverted established patterns of authority, the World Islamic Front reached out to Muslims as individuals rather than as members of politically organised communities."

On August 7, 1998, the eighth anniversary of the first deployment of U.S. troops into Saudi Arabia in preparation for the Persian Gulf War, two U.S. embassies in Africa were bombed. The explosions at embassy compounds in Nairobi, Kenya, and Dar es Salaam, Tanzania, occurred at the same time. They killed 224 people and wounded nearly 5,000. The group claiming responsibility called itself the Islamic Army for the Liberation of Holy Sanctuaries, but the attacks were quickly tied to bin Laden and al-Qaeda. U.S. officials began a long and costly effort to either capture bin Laden and try him in federal court or kill him. U.S. forces fired cruise missiles at training camps in Afghanistan and Sudan, but bin Laden himself was never in danger.

Osama bin Laden with his advisor, Ayman al-Zawahiri.
© REUTERS/CORBIS.

Al-Qaeda threats to international security continued. In 1999 an operative nearly succeeded in bringing a bomb into the United States from Canada as part of a plot to bomb Los Angeles International Airport in California and various other targets around the world on December 31, 1999. And on October 12, 2000, a group of men in Yemen pulled their small boat alongside the USS *Cole*, a navy destroyer docked in the port city of Aden for refueling, and detonated a bomb that ripped a huge hole in the side of the ship. The bomb killed seventeen and injured thirty-nine.

September 11, 2001

The attacks in 1999 and 2000 were dwarfed by the catastrophic attacks on the United States carried out on September 11, 2001. Nineteen men, most of them Saudi nationals, boarded four separate planes departing from Boston, Massachusetts; Newark, New Jersey; and Washington, D.C. Once in air, the men overtook the cockpits and cabin crews with the help of simple box cutter knives that they had smuggled aboard. At 8:46 AM the hijackers crashed American Airlines Flight 11 into the north tower of the World Trade Center in New York City. Sixteen minutes later, the hijackers on United Airlines Flight 175 flew their plane directly into the south tower. At 9:37 AM the hijackers on American Airlines Flight 77 crashed their plane into the Pentagon in Virginia. The hijackers on the fourth plane, United Airlines Flight 93, changed course over Ohio and began heading toward Washington, D.C. Investigators believe their target was either the White House or the U.S. Capitol, but they never made it. Cockpit audio tapes from the flight revealed that a group of passengers tried to retake control of the plane from the hijackers, and the plane crashed into an empty field in Pennsylvania. During the five-minute battle for control of Flight 93, meanwhile, the south tower of the World Trade Center began to collapse at 9:59 AM. Twenty-nine minutes later, the north tower also collapsed.

The total number of lives lost was 2,977. Both towers of the World Trade Center were destroyed, and the Pentagon was badly damaged. The plane that slammed into the ground in Pennsylvania had disintegrated on impact. U.S. intelligence officials identified the nineteen hijackers and pieced together their whereabouts over the previous years; all of them had ties to bin Laden or were known al-Qaeda operatives. Bin Laden knew of the attack, but the actual planning of it was likely carried out by Khalid Sheikh Mohammed. Mohammed was later captured in Afghanistan and

The Bin Laden Family and September 11th

Osama bin Laden's family had publicly distanced itself from him in the 1990s, as his increasingly radical statements on Islamic fundamentalism and calls for attacks on Western targets proved an embarrassment to the family's multibillion-dollar company, which had investments and projects in North America, the Middle East, Europe, and Asia. On September 11, 2001, several bin Laden family members were living in or visiting the United States. Among them were his half brothers Shafig, who was in Washington, D.C., for a conference, and Abdullah, a Harvard Law School graduate who lived in Boston, Massachusetts. There was also his half-sister Najiah, who lived in Los Angeles, California. Bin Laden's eldest brother Salem, who became head of the family upon their father's death, had died in an accident in Texas in 1988. The palatial home Salem had purchased in 1980 in Orlando, Florida, was still owned by the family in 2001. At the time of the September 11th attacks, bin Laden's half-brother Khalil was staying there. He was among the bin Laden family members who feared for their lives in the days following the September 11th attacks and contacted the Saudi Arabia ambassador to the United States for help in leaving the country on a private jet soon after the attacks.

remained in U.S. custody at a U.S. naval base in Guantanamo Bay, Cuba, indefinitely. Bin Laden asserted five days after September 11th attacks that he was not involved in the attacks or knew about them beforehand. A few months later, however, videotape footage from a meeting in Kandahar, Pakistan, between bin Laden and his supporters was found after a raid on a target in Jalalabad, Pakistan. On it he brags that he did know about the attacks before they happened. Of the World Trade Center bin Laden says, as quoted by an article on the *CNN* Web site, "I was thinking that the fire from the gas in the plane would melt the iron structure of the building and collapse the area where the plane hit and all the floors above it only. This is all that we had hoped for."

A hunted man

In October 2001 the United States launched a military offensive in Afghanistan with the goal of dislodging the Taliban from power and capturing bin Laden. They succeeded in ousting the Taliban but did not find bin Laden. He vanished after December 2001, when U.S. troops fought the Battle of Tora Bora, where bin Laden was believed to be hiding; this was the closest that U.S. forces came to finding him for the better part of a decade. For the next eight years bin Laden remained the world's number-one fugitive, with a fifty-million-dollar reward offered for his capture. He released videotaped messages to his followers from unknown locations. There were rumors he was living in a network of caves in Afghanistan or was somewhere in Pakistan.

On the moonless night of May 1, 2011, a team of U.S. Navy SEALS (Sea, Air, and Land) set out in Black Hawk helicopters from a base in Jalalabad, Afghanistan. The aircraft landed at a three-story compound in Abbottabad, a city in Pakistan's Khyber Pakhtunkhwa province in the

The compound in Abbottabad, Pakistan, where Osama bin Laden was killed by a U.S. Navy SEAL team on May 2, 2011. AAMIR QURESHI/AFP/ GETTY IMAGES.

northwest, near the border with Afghanistan. Their target was a house where an al-Qaeda courier was known to live with his family and some others. The tightly guarded house had no phone or Internet connection, and the occupants burned all of their trash. A tall man occasionally came out to pace in the yard. The man was thought to be either bin Laden or a senior-level al-Qaeda operative. Shortly after 1 AM on May 2, the SEALS stormed the house. One SEAL shot bin Laden in the chest, and a second shot him in the head. DNA testing later confirmed the man was bin Laden.

The SEALS departed Pakistan with bin Laden's body, which was then transported to a U.S. aircraft carrier. A Muslim crewmember supervised the Islamic burial rites and recited prayers before the body was buried at sea in the waters of the North Arabian Sea. Weeks later al-Qaeda confirmed the death of bin Laden and affirmed that Ayman al-Zawahiri had succeeded him as leader of the organization.

For More Information

BOOKS

Coll, Steve. *The Bin Ladens: An Arabian Family in the American Century.* New York: Penguin, 2008.

Randal, Jonathan. *Osama: The Making of a Terrorist.* New York: Knopf, 2004.

PERIODICALS

Fisk, Robert. "Was He Betrayed? Of Course." *Independent* (London, England; May 3, 2011). Available online at http://www.independent.co.uk/opinion/commentators/fisk/robert-fisk-was-he-betrayed-of-course-pakistan-knew-bin-ladens-hiding-place-all-along-2278028.html (accessed on November 30, 2011).

Mayer, Jane. "The House of Bin Laden." *New Yorker* (November 12, 2001). Available online at http://www.newyorker.com/archive/2001/11/12/011112fa_FACT3 (accessed on November 30, 2011).

Miller, John. "Greetings, America. My Name Is Osama bin Laden. Now That I Have Your Attention. . . . " *Esquire* (February 1999).

World Islamic Front. "Jihad against Jews and Crusaders." *Al-Quds al-Arabi* (February 23, 1998).

Zernike, Kate, and Michael T. Kaufman. "The Most Wanted Face of Terrorism." *New York Times* (May 2, 2011). Available online at http://www.nytimes.com/2011/05/02/world/02osama-bin-laden-obituary.html?scp=5&sq=osama+bin+laden&st=nyt (accessed on November 30, 2011).

WEB SITES

"Bin Laden's Fatwa." *PBS Newshour* (August 1996). http://www.pbs.org/newshour/terrorism/international/fatwa_1996.html (accessed on November 30, 2011).

Brahimi, Alia. "Al-Qaeda Is Its Own Worst Enemy." *Al Jazeera* (May 7, 2011). http://english.aljazeera.net/indepth/opinion/2011/05/20115783235763346.html (accessed on November 30, 2011).

Brahimi, Alia. "The 'Changing' Face of al-Qaeda." *Al Jazeera* (July 5, 2011). http://english.aljazeera.net/indepth/opinion/2011/07/20117316726986909.html (accessed on November 30, 2011).

"Hunting Bin Laden." *PBS Frontline.* http://www.pbs.org/wgbh/pages/frontline/shows/binladen/ (accessed on November 30, 2011).

Mahmoud Darwish

BORN: March 14, 1941 • Al-Birwa, Palestine

DIED: August 9, 2008 • Houston, Texas, United States

Palestinian poet

"The Israelis do not want to teach students that there is a love story between an Arab poet and this land. I just wish they'd read me to enjoy my poetry, not as a representative of the enemy."

For decades Mahmoud Darwish was hailed as the unofficial poet laureate (a poet honored by a state or group) of the Palestinian people. (Palestinians are an Arab [Arabic-speaking] people whose ancestors lived in the historical region of Palestine, comprising parts of present-day Israel and Jordan, and who continue to lay claim to that land.) In hundreds of poems published over the course of a career that spanned nearly fifty years, Darwish gave voice to the deep emotions of Palestinians living both inside and outside the borders of the country of Israel and its occupied territories. (The occupied territories are the lands under the political and military control of Israel, especially the West Bank and Gaza Strip.) He also wrote eloquently of the Israeli perpsective. Darwish's death in 2008 prompted an outpouring of grief, with Palestine Authority president **Mahmoud Abbas** (1935–; see entry) proclaiming a three-day period of

Mahmoud Darwish.
AP PHOTO/NADER DAOUD.

119

mourning. (The Palestinian Authority is the recognized governing institution for Palestinians in the West Bank and the Gaza Strip, established in 1993.) Abbas also delivered the eulogy at Darwish's funeral in Ramallah, a city in the West Bank.

Raised in a war-torn country

Mahmoud Darwish was born on March 13, 1941, in the village of al-Birwa, not far from the major city of Acre in Palestine. At the time, Palestine was a British mandate, a territory entrusted to foreign administration. The British left in 1948, just before the state of Israel was established there. Darwish was the son of a prosperous farmer and grew up with distinct memories of the period prior to the creation of Israel. A few years before his birth, his village had participated in the Arab Revolt of 1936–39, an uprising by Palestinian Arabs against British colonial rule and increasing Jewish immigration to Palestine, and suffered reprisals as a consequence, with several villagers executed for their participation. Al-Birwa had been populated for centuries, and its Arab residents were predominantly Muslims and their ancestors had lived in Palestine for centuries.

On June 11, 1948, Israeli forces captured al-Birwa and began the forcible removal of its residents to clear the way for Jewish settlement. The Darwish family was forced to flee to Lebanon but several months later returned, illegally, to find their village destroyed. The family was able to settle in Deir el Asad, where Darwish's father worked as a common laborer and the family eventually attained status as Arab residents of Israel. Darwish attended Israeli schools and learned Hebrew, the ancient language of the Jewish people and the official language of present-day Israel. It was a wrenching period of adjustment. "We were defined, and rejected, as refugees," Darwish said in a 2001 *New York Times* interview. (Refugees are people who flee their country to escape violence or persecution.) "This gave me a very strong bitterness, and I don't know that I'm free of it today."

The situations that Darwish experienced as a youth, such as eviction, exile, and an identity defined by an occupying power, proved to be powerful influences on his life. He first recorded his dislike of the inequalities faced by Arab children in a poem he wrote when he was fourteen years old. From that time on, Darwish wrote poetry that reflected the feelings he and his fellow Palestinians had about losing their land and the anger they felt at those who evicted them from that land and treated them with such violence and disdain.

A life in exile

In 1960 Darwish published *Asafir bala ajnihah* (Sparrows without Wings), his first collection of poetry. His second volume, *Awraq al-zaytun* (Olive Branches), in 1964, earned him a reputation as one of the leading voices of the growing Palestinian resistance movement. It featured one of his most famous poems, "Identity Card," which protests the law requiring Palestinians living in Israeli-controlled lands to carry identity papers and show them upon request. In the poem, available at *adab.com*, Darwish writes, "Beware . . . / Of my hunger / And my anger!"

Darwish spent much of the 1960s living in Haifa, a port city on the Mediterranean Sea in northern Israel. At age nineteen, he joined the Communist Party and, like many other young Arab men of his generation, allied with the Palestine Liberation Organization (PLO), political and military organization formed to unite various Palestinian Arab groups with the goal of establishing an independent Palestinian state. The late 1960s and early 1970s were a dark time for Palestinians. The 1967 Arab-Israeli War marked a turning point for the Israeli-Palestinian conflict, with Israel seizing large pieces of territory from its Arab neighbors. They took the Sinai Peninsula and the Gaza Strip from Egypt, the West Bank and East Jerusalem from Jordan, and the Golan Heights from Syria. This aggressive action galvanized the PLO into action, and its leader, **Yasser Arafat** (1929–2004; see entry), became one of the world's most famous resistance leaders. In Israel supporters of the PLO, like Darwish, were targeted and harassed for their public statements or covert actions in support of the Palestinian cause. After 1968 Darwish spent the majority of his time either in jail or under house arrest in Haifa, for various actions related to his literary efforts. By 1971, however, he saw that it would be impossible for him to continue writing his brand of subversive poetry within Israel, and he embarked on an exile that would last twenty-five years.

Darwish began his exile in Moscow, Russia, where he studied political economy for a year. He then moved to Cairo, Egypt, and from there to Beirut, Lebanon, the most cosmopolitan city in the Middle East at that time and home to a growing community of Palestinian refugees. From

Beirut he edited *Shu'un Filastiniyya*, a journal published by the Palestine Research Center that focused on Palestinian affairs. Years later, both a longtime friend of Darwish and a top PLO official said that it was Darwish who authored of one the most famous remarks ever uttered by Arafat. In November 1974 the PLO leader spoke before the United Nations (UN; an an international organization of countries founded in 1945 to promote international peace, security, and cooperation), and one passage from his speech was widely quoted in headlines around the world. "I have come bearing an olive branch and a freedom fighter's gun," Arafat told the UN General Assembly. "Do not let the olive branch fall from my hands."

Beginning in 1981, Darwish edited the respected journal *Al Karmel* and devoted time to promoting Palestinian political causes. By the early 1980s the PLO was waging war with Israel from Lebanon, and in 1982 Israel invaded Lebanon in an attempt to destroy the PLO. Darwish, who was by then a member of the Palestine National Council (PNC), the elected legislative body of the PLO, was forced to flee once again. He went to Paris, France, where he lived for a decade, and then he settled in Amman, Jordan.

Darwish's PNC colleagues elected him to serve on the executive committee of the PLO, and in 1988 his most notable involvement in Palestinian politics came when he authored the Algiers Declaration, also known as the Palestinian Declaration of Independence, which states the PLO's willingness to accept what is known as the two-state solution to the Arab-Israeli conflict. Before the Algiers Declaration, the PLO had insisted on the destruction of Israel and the creation of an Arab state in Palestine. The Algiers Declaration allowed for the existence of two states, one Jewish and one Arab. It also allowed many countries to officially recognize the existence of the PLO as representative of the Palestinian people.

The Algiers Declaration became the basis for the Oslo Accords, signed by the PLO and Israel in 1993. The accords laid out a rather vague plan for the Israeli government to grant Palestinian control in the occupied territories, or the lands under the political and military control of Israel, especially the West Bank and Gaza Strip. Darwish objected to the terms and withdrew from the executive committee of the PLO that same year. "There was no . . . clear commitment to withdraw from the occupied territories," he explained to *New York Times* writer Adam Shatz in 2001 regarding his opposition to the Oslo Accords. "I felt Oslo would pave the way for escalation" of hostilities between Jews and Arabs. "I hoped I was wrong. I'm very sad that I was right."

Darwish returned to the land of his birth in 1996, when the Israeli government, which had long banned him from the country, granted him permission to enter in order to participate in a documentary film involving one of his mentors, the Palestinian Christian writer Émile Habibi (1922–1996). Tragically Habibi died just prior to Darwish's arrival, and Darwish delivered the eulogy at his funeral. He also visited his own family and gave poetry readings to rapt Palestinians. "I went back to being a child," he told *New York Times* journalist Joel Greenberg, who met with him in Ramallah. "I touched the trees and the stones, and felt as if I hadn't left. Time had stopped, and the circle was closed." He was also overwhelmed by crowds who turned out to greet him at a reception in Judeida, where his family lived. "There were thousands of people in the soccer field, and they had signs that said, 'We love you, stay with us,'" he told Greenberg. "I cried. I felt guilty, and for the first time I apologized for leaving. In my speech I said: 'I'm sorry I left you. I'll never leave you again.'

Darwish was granted permission to stay in the West Bank. He settled in Ramallah and revived *Al Karmel*. He often remarked, however, that he found it difficult to write in a city under Israeli occupation. Although Darwish was famous for his protest poems, he also wrote sympathetically about Israelis, who had known nothing but life in a tightly guarded state with hostile neighbors. In 2000 his poetry became a source of controversy within Israel when that nation's minister of education, Yossi Sarid (1940–), recommended that two of Darwish's poems be included in the nation's high school curriculum. Members of the Knesset, Israel's legislative body, debated his poetry, and some even called for the resignation of President Ehud Barak (1942–) if Darwish's poems became part of the school curriculum. Eventually Barak declared that "Israel is not ready" to consider such poetry. In an interview with *Newsweek International* magazine, Darwish recognized that some Israelis would have difficulty accepting his poetry and said:

> "When a poet speaks about nostalgia and love for his country, it destroys what the Israelis have taught, which is that this country was empty when Israel was founded. My poems are a love story with this country. This clashes with their story. But we have to realize that this country belongs to two peoples. Everybody has the right to love it and to write poetry about it."

Mahmoud Darwish speaks to the Associated Press about a recommendation by the Israeli education minister to include two poems by Darwish, a Palestinian author, as part of the curriculum in Israeli schools. AP PHOTO/ JACQUELINE LARMA.

Poet of exile and loss

Throughout his years in exile, Darwish published a regular stream of works, including diaries, essays, and poetry. Over time, his work was embraced by Palestinians and by Arabs throughout the Middle East as the literary voice of displacement and loss. Darwish wrote in Arabic, and the intense emotion of his works inspired those in the Middle East who worried that Arabic was a declining language. Readers interpreted may of his poems as speaking of the sense of longing for his and their lost homeland, Palestine. Darwish told the *New York Times* in 2001 that Palestine became a metaphor "for the loss of Eden, for the sorrows of dispossession and exile, for the declining power of the Arab world in its dealings with the West."

Although all of Darwish's poetry relates to the loss of Palestine, critics have identified three distinct stages in his work. In the first stage, up to his departure from Israel in the early 1970s, many of Darwish's works are fierce and defiant, written out of a seeming desire to urge others to resist Israeli oppression. The most well-known among these is the poem "Identity Card." Verse he produced during the second stage of his career, between 1971 and 1982 when he lived in exile but still within the Arab world, echoes with a sense of loss and longing, as the poet tries to stay in touch with the sights and sounds of his place of birth. Many of the poems from this period are written about people, especially a female lover, but have been interpreted as being about Palestine. Darwish complained in the *New York Times* that readers sometimes misinterpreted his poems about people. "When I write a poem about my mother, Palestinians think my mother is a symbol of Palestine. But I write as a poet, and my mother is my mother. She's not a symbol."

After 1982 Darwish's poems grew in length, marking the start of the third stage of his literary career, and he demonstrated an ability to use his poetry to create narrative sagas. Critics commended him for using literary devices and symbols that spoke to universal longings for peace, and his works began to be translated more widely, including into English. Within the Arabic-speaking world he dazzled scholars with his gift for using the language and style of the Koran (also spelled Qur'an or Quran; the holy book of Islam) to interpret modern conditions. Darwish began to win notice throughout the world, even as his poems remained intensely political. A 1988 poem, "Those Who Pass between Fleeting Words," published in *Left Curve*, seemed to speak to Israeli occupiers, saying "Rid our time of yours, and be gone." Israelis were outraged by the poem and, not surprisingly, Palestinians readily embraced it. Interviewed in the *New York Times* by journalist Adam Shatz, Darwish stated, "I said what every human being living under occupation would say, 'Get out of my land.'"

Darwish's critics asserted his verse glorified acts of terrorism. He was habitually quick to dispel any notion that he supported the use of violence to reclaim Palestine for Arabs. "Nothing, nothing justifies terrorism," he said in an interview with writer Nathalie Handal for *Progressive* magazine.

He continued, "We should not justify suicide bombers. We are against the suicide bombers, but we must understand what drives these young people to such actions. They want to liberate themselves from such a dark life. It is not ideological, it is despair."

The publication in English of several of Darwish's collections, including *The Adam of Two Edens* (2000) and *Unfortunately, It Was Paradise* (2003), brought his work to a wider audience, especially outside of the Middle East. In 2001 Darwish was awarded the Lannan Foundation Award for Cultural Freedom. The award includes a $350,000 honorarium.

In the summer of 2008 Darwish traveled to Houston, Texas, in the United States to undergo heart surgery. He died there on August 9, 2008. He was sixty-seven years old. Palestinian president Abbas delivered a eulogy at his funeral in Ramallah. Thousands of Palestinians turned out in Ramallah to travel with Darwish's coffin in the procession to his final resting place, adjacent to the city's gleaming new Palace of Culture. "He was the most precious of men, who knew Palestine in all its facets," President Abbas asserted, according to an article in *Haaretz*, an Israeli newspaper.

For More Information

BOOKS

Darwish, Mahmoud. *If I Were Another*. Translated by Fady Joudah. New York: Farrar Straus & Giroux, 2009.

Lockman, Zachary. *Intifada: The Palestinian Uprising against Israeli Occupation*. Cambridge, MA: South End Press, 1990, p. 26.

Nassar, Hala Khamis, and Najat Rahman, eds. *Mahmoud Darwish, Exile's Poet: Critical Essays*. Northampton, MA: Olive Branch Press, 2008.

PERIODICALS

Alcalay, Ammiel. "Israel's Five-Poem War." *Nation* (April 10, 2000): 29.

Bronner, Ethan. "Mahmoud Darwish, Leading Palestinian Poet, Is Dead at 67." *New York Times* (August 10, 2008). Available online at http://www.nytimes.com/2008/08/11/world/middleeast/11darwish.html?scp=1&sq=mahmoud+darwish&st=nyt (accessed on November 30, 2011).

Darwish, Mahmoud. "Those Who Pass Between Fleeting Words." *Left Curve*, no. 13 (1988/89).

Greenberg, Joel. "Ramallah Journal: Suitcase No Longer His Homeland, a Poet Returns." *New York Times* (May 10, 1996). Available online at http://www.nytimes.com/1996/05/10/world/ramallah-journal-suitcase-no-longer-his-homeland-a-poet-returns.html?scp=55&sq=darwish&st=nyt (accessed on November 30, 2011).

Handal, Nathalie. "Mahmoud Darwish: Palestine's Poet of Exile." *Progressive* (May 2002): 24–27.

Hofmann, Paul. "Dramatic Session; P.L.O. Head Says He Bears Olive Branch and Guerrilla Gun." *New York Times* (November 14, 1974). Available online at http://select.nytimes.com/gst/abstract.html?res= F00E14FA3F5D12738DDDAD0994D9415B848BF1D3&scp= 1&sq=arafat+AND+olive+branch&st=p (accessed on November 30, 2011).

Rees, Matt, and Daniel Klaidman. "The Politics of Poetry." *Newsweek International* (March 20, 2000): 62.

Shatz, Adam. "A Poet's Palestine as a Metaphor." *New York Times* (December 22, 2001): A19.

WEB SITES

Bahaa, Maha. "Obituary: Mahmoud Darwish." *Aljazeera* (August 27, 2008). http://english.aljazeera.net/news/middleeast/2008/08/ 2008813174431509791.html (accessed on November 30, 2011).

Darwish, Mahmoud. "Identity Card." *adab.com.* http://www.adab.com/en/ modules.php?name=Sh3er&doWhat=shqas&qid=12 (accessed on November 30, 2011).

Khoury, Jack, and Avi Issacharoff. "Mahmoud Darwish: The Death of a Palestinian Cultural Symbol." *Haaretz* (August 14, 2008). http:// www.haaretz.com/print-edition/news/video-mahmoud-darwish-the-death- of-a-palestinian-cultural-symbol-1.251777 (accessed on November 30, 2011).

Mohamed ElBaradei

BORN: June 17, 1942 • Cairo, Egypt

Egyptian diplomat, politician

"Today we are proud of Egyptians. We have restored our rights, restored our freedom, and what we have begun cannot be reversed."

Mohamed ElBaradei.
© MICHELINE PELLETIER/
CORBIS.

Mohamed ElBaradei is an Egyptian diplomat and politician, and the former director general of the International Atomic Energy Agency (IAEA), an intergovernmental body affiliated with the United Nations (UN; an international organization of countries founded in 1945 to promote international peace, security, and cooperation). In that job ElBaradei played a prominent role in questioning the reasons for the 2003 invasion of Iraq by the United States. He and other senior IAEA officials publicly disputed U.S. claims that Iraq was producing weapons of mass destruction (WMDs). ElBaradei stepped down from the IAEA at the end of his third term in 2009 and was soon drawn into political and governmental changes unfolding in Egypt. In early 2011 mass demonstrations in his homeland succeeded in removing Egypt's longtime president **Hosni Mubarak** (1928–; see entry) from power, and ElBaradei became a candidate in the 2011–12 presidential race.

Early life and career

Mohamed Mustafa ElBaradei was born in 1942, in Cairo, Egypt, into a family of modest wealth and accomplishment. His father was an attorney, who served as president of Egypt's bar association (a professional body of lawyers), and ElBaradei had a French au pair as a toddler. (An au pair is a foreigner who lives with a family and is employed to help with housework and childcare.) During ElBaradei's childhood, the ruler of Egypt was King Farouk I (1920–1965), who was considered little more than a puppet of British colonial interests by many Egyptians. Farouk was ousted in a 1952 revolution started by a group of young Egyptian army officers led by **Gamal Abdel Nasser** (1918–1970; see entry). In 1956 Nasser became the second elected president of Egypt and remained in power until his death fourteen years later. Nasser was one of the most powerful figures in the Middle East, urging other Arab leaders to fight for self-rule and join what he envisioned as a powerful Arab coalition spanning from North Africa deep into the Middle East. (Arabs are people of the Middle East and North Africa who speak the Arabic language or who live in countries in which Arabic is the dominant language.)

Nasser had many critics, however, and ElBaradei's father was one of them. The attorney was a strong supporter of several key principles of democracy, including a free press and an independent judiciary, and under Nasser, political opponents faced the threat of jail and other reprisals. When Nasser died of a heart attack in 1970, he was succeeded as president by **Anwar Sadat** (also spelled al-Sadat; 1918–1981; see entry), who also dealt harshly with threats to his power. ElBaradei's father was critical of Sadat and his regime, as well.

During this period, ElBaradei was in school and participating in sports, excelling at both. At age nineteen he won Egypt's national youth squash championship. (Squash is a game in which two players use rackets to hit a small, soft rubber ball against the walls of a closed court.) A year later, in 1962, he earned his undergraduate degree in law from the University of Cairo. He went on to receive a graduate degree in international law from the Graduate Institute of International and Development Studies in Geneva, Switzerland. His education secured him a place with Egypt's Ministry of External Affairs, which he joined in 1964 as an associate with the country's Permanent Mission to the United Nations in New York City. After earning a law degree from New York University School of Law in 1974, he returned to Cairo and was appointed special assistant to foreign minister Boutros Boutros-Ghali (1922–), a post he held for the next four years.

Participates in the Camp David Accords

As special assistant to the foreign minister, ElBaradei was part of the Camp David Accords, peace talks between Egypt and its thirty-year enemy, Israel. Foreign Minister Boutros-Ghali was instrumental in the historic Camp David negotiations, which took place over a thirteen-day period in September 1978. ElBaradei was with the negotiating team that arrived with President Sadat at Camp David, the U.S. presidential retreat in Maryland, in the United States. The talks led to the 1979 Israel-Egypt Peace Treaty, which improved relations between the two nations. Israel withdrew its troops from Egypt's Sinai Peninsula, which it had taken in the 1967 Arab-Israeli War, while Egypt formally recognized Israel's right to exist as a Jewish state in the Middle East. (Since the creation of Israel in 1948, Arab nations had refused to recognize Israel as a legitimate nation, because the country had been established on land that was also claimed by Arabs.)

In 1980 ElBaradei was appointed a senior fellow (a member of a learned society) at the United Nations Institute for Training and Research in Geneva, Switzerland, as head of its international law program. A year later he accepted an adjunct professorship in international law with the faculty of New York University School of Law, a position he held for the next six years. He also joined the Secretariat of the International Atomic Energy Agency (IAEA) as a senior staff member. This UN-affiliated agency was created in 1957 in part as a response to the fears of a major nuclear catastrophe, because both the Soviet Union and the United States by then possessed the nuclear capability to annihilate one another.

The IAEA, headquartered in Vienna, Austria, employs some two thousand professionals from around the world who work to ensure that UN member countries use nuclear science and technology for positive goals, such as electricity and medicine, and work cooperatively with one another. It monitors nuclear-power reactors around the world to make certain operators follow safety and public-health guidelines, for example. The most important mission of the IAEA, however, is its inspection program. UN member countries must agree to inspection of their nuclear facilities and stockpiles of sensitive materials so the UN can ensure that they are not secretly building nuclear-weapons programs for military purposes. One key element in the IAEA mission is the Nuclear Non-proliferation Treaty (NNPT) of 1970, signed by the United States, the Soviet Union, Great Britain, China, and France. There are 184 other signees to the NNPT. Among the notably absent members are Israel, India, and Pakistan; North Korea was a signee, but withdrew in 2003.

Visits Iraq

In the early 1990s ElBaradei was part of the IAEA team sent to dismantle Iraq's nuclear, chemical, and biological weapons programs after the country's defeat in the Persian Gulf War (1990–91). He writes of his experiences in his memoir, *The Age of Deception: Nuclear Diplomacy in Treacherous Times*, noting that several weapons sites were discovered in the aftermath of the war in addition to two nuclear reactors built with Soviet and French help for energy purposes. "The IAEA was faulted for not having detected earlier these clandestine [secret] aspects of Iraq's nuclear program," he writes. "But the blame is mostly due to the limitations placed on the IAEA's inspection authority. The Agency was only expected to verify what a country declared. We had little authority, and few mechanisms, to search for undeclared nuclear materials or facilities."

With this in mind, the UN Security Council passed a resolution establishing a United Nations Special Commission (UNSCOM) to ensure that all of Iraq's stockpiles were eliminated, that no new research was being carried out, and that no new materials were being acquired by the government. There was a debate at the time over which UN agency would have primary authority, and as the IAEA's legal adviser, ElBaradei insisted that the IAEA handle nuclear matters, with UNSCOM given the task of investigating widespread evidence that Iraq was producing stockpiles of biological and chemical weapons. Because Iraq repeatedly refused to comply with UNSCOM inspection requests, the commission recalled its inspectors in 1998 and a joint U.S. and British military offensive on selected Iraqi installations was launched in December of that year in response to Iraq's continued refusal to comply with UN directives. Known as Operation Desert Fox, the joint air strikes targeted Baghdad and several other sites over a four-day period.

In his book ElBaradei writes of the struggles his team faced in Iraq, particularly with the UNSCOM personnel, before they were all recalled in 1998. He remembers in particular a July 1991 trip into the desert where Iraqi scientists showed where they had buried uranium-enrichment equipment before the war. "I witnessed a senior Iraqi scientist weeping in frustration at the treatment he was receiving from an UNSCOM inspector who had accused him publicly of lying," ElBaradei writes in *The Age of Deception.* He notes that the UNSCOM personnel were largely drawn from prestigious U.S. national scientific laboratories and "were highly qualified technically, but they had no clue about how to conduct international inspections or, for that matter, about the nuances of how to behave in different cultures. From their brash conversation, it was clear they believed that, having come to a defeated country, they had free reign to behave as they pleased."

Becomes IAEA Director

ElBaradei served as legal adviser at the IAEA until 1993, when he became the assistant director general for external relations. At the time, the IAEA was led by the former foreign minister of Sweden, Hans Blix (1928–), who took over in 1981. The directors general are elected to four-year terms by the IAEA General Council. ElBaradei was elected to succeed Blix in 1997 and won reelection in 2001 and 2005.

ElBaradei's role in inspecting Iraq took on a new urgency during his second term, especially after the terrorist attacks on the United States on September 11, 2001. In response to the attacks, U.S. president George W. Bush (1946–) declared a war on terrorism, and considered Iraq, which the United States suspected of stockpiling WMDs, as a possible threat to the safety and security of the nation. Prior to the 1998 missile attacks known as Operation Desert Fox, Iraqi leader **Saddam Hussein** (1937–2006; see entry) ordered an end to all IAEA and UN-sanctioned weapons inspections in Iraq.

UNSCOM was replaced by the United Nations Monitoring, Verification and Inspection Commission (UNMOVIC), which was authorized by a December 1999 UN Security Council resolution and headed by Blix. In late 2002 ElBaradei and Blix were part of high-level discussions with Iraqi diplomats and the Bush administration over a new team of inspectors to be sent to Iraq. ElBaradei requested clear terms of what the United States, the UN Security Council, and other interested parties expected from the new inspection reports. By that point Great Britain was siding with the Bush administration's stance against Saddam in Iraq and making statements about removing Saddam by force, if necessary, over his refusal to comply with UN inspections and a UN Security Council resolution barring any resurrection of Iraq's WMD program. At the time,

Mohamed ElBaradei with nuclear inspectors and safety experts. ElBaradei served as director of International Atomic Energy Agency (IAEA) from 1997 to 2009. © MICHELINE PELLETIER/CORBIS.

ElBaradei was attempting to maintain IAEA neutrality, especially after charges surfaced that UNSCOM had installed intelligence equipment in Iraq in the early 1990s. "I became deeply concerned that the reputation of international institutions, including the [IAEA], would be severely damaged by association—that we would be perceived as agents of the United States and its Western allies," he writes in his memoir of the preliminary meetings with U.S. and British officials.

Discredits yellowcake documents

One of the key charges against Saddam was a piece of intelligence claiming that Iraq had attempted to purchase five hundred tons of uranium oxide, also known as yellowcake, from the African nation of Niger. The two mines in Niger, however, produce it for the nuclear energy programs of France and other European nations, and the uranium oxide is sold before it is mined. The British claimed they had data that confirmed this information. ElBaradei and the IAEA demanded to see the proof. Finally, U.S. officials handed over a collection of documents to the IAEA's Iraq Nuclear Verification Office. "The problems were glaring," writes Seymour M. Hersh in the *New Yorker*. "One letter, dated October 10, 2000, was signed with the name of Allele Habibou, a Niger Minister of Foreign Affairs and Coöperation, who had been out of office since 1989. Another letter, allegedly from Tandja Mamadou, the President of Niger, had a signature that had obviously been faked."

On March 7, 2003, ElBaradei and Blix spoke at length to the UN Security Council in the debate over whether to allow the use of force against Iraq, as the United States and Great Britain were requesting, despite strong public sentiment against military action. Blix delivered an extensive report, followed by ElBaradei, who noted that Iraq's nuclear capabilities, based on 218 inspections at 141 different sites, were drastically diminished. Regarding the alleged yellowcake purchase, ElBaradei asserted, according to a *New York Times* article dated March 8, 2003, that "[T]hese specific allegations are unfounded." ElBaradei concluded, his report with these words: "[T]here is no indication that Iraq has attempted to import uranium since 1990."

Thirteen days later, a U.S.-led coalition invaded Iraq. The country's capital, Baghdad, fell under coalition control the second week of April. Saddam disappeared but was captured in December 2003. He was found guilty of war crimes by an Iraqi Special Tribunal and hanged in December 2006. No evidence of WMDs was ever found, which confirmed what ElBaradei and Blix had asserted before the UN Security Council in 2003.

In June 2005 ElBaradei was reelected for a third term as IAEA director general. Four months later, ElBaradei and the IAEA were awarded the Nobel Peace Prize for their joint "efforts to prevent nuclear energy from being used for military purposes and to ensure that nuclear energy, for peaceful purposes, is used in the safest possible way," according to a *New York Times* October 7, 2005, article.

Celebrity status

In 2009 ElBaradei stepped down after his third term as IAEA director general with a plan to ease his way into retirement, writing a memoir and working as a consultant. In February 2010 he went to Egypt and was greeted by large crowds at the airport, in open defiance of the country's

Mohamed ElBaradei poses with his Nobel Peace Prize.
BJORN SIGURDSON/AFP/
GETTY IMAGES.

Emergency Law, which places strict limits on public gatherings of five persons or more without a permit. The law had been in place since the 1981 assassination of Anwar Sadat by members of the Egyptian Islamic Jihad group, who opposed the 1979 Israel-Egypt Peace Treaty. Sadat was succeeded by his vice president, Hosni Mubarak, who was still in office in 2010, much to the dismay of many of Egypt's eighty-five million citizens. Elections had been marred by restrictions on candidates and allegations of blatant vote fraud at the polls. When ElBaradei arrived back home for a visit, there were rumors that Mubarak was gravely ill and was likely to soon hand over power to his son Gamal (1963–), a former investment banker who held a key position in the country's National Democratic Party.

ElBaradei dismissed rumors that he planned to challenge Mubarak in the next presidential election, noting that the current rules to win a spot on the ballot were not worth the time and effort. "I'm seeking to nudge Egypt toward democracy," he said in an interview with Joshua Hammer, a writer for the *New Yorker*. "To put it bluntly, democracy here is a farce." He took the opportunity to dismiss Gamal Mubarak's much-touted economic reforms over the previous few years: "The gap between rich and poor is widening dramatically," ElBaradei said. Before he left the country to return to Vienna, ElBaradei met with others and established the National Association for Change. The organization was not a political party; Egyptian political parties were tightly restricted by the Mubarak regime. Its first stated goal was the repeal of Egypt's Emergency Law.

In the spring of 2011 a wave of prodeomocracy uprisings spread throughout the Middle East and North Africa. These uprisings came to be known as the Arab Spring. First protests erupted in Tunisia in December 2010, and Tunisians successfully ousted longtime president Zine El Abidine Ben Ali (1936–) on January 14, 2011. That success sparked protests in Egypt on January 25, with scenes of demonstrations in Cairo's enormous Tahrir Square riveting the world.

A presidential contender

ElBaradei returned to Egypt on January 27, 2011, and after large-scale protests occurred the next day, he was among the thousands targeted by water cannons manned by Egypt's riot police. Two days later, he spoke before massive crowds calling for Mubarak to step down, asserting, "[W]e are on the right path, our strength is in our numbers. I ask you to be patient, change is coming," he said, according to a profile that appeared on the Web site *Al Jazeera.com* on January 31, 2011. For a time, he was placed under house arrest and confined to his villa on the Cairo-Alexandria Road by pro-Mubarak military troops.

Al Jazeera, a popular Arabic news network in the Middle East, reported that the National Association for Change had assigned ElBaradei the task of negotiating Mubarak's resignation and a handover of power to Egypt's Supreme Council of the Armed Forces. On February 11 Mubarak's vice president announced that Mubarak had stepped down, which prompted an outpouring of jubilation across Tahrir Square and throughout the rest of the world.

ElBaradei stated his opposition to some proposed changes to the Egyptian constitution, which he felt did not go far enough to ensure democratic freedoms in Egypt, but the measures agreed upon by the new post-Mubarak leaders passed in a referendum on March 19. In July 2011 ElBaradei was sworn in as one of fourteen new cabinet ministers in a provisional (temporary) government as the new head of the Ministry of Housing, Public Utilities and Urban Development. He continued to press for full constitutional reform, submitting a bill of rights to all political parties for their approval. Parliamentary elections began on November 28, 2011, and the long-awaited presidential election was slated to be held in the summer of 2012. ElBaradei declared his candidacy for president. He faced several well-qualified challengers, including former foreign minister Amr Moussa (1936–) and Hazem Salah Abu Ismail, a popular media figure formerly associated with the Muslim Brotherhood, an Islamic fundamentalist group organized in opposition to Western influence and in support of Islamic principles. While ElBaradei is considered an integral figure in helping Egypt move toward democracy, political analysts do not deem him likely to be elected president, because he spent nearly three decades out of the country during his career with the United Nations and IAEA.

For More Information

BOOKS

ElBaradei, Mohamed. *The Age of Deception: Nuclear Diplomacy in Treacherous Times.* New York: Metropolitan Books, 2011, pp. 5–6, 9–10, 23, 85.

PERIODICALS

ElBaradei, Mohamed. "Saving Ourselves From Self-Destruction." *New York Times* (February 12, 2004). Available online at http://www.nytimes.com/2004/02/12/opinion/saving-ourselves-from-self-destruction.html?scp=222&sq=%22elbaradei%22&st=nyt (accessed on November 30, 2011).

Hammer, Joshua. "The Contenders." *New Yorker* (April 5, 2010). Available online at http://www.newyorker.com/reporting/2010/04/05/100405fa_fact_hammer#ixzz1VOFUvfZ6 (accessed on November 30, 2011).

Hersh, Seymour M. "Who Lied to Whom?" *New Yorker* (March 31, 2003). Available online at http://www.newyorker.com/archive/2003/03/31/030331fa_fact1#ixzz1VOXkWF31 (accessed on November 30, 2011).

"In a Chief Inspector's Words: 'A Substantial Measure of Disarmament.'" *New York Times* (March 8, 2003). Available online at http://www.nytimes.com/2003/03/08/world/threats-responses-chief-inspector-s-words-substantial-measure-disarmament.html?scp=4&sq=%22hans+blix%22&st=nyt&pagewanted=all (accessed on November 30, 2011).

'Nuclear Watchdog Wins Nobel Peace Prize.' *New York Times* (October 7, 2005). Available online at http://www.nytimes.com/2005/10/07/world/europe/07iht-web.1007nobel.html?scp=1&sq=%22efforts%20to%20prevent%20nuclear%20energy%20from%20being%20used%20for%20military%20purposes%22&st=cse (accessed on November 30, 2011).

WEB SITES

"Profile: Mohamed ElBaradei." *Al Jazeera* (January 31, 2011). http://english.aljazeera.net/news/middleeast/2010/02/2010219162148390306.html (accessed on November 30, 2011).

"Wafd Party Approves ElBaradei's Human Rights Charter." *Al-Masry Al-Youm* (June 30, 2011). http://www.almasryalyoum.com/en/node/473070 (accessed on November 30, 2011).

Recep Tayyip Erdoğan

BORN: February 26, 1954 • Istanbul, Turkey

Turkish prime minister

"A political party cannot have a religion. Only individuals can. Otherwise, you'd be exploiting religion, and religion is so supreme that it cannot be exploited or taken advantage of."

Recep Tayyip Erdoğan. DAVID GANNON/AFP/GETTY IMAGES.

Turkey's prime minister since 2003, Recep Tayyip Erdoğan (pronounced ERR-doe-wan) is a political leader firmly committed to the religion of Islam. He leads a nation of seventy-three million people, most of them Muslim. Formerly a mayor of the city of Istanbul, Turkey, Erdoğan has won praise for maintaining steady economic growth, improving foreign relations with Turkey's neighbors and with the West, and placating the more conservative members of Turkish society. The Justice and Development Party he leads secured a resounding victory during the 2011 election, in which Erdoğan was elected to his third term as prime minister. "Before anything else, I'm a Muslim," he told Deborah Sontag of the *New York Times.* "As a Muslim, I try to comply with the requirements of my religion. I have a responsibility to God, who created me, and I try to fulfill that responsibility. But I try now very much to keep this away from my political life, to keep it private."

Early life and political ambitions

Erdoğan was born on February 26, 1954, and raised in the working-class Kasimpaşa neighborhood of Istanbul. He grew up playing soccer and played at the semiprofessional level for several years as a young adult. His father, Ahmet, was a captain with Turkish Maritime Lines, a cargo and passenger shipping company.

The modern nation of Turkey was just three decades old when Erdoğan was born. Istanbul had been the centuries-old capital of the Byzantine and Ottoman empires under its former name of Constantinople. The Ottoman Empire (the vast empire of the Ottoman Turks which included southwest Asia, northeast Africa, and southeast Europe, and lasted from the thirteenth century to the early twentieth century) collapsed in the years following World War I (1914–18; a global war between the Allies [Great Britain, France, and Russia, joined later by the United States] and the Central Powers [Germany, Austria-Hungary, and their allies]), and a young, dynamic leader named **Mustafa Kemal Atatürk** (1881–1938; see entry) united several regions into modern Turkey in 1923, becoming its first president. Firmly committed to joining the Western world, Atatürk used his executive powers to enact sweeping changes that erased the final traces of Ottoman rule. Religious courts were abolished, women's suffrage (right to vote) went into effect, and the Latin alphabet was adopted. The fez (the traditional Turkish hat) was banned, while women were encouraged to adopt Western dress. Secularism, the concept that religion and religious affairs should play no role in political life, was incorporated into a new constitution.

In his youth Erdoğan was a talented soccer player, but he also demonstrated a devotion to his faith. His teachers recommended him for entry into Istanbul's İmam Hatip (Prayer Leaders and Preachers School), a government-run religious school. Erdoğan completed his secondary education in 1973 and went on to Marmara University, where he earned a degree in business administration and became active in politically oriented student groups.

During his college years, Erdoğan became active in the youth wing of the Islamist National Salvation Party. The party was founded in 1972 by Turkish politician Necmettin Erbakan (1926–2011). As an Islamist political party, it was based on the belief that Islam should provide the basis for political, social, and cultural life in Muslim nations. Within five years the Islamist National Salvation Party had captured enough popular support to win 24 of the 550 seats in Turkish Grand National Assembly. Erdoğan headed the party's youth wing, and Erbakan became a mentor to him.

1978 Erdoğan married Emine Gülbaran and began a family that would eventually include four children. He played semiprofessional soccer in the years before he finished his management degree at Marmara University in 1981. He then went to work for Ülker, a large candy, confectionery, and beverage manufacturer.

After a third military coup (overthrow of the government) in September 1980, all political parties were banned for a time. The Islamist National Salvation Party was dissolved, but Erbakan returned to politics a few years later as one of the founders of the Welfare Party. Erbakan encouraged Erdoğan's political ambitions. In 1985 Erdoğan became chair of the Welfare Party in Istanbul and a year later ran for a seat in the Turkish Grand National Assembly (TGNA), but lost. He entered the 1989 mayoral race in Istanbul, which he also lost, then suffered a third and final defeat in 1991 for seat in the TGNA.

Elected mayor of Istanbul

Erdoğan ran for Istanbul mayor again as the Welfare Party candidate in 1994 and won, becoming the first Islamist mayor of the city. His four years in office resulted in some noteworthy reforms inside the growing metropolis of nine million, which straddles two continents and had become famously congested in population as Turkey's economy grew during the 1980s and 1990s. As mayor, Erdoğan improved vital services, including the waterworks, and made some progress in reducing the city's congested traffic. Although Turkey's population is predominantly Muslim, Istanbul is a cosmopolitan city and tourist destination with both nightclubs and brothels, rarities in an urban setting with an Islamic orientation. Erdoğan's failure to remake the city into a more Islamic showcase by restricting its nightlife and introducing alcohol consumption regulatory measures, as some had feared with his election, seemed to sway undecided Turks toward the Welfare Party, which won 158 seats in the TGNA in the parliamentary elections.

In 1996 Erbakan formed a coalition government and became the country's first Islamist prime minister. He quickly asserted that Turkey should not model its politics on Western democracies. That statement and other actions prompted yet another military coup on February 28,

1997. This time, parliament was not dissolved, although the Welfare Party was banned and Erbakan's coalition government was disassembled. It was the fourth and final time that the Turkish military intervened to oust a democratically elected government in the twentieth century.

Jailed because of a poem

In December 1997 Erdoğan visited Siirt, the hometown of his wife's family. While there, he delivered a public speech in which he read aloud a poem by Turkish poet Ziya Gökalp (1876–1924), who had been a contemporary of Atatürk's and helped shape the idea of Turkish nationalism. (Nationalism is devotion and loyalty to the nation and its culture.) Back in his youth, Erdoğan had won poetry reciting contests, and Gökalp's work was a favorite. On that day he quoted from the 1912 poem "Asker Duasi" (The Soldier's Prayer), altering some lines in its first stanza. Erdoğan's altered version was:

> The mosques are our barracks
> the domes our helmets
> the minarets our bayonets
> and the believers our soldiers.

He also made a remark that any attempt to stifle prayer in Turkey would spark an uprising he likened to a volcanic eruption.

Erdoğan's speech was widely reported in the media, and a few months later local prosecutors in Diyarbakir charged him with subversion (attempting to undermine or overthrow the government) and the incitement of religious hatred. In a shocking decision, the court sentenced him to ten months in prison, a relatively harsh penalty for an elected official. The State Security court also banned him from any future political activity. He was forced to resign as mayor of Istanbul in November 1998. He made several attempt to have the sentence repealed, but when these failed he reported to a jail in Thrace on March 21, 1999. He served four months in prison but was granted early release on July 24, 1999.

Founded political party

After his release and despite the ban on his political participation, Erdoğan joined the Virtue Party, an Islamist party founded in 1998, just as the party was becoming divided over its future direction. The two factions were *yenilikciler* (renewalists), who wanted to remake it in conservative democratic fashion, and *gelenekçiler* (traditionalists), who argued in favor of keeping the strict Islamist outlook. Erdoğan sided with the renewalists and helped reshape the party for the coming 2002 election, but in June 2001 a high court outlawed the party entirely, declaring it an obvious successor to Erbakan's banned Welfare Party. In response, Erdoğan and the renewalist faction organized a new party, the Justice and Development Party, in August 2002. The traditionalist faction from the Virtue Party, meanwhile, formed their own party, Felicity.

The Justice and Development Party chose a light bulb as its logo, instead of a religious symbol. "A political party cannot have a religion," Erdoğan explained to Sontag about the party and Turkey's new direction. "Only individuals can. Otherwise, you'd be exploiting religion, and religion is so supreme that it cannot be exploited or taken advantage of."

When the Justice and Development Party swept the November 2002 elections, winning 34 percent of the vote and a historic 363 TGNA seats, Erdoğan was still under the ban on any political activity, including holding political office. Fortunately the Justice and Development Party held enough of a majority to spearhead a constitutional amendment that reversed the ban. In the interim party cofounder and former Welfare Party colleague Abdullah Gül (1950–) served as acting prime minister. In a February 2003 election, Erdoğan won a TGNA seat and Gül became his Minister for Foreign Affairs.

Once the constitutional amendment went into effect, Erdoğan took over from Gül and became prime minister on March 14, 2003. This was one of the most crucial moments in U.S.-Turkish foreign relations. U.S. president George W. Bush (1946–) expected Turkey to allow the use of U.S. military bases in Turkey as a staging ground for the invasion of Iraq. The bases were American, but under the terms of the agreement between the United States and Turkey their activities were carefully delineated; using them to launch a war against one of Turkey's regional neighbors was prohibited unless Turkey agreed. The Iraq War (2003–2011) was launched just a week after Erdoğan took office, on the grounds that Iraqi leader **Saddam Hussein** (1937–2006; see entry) was harboring weapons of mass destruction (WMDs). The TGNA rejected Bush's plan, however, and Turkey lost a projected fifteen billion dollars worth of U.S. aid that Bush administration officials had offered as part of the deal.

The Head Scarf Debate

In the 1920s president **Mustafa Kemal Atatürk** (1881–1938; see entry) banned the wearing of certain items of clothing. The fez, a brimless hat for men that had become ever-present in the Ottoman era, was prohibited because of its association with the Greeks, with whom Turks had warred recently. Similarly, Atatürk outlawed traditional Muslim head scarves on women, but in the 1970s and 1980s Turkish women of Recep Tayyip Erdoğan's own generation adopted them again as a sign of their faith. Erdoğan's wife covers her head, as does the spouse of Turkish president Abdullah Gül (1950–). Any woman who wears a head covering is banned from entering universities in Turkey and from holding civil-service jobs. In 2006 the country's president, Ahmet Necdet Sezer (1941–), refused to allow Erdoğan's wife and those of other Justice and Development Party members from attending a special-occasion event at the Presidential Palace that commemorated Turkey's independence. The Presidential Palace was a government building and thus included in the rules about headscarves; the president's decision in favor of secularists was viewed as an insult to Erdoğan's wife and other spouses.

The head scarf controversy also impacted the lives of Erdoğan's two daughters, who chose to attend foreign universities where they were allowed to wear their headscarves. At the 2004 wedding of Esra, the eldest, heads of state from across the region celebrated the nuptials in which the bride wore a traditionally styled dress and head covering. "The people at this ceremony reflect this country: They're from East and West, with their heads covered and uncovered," the father of the bride told the seven thousand guests, according to the Associated Press.

Erdoğan pledged to lift the ban on wearing headscarves in public during his 2007 reelection campaign to win a second term as prime minister, but massive protests erupted as the TGNA debated the measure. An amendment passed in February 2008 that lifted the ban, but the Republican People's Party immediately issued a legal challenge, and the constitutional court annulled the terms of the proposed amendment

Pressed for European Union membership

During his first months in office, Erdoğan visited several European cities and affirmed his support for Turkey's admittance to the European Union (EU; an economic and political association of European countries). This was an issue that had deeply divided a country that for centuries had felt torn between Europe and the Middle East and Asia, and caused considerable consternation within the member countries of the EU. His public-relations tour sought to quell fears that his party was a moderate political organization in name only, actually concealing its Islamist agenda to evade the strict secular (nonreligious) laws of Turkey's constitution. These fears stem from a concept in Islamic philosophy referred to as *takiyye,* or "the idea that a Muslim can hide his real opinion to gain a

four months later. University officials across Turkey, however, generally still permit women to study and sit for exams while wearing head scarves and do not impose fines or sanctions, although there is the occasional headline-generating arrest.

Recep Tayyip Erdoğan and his wife Emine greet supporters at a rally in 2007. Emine Erdoğan, like many Muslim Turkish women, has adopted wearing the headscarf as a sign of her faith. This piece of clothing was outlawed in the 1920s and has recently been a point of controversy in Turkish society. DIMITAR DILKOFF/AFP/GETTY IMAGES.

practical advantage," explains Chris Morris in an article on the *BBC News* web site. Erdoğan refuted these claims. "We did not establish our party as a party based on religion," he said in an interview with Helena Smith for the *Guardian*. "Politicians can be religious, but religion should not establish the basis of politics. There are 1.5 billion Muslims in the world. Turkey's model will prove to them, and Europe, that Islam and democracy can coexist harmoniously."

There were several requirements for Turkey to meet before becoming fully eligible to join the EU. Member states of the EU must be fully democratic and in sound fiscal health. To help Turkey move more quickly toward EU admission, Erdoğan sought to mend troubled relations with one neighbor, Greece. For centuries the two had been

magazine/the-Erdoğan-experiment.html?scp=1&q=Erdoğan+AND+
Kasimpasa&st=nyt&pagewanted=print (accessed on November 30,
2011).

WEB SITES

Associated Press Staff. "Wedding Turns into Diplomatic Fest." *Taipei Times*
(July 13, 2004). http://www.taipeitimes.com/News/world/print/2004/07/
13/2003178824 (accessed on November 30, 2011).

Morris, Chris. "Turkey's Leading Man." *BBC News* (September 30, 2004).
http://news.bbc.co.uk/2/hi/programmes/from_our_own_correspondent/
3701606.stm (accessed on November 30, 2011).

Faisal ibn Abd al Aziz ibn Saud

BORN: c. 1905 • Riyadh, Saudi Arabia

DIED: March 25, 1975 • Riyadh, Saudi Arabia

Saudi king

Faisal ibn Abd al Aziz ibn Saud. THOMAS J. ABERCROMBIE/NATIONAL GEOGRAPHIC/GETTY IMAGES.

"It has reached the point where people believe that he who wants American aid should proclaim enmity [hostility] to the United States."

King Faisal ibn Abd al Aziz ibn Saud of Saudi Arabia pushed his oil-rich kingdom into the modern age. Ruling for a little over a decade, from 1964 to 1975, Faisal used the seemingly unlimited wealth from the country's oil to bring prosperity to Saudi Arabia. His reign coincided with an explosive media interest in his family from the Western world, because of the power the kingdom wielded as one of the founding members of the Organization of the Petroleum Exporting Countries (OPEC), an organization formed in 1960 by the world's major oil-producing nations to coordinate policies and ensure stable oil prices in world markets. A devout Muslim who opposed both the existence of the country of Israel in the Middle East and the military aid Israel received from other countries, Faisal pushed other OPEC member nations to restrict their supplies of oil to the rest of the world, which prompted an

Wahhabism: Saudi Fundamentalism

The Saudi royal family follows a branch of Islam known as Wahhabism, which makes their country one of the most conservative of the Islamic nations. Wahhabism is named after its founder, Muhammad ibn Abd al-Wahhab. Al-Wahhab and his followers preached a fundamentalist version of Islam. (Fundamentalism is a movement stressing adherence to a strict or literal interpretation of religious principles.) He wanted Muslims to revere only the prophet Muhammad (c. 570–632) and to follow sharia, or Islamic religious law, very closely. Wahhabis believe in strict observance of daily prayers and in the careful separation of women and men in most areas of life.

For the Saudis, balancing religious fundamentalism with their desire to be participants in the world community has always been difficult. Many Saudis have privately supported Islamic fundamentalist movements that are directly opposed to the United States, including the 1979 Iranian Revolution (also known as the Islamic Revolution) and the rise of al-Qaeda, an organization that proclaims jihadism, or armed struggle against the non-Muslim world, as its goal. Al-Qaeda was led by its founder **Osama bin Laden** (1957–2011; see entry) until his death in 2011. Bin Laden was a Saudi-born follower of Wahhabism, who forged deep contacts inside Saudi Arabia. Bin Laden's call for revolution within Saudi Arabia, however, cost him the support of the Saudi government, and he was exiled in 1992.

energy crisis in the West from 1973 to 1974. OPEC had demonstrated its ability to use oil as a political tool.

Son of a national hero

Faisal's family has long-standing claims to power in the Middle East. From the time that Islam spread throughout the Middle East in the seventh century CE, numerous sheikhs (Arab tribal leaders), had vied for power in the largely desert lands that make up present-day Saudi Arabia. In the middle of the eighteenth century one powerful sheikh, Muhammad ibn Saud (died 1765), allied himself with the Muslim religious leader Muhammad ibn Abd al-Wahhab (1703–1792), whose followers were known as Wahhabis. Saud's followers and the Wahhabis joined in a powerful alliance that battled intermittently for local dominance on the Arabian Peninsula throughout the eighteenth and nineteenth centuries. By 1904 a powerful member of the Saud family, Abd al Aziz ibn Saud (1876–1953), took control of the region known as the Nejd, defeating another Arab sheikh and troops from the powerful Ottoman Empire, which ruled much of the Middle East. After 1904, Ibn Saud, as he was popularly known, pursued his goal of bringing centralized control to the Arabian Peninsula.

Faisal was born around 1905 to Ibn Saud (1876–1953) and his wife, Tarfa bint Abduallah bin Abdulateef al Sheekh, herself a descendant of Muhammad ibn Abd al-Wahhab. Tarfa was the second of Ibn Saud's multiple wives, and Faisal had at least forty-five brothers and half brothers, as well as an unknown number of sisters. As Ibn Saud's third son, Faisal was third in line to succeed his father as ruler of the Saudi clan.

Faisal's mother died when he was very young, and the boy was raised by his mother's parents, who followed the strict religious teachings of Wahhabism. Faisal memorized large parts of the Koran (also spelled Qur'an or Quran; the holy book of Islam); debated with religious scholars; and learned to love poetry as he grew up in the city of Riyadh, now the capital of Saudi Arabia. The Riyadh of Faisal's youth was primitive. Houses were made of mud brick, and woven rugs and mats were the only furniture. The entire city was surrounded by a great stone wall, a symbol of its isolation that endured into the modern era.

Faisal was small and thin as a boy, but very brave. He is said to have ridden the feared horse of his brother, Turki, around the city walls and to have jumped into a deep well to demonstrate his courage. He also learned to be a wise negotiator and leader of people. Faisal spent a great deal of time with Ibn Saud, who was beloved by the nomadic sheepherders and traders who made up the small population of the Arabian Peninsula. (Nomads are people who move from place to place, with no fixed home.) He saw how his father won his people's loyalty, and Faisal saw him lead soldiers into battles to extend Saudi power throughout the Arabian Peninsula. In 1919 Ibn Saud even sent the fourteen-year-old Faisal to represent him on a diplomatic mission to Great Britain. The teenager and his entourage were welcomed by King George V (1865–1936) and shown the marvels of British science and industry, which made a deep impression on Faisal. He saw snow for the first time in Wales and was entranced by the escalators in London, England, that carried people into and out of the underground subway stations.

House of Saud fills the Ottoman vacuum

The Saudis were not directly involved in World War I (1914–18; a global war between the Allies [Great Britain, France, and Russia, joined later by the United States] and the Central Powers [Germany, Austria-Hungary, and their allies]), but they were deeply influenced by the outcome. The Ottoman Empire had collapsed, and the British and French now exerted political power over its lands in the Middle East. (The Ottoman Empire was the vast empire of the Ottoman Turks which included southwest Asia, northeast Africa, and southeast Europe, and lasted from the thirteenth century to the early twentieth century.) In 1921 the Europeans divided up the Middle East, forming new nations, including Iraq,

Lebanon, Palestine, Syria, and Transjordan (present-day Jordan). They divided the Arabian Peninsula into kingdoms controlled in part by the Saudis and in part by rival families. Although Ibn Saud did not want to anger the Europeans, especially the British, he wanted to take control of the peninsula from his rivals. Faisal would prove a valued aide and soldier.

Faisal's first military mission came in 1921, when he joined a group of his father's soldiers as they took control of the province of Asir, on the Red Sea. In 1924, at age twenty, Faisal led his own troops in the region. By 1926 Faisal, his brothers, and his father had wrested control of much of the Arabian Peninsula from their enemies, including the cities of Mecca and Medina, considered two of Islam's holiest cities. Ibn Saud declared himself sultan (later king) of Nejd and Hejaz, two of the largest regions on the Arabian Peninsula. When a number of European countries recognized his leadership, Ibn Saud named Faisal his foreign minister, and in 1926 Faisal made his second trip to Europe, this time as the official representative of his land.

The final step in the unification of the Arabian Peninsula came in 1932, when Ibn Saud's troops defeated the lone remaining resisters to his rule. That year, he declared his nation to be the Kingdom of Saudi Arabia, making it the world's only nation to be named after a family. Ibn Saud was king, and his second eldest son, Saud bin Abdul-Aziz Al Saud (1902–1969), was declared heir to the throne (The king's eldes son, Prince Turki I bin Abdul-Aziz Al Saud, died in 1919.) With the creation of Saudi Arabia as an independent nation, Faisal became his nation's representative to the world. He traveled to the Soviet Union, which was the first country to recognize his nation, but also communicated with governments throughout the world.

Like many wealthy Arab men, Faisal took multiple wives. His first two marriages, in the 1920s, were largely to secure alliances with other families. His third and happiest marriage, to Iffat Al-Thuniyyan, began in 1932. The couple lived in the holy city of Mecca and, when Faisal later became king, Queen Iffat was very popular among the Saudi people. Faisal's first two marriages produced several sons, including Abdullah, Khalid, and Saud, and eight daughters. With Iffat he would have nine more children.

An uneasy relationship with the United States

Saudi Arabia was not a wealthy country at the start of the 1930s. Most of the kingdom's wealth came from fees paid by Muslims visiting the holy shrines in Mecca and Medina and from a tax paid by every citizen. But when geologists discovered oil, the kingdom's financial situation changed dramatically. Representatives from Great Britain and the United States both tried to win concessions to drill for Saudi oil. (An oil concession allows a foreign company to provide the equipment and skill needed to extract and sell oil in exchange for a fee paid to the government.) The United States, with a down payment of about $250,000, won the concession, thus beginning a long relationship with Saudi Arabia. Over the years oil drilling would bring millions, then billions, of dollars into the kingdom.

The relationship between Saudi Arabia and the United States has not always been easy. While the U.S. oil concession brought great wealth to Saudi Arabia, especially to the royal family which retained sole control over its share of the oil revenues, the two countries are unlikely allies. Saudi Arabia is a devout Muslim country, allowing few rights to women and insisting on strict observance of Islamic law from all its citizens. The United States promotes full rights and religious freedom for all its citizens. It also has laws which separate religion and government. Additionally, the two nations have very different views about an important political issue: the existence of Israel.

Jews had called for a homeland in Palestine, a historical region in the Middle East on the eastern shore of the Mediterranean Sea, comprising parts of present-day Israel and Jordan, since the late nineteenth century in a movement known as Zionism. In May 1948 Jewish leaders in Palestine declared the establishment of the independent state of Israel. Arab nations, including Saudi Arabia, were outraged. They felt that a Jewish homeland amounted to stealing land and political power from the Arabs (people who speak the Arabic language) who had lived there for centuries. When Egypt, Syria, Iraq, and several other Arab nations went to war to crush the emerging Jewish state, Saudi Arabia provided financial support, but no soldiers. However, Jewish forces won the war and established the nation of Israel. Ever since the 1948 Arab-Israeli War, Saudi Arabia has provided financial assistance to Palestinians (the Arab people whose ancestors lived in the historical region of Palestine and who continue to lay claim to that land) and urged Great Britain, France, Canada, the United States, and other Western nations to cease their support for Israel.

The cultural and political differences between Saudi Arabia and the United States made for a difficult relationship. Faisal, in his job as representative of Saudi interests, often had to express his displeasure with U.S.

actions. Yet Saudi Arabia typically did not let political disagreements interrupt economic cooperation.

From diplomat to king in waiting

Faisal was named his country's ambassador to the United Nations in 1945, and he worked hard to represent Saudi Arabia in the issues that faced the world's new political order. He became widely respected for the reasonable way he presented Arab objections to the existence of Israel. Faisal also played an important role within Saudi Arabia. In the late 1940s and early 1950s his father, Ibn Saud, slowly withdrew from a direct role in governing the kingdom. Yet the aging king was also growing uneasy about his newly wealthy clan's eager embrace of Western material goods. Ibn Saud recognized that it would be difficult for his children and his country to pursue oil riches while remaining devout Muslims. When he passed on the role of king to his son, Saud, in 1953, this contradiction between wealth and religion became a significant problem.

Faisal had long clashed with his older brother Saud. Saud was impulsive and loved to spend money; Faisal thought through his actions carefully and lived the simple life of a devout Muslim. Their differing styles soon became apparent to those inside and outside Saudi Arabia. King Saud was even exposed as attempting to bribe a Syrian colonel to assassinate Egyptian leader **Gamal Abdel Nasser** (1918–1970; see entry). In 1958 family members convinced King Saud to let Faisal run the country. Faisal placed limits on the royals' frivolous spending, used oil money to make improvements that helped ordinary Saudis, and in 1960 agreed to become one of the five founding nations of OPEC. In 1962 he abolished the practice of slavery, which had existed in the area for thousands of years and remained in practice in some households. Faisal was well liked for all of his efforts, but he was not yet king.

King Saud resented his brother's obvious leadership skills. Twice he reclaimed his position, but both times family members and influential religious leaders stepped in. Finally, in October 1964, supporters of Faisal insisted that Saud formally step down as king. Faisal had always avoided criticizing his brother out of family loyalty, and he kept his distance from the plotting against Saud. When he was told that Saud had been stripped of his title, Faisal was upset at the impact this had on his family, but he accepted the throne.

Faisal and his brothers arrive at an airport in New York. Faisal was often in the United States due to his title of ambassador to the United Nations in the late 1940s and early 1950s. © BETTMANN/CORBIS.

Arab leader

As king, Faisal settled a long-simmering conflict with Egypt over its attempt to overthrow the government of Yemen, which lay to the south of Saudi Arabia. He also began a program of social and economic reforms. He encouraged public education through newly launched, state-run, newspapers, radio, and television. With the help of his wife, Iffat, he introduced reforms that allowed women access to education, although women were still kept apart from men in most public places. He also sought ways to help his nation develop agriculture and industry so that it would not be overly dependent on the income it earned from oil. His most important achievements as king, however, were the role he played in promoting Arab issues to the world and the power he helped oil-producing nations claim through OPEC.

The Arab countries of the Middle East had long been torn between competing bids for their allegiance. Egypt's president Nasser, the one genuine rival to the House of Saud in the region, wanted secular, or nonreligious, governments to lead a movement for the unification of all Arab countries under a socialist economic system, in which the government owns the means of production and controls the distribution of goods and services. Nasser also tried to persuade Arab countries to ally themselves with the Soviet Union, which practiced a form of socialism. Faisal countered Nasser's ideas. He wanted the Islamic religion to be at the center of his nation. He also wanted Arab nations to work together to promote their economic interests, and he remained a strong ally of the United States.

When Nasser died in 1970, Faisal was now the senior Arab leader in the Middle East. He used his skills to organize Arab nations via the Arab League and other multinational groups and to help other countries resolve their disputes. In 1967 Faisal helped organize the first face-to-face meeting between the leaders of all the Islamic countries. The nations met in Morocco to protest the Israeli occupation of Muslim holy places in Jerusalem. They also established a news agency. Faisal increasingly served as a spokesman for Palestinians, many of whom had become refugees (people who flee their country to escape violence or persecution) after the state of Israel was established in 1948, and even called for jihad with the goal of taking back Jerusalem for Muslims. Faisal's government was generous with foreign aid dollars to the displaced Palestinians and to the nations like Syria that had opened their borders to the refugees.

The oil king

Faisal's most notable achievement as an Arab leader was his use of OPEC as a bargaining tool with the West. Ever since Western oil companies had begun drilling oil in Arab countries, they had controlled the amount and price of oil. Faisal and his oil minister, Ahmed Zaki Yamani (1930–), believed that it was time for the oil-producing countries to gain more

The Oil Crisis in the United States

Before 1973, consumers in the United States took the availability of oil for granted. They rarely worried about being able to find gasoline (which is produced from oil) to operate their cars or about how much gasoline cost. The Arab oil embargo of 1973, and the oil crisis that followed, forever changed Americans' untroubled relationship with oil and with Saudi Arabia.

When Saudi Arabia and other countries cut the flow of oil to protest U.S. support for Israel during the 1973 Arab-Israeli War, the oil market responded immediately. Supplies went down and prices skyrocketed. Soon gasoline was rationed, which meant that people could only buy gas on certain days and only in certain amounts. Across the United States, long lines formed at gas stations. People began turning off lights and turning down the heat to save on heating oil. The higher fuel costs echoed throughout the economy, causing the prices of all goods to rise. The oil embargo affected the entire economy of the United States and the world.

The embargo ended in March 1974, but oil prices never returned to their earlier low levels. Saudi Arabia and other oil-producing countries grew rich. An article in *Time* magazine notes that the oil embargo led to the "greatest and swiftest transfer of wealth in all history: the 13 OPEC countries earned $112 billion from the rest of the world." People in the United States and elsewhere became far more conscious about their use of oil, gas, and other forms of energy. Automobile manufacturers worked to make cars more fuel efficient, a process led by the Japanese, who dramatically increased their share of the world automobile market. The oil embargo also gave a boost to the environmental movement, which supported the conservation of energy wherever possible.

"FAISAL AND OIL." *TIME* (JANUARY 6, 1975). HTTP://WWW.TIME.COM/TIME/ MAGAZINE/ARTICLE/0,9171,912630,00. HTML (ACCESSED ON NOVEMBER 30, 2011).

control over oil production, price, and profits. By the early 1970s, they had convinced other OPEC nations to act.

In October 1973 war broke out between Israel and the combined forces of Egypt and Syria in what became known as the 1973 Arab-Israeli War. The United States and other Western countries supported Israel. Sensing an opportunity to promote his economic interests and support Palestinians at the same time, Faisal and the OPEC chiefs ordered an embargo (stoppage) on oil exports to supporters of Israel. OPEC also raised the price of oil dramatically, from $3.01 per barrel to $11.65 per barrel within a few weeks' time. The impact on the world oil market was dramatic. Prices for gasoline and other oil products soared, and governments in many nations ordered rationing, or the limiting of supplies. With his actions, Faisal instantly turned Saudi Arabia into a powerful new force in world politics. From this point forward, Western oil companies no longer dictated the terms of Arab oil production.

Faisal was much loved in Saudi Arabia. He had shown that it was possible to use the country's oil wealth wisely, such as to promote social and economic programs that helped the Saudi people. Although some complained that there were few freedoms in Saudi Arabia's conservative society, Faisal said, "If anyone feels wrongly treated, he has only himself to blame for not telling me. What higher democracy can there be?" according to the *King Faisal Foundation* Web site. Unlike his older brother, Saud, who spent money lavishly, Faisal was not corrupted by wealth. He lived simply and was a devout Muslim throughout his life, even opting not to live in a lavish new palace built in Jeddah for his family. This was perhaps his greatest feat, demonstrating that great wealth did not have to corrupt strict Islamic values.

On March 25, 1975, one of Faisal's nephews came to visit the king. The young man's brother had been killed a decade earlier in riots in Riyadh related to the launch of a new television station, which the kingdom's clerics (ordained religious officials) viewed as a potentially corrupting influence on Saudi society. Yet this surviving brother was among the younger princes whose lifestyle choices, including alcohol consumption, Faisal looked upon with disapproval. The young man had even been arrested in the United States during his college years on a drug charge. As the two prepared to embrace, the nephew pulled out a gun and shot his uncle. Within an hour, Faisal was dead. Before he died, Faisal asked that the nephew be spared the death penalty, but twenty thousand Saudis turned out to watch the public beheading of the nephew on June 18, 1975. Faisal was buried in a simple grave on the outskirts of Riyadh. Faisal's half brother Khalid succeeded him as king.

For More Information

BOOKS

Holden, David. *The House of Saud: The Rise and Rule of the Most Powerful Dynasty in the Arab World*. New York: Holt, Rinehart, and Winston, 1982.

Mackey, Sandra. *The Saudis: Inside the Desert Kingdom*. New York: Norton, 2002.

Weston, Mark. *Prophets and Princes: Saudi Arabia from Muhammad to the Present*. Hoboken, NJ: Wiley, 2008.

PERIODICALS

"Faisal and Oil." *Time* (January 6, 1975). Available online at http://www.time.com/time/magazine/article/0,9171,912630,00.html (accessed on November 30, 2011).

Middleton, Drew. "Faisal Says U.S. Policies Spur Rampant Mideast Communism." *New York Times* (May 23, 1968). Available online at http://select.nytimes.com/gst/abstract.html?res=F70611F93954157493C1AB178ED85F4C8685F9&scp=4&sq=%22faisal+said%22&st=p (accessed on November 30, 2011).

WEB SITES

Danish, Paul. "CU's Most Famous Alum." *Coloradan Magazine* (March 5, 2009). http://www.coloradanmagazine.org/2009/03/05/cu%E2%80%99s-most-infamous-alum/ (accessed on November 30, 2011).

"King Faisel bin Abdulaziz Al Saud." *King Faisal Foundation.* http://www.kff.com/EN01/KingFaisal/KingFaisalIndex.html (accessed on November 30, 2011).

Pierre Gemayel

BORN: November 6, 1905 • Mansoura, Egypt

DIED: August 29, 1984 • Bifkayya, Lebanon

Lebanese politician

Pierre Gemayel. © CLAUDE SALHANI/SYGMA/CORBIS.

"The Christian psychosis of fear is internalized, visceral, and tenacious. We can do nothing about it. It is the Moslems' task to reassure us."

Pierre Gemayel was a Lebanese political leader and cofounder of the Phalange Party, also known as the Kataeb Party. Gemayel gave Lebanese Christians a forceful political voice in a country dominated by a restless Muslim majority. His efforts to secure his people's place in Lebanon inspired his followers to call him "the rock on which Lebanon is to be built," according to Eric Pace in the *New York Times*. Under Gemayel's charismatic leadership, the Phalange Party, whose goal was to unite Maronite Christians against domination by foreign or religious rivals, played a significant role in winning Lebanon its independence from France. (Maronites are members of an Arabic-speaking group of Christians, living mainly in Lebanon, who are in communion [share essential doctrines] with the Roman Catholic Church.) It also protected Christians during the extended Lebanese Civil War (1975–90) and dominated Lebanese politics into the 1980s.

A family of political influence

The Gemayel family has a long history in Lebanon. Their ties to the village of Bifkayya, about 15 miles (24 kilometers) northeast of Beirut, dates back to the sixteenth century, and in the twenty-first century the family still owns a house on Mount Lebanon built by their ancestors in 1540. The Gemayels were also leaders among the Lebanese Maronite community. This Christian group's origins in this region date back to the fifth century CE.

Pierre Gemayel grew up surrounded by strong, outspoken men. For their opposition to the Ottoman Empire's rule over their land, both Gemayel's father and uncle were sentenced to death. (The Ottoman Empire was vast empire of the Ottoman Turks which included southwest Asia, northeast Africa, and southeast Europe, and lasted from the thirteenth century to the early twentieth century.) To escape their fate, the two fled with their families to Mansourah, Egypt, where Gemayel was born in 1905. After the defeat of the Ottoman Empire in World War I (1914–18; a global war between the Allies [Great Britain, France, and Russia, joined later by the United States] and the Central Powers [Germany, Austria-Hungary, and their allies]), the Gemayels returned to their Lebanese home and to a place of prominence in the community.

Lebanon has more than a dozen different religious communities, but the largest differences in faith are between Muslims and Christians. When World War I ended, Western nations were given the authority to administer the affairs of the regions that had formerly been under the control of the Ottoman Empire. France was granted the mandate (administrative authority) for Lebanon. France grouped the various populations living in Beirut and other towns along the coast of the Mediterranean Sea, the Bekaa Valley, and the mountainous area including Mount Lebanon into a French protectorate called Greater Lebanon. (A protectorate is a state that is controlled and protected by another, stronger country.) In 1926 France created a constitution that divided political power among the various religious factions in Lebanon, declaring that the Lebanese president must be a Maronite, the prime minister a Sunni Muslim (a follower of the Sunni branch of the religion of Islam), and the speaker of the chamber a Shiite Muslim (a follower of the Shia branch of Islam). Although the government shared power between these groups, it was an unequal arrangement. France was a predominantly Roman Catholic country, so the Maronites were viewed as protected by the French. The constitutional division of power in the Lebanese government would become the source of much struggle during Gemayel's political career.

Gemayel was educated by the Roman Catholic Jesuit order at St. Joseph University in Beirut and went on to earn a degree in pharmacy from the French School of Medicine, also in Beirut. He worked at a hospital and at a Gemayel family-owned drugstore in Beirut. Although Gemayel had concentrated on his studies and entered into a suitable profession, he never lost his youthful passion for playing soccer (called football in Lebanon), and he organized a soccer league called the Lebanese Football Federation. In 1936 he represented Lebanon as an observer at the Summer Olympic Games, which were held in Berlin, Germany.

Lebanese nationalism

While in Berlin, Gemayel was impressed by the nationalistic attitude of the Germans. (Nationalism is devotion and loyalty to the nation and its culture.) "I was struck with admiration," Gemayel said of his visit, as quoted by *New York Times* journalist John Kifner. "We . . . are, by nature, an unruly and individualistic people. In Germany, I witnessed the perfect conduct of a whole unified nation." Gemayel may have been especially struck by German nationalism, because nationalistic sentiment was growing in Lebanon at the time. In 1936 Lebanon negotiated a three-year period of transition, after which time France would grant it independence. Although Lebanon would not actually obtain its independence until 1943, such prospects kindled the emergence of nationalistic feelings in Lebanon.

With four friends, Gemayel founded the Phalange Party in 1936, with the goal of developing a Lebanese nationalistic attitude, physical discipline, military expertise, and a democratic philosophy among its members. The party adopted the motto "God, Family, Nation." Gemayel and his friends shaped the goals of the Phalangists in an attempt to guard the freedoms of Lebanese Christians in a Middle East dominated by Muslims. Indeed, the threat seemed very real, because in Beirut that year Muslims convened in a conference and, according to author Helena Cobban in *The Making of Modern Lebanon*, Muslims "almost unanimously demanded the re-integration of Lebanon's Muslim districts with Syria," its neighbor to the east.

In 1937 Gemayel took leadership of the Phalange Party. For demonstrating against French rule that year he spent a brief period in prison.

But the Phalangists continued to grow, and membership increased to thirty-five thousand by 1942. The Phalangists maintained a disciplined, tight-knit group, with regular military training near Mount Lebanon. Although the group presented its ideas as nonsectarian (inclusive of all religious groups), the vast majority of its members were Maronites. Gemayel drew support for the party in the 1940s by championing Lebanese independence, but the Phalangists would remain pro-Western even as it rejected French rule. Gemayel and other leaders of the organization considered Western countries, such as Great Britain, France, and the United States, as sources of support for the defense against Pan-Arabism, a movement for the unification of Arab peoples and the political alliance of Arab states.

When Lebanon gained its independence in 1943, it kept the power-sharing model of government that it had used under French rule. The government was structured so that no one party could dominate Lebanese politics. Members of Lebanon's various religions all won seats in the government and had to form coalitions with each other in order to rule effectively. Gemayel realized that the balance of power in Lebanese government could only be tipped by a stronger party, and he worked to increase his party's membership and develop relationships with other parties. In 1951 he allied the Phalangists with other Maronites and Druze (members of a small sect of Islam) to form the Socialist Front. The Socialist Front suspected Lebanon's first president of corruption and successfully called for his resignation.

By the 1950s the Phalangists had become the largest and most powerful political party in Lebanon, with nearly forty thousand members and a trained private army; it remained the strongest partner inside the Socialist Front. The Phalangists' strength was rewarded in 1958. That year Egypt and Syria, having united as the United Arab Republic under Egyptian president **Gamal Abdel Nasser** (1918–1970; see entry), encouraged a Muslim revolt in Lebanon. The Phalangists feared that the Pan-Arabism promoted by Nasser would swallow up the Christian communities in Lebanon. A civil war broke out in Lebanon, and the Phalangists' army fought against Muslim demonstrators and held general strikes in Beirut. To quell fears of Arab domination, the newly appointed Lebanese prime minister Rashid Karami (1921–1987) chose to lead the government with a coalition of four men of varying religious backgrounds. Two of the members, including Karami, were Sunni Muslims, while the other two members, Fuad Chehab (1902–1973) and Gemayel, were Christians.

Palestinians provoke the Phalangists

Gemayel remained in the upper levels of Lebanese government for more than two decades, and other Phalange Party members also won seats in the government. In the late 1960s about 10 percent of the Lebanese population was Palestinian refugees, who had fled Israel following its independence in 1948 or after the 1967 Arab-Israeli War. (Palestinians are an Arab people whose ancestors lived in the historical region of Palestine, comprising parts of present-day Israel and Jordan, and who continue to lay claim to that land.) Palestinians formed the Palestine Liberation Organization (PLO), a political and military organization formed to unite various Palestinian Arab groups with the goal of establishing an independent Palestinian state. The PLO had operated from Jordan, but was expelled from that nation in 1970. Then Lebanon became home to the group's headquarters. Palestinians flooded into Lebanon. The PLO irritated the Lebanese population and provoked Israel to invade Lebanon in retaliation against PLO attacks along the Lebanon-Israeli border in 1973. The private armies of various political parties, including the Phalangists, recruited men and increased their weapons supplies in preparation for a battle to rid Lebanon of the PLO. Israel allied itself with the Phalangists and pledged its support against the PLO and against the intervention of Syria, which had dispatched military forces to provide security during the 1967 Lebanese presidential elections.

Gemayel played a leading role in these developments through the Phalangists, which he continued to lead. He was elected to parliament in 1960 and held cabinet positions throughout the decade. There were also two failed bids for the presidency, in 1964 and 1970. As a member of the Lebanese government, Gemayel advocated for the Lebanese army to move against the PLO, but when his pleas were rejected Gemayel prepared his party's private army to fight. By the 1970s the Phalange Party had nearly sixty-five thousand members and an army of ten thousand men.

On April 13, 1975, Gemayel was nearly killed in an incident that erupted outside a Maronite church in a eastern suburb of Beirut; the gunmen missed Gemayel but hit and killed four others. Later that day the Kataeb Regulatory Forces (also known simply as the Phalangist militia), led by Gemayel's son Bashir, ambushed a busload of Palestinians on its way back to the Sabra refugee camp and opened fire, killing twenty-six

Gemayel's Political Legacy: His Sons

"There were always some in the Maronite community who thought that the [Gemayels] really aimed at replacing the many 'big families' with the rule of just one 'big family'—their own," according to Helena Cobban, a *New York Times* journalist who covered Lebanon in the 1970s and wrote about it in a 1985 book, *The Making of Modern Lebanon*. Indeed, Pierre Gemayel's two sons followed his example and rose to positions of leadership in Lebanon. Bashir Gemayel (1947–1982) was a skilled fighter and an admired leader of the Phalangist militia. Even though, in keeping with Lebanese tradition, Bashir was not groomed for public office, because he was the second son, he nevertheless came to prominence in Lebanese politics as the leader of the Lebanese Front, which was formed in 1976. He was considered a hero by his followers but was often described in less-than-favorable terms by his many opponents. Bashir used bloody force against his enemies and even against rival factions of his own party. He masterminded violent attacks against other Maronites, which drove a wedge between them in the late 1970s and early 1980s. Bashir was elected to the Lebanese presidency on August 23, 1982 but was assassinated by a bomb that

detonated at an event at which he was speaking on September 14.

The eldest son of Pierre Gemayel, Amine (1942–), prepared to follow in his father's footsteps. Educated as a lawyer, Amine proved himself a skillful debater and a savvy businessman. Amine won election to parliament in 1970 and developed diplomatic relations between the Phalangists and others in the government. Although a polished and sophisticated man, Amine did not possess the charisma of his younger brother. He stood in his brother's shadow as Bashir rose to power in the early 1980s. Elected to the presidency after his brother's assassination, Amine did not succeed in unifying the different parties in his government to support national projects, and he left office in 1988. After spending years in exile in the United States and France following the assassination of his brother, Amine returned to Lebanon in 2000 and reentered the political scene by founding a party he deemed the genuine successor to the Phalange Party. His own son, Pierre, was elected to parliament in 2000 and assassinated by unknown militants in 2006.

people. This day marks the formal start of the Lebanese Civil War, which lasted fifteen years.

Formed the Lebanese Front

In January 1976 Gemayel and other Maronites, including former Lebanese president Camille Chamoun (1900–1987), formed a new coalition, the Lebanese Front, made up of Christian-oriented parties, including the Phalangists and the National Liberal Party. The parties combined their militias to fight in the civil war. Gemayel's son Bashir was named the leader of the Lebanese Front. Bashir proved himself to be a strong, charismatic leader, and he rose to a position of some fame in Lebanon.

Although never the only "big" political family in Lebanon, the Gemayels have continued to play a significant role in Lebanese political life.

COBBAN, HELENA. *THE MAKING OF MODERN LEBANON*. LONDON: HUTCHINSON, 1985.

While many people felt that Pierre Gemayel and his family helped Lebanon through difficult times, others believed that they were ruthless leaders. Many paintings and murals of the Gemayels were disfigured during the Lebanese Civil War.
© CHRISTINE SPENGLER/CORBIS.

The civil war, which resulted in a starkly divided Beirut, was further complicated by the invasion of troops from Syria to support the Phalangists. Syria's president, **Hafez Assad** (also spelled al-Assad; 1930–2000; see entry), skillfully played both sides of the conflict, quietly aiding Palestinian forces, too. Israel entered the fray in 1978, and launched a full-scale invasion of southern Lebanon in June 1982, after a failed assassination attempt on their ambassador to Great Britain by a group with ties to the PLO. Like Syria, Israel officially sided with Gemayel and Phalange Party.

Gemayel's son, Bashir, was elected to the presidency in 1982, but his assassination nine days before his inauguration revealed how divided the communities in Lebanon had become. In addition to the tensions between

Christian and Muslim factions in Lebanon, the leading Christian families had long feuded with each other for power. These feuds turned bloody by the late 1970s, and Bashir was targeted. One bungled attempt on his life in 1980 killed Bashir's young daughter in a car-bomb attack. Bashir's enemies finally succeeded in killing him on September 14, 1982, just before he was to be sworn in as president.

Two days after Bashir's death, the Phalange Party nominated his older brother, Amine (1942–), to run for the presidency. Amine remained in office until stepping down in 1988 due to Lebanon's increasingly fractious and violent political sphere. The situation deteriorated even further after that, with rival governments controlled by Christian and Muslim sides. Even though his sons eclipsed his power in government, Gemayel remained a prominent figure in Lebanese politics until his death. He died of heart failure just hours after attending a cabinet meeting on August 29, 1984.

For More Information

BOOKS

Cobban, Helena. *The Making of Modern Lebanon.* London: Hutchinson, 1985.

Harel, Amos, and Avi Issacharoff. *34 Days: Israel, Hezbollah, and the War in Lebanon.* Translated by Ora Cummings and Moshe Tlamin. New York: Macmillan, 2009.

Young, Michael. *The Ghosts of Martyrs Square: An Eyewitness Account of Lebanon's Life Struggle.* New York: Simon & Schuster, 2010.

PERIODICALS

Kempe, Frederick. "Mideast Losers? Lebanon's Christians Are Bitter at the U.S., Fearful About the Future—Discord Among Top Leaders and Rise in Population of Moslems Worry Them—But Some Vow to Fight On." *Wall Street Journal* (February 28, 1984): 1.

Kifner, John. "Lebanese Christians Bury Chief in Mountain Town." *The New York Times* (August 30, 1984): A4.

Page, Eric. "Pierre Gemayel, a Courtly Chieftain of Christians." *New York Times* (August 30, 1984): A10.

Wallace, Charles P. "Lebanon's Gemayel: A Leader Looks Around, Sees No One Following." *Los Angeles Times* (September 22, 1985): 24.

WEB SITES

kataeb.org. http://www.kataeb.org/EN (accessed on November 30, 2011).

"Lebanon: The Family Business." *Aljazeera* (June 9, 2009). http://english. aljazeera.net/programmes/general/2009/05/20095317388560607.html (accessed on November 30, 2011).

McCarthy, John. "Lebanon's 'Old' and 'New' Politics." *BBC News* (May 3, 2011). http://www.bbc.co.uk/news/world-13271857 (accessed on November 30, 2011).

Moubayed, Sami. "Amin Gemayel Says His Family's History 'Runs Parallel to Lebanon's.'" *Washington Report on Middle East Affairs* (October 2001). http://www.wrmea.com/archives/october01/0110029.html (accessed on November 30, 2011).

Theodor Herzl

BORN: May 2, 1860 • Budapest, Hungary

DIED: July 3, 1904 • Edlach, Austria

Hungarian author, activist

"The Jewish State is essential to the world; it will therefore be created."

Theodor Herzl. ERICH LESSING/ART RESOURCE, NY.

Theodor Herzl was a leading force in the late-nineteenth-century Zionism, an international political movement that called for the creation of an independent Jewish state in Palestine. (Palestine is a historical region in the Middle East on the eastern shore of the Mediterranean Sea, comprising parts of present-day Israel and Jordan.) Herzl was not the first to suggest Jewish migration to Palestine, nor did he live to see the creation of the Jewish state of Israel in Palestine in 1948, but he was instrumental in marshaling support from Europe's wealthy assimilated Jews (Jews who had successfully blended into society) and high-level diplomats for the cause. Herzl was not a particularly religious man, but he dreamed of a homeland where Jews would be free from the discrimination that had followed them for centuries. A journalist and author of several influential publications, including a pivotal 1896 work called *The Jewish State*, Herzl was the first president of the World Zionist Organization, an organization that lobbied for support of the Zionist cause throughout the world. For his efforts he is hailed as one of the founding fathers of Israel.

Grew up facing anti-Semitism

Herzl lived at a time when Jews in Europe and Russia were the frequent targets of discrimination. The American Revolution (1775–83) in the United States and the French Revolution (1789–92) in France unleashed major currents of change across the Western world. People in the West challenged the rule of kings and queens and called for political representation. They identified strongly with the cultural values of their nation, a trend called nationalism. But nationalism's darker side was discrimination of those considered outsiders, and Jews were always considered outsiders. In ancient times, the Jews had made their home in Eretz Yisrael ("Land of Israel" in Hebrew; the ancient kingdom of the Jews), but had been driven out of their homeland by the Romans. Jews settled in a wide variety of locations across the world. Both Christian- and Muslim-oriented nations openly discriminated against them, and in many places the level of education, professional opportunities, religious practices, and location of homes for Jews were restricted by law. As European nations moved out of the Middle Ages (c. 500–c. 1500), the Roman Catholic Church maintained strict rules against usury, or the charging of interest or fees for lending money. This helped a small group of successful Jewish entrepreneurs amass great banking fortunes. Jews were also local shopkeepers, regional merchants, and other business entrepreneurs, because discriminatory practices had barred them from many other trades. In the early nineteenth century, resentful lower classes often targeted local Jews in pogroms (racially-motivated riots in which mobs, usually organized and sanctioned by the state, attack a minority group, most often Jews). These attacks persisted in places like Poland and Russia into the twentieth century. Anti-Semitism (prejudice against Jews) was a regular part of life throughout Europe, Russia, and in many other parts of the world where Jews made up a minority of the population.

Theodor Herzl was born on May 2, 1860, in Budapest, Hungary. His father, Jacob, was the wealthy owner of a trading company. Jacob was raised as an Orthodox Jew but shed much of the customs and observances as he assimilated; Herzl's mother, Jeanette, also did not observe these strict religious traditions. Like other assimilated Jews of bustling Budapest, Herzl grew up with little knowledge of his religious heritage. When he was about to turn thirteen years old, the age at which Jewish boys participate in a coming-of-age ceremony called the bar mitzvah, his family had to hire a tutor to give him a quick course in Judaism, the Jewish religion. Herzl never fully embraced Judaism, but over time he grew to more fully embrace his Jewish cultural identity.

Herzl was highly intelligent, but was an indifferent student. He attended a scientific school in Budapest starting in 1870, but by 1875 his lack of interest in science and the anti-Semitism of his peers caused him to transfer to a gymnasium, which was a standard secondary school. In 1878 his sister, Pauline, died, causing great trauma in the family. Also in 1878 the family moved to Vienna, Austria, and Herzl entered law school at the University of Vienna. His parents were pleased that he was studying law, as it seemed likely to help Herzl blend into Austrian society. But assimilation (blending in) was not easy. He joined a student political society favored by other law students but, faced with persistent anti-Semitism, he eventually dropped out. During law school, Herzl read the book *The Jewish Problem as a Question of Race, Morals, and Culture*, written by Karl Eugen Dühring (1833–1921), and it had a great impact on him. The book offers a pseudo-scientific explanation for anti-Semitism and concludes that the Jewish race is without merit. Herzl wrote in his diary at the time, as quoted in the 1946 edition of his book *The Jewish State*, "If Dühring, who unites so much undeniable intelligence with so much universality of knowledge, can write like this, what are we to expect from the ignorant masses?" It was a question that puzzled him for many years. Although he completed his law degree in 1884, Herzl realized that anti-Semitism would prevent him from ever being fully accepted into the legal profession, and he began to dream of a career as a writer.

Begins writing career

Herzl first wrote short stories and plays. By the mid–1880s he had a number of his plays produced in Prague, Czechoslovakia; Berlin, Germany; Vienna, Austria; and New York, in the United States. One play, *Seine Hoheit* (His Highness), a satirical comedy about the corrupting powers of money, received some critical acclaim and earned Herzl the income to travel widely. He visited Germany, Switzerland, Holland, Belgium, Italy, France, and Great Britain. He met and courted Julie Naschauer, a wealthy Viennese woman, beginning in 1886, and they were married in 1899. In 1891, in search of a stable income, Herzl took a position as the Paris,

France, correspondent for one of Vienna's best-known newspapers, *Neue Freie Presse* (New Free Press).

In Paris Herzl grew ever more aware of the social and political problems facing European Jews. His articles in *Neue Freie Presse* increasingly reported on the growing anti-Semitism in France. In 1893 he wrote, as quoted in the introduction to the 1946 edition of *The Jewish State*, "[Anti-Semitism] is no longer—and it has not been for a long time—a theological matter. It has nothing whatsoever to do with religion and conscience. What is more, everyone knows it. The Jewish question is neither nationalistic nor religious. It is a social question." In 1895 Herzl condensed some of his thinking on this issue into a play called *Das Neue Ghetto* (*The New Ghetto*). According to Morris B. Margolies, author of *Twenty Twenty: Jewish Visionaries through Two Thousand Years*, Herzl's play reveals that "the Jew still found himself in a ghetto, a ghetto surrounded by the hatred and animosity of the people in whose midst he lived." (A ghetto is a poor area of a city, usually occupied by minorities.)

The event that solidified Herzl's ideas about the problems facing Jews was the Dreyfus Affair. In 1894 Alfred Dreyfus (1859–1935), a Jewish French army captain, was charged with treason. Although Dreyfus insisted on his innocence, he was convicted of betraying his country to Germany during the Franco-Prussian War (1870–71) and sentenced to life in prison. A few years later evidence surfaced that showed another officer was indeed responsible for the breach of security, and that this information had been withheld during the trial. French military officials actually conspired to hide this fact, and the other officer was tried and acquitted. In Dreyfus trial-related demonstrations on the streets of Paris, crowds called out "Death to the Jews!" Witnessing this hatred, Herzl came to the crucial realization that Jews would only find peace when they could create a country of their own. From that time on, he dedicated his life to making a Jewish state a reality.

Embracing Zionism

In the early 1880s Russian Jews began emigrating in order to escape the pogroms in their country. Many moved to Palestine and built small settlements. In 1881 Polish Jew Leo Pinsker (1821–1891) wrote *Autoemancipation*, suggesting that all Jews relocate to Palestine. (Herzl claimed not to have read this publication until later in his life.) However, Herzl was the one who translated these ideas into action. With the publication of *The Jewish State* in 1896, Herzl launched the movement that would one day make the nation of Israel a reality.

The Jewish State was first published in Germany as *Der Judenstaat* in 1896, and it was rapidly translated and distributed, soon numbering some eighty editions in eighteen languages. Herzl's book, whose English translation bore the subtitle *Proposal of a Modern Solution for the Jewish Question*, was a radical prescription for the anti-Semitism faced by Jews everywhere. According to Herzl, anti-Semitism distorted the lives of Jews in every country in which they lived, but it also hurt the host countries by bringing social unrest. Both Jews and gentiles (non-Jews) would be better off if Jews were to establish a homeland of their own (although Herzl was not yet specific about where that homeland would be). Herzl did not believe that simply forming small settlements in Palestine was enough; he wanted Jews to use diplomacy to persuade powerful countries like Great Britain, France, and Germany to officially recognize a new Jewish nation. Herzl writes that the Jews, "once settled in their own State, would probably have no more enemies." He concludes his book with these words:

> The Jews who wish for a State will have it. We shall live at last as free men on our own soil, and die peacefully in our own homes. The world will be freed by our liberty, enriched by our wealth, magnified by our greatness. And whatever we attempt there to accomplish for our own welfare, will react powerfully and beneficially for the good of humanity.

Neither Jews nor gentiles were immediately swayed by the optimism of Herzl's conclusions about the future of a Jewish state. The *Wiener Allgemeine Zeitung* newspaper called the plan a "desperate delusion," and other critics disdained the idea that other nations would give formal diplomatic recognition to such a self-described state. Those who favored establishing small settlements practiced what was called "cultural Zionism." They thought that Herzl's plan, called "political Zionism," was doomed to failure because powerful nations would never support it. Many middle-class Jews in Europe did not want to leave their settled lives to move to a foreign land or worried that if they embraced Herzl's form of Zionism they would be considered traitors to their present country.

Despite their misgivings, many young Jews in Austria, Germany, and other European nations embraced Herzl's plan. Their enthusiasm soon spread, and Herzl found himself acclaimed as the leader of a new

Political Zionists versus Cultural Zionists

During the years that Theodor Herzl championed Zionism, the movement calling for the creation of an independent Jewish state, and for many years thereafter, Zionists (supporters of Zionism) disagreed over how that state should be created. Herzl and his followers were political Zionists. They wanted to gain international support for the creation of a Jewish state, Only when powerful nations recognized their claims to a state, they reasoned, would that state be secure enough to offer Jews the shelter and protection they needed. Political Zionists thus formed an organization that could lobby diplomats, monarchs, and presidents for support. This was the First Zionist Congress, which evolved into the World Zionist Organization.

Cultural Zionists took a very different approach. They believed that Jews needed to form settlements or colonies in Palestine to spread Jewish culture in the region. The presence of Jewish settlements would allow the spread of Hebrew (ancient language of the Jewish people), and Jews would be attracted to a place where

their culture was flourishing. Cultural Zionists did not wish to entrust non-Jewish politicians with the task of building a nation on their behalf. The cultural Zionists would make a state for themselves, settlement by settlement, until the existence of a nation was accomplished.

In the end, it took both political Zionists and cultural Zionists to accomplish their shared dream. Cultural Zionists, led by Ahad Haam (1856–1927), built Jewish settlements in Palestine, which helped make Zionism a reality. Others, such as Chaim Weizmann (1874–1952), encouraged settlement along with political solutions. Weizmann helped win the support of the British, who in 1917 issued the Balfour Declaration, which guaranteed British support for a Jewish homeland. Finally, in 1948, the United Nations recognized the state of Israel. (The United Nations is an international organization of countries founded in 1945 to promote international peace, security, and cooperation.) Weizmann became Israel's first president.

political movement. Seeking to take advantage of the excitement, Herzl took several steps to make his plans a reality. In June 1896 he visited Constantinople, the capital of the Ottoman Empire, which ruled over the region called Palestine. (The Ottoman Empire was the vast empire of the Ottoman Turks which included southwest Asia, northeast Africa, and southeast Europe, and lasted from the thirteenth century to the early twentieth century.) His journalism credentials helped him secure meetings with high-level officials, but he was unable to meet with the Ottoman sultan (ruler), Abdul Hamid II (1842–1918). Herzl came with a proposal for the sultan that involved the establishment of a Jewish state under the jurisdiction of the Ottoman Empire in exchange for retiring the massive Ottoman Empire debt. When this plan failed, Herzl turned to other means.

Leading the Zionist cause

After Constantinople, Herzl set about rallying public opinion in Europe. He traveled throughout the continent trying to persuade prominent leaders and diplomats to support the Zionist cause. Early in 1897 he created *Die Welt* (The World), a weekly newspaper dedicated to the spread of Zionist ideas. Herzl financed and edited the paper, which became a powerful tool for building support. Also in 1897, Herzl decided to organize the First Zionist Congress. Held in Basel, Switzerland, in August 1897, the meeting attracted two hundred delegates from nearly twenty countries. It also drew journalists from twenty-six newspapers, who reported the events to the world.

The congress was a media-ready spectacle. Herzl insisted that the delegates follow standard formal-dress rules for high-level diplomatic summits and arranged for a giant blue-and-white banner featuring the

Theodor Herzl addressing the Zionist Congress in Basel, Switzerland, in 1897. Herzl was the organizer of the Congress, which brought together Jewish leaders from various countries to discuss a Jewish state. GOVERNMENT PRESS OFFICE OF ISRAEL.

Star of David (a Jewish symbol consisting of a six-pointed star formed from two equilateral triangles) to be hung in the hall; the design would later become the flag of Israel. But the congress was also very productive. Delegates formed the World Zionist Organization with Herzl as the president, and they affirmed that their goal was to establish "a home for the Jewish people in Palestine secured under public law," according to Naomi Pasachoff, author of *Links in the Chain: Shapers of the Jewish Tradition*. Herzl sums up his assessment of the First Zionist Congress, as quoted in the introduction to the 1946 edition of *The Jewish State*: "In Basle I created the Jewish State. Were I to say this aloud I would be greeted by universal laughter. But perhaps five years hence, in any case, certainly fifty years hence, everyone will perceive it. The state exists as essence in the will-to-the-state of a people."

For the remaining seven years of his life, Herzl worked to make this concept a reality. He lobbied statesmen and wealthy Jewish leaders, and each year he led an annual Zionist congress, which brought together the leading figures in the movement. In 1902 he published another important book, *Altneuland* (*Old-New Land*), which introduces the motto "If only you will it, it is no dream." In 1903 Herzl thought that he had found the opportunity to create a Jewish state. A new pogrom in Russia prompted many Jews to flee that country, and British and Russian officials neared agreement on establishing a Jewish colony in British East Africa (present-day Uganda). But when Herzl presented the British and Russian proposal at the Sixth Zionist Congress, he was vigorously attacked by those who believed that the only legitimate Jewish settlement must be in Palestine, the ancient Jewish homeland. The proposal was put to a vote and resoundingly defeated, and from that point onward Palestine was the only place seriously considered for a Jewish state.

Herzl would not live to see his dream realized. He died on July 3, 1904, at the age of forty-four, in the Austrian resort town of Edlach. The state of Israel was proclaimed on May 14, 1948. It had taken some fifty years, but an independent Jewish nation finally existed. Neighboring Arab (Arabic-speaking) nations, however, did not recognize Israel as a legitimate state. The 1948 Arab-Israeli War followed, as Arab nations attempted—and failed—to take back the land they felt the Jews had stolen. Many Arab Palestinians became refugees (people who flee their country to escape violence or persecution), and they have sought the return of their land ever since. Their cause was taken up by the Arab world and conflict

Herzl's Tragic Family

Theodor Herzl did not live to witness the tragedies that afflicted his own offspring. Herzl and his wife Julie Naschauer had three children, beginning with the birth of Pauline in 1890. She was fourteen years old when her father died, and she suffered from a number of personal problems, including an addiction to opiates (a type of a narcotic drug). She died in 1930 at the age of forty. On the day of her funeral, Herzl's only son, Hans, committed suicide, leaving a note that affirmed his Jewish faith, which he had rejected for many years.

An even worse fate was to befall Herzl's two remaining descendants. His youngest daughter was Margarethe, born in 1893 and nicknamed Trude. She was suffered from manic-depressive disorder and was hospitalized for much of her adult life after the birth of her son, Stephen Theodor Neumann, in 1918. Both Trude and her husband, Richard Neumann, were victims of the Holocaust, the mass murder of European Jews and other groups by the Nazis during World War II (1939–45). They were sent to the Terezín concentration camp in the present-day Czech Republic. (Concentration camps are complexes built by the Germans for the continement and extermination of political opponents and ethnic minorities, especially Jews.) At one point, an enraged Trude shouted at her captors, according to eyewitness reports, "Do you know who I am?

I am the daughter of Herzl!" according to Egon Redlikh's book *The Terezin Diary of Gonda Redlich*. She died at Terezín on March 15, 1943; her husband also died there.

Trude's son Stephen managed to escape the Nazis with the help of sympathetic Zionists and settled in England in the mid–1930s. He did not know of his parents' fate for some time after World War II ended. He served in the British army during the war and visited Palestine shortly after the war's end. He planned to settle there, but was prevented from doing so by unrest in the region. In the summer of 1946 he finally received confirmation that both his parents had died at Terezín. On November 26, 1946, Stephen committed suicide, leaping from the Massachusetts Avenue Bridge over Rock Creek in northwest Washington, D.C., in the United States. His and his father's remains, along with those of other relatives, are interred at Mount Herzl, Israel's national cemetery. Trude's remains, like the majority of the six million Jews who perished in the Holocaust, were never identified.

REDLIKH, EGON. *THE TEREZIN DIARY OF GONDA REDLICH*. EDITED BY SAUL S. FRIEDMAN AND TRANSLATED BY LAURENCE KUTLER. LOUISVILLE: UNIVERSITY PRESS OF KENTUCKY, 1992, P. 54.

between Arabs, Jews, and Palestinians has shaped the political, economic, and cultural landscape of the Middle East well into the twenty-first century.

For More Information

BOOKS

Cohen, Israel. *Theodor Herzl, Founder of Political Zionism*. New York: T. Yoseloff, 1959.

Elon, Amos. *Herzl.* New York: Holt, Rinehart and Winston, 1975.

Finkelstein, Norman H. *Theodor Herzl: Architect of a Nation.* Minneapolis, MN: Lerner, 1991.

Herzl, Theodor. *Old-New Land.* New York: Bloch, 1941.

Herzl, Theodor. *The Jewish State: An Attempt at a Modern Solution of the Jewish Question.* New York: American Zionist Emergency Council, 1946, p. 37.

Levenson, Alan T., and Roger C. Klein. *An Introduction to Modern Jewish Thinkers: From Spinoza to Soloveitchik,* 2nd ed. Oxford: Rowman & Littlefield, 2006.

Margolies, Morris B. *Twenty Twenty: Jewish Visionaries through Two Thousand Years.* Northvale, NJ: Aronson, 2000.

Pasachoff, Naomi. *Links in the Chain: Shapers of the Jewish Tradition.* New York: Oxford University Press, 1997, p. 178.

Redlikh, Egon. *The Terezin Diary of Gonda Redlich.* Edited by Saul S. Friedman and translated by Laurence Kutler. Louisville: University Press of Kentucky, 1992, p. 54.

Vital, David. *The Origins of Zionism.* Oxford: Clarendon Press, 1975.

PERIODICALS

Elon, Amos. "Israelis & Palestinians: What Went Wrong?" *New York Review of Books* (December 19, 2002). Available online at http://www.nybooks.com/articles/archives/2002/dec/19/israelis-palestinians-what-went-wrong/ (accessed on November 30, 2011).

WEB SITES

"The Impresario of Zionism." *Jewish Ideas Daily* (April 28, 2010). http://www.jewishideasdaily.com/content/module/2010/4/28/main-feature/1/the-impresario-of-zionism (accessed on November 30, 2011).

Massad, Joseph. "The Rights of Israel." *Aljazeera* (May 6, 2011). http://english.aljazeera.net/indepth/opinion/2011/05/20115684218533873.html (accessed on November 30, 2011).

"Theodor (Binyamin Ze'ev) Herzl." *Jewish Virtual Library.* http://www.jewishvirtuallibrary.org/jsource/biography/Herzl.html (accessed on November 30, 2011).

OTHER SOURCES

The Spielberg Jewish Film Archive—Theodor Herzl—Father of the Jewish State. YouTube. http://www.youtube.com/watch?v=47tgrvMWbRg (accessed on November 30, 2011).

Amin al-Husayni

BORN: 1893 • Jerusalem, Palestine

DIED: July 4, 1974 • Beirut, Lebanon

Palestinian religious leader, politician

"The Arabs...will oppose until the end the establishment of the Jewish state, no matter what forces may combine against them."

Amin Al-Husayni. © NIK WHEELER/SYGMA/CORBIS.

From 1922 to 1948 Amin al-Husayni (also spelled Haj Āmin al-Husayni) wielded enormous influence as the Grand Mufti (Muslim religious leader) of the ancient city of Jerusalem in Palestine, a historical region in the Middle East on the eastern shore of the Mediterranean Sea, comprising parts of present-day Israel and Jordan. He was a leader of Muslims in the region and the guardian of the Muslim holy sites of Jerusalem. In the 1920s and 1930s he encouraged armed resistance to Jewish settlement in Palestine and was finally exiled in 1937. His most controversial action came four years later, when he sought the aid of Nazi Germany in his bid to help Arabs (people who speak the Arabic language) who lived in Palestine to repel Jewish claims to the land.

Born to privilege

Al-Husayni was born in 1893, in Jerusalem, Palestine, which was then under the rule of the Ottoman Empire, the vast empire of the Ottoman Turks which included southwest Asia, northeast Africa, and southeast Europe, and lasted from the thirteenth century to the early twentieth century. The al-Husayni family was one of the wealthiest and most respected Arab Muslim families in Palestine, tracing their heritage back to the founder of Islam, the prophet Muhammad (c. 570–632). By the end of the eighteenth century, members of his family had risen to positions of political and religious power in Jerusalem. At the time of al-Husayni's birth his father, Mohammed Tahir al-Husayni (1842–1908), held the post of Grand Mufti of Jerusalem and was one of the first figures to question the wisdom of selling land to foreigners. The Zionist movement, an international political movement that called for the creation of an independent Jewish state in Palestine, was at the time gaining traction among some key figures in Europe and North America thanks to Jewish author and Zionist activist **Theodor Herzl** (1860–1904; see entry).

Al-Husayni's father was succeeded as Grand Mufti by his son, Kamil (1867–1921), who was al-Husayni's older brother. The Grand Mufti, while serving as guardian of religious sites in Jerusalem, also interpreted sharia, or Islamic religious law. The city had been in Muslim hands since 1187 CE. Jerusalem was the coveted crown jewel for the Crusaders, Western armies who participated in a series of military campaigns ordered by the Roman Catholic Church between 1095 and 1291 with the main goal of taking the Holy Land (an area that includes sacred sites for Jews, Christians, and Muslims) from the Muslims. Subsequent treaties allowed all three faiths who claimed the city as holy ground to enjoy access to their respective places of religious significance. But the powerful Ottoman Empire firmly held the Middle East well into the twentieth century.

Al-Husayni was educated in a traditional Islamic school in Jerusalem before enrolling at Al-Azhar University in Cairo, Egypt. He studied sharia under Rashid Rida (1865–1935), a well-known scholar who urged that Islam be given a central role in any Arab state. Al-Husayni's allegiance to this idea would place him at the center of one of the great debates among Arab states in the twentieth century, over the place of religion in government.

Wrestling with the central problem of his time

Al-Husayni lived at a time when Zionism was a new political movement just beginning to demand the attention of the world. Beginning in the 1880s, a few influential Jews, weary of the centuries of discrimination and even violence they had endured while living in predominantly Christian lands, began to call for an independent Jewish state. While Argentina and East Africa were briefly considered as potential locations, most Zionists were adamant that the Jewish homeland needed to be in Palestine, the location of the ancient Jewish homeland. The problem was that the population of Palestine was made up of predominantly Arab Muslims.

During his college years in Cairo, al-Husayni became deeply enmeshed in the Arab-Zionist debate. He emerged as an outspoken activist, organizing a campus group of Arabs whose goal was to awaken other Arabs to the perceived dangers of Zionism. He left college in 1913 in order to make the pilgrimage (religious journey) to Mecca, a city near the coast of the Red Sea where the prophet Muhammad was born. This pilgrimage, called the hajj, is considered a sacred duty for every Muslim.

When World War I (1914–18; a global war between the Allies [Great Britain, France, and Russia, joined later by the United States] and the Central Powers [Germany, Austria-Hungary, and their allies]) erupted, al-Husayni enlisted in the Ottoman forces and served as an artillery officer. As the war progressed, many Arabs in Palestine felt that they had a better chance to create an independent Arab state if they joined forces with the British. On medical leave from the Ottoman forces in 1916— really a cover to organize sympathizers to his mission in Jerusalem— al-Husayni was captured by British forces and detained, eventually joining the army of Husayn ibn 'Ali (also spelled Hussein bin Ali; c. 1854–1931), the sharif of Mecca, who was leading an Arab rebellion against Ottoman rule. (A sharif is a nobleman and political leader chosen from among descendants of the Muslim prophet Muhammad [c. 570–632].) When the war ended, the victorious Allies divided up the former Ottoman lands. They created new, independent nations, including Egypt, Turkey, and Saudi Arabia. They placed others, such as Syria, Iraq, Transjordan (present-day Jordan), and Palestine, under a mandate, granting one country the authority to administer the affairs of another country. The British assumed control of Transjordan and Palestine.

The British made a number of promises during World War I. They promised the Arabs that they would help them to create Arab nations in the Middle East. But they also promised Jews that they would help them create a national home in Palestine. Both Jews and Arabs in Palestine fought to ensure that Great Britain lived up to its contradictory promises.

From exile to leadership

Al-Husayni emerged from his experiences in the war more confident and mature and even more committed to the idea that Arabs must resist Zionism, which he felt threatened to turn Arab Palestinians into second-class citizens in their own land. During these postwar years, he taught high school and wrote for *Suriyya al-Janubiyya* (Southern Syria), a newspaper founded in Jerusalem in 1919. In April 1920 he took part in a protest march against Jewish immigration to Palestine and the terms of the Balfour Declaration and delivered a particularly vehement speech against allowing Jews to pray at the Western Wall (also known as the Wailing Wall), one of Judaism's holiest sites. The march turned violent, and British police moved in to disperse the protesters. Nine people were killed and dozens were wounded. The demonstration and its aftermath cemented al-Husayni's reputation. Arabs saw him as a leader in their quest for independence, but Jews saw him as an anti-Semite, who wanted to drive them out of British-controlled Palestine. For a time al-Husayni was forced to flee to Transjordan.

Al-Husayni did not remain away for long. The British needed Arab cooperation if they were to successfully manage Palestine. They needed someone from a highly placed and well-respected Arab family to lend credibility to their foreign presence in the region. **Herbert Louis Samuel** (1870–1963; see entry), British high commissioner of Palestine, issued a pardon for al-Husayni regarding his 1920 speech and allowed him to return to Jerusalem during the winter of 1920–21, where his brother, Kamil, still presided as Grand Mufti. Upon Kamil's death in March 1921, Samuel used his power to appoint al-Husayni as Grand Mufti of Jerusalem. In 1922 al-Husayni was appointed head of the Supreme Muslim Council, the highest body in charge of Muslim community affairs in Palestine. Al-Husayni was now the most influential religious and political leader of Muslims in Palestine. The British wanted an agreeable Grand Mufti, and al-Husayni pledged his cooperation.

Serving two masters

Al-Husayni took office pledging to work with the British to ensure peace in Palestine. The British had promised in the Balfour Declaration not to "prejudice the civil and religious rights of the existing non-Jewish communities in Palestine," yet they were under constant pressure from prominent British Jews and from Zionists in Palestine and around the world to allow more Jewish immigration to Palestine and to protect and expand the rights of Jews in Palestine. Al-Husayni, on the other hand, believed that Zionism posed a real threat to Arabs, thinking that the Jews would to buy up Arab land and dominate the economy.

Al-Husayni managed to balance these interests throughout the 1920s. Although he spoke out and wrote articles in favor of limiting the Jewish population in Palestine, he quelled Arab demonstrations and attacks against the Jewish population. But by the late 1920s, Arabs were becoming increasingly agitated at the growing Jewish settlements, fearing that they would lose control of the area to the Jews entirely.

During the 1920s al-Husayni led a fund-raising campaign to restore the Temple Mount, known to Muslims as the Haram ash-Sharif. It is the holiest site in Judaism, the third holiest site in Islam, and also important to the Christian faith. The long-neglected mosques there, Al Aqsa and the Dome of the Rock, were renovated as part of his plan to firmly embed Muslim allegiance to a geographic site in Jerusalem's Old City. During this time, the Jews were working to gain access to the Western Wall. It was technically under the control of Muslim officials in Jerusalem, like al-Husayni. The wall once surrounded a temple built by King Solomon in the tenth century BCE, and Jews make pilgrimages to the site and to the Temple Mount. During the renovation and reconstruction period, tensions periodically erupted between Jews and Arab Palestinians over access and alterations to these sites.

The Western Wall became a symbol and source of strife for both Jews and Arabs. The Jews pushed the British to guarantee their access to the site, and Arabs depicted Jewish claims as another attempt to drive the Arab Palestinians out of Palestine. Tensions developed into violence in what became known as the Palestinian Riots of 1929. Violence also erupted in several other cities, including Hebron in the West Bank, where Palestinians killed sixty-nine Jewish residents. Al-Husayni was caught in the middle, supportive of Arab groups who despised the growing power of the Jews but trying to keep the peace for the British. Some believed that al-Husayni orchestrated attacks on Jews, but a British commission assembled to investigate the riots exonerated him, although it did blame Arab agitators for inciting the riots. A wave of reprisals began, with British authorities arresting Palestinians and ordering punitive measures against entire Arab villages.

Many Palestinians believed that the time had come to fight openly against British control of Palestine. Al-Husayni did not agree. He continued to try to work with the British to secure rights for Palestinians. In negotiations for a legislative body, he constantly pushed for representation based on population, which would give some seven hundred thousand Arab Palestinians control over their political destiny. He traveled to other Arab countries in an attempt to persuade their leaders to provide support for the Palestinians. In 1931 he organized a World Islamic Congress to promote cooperation among Arab nations. But al-Husayni's efforts to use political pressure to secure his goals ultimately failed. The British authorized a continued flow of Jewish immigration to Palestine. The number of immigrants increased steadily, rising from 4,075 in 1931 to 61,854 in 1935. By this point more militant Palestinians began to advocate outright war to remove the Jewish settlements.

Leading the Arab Revolt

Throughout the early 1930s, Palestinian politics and British policies were pulled in opposite directions. Radical political factions within Palestine called for increased resistance to Zionism, while events in Europe, especially the rise of the Nazi Party in Germany, caused increasing violence against Jews, lending more weight to the calls for Jewish immigration to Palestine. Finally in 1936 the fragile agreement that al-Husayni had brokered between British authorities and Palestinians was shattered. Sheikh Muhammad Izz al-Din al-Qassam (1882–1935), a radical Muslim scholar, was killed by the British after he called for jihad (meaning armed struggle) against the Jews and the British. His death provoked an uprising among Palestinians, including frequent demonstrations against Jewish and British interests in Palestine. Finally, in April 1936 various Palestinian groups called for a wave of protests, strikes, and the withholding of taxes in their effort to end British and Jewish influence in the region.

In the midst of this general uprising, al-Husayni recognized that it was no longer possible for him to please both sides. On April 25, 1936, he became leader of the Arab Higher Committee, an organization created to express the united interests of the Palestinians. According to author Philip Mattar in *The Mufti of Jerusalem*, the committee "declared its determination to achieve three major demands: a complete halt to Jewish immigration, prohibition of the transfer of Arab lands to Jews, and the establishment of a national government responsible to a representative council." Al-Husayni thus became the leading figure in the organized opposition to British policy and Jewish interests.

These events spiraled into what is known as the Arab Revolt of 1936–39. For the next several years Palestinians engaged in a multifaceted attack on the British and on Jews. They staged a general strike and boycott, refusing to work for or buy from the British or the Jews. They held demonstrations and protests against the British and the Jews. In 1937 the revolt became even more intense. Al-Husayni officially called for an end to British rule in Palestine, and Palestinians launched a military offensive that took control of a number of Arab villages and towns. In 1938, however, British army units counterattacked, recapturing territory and killing many Palestinians. By the time the revolt ended in 1939, approximately five thousand Palestinians had been killed, the same number taken prisoner, and some fifteen to twenty thousand were wounded. Meanwhile, Jewish militia groups gained crucial experience in organizing and fighting.

Al-Husayni became a hero to Palestinians and to many pro-Palestinian Arabs throughout the Middle East as a result of his leadership of the Arab Revolt. He rejected British attempts to negotiate a compromise in 1938 and 1939, insisting that only complete Palestinian independence was an acceptable outcome. There was also an incident in July 1937 when British authorities issued an arrest warrant for al-Husayni, because of his involvement in a widespread crackdown on political and religious dissent in the city. Al-Husayni learned about it shortly before, and took refuge inside the Haram ash-Sharif holy site. British military officials considered arresting him there but decided the act might provoke further violence. Finally, al-Husayni escaped to the port city of Jaffa clad in the robes of a simple Bedouin nomad in October 1937. (Nomads are people move from place to place, with no fixed home.) From there he went to Lebanon in 1937, and in 1939 he escaped to Iraq. From Iraq al-Husayni became a leader of the anti-British, pro-Arab movement that dominated the Middle East throughout World War II (1939–45; a war in which the Allies [Great Britain, France, the Soviet Union, the United States, and China] defeated the Axis Powers [Germany, Italy, and Japan]). He encouraged the Iraqi government to ally itself with the Axis Powers. After the British invaded Iraq in 1941, al-Husayni issued a fatwa (official religious decree) calling on all Muslims to come to the aid of Iraqis.

Al-Husayni allies with the Nazis

After the British conquest of Iraq, al-Husayni fled to Iran. But Iran was not safe for al-Husayni, and he fled again, in disguise, first to Turkey and then to Italy. From Italy al-Husayni began a relationship with the Nazis that would forever taint his reputation. As early as 1940, al-Husayni had been in contact with German officials, hoping to gain support for his efforts to drive the British out of Palestine. Al-Husayni now entered into direct talks with Italian leader Benito Mussolini (1883–1945) and German chancellor Adolf Hitler (1889–1945). He pledged Arab cooperation in fighting the British in exchange for German support for the creation of independent Arab states after the war. Hitler would not sign an agreement with al-Husayni, but he pledged his support for Arab independence and for the elimination of the Jewish settlements in Palestine.

For the remainder of the war, al-Husayni worked to help Germany in the Middle East. From his new home in Berlin, Germany, he urged Arabs to revolt against British and French influence in the Middle East, and delivered speeches supporting the Germans that were broadcast on the radio in the Middle East. But Arab resistance to the British was minimal, and the Allies defeated the Axis Powers in 1945. The defeat of the Germans sent al-Husayni on the run once again, first to Austria, then to Switzerland, then France, and finally back to Palestine.

Decline after World War II

After the war, world opinion changed regarding Palestine and Zionism. The German attempt to exterminate all Jews in Europe, known as the Holocaust (the mass murder of European Jews and other groups by the Nazis during World War II), had created an immense groundswell of support for the creation of a safe homeland for Jews in Palestine. Western governments, including the United States, supported the United Nations when it called for the division of Palestine into Jewish and Arab states in 1947. (The United Nations is an international organization of countries founded in 1945 to promote international peace, security, and cooperation.) Al-Husayni, who played an important though weakened role in postwar Palestine, resisted the plan and, along with others, called again

Al-Husayni and Hitler

The blackest mark on the record of early Palestinian leader Amin al-Husayni was his relationship with Germany during World War II (1939–45). That relationship was captured in a photograph of him in a conversation with German chancellor Adolf Hitler taken on November 28, 1941. The photograph of them deep in discussion was shown, in enlarged format, for many years in a prominent gallery at Yad Vashem, a museum in Jerusalem dedicated to the Holocaust, the mass murder of European Jews and other groups by the Nazis during World War II.

There were calls to charge al-Husayni with war crimes for supporting Hitler and his genocidal policies. (Genocide is the deliberate and systematic destruction of a group of people based on religion, ethnicity, or nationality.) Al-Husayni's enemies produced evidence that al-Husayni had written letters urging that Jews not be allowed to immigrate and settle in Palestine, suggesting that they be sent instead to Poland. At the time, Poland was one of the nations where German concentration camps were located. (Concentration camps are complexes built by the Germans for the confinement and extermination of political opponents and ethnic minorities, especially Jews.) They also produced a letter from a German official claiming that al-Husayni cooperated with efforts to exterminate European Jews. British officials judged this evidence inconclusive. There was no proof that al-Husayni knew of the concentration camps, and it seems likely that the German official mistook al-Husayni for an Arab religious leader in another Middle Eastern country.

Al-Husayni allied with Nazi leader Adolf Hitler during World War II in an attempt to defeat the British and drive them out of Palestine. © GETTY IMAGES.

for outright war against Jews in Palestine when the British departed and Jews created the nation of Israel on May 14, 1948.

Al-Husayni's political efforts following the creation of Israel were increasingly futile. He was instrumental in the creation of the Palestine National Council, and this quasi-government issued a Palestinian Declaration of Independence on October 1, 1948. But the Palestine National Council had no real power, for it controlled no territory and had neither money nor an army. In the years that followed, al-Husayni scrambled to ally himself with other Arab political leaders to gain support for Palestinian resistance to Israeli rule. Increasingly, however, he was seen as a figure from the past. Younger, more radical Arab leaders like Egyptian president **Gamal Abdel Nasser** (1918–1970; see entry) and Palestinian leader **Yasser Arafat** (1929–2004; see entry) earned the loyalty of those Arabs who once might have supported al-Husayni.

After leaving Palestine in 1937, al-Husayni spent his remaining years in exile, living first in Transjordan, then Lebanon. He remained head of the World Islamic Congress until his death on July 4, 1974, in Beirut, Lebanon.

For More Information

BOOKS

Dalin, David G., and John F. Rothmann. *Icon of Evil: Hitler's Mufti and the Rise of Radical Islam.* New York: Random House, 2008.

Mattar, Philip. *The Mufti of Jerusalem: Al-Hajj Amin al-Husayni and the Palestinian National Movement,* rev. ed. New York: Columbia University Press, 1992, p. 71.

Pappé, Ilan. *The Rise and Fall of a Palestinian Dynasty: The Husaynis, 1700–1948.* Los Angeles: University of California Press, 2011.

PERIODICALS

Byrnes, Sholto. "Family Fortunes." *New Statesman* (December 6, 2010): 54.

"Grand Mufti Urges War." *New York Times* (July 17, 1948). Available online at http://select.nytimes.com/gst/abstract.html?res=F70E16FC3A5C167B 93C5A8178CD85F4C8485F9&scp=2&sq=%22grand+mufti%22&st=p (accessed on November 30, 2011).

Segev, Tom. "Courting Hitler." *New York Times Book Review* (September 28, 2008): 34. Available online at http://www.nytimes.com/2008/09/28/books/ review/Segev-t.html?scp=1&sq=hitler%27s+mufti&st=nyt (accessed on November 30, 2011).

WEB SITES

Bard, Mitchell. "The Mufti and the Führer." *Jewish Virtual Reference Library.* http://www.jewishvirtuallibrary.org/jsource/History/muftihit.html (accessed on November 30, 2011).

Hussein I

BORN: November 14, 1935 • Amman, Transjordan

DIED: February 7, 1999 • Amman, Jordan

Jordanian king

King Hussein I of Jordan. TIM GRAHAM/GETTY IMAGES.

"This is peace with dignity. This is peace with commitment. This is our gift to our peoples and the generations to come."

Jordan's King Hussein I was one of the longest serving leaders in the Middle East before his death in 1999. Handed the responsibility of leading his country when he was just a teenager, he ruled the small Hashemite Kingdom of Jordan for forty-six years and spent much of that time trying to maintain stability within the country and broker peace between neighboring nations. Hussein was the target of several assassination plots, and was just fifteen years old when he witnessed the assassination of his grandfather. "Hussein was driven by a single imperative: determination to preserve his own throne and the Hashemite dynasty," writes Max Hastings in the *Times* of London, England. (A dynasty is a series of rulers from the same family, in this case the Hashemites.) "His success in achieving this, amid relentless murder plots and upheavals, and against every prediction of foreign intelligence services and diplomats, inspired admiration in the West, if not in the Arab world." (Arabs are people of the Middle East and North Africa who speak the Arabic language or who live in countries in which Arabic is the dominant language.)

Hashemite family history

Hussein ibn Talal was born into the Hashemite royal family. The Hashemites trace their ancestry to Hashim ibn Abd al-Manaf (died c. 510), the great-grandfather of the Muslim prophet Muhammad (c. 570–632) and are descended from Muhammad through his daughter Fatima. For centuries the Hashemites were one of Islam's leading dynasties, as the descendants of Muhammad took on the role of caliph, the spiritual, political, and military leader of the world's Muslims. For thirteen hundred years the Hashemites controlled the lands of Hejaz, coastal region on the western Arabian Peninsula that includes the Muslim holy cities of Mecca and Medina. The sharif (a nobleman and political leader chosen from among descendants of the Muslim prophet Muhammad) of Mecca and the emir (a ruler, chief, or commander in some Islamic countries) were by tradition chosen from among the Hashemite princes. Their major rival for dominance in the region was the Saud family, united under Abd al-Aziz ibn Abd al-Rahman (1876–1953), more commonly known as Ibn Saud.

During World War I (1914–18; a global war between the Allies [Great Britain, France, and Russia, joined later by the United States] and the Central Powers [Germany, Austria-Hungary, and their allies]), Hussein's great-grandfather Husayn ibn 'Ali (also spelled Hussein bin Ali; c. 1854–1931), the sharif of Mecca, struck an alliance with the British. Husayn would lead an uprising against the Ottoman Empire, who controlled the Arabian Peninsula and fought on the side of the Central Powers. In exchange, once the war was over, the British would recognize the independence of Arab lands. Husayn successfully led the Arab Revolt of 1916, which ended in October 1919 when Arab armies captured the city of Damascus, in Syria. Husayn proclaimed Arab independence and declared himself king. The British, however, had other plans for the region. In 1921 British politician and future prime minister Winston Churchill (1874–1965) arranged for the Hashemites to be given their own dual kingdoms. In 1923 Abdullah bin Husayn (1882–1951), Husayn ibn 'Ali's son, was installed as the king of the newly created Emirate of Transjordan (present-day Jordan). Abdullah's brother, Faisal (1885–1933), was similarly installed in Baghdad as king of Iraq. In 1924 Ibn Saud and his militia successfully seized Hejaz. In 1932 he united the Nejd (the central area of the Arabian Peninsula) with the Hejaz and named the new kingdom Saudi Arabia. The Saud family continued to rule Saudi Arabia into the twenty-first century.

Hussein was the first Hashemite prince born outside of Hejaz. He was born in Amman, the capital of Transjordan, on November 14, 1935. Although his family had royal status, they possessed little else. Transjordan was a small country with no natural resources, and poverty was widespread. Hussein's parents, Princess Zein and Crown Prince Talal, lived simply. Hussein's little sister died of pneumonia as an infant during one cold period in Amman. Their house lacked central heating.

Growing up during a time of change

Transjordan was administered by the British. It was considered part of Palestine, a historical region in the Middle East on the eastern shore of the Mediterranean Sea, comprising parts of present-day Israel and Jordan. In 1946 Transjordan was granted independence by the British, who nevertheless hoped to remain in the region and protect their interests, particularly the oil fields in the Arabian Desert that had been discovered earlier in the century. Abdullah, Hussein's grandfather, was actually paid a salary by the British to rule the country, although it was not enough money to give him much power. In 1949 Transjordan took control of the West Bank, an area between Israel and Jordan on the west bank of the Jordan River, and Abdullah officially renamed his country the Hashemite Kingdom of Jordan, commonly referred to simply as Jordan.

Jordan was one of the Arab nations that participated in the 1948 Arab-Israeli War. Jews had long been working to establish a Jewish homeland in Palestine, the site of the ancient Jewish kingdom. When the British left Palestine in 1948, Jews declared the establishment of the state of Israel. Palestine, however, was also home to predominantly Muslim Arabs who had lived in the region for centuries. Neighboring Arab nations, including Jordan, invaded Israel in an attempt to reclaim the region for Arab Palestinians. Israel won the war, and some 750,000 Palestinians became refugees, people who flee their country to escape violence or persecution. These Palestinians sought refuge is several Arab states, including Jordan. Abdullah was faced with the challenge of providing for thousands of refugees. In addition, his overtures of cooperation toward Israel, which would engage in several wars with its Arab neighbors over the next several decades, roused the hatred of Arab extremists.

In the meantime Hussein had a difficult youth. His father, Talal, who was educated in England, resented the British hold on Jordan and fought bitterly with Abdullah. Hussein's grandfather thought that young Hussein was better suited to eventually rule the kingdom than Crown Prince Talal and began supervising his studies. Hussein grew close to his grandfather. He attended Victoria College in Alexandria, Egypt, a British-style boarding school. Hussein thrived there and even won the school's fencing prize, and for this his grandfather awarded him the Jordanian Star First Class medal.

Abdullah had been warned to stay away from Jerusalem's Al-Aqsa Mosque on July 20, 1951, due to rumors of an assassination plot against him. (A mosque is a Muslim place of worship.) He ignored the warnings and took fifteen-year-old Hussein with him to visit the mosque. Earlier that day Hussein had donned a suit and tie for the trip to Jerusalem, but his grandfather insisted he change and wear his military uniform instead. Once they were inside the famous holy site, a gunman emerged from the crowd, raised a pistol to Abdullah's head, and pulled the trigger. The king collapsed and died almost instantly. The assassin then turned and fired a single bullet at a stunned Hussein, who felt the bullet hit him. But the assassin had fired at an angle, and the bullet bounced off the prince's Jordanian Star First Class medal. It was a traumatic experience, and Hussein has described it as the pivotal event of his life. Seeing his grandfather shot to death at close range was horrifying, but it was the reaction of those around them that most profoundly affected the prince. In his autobiography, *Uneasy Lies the Head: An Autobiography of King Hussein of Jordan*, Hussein writes, "I can see them now, those men of dignity and high estate, doubled up, cloaked figures scattering like bent old terrified women." He continues, "That picture, far more distinct than the face of the assassin, has remained with me ever since as a constant reminder of the frailty of political devotion."

Underprepared to lead

At the time of Abdullah's assassination, Hussein's father was a patient in a psychiatric clinic in Switzerland. Talal was said to have suffered from paranoid schizophrenia (a severe mental illness typically characterized by delusions and hallucinations), but there are some claims that rumors about the crown prince's mental health were spread by the British and others who knew he was not easily influenced by the West. Talal returned to Amman and was crowned king. Hussein, the new crown prince, went off to Harrow, an elite private academy in north London, to finish his education. A little over a year after Abdullah's assassination, Jordan's parliament (legislature) declared King Talal unfit to rule, and on August 11, 1952, Hussein was proclaimed king of Jordan. He went on to attend Great Britain's elite Royal Military Academy at Sandhurst, while a council of regents ruled for him in Amman. (A regent is someone who rules for a king or queen when the monarch is absent, too young, or unable to rule.) He was installed as King Hussein I on May 2, 1953.

The inexperienced Hussein faced many challenges in his early years as ruler of Jordan. During his first twelve months on the throne, he took steps to bring greater freedoms to his country. He demanded that his prime minister allow all political parties to operate freely within the kingdom. He called for immediate, free, fair, and open elections. King Hussein was faced also with the problem of Palestinian refugees in Jordan. They had lost their homes, their money, and most of their rights as they fled from their former homes in Israel. Finally, Hussein was challenged by two popular movements that had originated on other Middle East nations, but gained support in Jordan: Nasserism and Ba'athism. Neither of these movements looked favorably on monarchies, especially those that owed their origins to decisions made by British colonial authorities.

Egyptian president **Gamal Abdel Nasser** (1918–1970; see entry) had overthrown King Farouk of Egypt, just a month before King Hussein took power in Jordan. Nasser emerged as a powerful proponent of Pan-Arabism, a movement for the unification of Arab peoples and the political alliance of Arab states. Nasser was such a strong voice for the Pan-Arab movement that his own brand of Pan-Arabism became known as Nasserism. Hussein found it difficult to assert his legitimacy while Nasserism was sweeping the region and millions looked to Egypt as a symbol of what Arab countries might become.

Ba'athism was a similar movement originating with the creation of the Ba'ath Party in Syria. (The Ba'ath Party is a secular [nonreligious] political party founded in the 1940s with the goal of uniting the Arab world and creating one powerful Arab state.) It differed from Nasserism in that it was based on socialism, an economic system in which a government owns all means of production and distribution. However, both Nasserism and Ba'athism were opposed to cooperation with the West and to acknowledging the existence of Israel.

When protests erupted in Amman, Hussein swiftly abandoned his liberal policies. He sent the army out to stop the protests, and hundreds of people were arrested. Even larger protests in Amman and in many other Arab capitals erupted as a result, and there were event attempts to remove Hussein from power in unsuccessful coups (overthrow of the government). In a move to secure full control of the Jordanian army, Hussein fired the renowned British John Bagot Glubb (1897–1986), known as Glubb Pasha, from his position as head of the army in 1956, a move that stunned the British.

Hussein teamed with his cousin, Iraq's King Faisal II (1935–1958), to form the short-lived Arab Federation of Iraq and Jordan, also called the Arab Union, which lasted from February 1958 to August 1958. In July 1958 Faisal was killed by Ba'ath Party revolutionaries. Fearing a similar uprising in Jordan, Hussein called on the British army to help him. British troops flooded back into the country, securing Hussein's rule but costing him a great deal of the popularity he had won among his own people earlier in his reign.

Loses the West Bank to Israel

In the early 1960s the conflicts between Israel and its Arab neighbors continued. As Israel's closest neighbor, Jordan absorbed many of the resulting refugees. In an attempt to make peace with Nasser and calm the civil unrest in his own country, Hussein flew to Cairo, Egypt, and signed a secret defense pact with the Egyptians. Then, in 1967, Hussein sided with the Egyptians and Syrians as they prepared to wage war against Israel, a decision which he would later describe as the most devastating diplomatic error of his long rule.

Allied Arab armies gathered on Israel's borders in 1967, preparing to carry out a full-scale war in the hope of regaining land for the Palestinians that was seized by Israel in the 1948 Arab-Israeli War. But Israel struck first and, despite being outnumbered, Israeli troops triumphed, capturing the Sinai Peninsula and the Gaza Strip from Egypt, the West Bank from Jordan, and the Golan Heights from Syria within just six days. The outcome of this war, the 1967 Arab-Israeli War, was a devastating and humiliating blow to the Arab armies. Thousands of Palestinian refugees spilled over the border into Jordan, increasing the country's population by about half. Faced with this crisis, Hussein offered the refugees citizenship and passports. He was particularly pained at the

King Hussein I inspects an Israeli tank that was left behind during a skirmish after the 1967 Arab-Israeli War. Jordan was one of many countries that frequently battled with Israel over land and resources. © BETTMANN/CORBIS.

loss of the West Bank and its major cities of Jerusalem, Bethlehem, Ramallah, Hebron, and Nablus.

The Palestinian problem

A Palestinian named **Yasser Arafat** (1929–2004; see entry) rose to become the leader of a generation of Palestinians with no country of their own. He became head of the Palestine Liberation Organization (PLO), a political and military organization formed to unite various Palestinian Arab groups with the goal of establishing an independent Palestinian state. The PLO was formally founded in 1964, and Arafat built a base in Amman. Arafat was vocal about his dislike of Hussein, even though the king was the only Arab leader who offered the Palestinians citizenship.

The 1967 Arab-Israeli War had brought an influx of new Palestinian refugees into Jordan. Some of them had spent their entire lives in refugee camps in the West Bank and emerged as militant young adults. Under the supervision of the PLO, they launched attacks across the border at Israel. In early September 1970 Palestinian militants hijacked four airliners that had departed from European airports and diverted them to a strip of airfield in the Jordanian desert once used by British military aircraft. The militants released the hostages, blew up the planes for the benefit of invited media, and declared a Palestinian republic. After being warned of a PLO assassination plot against him, Hussein decided to expel the PLO from Jordan. On the morning of September 17, 1970 in an event that came to be called Black September, Hussein sent Jordanian armored units to attack PLO bases in Amman. Syria invaded Jordan three days later. In the end, some thirty-four hundred Palestinian militants were killed. Hussein formally expelled the PLO, and many in the Arab world sharply criticized him for failing to support the Palestinian cause.

Seeking a solution with Israel

Hussein had been instrumental in drafting the terms of the United Nations Security Council Resolution 242 after the 1967 Arab-Israeli War. (The United Nations is an international organization of countries founded in 1945 to promote international peace, security, and cooperation.) Resolution 242 urged Israel to relinquish the territories it had taken from Egypt, Syria, and Jordan, In return Israel would secure formal recognition of its right to exist from its Arab neighbors. This, too, displeased Palestinian supporters. In 1974 the Arab League (a regional political alliance of Arab nations formed in 1945 to promote political, military, and economic cooperation within the Arab world) voted to remove Jordan's authority to negotiate on behalf of Palestinians. Arafat and PLO were granted this authority instead.

In the meantime Hussein began secretly meeting with Israeli leaders. Conducted under the tightest security, these informal talks occurred on ships in the Gulf of Aqaba, in hotels, and in one instance a safe house (houses in a secret location, used as hiding places or a secure refuge) in Israel run by Mossad, Israel's intelligence service. The meetings remained unknown to the rest of the world until former Israeli foreign minister

Moshe Dayan (1915–1981) wrote *Breakthrough: A Personal Account of the Egypt-Israel Peace Negotiations*, which was published in 1981.

In 1978 Egyptian president **Anwar Sadat** (also spelled al-Sadat; 1918–1981; see entry) participated in the Camp David Accords, peace negotiations between Egypt and Israel at Camp David, the U.S. presidential retreat in Maryland. In 1979 Egypt became the first Arab nation to sign a peace treaty with Israel. Hussein was critical of the treaty, as were many in the Arab world. There was a belief that Sadat had traded the future of the West Bank and Jerusalem in a deal that returned the Sinai Peninsula to Egypt. The Egyptian president would pay for his decision with his life; he was assassinated in October 1981.

Hussein fared somewhat better in his own peace treaty with Israel, which was signed many years later under dramatically different circumstances. In July 1994 he appeared with Israeli prime minister **Yitzhak Rabin** (1922–1995; see entry) on the lawn of the White House in the United States to announce the preliminary terms of the deal, along with U.S. president Bill Clinton (1946–), who had arranged the talks. The actual treaty was signed in a ceremony at Wadi Arava, on the Israel-Jordan border, on October 26, 1994. "God willing, and with God's blessing of us all to remember this day as long as we live and for future generations—Jordanians, Israelis, Arabs, Palestinians—all children of Abraham to remember it as the dawning of the new era of peace," Hussein said that day, as quoted in a 1994 *New York Times* article. "Mutual respect between us all, tolerance, and the coming together of people, of generations to come beyond this time to build and achieve what is worthy of them. . . . This is peace with dignity. This is peace with commitment. This is our gift to our peoples and the generations to come."

Death and legacy

Hussein's urge to leave a worthy achievement in the Arab-Israeli peace process was prompted by fears about his own mortality. Diagnosed with non-Hodgkin's lymphoma, a type of cancer, in 1992, he had undergone treatment and lost a kidney. The disease returned in 1998, and he died on February 7, 1999, at a military hospital on the outskirts of Amman. Thousands of Jordanians turned out to mourn his death, and his funeral was attended by heads of state and dignitaries from around the world,

King Hussein I and Yitzhak Rabin shaking hands after peace talks between Israel and Jordan in Washington, D.C., in 1994. © DAVID RUBINGER/ CORBIS.

including President Clinton, Syrian president **Hafez Al-Assad** (also spelled al-Assad; 1930–2000; see entry). Israeli prime minister **Benjamin Netanyahu** (1949–; see entry), and even PLO leader Arafat, who paid his respect with a bow before Hussein's coffin and a military salute.

Hussein was twice divorced, once widowed, and the father of eleven children. In 1978 he married his fourth wife, an American woman named Lisa Halaby (1951–), who became known as Queen Noor. His first-born son succeeded him as King Abdullah II (1962–).

For More Information

BOOKS

King Hussein I. *Uneasy Lies the Head: An Autobiography of King Hussein of Jordan.* London: Heinemann, 1962.

Shlaim, Avi. *Lion of Jordan: The Life of King Hussein in War and Peace.* London: Penguin, 2007.

PERIODICALS

Bronner, Ethan. "Jordan Faces a Rising Tide of Unrest, but Few Expect a Revolt." *New York Times* (February 4, 2011). Available online at http://www.nytimes.com/2011/02/05/world/middleeast/05jordan.html?scp=2&sq=%22king+abdullah%22+AND+father&st=nyt (accessed on November 30, 2011).

Hastings, Max. "*Lion of Jordan: The Life of King Hussein in War and Peace* by Avi Shlaim (review)." *Times* (London; November 11, 2007).

"The Jordan-Israel Accord: The Remarks." *New York Times* (October 27, 1994). Available online at http://www.nytimes.com/1994/10/27/world/jordan-israel-accord-remarks-3-leaders-offer-words-hope-for-future.html?scp=2&sq=%22King+hussein%22&st=nyt&pagewanted=all (accessed on November 30, 2011).

Newhouse, John. "Monarch." *New Yorker* (September 19, 1983): 49. Available online at http://www.newyorker.com/archive/1983/09/19/1983_09_19_049_TNY_CARDS_000338533#ixzz1VsAUrdZb (accessed on November 30, 2011).

WEB SITES

"King Hussein: A Man of Peace." *PBS NewsHour.* http://www.pbs.org/newshour/bb/middle_east/jan-june99/hussein_index.html (accessed on November 30, 2011).

"Special Report: Death of a King." *BBC News* (February 13, 1999). http://news.bbc.co.uk/2/hi/middle_east/272709.stm (accessed on November 30, 2011).

Saddam Hussein

BORN: April 28, 1937 • Al-Awja, Iraq

DIED: December 30, 2006 • Iraq

Iraqi president

"Iraq is not the only target in this confusion, even if the noise is meant to intimidate us and to cover the aggression. . . . The objective is rather to subject the Arab Gulf area to a full, complete and physical occupation."

Saddam Hussein. AP PHOTO/ INA.

Saddam Hussein, usually referred to simply as Saddam, was the president of Iraq for more than three decades. He was a ruthless and aggressive leader who pushed his oil-rich, once-prosperous nation to an extreme level of deterioration. Saddam tightly controlled the Ba'ath Party in Iraq and brutally suppressed political opposition inside his country. (The Ba'ath Party is a secular [nonreligious] political party founded in the 1940s with the goal of uniting the Arab world and creating one powerful Arab state.) He engaged in a long and costly battle with neighboring Iran for much of the 1980s. The United States led two large-scale military efforts to remove him from power, the second of which succeeded in 2003. In 2006 an Iraqi tribunal declared him guilty of war crimes against his own people and issued a sentence of death. Saddam was hanged on

December 30, 2006. In the years following his death Iraq was a divided, perilous place, struggling to rebuild its economy amid a violent insurgency (an uprising, or rebellion, against a political authority).

Born into poverty

Saddam Hussein Abd al-Majid al-Tikriti was born on April 28, 1937. Many of the circumstances of Saddam's early life are unclear. For example, little is known about Saddam's father, Hussein Abdel Majid. A peasant sheepherder, he is thought to have died shortly before his son was born. (Some accounts say he abandoned the family.) An older brother died of cancer. Saddam's mother, Sabha Tulfah al-Mussallat, eventually remarried. The family lived in a mud hut without electricity or running water. His stepfather beat Saddam and forced him to steal to help the family. In 1947 Saddam ran away to the city of Tikrit, the home of his maternal uncle, Khairallah Talfah (also spelled Tolfah or Tilfah), who agreed to take him in. Tikrit is about a 100 miles (161 kilometers) north of the Iraqi capital of Baghdad, and Saddam would later claim Tikrit as his birthplace, instead of the poverty-ridden village of al-Awja where he was born.

Saddam's uncle was a respected local figure in Tikrit and a retired army officer. He sent Saddam to school for the first time, where classmates teased him for his lack of education. Saddam was close to his cousin, Adnan Khayr Allah Talfa (1949–1989), who would later become the country's minister of defense. When he completed one level of his education at age eighteen, Saddam applied to the Baghdad Military Academy but failed the entrance examination. By this point, he and others in his family were swept up by a new nationalist fervor inspired by Egypt's **Gamal Abdel Nasser** (1918–1970; see entry), who had led a 1952 army coup (overthrow of the government) to oust Egypt's king and became president of Egypt in 1956. Nasser's message was one of Arab nationalism, or devotion and loyalty to the Arab culture. (Arabs are people of the Middle East and North Africa who speak the Arabic language or who live in countries in which Arabic is the dominant language.) Nasser urged Arabs in Egypt and the Middle East to unite against Western influence and domination. This movement for the unification of Arab nations is known as Pan-Arabism. It gained significant momentum in the region. In 1958 a group of Iraqi army officers, members of the Ba'ath Party, killed Iraq's King Faisal II (1935–1958).

Pan-Arabism and the Ba'ath Party

Arab frustration with foreign interference in Middle Eastern affairs grew exponentially along with the discovery of new oil fields beneath the sands of the Arabian, Syrian, Iranian, and Iraqi deserts in the first decades of the twentieth century. American and British companies struck favorable deals with local leaders for drilling rights. After World War I (1914–18), much of the Middle East came under British or French mandate (administrative authority). To protect their oil interests, foreign governments sought to maintain a balance of power in the region, and that effort turned into full-scale conflict after Jewish settlers in Palestine (a historical region in the Middle East on the eastern shore of the Mediterranean Sea, comprising parts of present-day Israel and Jordan) established the country of Israel there in 1948. Arab leaders went to war against Israel in a failed effort to take back the land that they believed rightfully belonged to the Arab Palestinians who had lived there for hundreds of years. The 1948 Arab-Israeli War spurred the development of Pan-Arabism, a movement for the unification of Arab peoples and the political alliance of Arab states. Only a united

Arab front, Egyptian president **Gamal Abdel Nasser** (1918–1970; see entry) and others believed, could bring an end to foreign dominance and return the land of Israel to the Palestinians.

In Syria and Iraq, similar ideas were promoted by a new political party, the Ba'ath Party, whose name means "rebirth" or "renaissance" in Arabic. Founded in 1947 by two Syrians, Michel Aflaq (1910–1989) and Salah al-Din al-Bitar (1912–1980), the party aimed to unite the Arab world and create one powerful Arab state. The party gained support in Iraq, and Iraqi army officers with links to the party were involved in the 1958 coup (overthrow of the government) in which king Faisal II (1935–1958) was killed. This event came to be known as the 14 July Revolution.

One significant difference between the Ba'athism and other new revolutionary movements in the Middle East at this time was that Ba'athism promoted a secular (nonreligious) government. This put the Ba'athists in conflict with Islamic fundamentalists whose goal was to use sharia (Islamic religious law) as the basis of government.

Swept up in Nasserist fervor

Saddam joined the Ba'ath Party in 1957 and two years later was among a group that attempted to assassinate a top Iraqi general and the country's prime minister, Abdul Karim Qassem (1914–1963). When the attempt failed, Saddam and his coconspirators fled to Cairo, Egypt. He completed his high school education there in 1961, when he was twenty-four years old. He then studied law at the University of Cairo. In 1963, when the Ba'ath Party in Iraq succeeded in overthrowing the Iraqi government, Saddam's powerful cousin, Ahmad Hassan al-Bakr (1914–1982), gave him a position in the Ba'ath regional command. That year Saddam also married his cousin, Sajida Khairallah Tulfah. Over the years they would have five children: sons Uday and Qusay, and daughters Raghad, Rina, and Hala. Family ties and political loyalty provided Saddam with a web of connections that he would skillfully exploit in the coming years.

Just nine months after the February 1963 government takeover, the Ba'athists in Iraq were ousted in a military coup. Saddam and several others were jailed in 1964, and the party was outlawed. During this period the Ba'athists established a loyal security force, the Jihaz al Khas (Special Apparatus), and after a prison escape around 1967, Saddam was installed as its head. On July 17, 1968, the Ba'ath Party and the military joined together to take control of the Iraqi government. Saddam's cousin al-Bakr became president, and Saddam served as his deputy. The Jihaz al Khas became part of the government as the Da'irat al Mukhabarat al Amah (General Intelligence Department), known by its shortened name, Mukhabarat.

Under al-Bakr, the Ba'athists established control over all areas of Iraqi life, systematically eliminating their political rivals, frequently by force and with the help of Mukhabarat intelligence. Saddam played a key role as deputy chair of the Revolutionary Command Council, the Ba'ath Party's ruling body, a job he secured in 1969 at the age of thirty-two. Three years later, al-Bakr's government moved to nationalize (bring under government ownership and control) Iraq's oil industry, taking over the Iraqi Petroleum Company and the enormously profitable Kirkuk oil fields.

Despite its ruthless methods to suppress political rivals, Ba'athist Iraq emerged as a prosperous, even progressive Arab country in the 1970s, with a secure economy and an impressive social-welfare network. With a steep increase in the price of crude oil on the world market, the country was becoming wealthy, and those revenues paid for the construction of schools, roads, and hospitals. As a secular government, Iraq placed fewer limits on the role of women, unlike some of its stricter Muslim neighbors, and Iraqi women began to obtain university degrees and enter the workforce in large numbers.

Becomes president

Al-Bakr's health began to fail in the 1970s. Saddam assumed more duties, and on July 16, 1979, al-Bakr announced his resignation. Saddam became president of Iraq, prime minister, head of the Ba'ath Party, and chair of the Revolutionary Command Council. It was a masterful sweep of control, and his grip on Iraq would last nearly a quarter century.

Once in power, Saddam moved quickly to eliminate his rivals inside the Ba'ath Party. In early August 1979 he announced at a party conference there were treasonous elements inside the party working with Syria to unseat him and unite the two countries. He read sixty-eight names from a list, and those Ba'athists were escorted out of the hall. Brought up on treason charges, twenty-two of them were executed by firing squad within days. An estimated five hundred more were detained.

Saddam distrusted even his closest associates, which made party leaders and even top military officials fearful for their lives. Saddam could even be ruthless with members of his own family. To secure wider respect he had statues and murals of himself placed throughout the country. He also had songs and poems written about his early life, to make it seem natural that he had emerged as Iraq's most admired leader.

Saddam did command some respect in the Arab world. He denounced the 1978 Camp David Accords between Egypt and Israel, which made Egypt the first Arab nation to make peace with Israel. In November 1978 Saddam successfully urged other members of the Arab League (a regional political alliance of Arab nations formed in 1945 to promote political, military, and economic cooperation within the Arab world) to expel Egypt for making a deal with Israel, which was viewed by much of the Middle East as a bargain that Egypt entered into merely to secure the return of Egyptian territory that had been lost to Israel in the 1967 Arab-Israeli War. The Arab League even moved its headquarters from Cairo to the Tunisian capital of Tunis. When the shah of Iran, **Mohammad Reza Pahlavi** (1919–1980; see entry), was removed from power in January 1979, Saddam emerged as one of the key shapers of policy in the Middle East.

War with Iran

The shah of Iran was ousted during the 1979 Iranian Revolution (also known as the Islamic Revolution). This revolution transformed Iran from a secular nation into an Islamist state, based on the belief that Islam should provide the basis for political, social, and cultural life in Muslim nations. Iran's new leader, **Ayatollah Ruhollah Khomeini** (1900–1989; see entry), established the Islamic Republic of Iran. (An ayatollah is a high-ranking Shiite religious leader.) The revolution threatened to spill across Iran's border into Iraq, and Khomeini took a number of steps that Saddam perceived as hostile. Khomeini was openly critical of Saddam, called on Shiites within Iraq to lead a revolution there, and supported Kurds

Shiites and Sunnis in Iraq

The religion of Islam has two major branches, Shia and Sunni. The main difference between these branches is their belief in who should be the leader of Islam. Shiites, followers of the Shia branch of Islam, believe that only direct descendants of the prophet Muhammad (c. 570–632) are qualified to lead the Islamic faith. Sunnis believe that elected officials, regardless of their heritage, are qualified to lead Islam. In Iraq Shiites are in the majority, making up about 60 percent of the population. Sunnis, however, have traditionally held most of the wealth and power in the nation, thanks in large part to the rule of Saddam Hussein, who is from a Sunni family.

Sunnis and Shiites played a large role in the 1980–88 Iran-Iraq War, the Persian Gulf War (1990–91), and the Iraq War (2003–11). Iran encouraged Shiites inside Iraq to support Iran during the Iran-Iraq War. During the Persian Gulf War, the United States supported Shiite groups who opposed Saddam and Sunni dominance. After the withdrawal of U.S.-led coalition forces in that war, Saddam retaliated by increasing persecution of Shiites in Iraq. In early 2005 Shiites in Iraq gained some political power when their party won close to 50 percent of the seats in the newly formed Iraqi National Assembly during the elections held after Saddam was removed from power. This resulted in increased Sunni-led attacks against the Iraqi interim government officials that had been occurring since Saddam's government was overthrown in 2003. An effort to forge a lasting peace between Shiites and Sunnis consumed much of Iraq's politics after 2003.

(a non-Arab ethnic group) in northern Iraq who had long desired independence. (Shiites are followers of the Shia branch of Islam.) In April 1980 Saddam's deputy foreign minister, Tariq Aziz (1936–), was the target of an assassination attempt. Members of Al Dawa Al Islamiyah (Islamic Call), a Shiite group, were blamed for the attempt, and Iraq's leading Shiite cleric, Ayatollah Mohammad Bakr al-Sadr (1935–1980), was arrested and executed a week later.

In September 1980 Saddam invaded Iran, in part because of a long-unresolved border dispute. Iraq had significant military advantages over Iran. It had a much more powerful army and received weapons and supplies from the United States, the Soviet Union, and other Arab countries who feared the spread of Iran's Islamic Revolution. Iran, however, proved a strong opponent, and the war reached a stalemate (a situation in which no progress can be made) early on. It was during this period that Saddam ordered the development and use of chemical weapons (toxic chemical substances used during armed conflict to kill, injure, or incapacitate an enemy) against Iranians and against Kurds within Iraq. He threatened the use of nuclear weapons, as well. In 1981 Israel bombed Iraq's only nuclear reactor, which was then under construction.

Iraq's economy was devastated by the long war with Iran, which finally concluded with a 1987 cease-fire and a treaty signed the following year. By 1990 Iraq owed more than eighty billion dollars to other countries. Saddam tried to convince other Arab nations to extend more credit and forgive Iraq's debts, arguing that he alone had been willing to stand up to Islamic fundamentalism. Although some Arab nations provided monetary assistance, the rich country of Kuwait, just to the south of Iraq, refused. In retaliation Saddam claimed that Kuwait was stealing oil from Iraqi oil fields, and that Kuwait was actually a historic province of Iraq. On August 2, 1990, Iraq's still-powerful military invaded Kuwait. Saddam proclaimed that he was freeing Kuwait from the oppressive rule of the al-Sabah family. But world opinion soon turned against him.

The Persian Gulf War

The United Nations (UN; international organization of countries founded in 1945 to promote international peace, security, and cooperation) denounced Iraq's invasion of Kuwait. U.S. president George H.W. Bush (1924–) led a call for Saddam to remove his troops. Saddam did not believe the United States was willing to go to war over Kuwait, and he dared the United States to attack. To Saddam's surprise, it did. The United States did not challenge Iraq alone, however. Bush organized a coalition of nations that coordinated their military forces against Iraq. Many expected a long and bloody conflict, but the war ended very quickly. Coalition air strikes paralyzed the Iraqi air force, and ground forces quickly subdued the Iraqi army. By February 27, 1991, after just a few days of fighting, Iraq submitted to the demands of the coalition, and the war was over.

As part of the agreement to end the war, Saddam agreed to allow UN weapons inspectors to enter the country to ensure that Iraq had destroyed all of its biological, chemical, and nuclear weapons. For nearly ten years Saddam alternately allowed and impeded inspections, accusing the United States of using the inspection teams as an excuse to spy on Iraq. UN-imposed sanctions made it difficult for Iraq to provide enough food or medical care for its people, and in the eyes of many world observers, Saddam's resistence had set his nation on a backward economic path. (Sanctions are punitive measures adopted by the international community against a nation that has violated international law, usually in the form of diplomatic, economic, or social restrictions.)

In late 1998 U.S. and British forces conducted air strikes in Iraq in response to Saddam's stubborn refusal to comply with numerous UN Security Council resolutions concerning its weapons of mass destruction (WMDs). Foreign relations between Saddam and the West deteriorated further as the twenty-first century began. The first sign of trouble from Saddam's point of view was the election of George W. Bush (1946–) as the forty-third president of the United States in 2000. He was the son of former U.S. president George H.W. Bush, who had failed to remove

An American soldier stands in front of a mural of Saddam Hussein near the border between Iraq and Kuwait. U.S.-led coalition forces defeated Iraq in the Persian Gulf War. © PETER TURNLEY/CORBIS.

Saddam from power during the Persian Gulf War. Once in office, the new president pressured the UN to step up its weapons inspections in Iraq, asserting that Saddam had restarted its nuclear, chemical, and biological weapons programs. This foreign-policy imperative unintentionally came at the same time as a major catastrophic event in the United States—the September 11, 2001, terrorist attacks, which killed nearly three thousand people. In response to the attacks, Bush announced a war on terror, and cited Saddam's WMDs as a possible threat to U.S. safety and security.

Suspected of stockpiling WMDs

After the September 11th attacks, the Bush administration continued to call for the UN Security Council to deal with the possibility that Iraq was harboring WMDs. By September 2002 Bush was urging direct military intervention. UN officials, however, felt that even though Saddam had hindered investigations in the past, he was finally allowing teams of weapons inspectors to enter Iraq and inspect facilities. U.S. and British officials asserted there were documents showing that Iraq had attempted to purchase five hundred tons of uranium oxide, also known as yellowcake, from Niger, a West African producer of the mineral. Niger had a pair of mines containing uranium oxide, and it extracted the mineral for Western European countries with nuclear energy programs. When the classified documents were finally turned over to the International Atomic Energy Agency (IAEA), a United Nations-affiliated body, IAEA officials discredited the documents.

Saddam defended himself in an interview with British journalist Tony Benn for Great Britain's Channel 4 in early February 2003. Saddam explained:

> No Iraqi official or ordinary citizen has expressed a wish to go to war. The question should be directed at the other side. Are they looking for a pretext so they could justify war against Iraq? If the purpose was to make sure that Iraq is free of nuclear, chemical and biological weapons then they can do that. These weapons do not come in small pills that you can hide in your pocket. These are weapons of mass destruction and it is easy to work out if Iraq has them or not.

Various intelligence sources, some of which were later discredited, still asserted that Iraq was stockpiling WMDs. The United States led a combined force of troops from the United States, Great Britain, Australia and Poland to invade Iraq. Aerial bombing of Iraq began on March 20, 2003. Four days later, as coalition troops neared Baghdad, Saddam appeared on state-run television appealing to his army and the citizens to defend the city. He claimed U.S. forces had already suffered heavy losses and pledged to drag the conflict out for as long as possible. "The enemy is trapped in the sacred land of Iraq which is being defended by its great people and army," he said, according to the *Guardian*. "O brave fighters, hit your enemy with all your strength. O Iraqis, fight with the strength of the spirit of jihad which you carry in you and push them to the point where they cannot go on."

Escapes heavy bombing

Tank battalions entered Baghdad in the first week of April, taking control of the international airport that bore Saddam's name and then the presidential palace. Saddam was thought to be hiding in underground bunkers, and he was last photographed in public as Iraq's leader on April 7, when he surfaced in the neighborhood of Mansour, which was hit that same day with heavy bombs. Two days later, U.S. military officials proclaimed that coalition forces had control of Baghdad. Many Iraqis celebrated the removal of Saddam from power, especially the Shiites and Kurds, long the victims of violence under Saddam's rule. Soon, however, rumors circulated that Saddam was alive and helping to organize the insurgency that continued to prove deadly for coalition forces. There were also rumors that he had died. His sons, Uday and Qusay, two of the most feared figures in his regime, were killed in raids in July 2003.

On December 13, 2003, a U.S. military effort code-named Operation Red Dawn sectioned off an area on the outskirts of Tikrit and began searching a rundown farm. Saddam was discovered hiding in an 8-foot-deep (2.4-meter) hole in the ground. In his possession were a pistol and a semiautomatic weapon, but he surrendered without resistance. On June 30, 2004, legal custody of Saddam was turned over to the Iraqi Interim Government, although physically Saddam remained in U.S. military custody. A few weeks later an Iraqi Special Tribunal indicted (formally charged) him on charges of war crimes related to a massacre he ordered back in July 1982, after gunmen in the Shiite city of Dujail opened fire on his presidential motorcade. Saddam ordered brutal reprisals, and the charges against him included 148 deaths and the torture of women and children at Abu Ghraib prison. Other charges the tribunal levied against him included a chemical-weapons attack on the Kurdish town of Halabja in March 1988 that killed between three thousand and five thousand civilians and the illegal invasion of Kuwait in 1990.

"What does this court want?"

Saddam remained defiant and unrepentant throughout his trial. In the opening statements, he was told to stand and identify himself. "What does this court want?" he responded, as quoted by Michael A. Newton and Michael P. Scharf in *Enemy of the State: The Trial and Execution of Saddam Hussein*. "I don't answer [to] this so-called court, with all due respect, and I reserve my constitutional rights as the president of the country of Iraq. I don't acknowledge either the entity that authorizes you or the aggression, because everything based on a falsehood is a falsehood." Among Saddam's defense attorneys was Ayesha al-Gaddafi (1976–),

Saddam Hussein after his capture by U.S. forces in Iraq in 2003. Saddam was forced from power by the U.S. military earlier in the year and had been a fugitive until his capture. © HANDOUT/CNP/ CORBIS.

daughter of Libyan leader **Mu'ammar al-Qaddafi** (also spelled Moammar al-Gaddafi; 1942–2011; see entry).

Saddam was found guilty of war crimes on November 5, 2006, and sentenced to death. His legal team filed an appeal, but Iraq's Supreme Court of Appeal affirmed the decision. He was hanged at Camp Justice, a joint Iraqi-U.S. military facility, on December 30, 2006. The Iraqi government released official video footage of part of the execution, but an unauthorized clip emerged soon afterward, made by one of the guards in the facility, revealing that members of the new Iraqi National Police had heckled Saddam before his death as he recited the Islamic creed of belief known as the Shahada. Images also surfaced that showed his body may have been stabbed after it was removed from the gallows. He was buried the next day in Tikrit alongside his sons. His three daughters had previously fled to Jordan, and his wife Sajida had gone to Qatar.

Iraq's new prime minister, Nouri al-l-Maliki (1950–), and political leaders in the West voiced relief that Saddam had been brought to justice for his actions, hailing it as the start of a new era for Iraq. Others in the Middle East condemned the act and criticized the date of his execution, which coincided with the start of the Muslim holy day of Eid al-Adha (Festival of Sacrifice). Abdel-Bari Atwan, the editor of *Al-Quds al-Arabi*, an Arab newspaper published in London, England, called the decision to carry out the death sentence on Eid al-Adha as "an affront to all Arabs and Muslims," according to a December 30, 2006, article in the *Guardian*. The Iraq War officially came to an end in December 2011. No weapons of mass destruction were ever found in Iraq.

For More Information

BOOKS

Aburish, Saïd K. *Saddam Hussein: The Politics of Revenge.* New York: Bloomsbury, 2000.

Moore, Robin. *Hunting Down Saddam: The Inside Story of the Search and Capture.* New York: St. Martin's, 2004.

Newton, Michael A., and Michael P. Scharf. *Enemy of the State: The Trial and Execution of Saddam Hussein.* New York: Macmillan, 2008, pp. 3, 5.

PERIODICALS

Benn, Tony. "Full Text of Saddam Interview." *Guardian* (February 5, 2003). Available online at http://www.guardian.co.uk/world/2003/feb/05/iraq.politics (accessed on November 30, 2011).

"'The Enemy Is Trapped in the Sacred Land of Iraq.'" *Guardian* (March 24, 2003). Available online at http://www.guardian.co.uk/world/2003/mar/24/iraq4 (accessed on November 30, 2011).

"Full Text: Saddam Hussein's Speech." *Guardian* (January 6, 2003). Available online at http://www.guardian.co.uk/world/2003/jan/06/iraq1 (accessed on November 30, 2011).

Gibbs, Nancy. "Ladies and Gentlemen, We Got Him." *Time* (December 22, 2003).

Maass, Peter. "The Toppling." *New Yorker* (January 10, 2011). Available online at http://www.newyorker.com/reporting/2011/01/10/110110fa_fact_maass (accessed on November 30, 2011).

McGeary, Johanna. "Inside Saddam's Head." *Time* (March 31, 2003).

"Reaction to Saddam's Execution." *Guardian* (December 30, 2006). Available online at http://www.guardian.co.uk/world/2006/dec/30/iraq2 (accessed on November 30, 2011).

WEB SITES

"A Letter Written on 5 November by Saddam Hussein Has Been Released by the Former Iraqi Leader's Lawyers." *Islam for Today* (December 28, 2006). http://www.islamfortoday.com/saddam01.htm (accessed on November 30, 2011).

Butt, Gerald. "Saddam Hussein Profile." *BBC News.* http://news.bbc.co.uk/1/hi/world/middle_east/1100529.stm (accessed on November 30, 2011).

"The Saddam Hussein Sourcebook." *National Security Archive.* http://www2.gwu.edu/~nsarchiv/special/iraq (accessed on November 30, 2011).

Meir Kahane

BORN: August 1, 1932 • New York, United States
DIED: November 5, 1990 • New York, United States

Israeli rabbi, activist, politician

"For Arabs and Jews of Eretz Yisrael ["Land of Israel" in Hebrew] there is only one answer: separation, Jews in their land, Arabs in theirs. Separation. Only separation."

Meir Kahane was one of the most controversial figures in Israeli politics in the 1980s. As the head of the Kach Party, he ran for and won a seat in the Knesset, Israel's legislature, by voicing opinions no one else dared state aloud: that Jews should evict all Arabs from Israel and that a Jewish state does not need to be democratic. He was later banned from public office in Israel for promoting racism and opposing democracy. People from across the political spectrum denounced his views as dangerous, yet a minority of Israeli voters expressed support for his views. Kahane was assassinated in 1990.

Early life

Meir Kahane was born Martin David Kahane on August 1, 1932, in Brooklyn, New York. His childhood was relatively normal, with his days filled with school and athletic pursuits like ping-pong and basketball. His

Meir Kahane. © LES STONE/
SYGMA/CORBIS.

father, Charles, was an ordained rabbi (a Jewish scholar, teacher, and religious leader) and a respected scholar of Jewish law and philosophy. Charles was also an ardent supporter of Zionism, the international political movement originating in the late nineteenth century that called for the creation of an independent Jewish state in Palestine. (Palestine is a historical region in the Middle East on the eastern shore of the Mediterranean Sea, comprising parts of present-day Israel and Jordan.) Kahane's mother, Sonia, was intelligent and opinionated. Charles and Sonia were equally strong-willed. They fought constantly and then lavished Kahane with special attention, repeatedly reminding him of their high expectations for his future.

Kahane readily took up the Orthodox Jewish faith of his father and grandfather, who was also a rabbi, and even developed his own set of ideas about interpreting religious standards, including a stricter separation of men and women. By his teens he had evolved into an opinionated, intense, and driven young man. He criticized the lack of rigor in the teachings at the Brooklyn Talmudical Academy, where he attended high school, and stirred debate among his fellow students with his dramatic statements about Zionism. Kahane went on to earn his diploma from the Yeshiva University High School for Boys.

Politics and religion

Around 1946 Kahane joined a Zionist youth group called Betar. In Betar, Kahane trained in self-defense and prepared for the day when Jewish youths would become soldiers in the fight to create a Jewish nation in Palestine. Kahane, his brother, and his cousins were all ardent Betar members, joining in marches and protests in support of Zionism. In 1947 Kahane and several other Betar members pelted the car of British foreign minister Ernest Bevin (1881–1951) with eggs and tomatoes at a Manhattan pier in protest against a British policy of refusing to allow Jewish refugees from Europe to immigrate to Palestine. (At the time, Palestine was a mandate, or a territory entrusted to foreign administration, controlled by the British.) Police arrested Kahane, whose photo appeared in the *New York Daily News* newspaper. By the time he was seventeen years old, Kahane hoped to command his own wing of Betar. When his attempt to do so failed, Kahane quit, vowing to create his own Zionist group to promote a religiously "pure" Jewish state, meaning a state only for Orthodox Jews.

Kahane's dreams of political and religious activism fueled his higher education, which consumed much of his life from the late 1940s through most of the 1950s. He pursued studies to become a rabbi at Mir Yeshiva, an ultra-Orthodox Jewish seminary in New York City. Kahane was not a distinguished student; his interests were too diverse, and his focus was too scattered. But he was devout and hardworking, spending long hours at the school, and he eventually finished his studies. During the evenings, he attended Brooklyn College, earning a bachelor's degree in political science in 1954, and then he attended New York Law School, where he completed a law degree in 1957. He failed in his one attempt to pass the New York State bar exam, a necessary step in becoming a lawyer, and he later claimed that he no intention of becoming a lawyer. In order to support himself and his wife, Libby, whom he married in 1956, Kahane took a job in 1958 as a rabbi at the Howard Beach Jewish Center in Queens, New York.

Kahane's time at Howard Beach was brief and stormy. The Howard Beach congregation was part of the conservative Jewish movement, which followed a less-strict interpretation of the Torah (the Hebrew Bible) than did Orthodox Judaism. Kahane toned down his ultra-Orthodox religious views for the adults in his congregation, and he helped increase membership with his energetic leadership. At the same time, he inspired the youthful members at Howard Beach with dramatic stories of Jewish nationalism. (Nationalism is the belief that a people with shared ethnic, cultural, and/or religious identities have the right to form their own nation.) Soon parents charged that he was brainwashing their children, turning them against their parents, and Kahane was fired. Then he wrote an article in which he boasted that he brought true religion to

Betar

Betar was a militant youth group founded by Vladimir Ze'v Jabotinsky (1880–1940), a champion of Zionism. Banned from Palestine by British authorities, who administered the region, in 1920 for leading uprisings against Arabs, Jabotinsky devoted himself to building support for Zionism in Jewish communities throughout the world. He was adamant in the belief that the only way to create a Jewish state was to claim it by force. Thus in 1923, in Riga, Latvia, he founded Betar to train young Jews in the skills they would need to claim and defend a Jewish state but also to defend themselves against the anti-Semitism (prejudice against Jews) that they experienced in their own countries.

In the years that followed, Betar groups formed in nations throughout Europe and elsewhere. The U.S. chapter of Betar was based in New York City and had a training camp upstate, in the Catskill Mountains. Members learned self-defense and military tactics at the camp and were schooled in Zionist ideology. During World War II (1939–45), as news reached the United States about the Holocaust (the mass murder of European Jews and other groups by the Nazis during World War II), the need to take up arms became even more evident to members of Betar and other Jews. During the mid– and late–1940s, Betar members devoted themselves to smuggling weapons to Jewish groups fighting in Palestine. After the creation of the Jewish state of Israel in Palestine in 1948, Betar became even more vocal in its support of armed resistance against Israel's enemies. The organization still exists in the twenty-first century.

an ignorant congregation. When the article was published in a local Jewish newspaper, Kahane became something of a hero in the local Orthodox community.

For a few years after his dismissal from Howard Beach, Kahane wrote articles for the weekly newspaper *The Jewish Press*. His interest in espionage led him to adopt a second identity as "Michael King." As King, he took an apartment in Manhattan, shed his yarmulke (a type of hat that Orthodox Jews wear) and became involved with a model named Gloria Jean D'Argenio, a Gentile (non-Jew). When he ended the affair, she committed suicide by jumping from the Queensboro Bridge. Also under the name of King, Kahane opened a consulting firm with a New York friend of Syrian Jewish roots, Joseph Churba (1934–1996), offering to spy and gather intelligence for U.S. federal agencies. The two engaged in a range of schemes, and their company won job contracts with the U.S. government. The pair also wrote papers, encouraged actions supportive of U.S. efforts in the Vietnam War (1954–75) and endorsed U.S. support for Israel. Kahane later claimed that he was employed by the U.S. Federal Bureau of Investigation (FBI), although FBI officials insisted that Kahane was merely an informant. He and Churba also wrote a book titled *The Jewish Stake in Vietnam*, published in 1967. The book lists Churba, Michael King, and Meir Kahane as authors.

Kahane went on to write more books under his own name, all of them promoting his radical views about the need for Jews to defend themselves and to fight for Israel. The best known of his books are *Never Again! A Program for Survival* (1971), *They Must Go* (1981), and *Uncomfortable Questions for Comfortable Jews* (1987).

Founds the Jewish Defense League

Around 1967 Kahane broke with Churba and returned to his more traditional roots. He became the rabbi at the Rochdale Village Traditional Synagogue in Queens, New York. There Kahane's orthodox interpretations of Judaism matched those of his lower middle-class congregation. But Rochdale and other parts of Queens were transitioning into a more ethnically diverse community, and tensions arose between older residents and African American newcomers. Kahane railed against what he viewed as attacks on the Jewish community and founded the Jewish Defense League (JDL) in 1968. "The [JDL] mounted 'anti-mugger' patrols in neighborhoods bordered by black areas," notes Kahane's obituary,

Meir Kahane at a Jewish Defense League protest of the treatment of Jews in Russia. Meir Kahane was the founder of the Jewish Defense League and was often the organizer of its protests and rallies. © BETTMANN/CORBIS.

published in the *New York Times* in 1990. "[JDL members] escorted Jewish teachers through black neighborhoods with baseball bats, taught riflery and karate to rabbinical students and invaded Soviet diplomatic offices here to protest the treatment of Jews in the Soviet Union."

The JDL was modeled on the Betar of Kahane's youth. It was structured like a military organization, complete with a weapons training camp in the Catskill Mountains, and it operated under the slogans "Every Jew a .22" (referring to a .22-caliber rifle) and "Never Again!" (appealing to the Jewish desire to never again become the victim of attempted genocide (the deliberate and systematic destruction of a group of people based on religion, ethnicity, or nationality), as they had during the Holocaust, the mass murder of European Jews and other groups by the Nazis during World War II (1939–45). The JDL appealed to young Jews who felt threatened by the changing ethnic makeup of their neighborhoods, but it also appealed to Zionists, who now expressed support for Israel in its conflict with the Arab nations surrounding it. After the creation of the state of Israel in 1948, Arab nations invaded Israel in an attempt to take back the region, which they believed Israel had stolen from Arabs. Several Arab-Israeli wars and other conflicts followed, as Palestinians (an Arab people whose ancestors lived in the historical region of Palestine and who continue to lay claim to that land) struggled to gain recognition within and outside Israel's borders.

By the early 1970s the JDL had grown dramatically in both size and strength, receiving large donations from those who supported the group's aims. Kahane used the money to increase membership, which grew into the thousands. His followers embraced Kahane's central thesis: that Jews should unite to combat, with force, any challenge to their rights, whether it be in Israel or anywhere else. With this in mind, the JDL bombed Palestine Liberation Organization (PLO) offices in New York and sent assassins to target PLO targets in other countries. (The PLO is a political and military organization formed to unite various Palestinian Arab groups with the goal of establishing an independent Palestinian state.) The JDL also mounted a campaign of violence against Soviet targets in the United States in protest against Soviet persecution of Jews. Within a short period of time Kahane and a number of other JDL members were arrested and charged with a string of criminal charges, including conspiracy to manufacture explosives and illegal possession of weapons. Kahane was convicted and sentenced to one year in prison. After his release, he moved to Israel, where his younger brother, Nachman, lived and worked as a rabbi and a civil servant with the Ministry of Religious Affairs.

Moves to Israel

Kahane received a mixed welcome upon his arrival in Israel. Conservatives in Israel greeted him warmly, many feeling that Kahane's outlook was what was needed to maintain a secure Jewish state. Kahane was courted by politicians from a variety of conservative parties, including **Menachem Begin** (1913–1992; see entry), who hoped that Kahane could help bolster support for their vision of a strong Israel that would deny any Arab claims to territory. Instead Kahane founded his own party, which he called Kach (meaning "thus" in Hebrew). It comes from the slogan, *Raq Kach!* (Only Thus!), of the Irgun Zvai Leumi, a militant underground group founded in 1931 that worked to secure Israeli independence by staging violent attacks on British and Arab targets.

Kahane spent his first several years in Israel building support for his Kach Party and encouraging violence against Arabs. In the late summer of 1972, just a year after he arrived in Israel, a militant Palestinian group known as Black September took several Israeli athletes hostage at the 1972 Olympic Games in Munich, West Germany, all of whom were killed by the kidnappers during a failed rescue attempt. The hostage crisis was broadcast to the world thanks to network coverage of the Olympics. The event angered Kahane and others. He plotted to avenge the deaths, but his plans were foiled and he stood trial for attempted weapons smuggling in connection to a plan to organize a group to fight Arab terrorists; he was convicted in 1974. Israeli authorities detained him on several occasions, but his movement gained traction in an increasingly violence-plagued Jewish state. In the 1973 Knesset elections, the Kach Party garnered some twelve thousand votes, although this was less than the 1 percent needed to win at least one seat.

Kahane's frequent arrests and the publicity made him a hero to extremists in Israel. Kahane took advantage of his high public profile to promote the idea of transfer, one of the most controversial ideas in Israeli politics. Supporters of transfer believed that the only way to bring peace was to remove, forcibly if necessary, all Arabs from within the borders of Israel. "I don't want to kill Arabs, I just want them to live happily, elsewhere," Kahane's obituary in the *New York Times* quotes him as saying at rallies. "Give me the strength to take care of them once and for all." The idea of transfer was an abrupt dismissal of United Nations Resolution 194, adopted in 1948, which gives Palestinian refugees, who had fled their homes in Palestine during the violence of the Arab-Israeli wars, the so-called right of return. If all Palestinians were permitted to return, however, their population would outnumber that of the Israelis.

Wins a seat in the Israeli legislature

Moderates in Israel branded Kahane a lunatic and an agitator, whose words and actions threatened to derail efforts for peace between Israelis and Palestinians. Yet his beliefs resonated with newer immigrants, particularly working-class Sephardic Jews, who were of African, Asian, Spanish, or Middle Eastern descent. In contrast to the Ashkenazi Jews of European background, many Sephardim had fled Arab regimes to settle in Israel and had grown up with a deep mistrust of Arabs and Muslims. By 1984 Kahane had attracted enough support to gain 25,907 votes in the Knesset election, enough to win him a seat in the Knesset. His victory was greeted with disgust by most politicians within Israel.

Although Kahane's support was drawn from the extremist fringe of the Israeli right, some feared that his ideas secretly appealed to many within Israel who believed that their country could never prosper as long as it maintained a large Arab minority that posed a persistent security threat. Kahane's election caused a moral dilemma inside Israel. Many were proud of their country's constitution and democratic principles but realized the nation seemed incapable of incorporating Arabs into the political process. Kahane insisted that "Western democracy as we know it is incompatible with Zionism," as quoted by Kifner in the *New York Times*. "Zionism came into being to create a Jewish state. Zionism declares that there is going to be a Jewish state with a majority of Jews, come what may. Democracy says 'No, if the Arabs are the majority then they have the right to decide their own fate.' So Zionism and Democracy are at odds."

As a member of the Knesset, Kahane seemed to enjoy provoking his colleagues and drawing the attention of the media. He introduced laws that would revoke Israeli citizenship for non-Jews, as well as a ban on marriages between Jews and non-Jews, which failed to gain much support from fellow lawmakers. Kahane led marches and protests in the streets of Israeli cities, and his support grew, particularly after the onset of the First Intifada, a Palestinian uprising in the occupied territories that began in 1987 and would last for another six years. (The occupied territories are the lands under the political and military control of Israel, especially the West Bank and Gaza Strip.) Polls predicting Kach support in the next election hinted Kahane's party might win three or even four seats in the Knesset.

In 1985 there was an attempt to disqualify Kahane from the ballot with a law that banned parties whose platform included either promoting "negation of the democratic character of the State" or inciting racism, according to Thomas W. Simon, who quotes the law in *Democracy and Social Injustice: Law, Politics, and Philosophy*. In October 1988 the country's Central Election Commission, which carries out Knesset elections, upheld the ban, effectively shutting Kahane out of the upcoming elections. His supporters were outraged, and Kahane continued to denounce moderate Jews, Muslims, and others who opposed his political beliefs.

Assassination and legacy

In November 1990 Kahane returned to the United States on a fund-raising mission. While leaving a Marriott hotel in New York, he was shot and killed. Egyptian-born El Sayyid Nosair (1955–), a U.S. citizen, was arrested and charged with the murder. He was found not guilty of the murder charge, but was convicted on lesser charges. At Kahane's funeral supporters chanted "Mavet La'aravim," which is Hebrew for "death to the Arabs."

Kahane's son, Binyamin, took over a splinter group of the Kach Party called Kahane Chai (Kahane Lives). Binyamin and his wife were shot and killed in the West Bank in December 2000.

Kahane's followers continue to seek elected office, but usually fail to gain enough votes to win a Knesset seat. Israel's 2004 decision to withdraw from the Gaza Strip reignited tensions in the country, and a former student of Kahane's named Michael Ben Ari (1963–) won a Knesset seat as part of the National Union Party. The Kahane Movement (Jewish extremist groups that follow Kahane's political ideas) resurfaced for a time after this, with followers attempting to win Israeli Supreme Court approval to conduct marches through predominantly Muslim towns. They reject the proposed two-state solution to the Arab-Israeli conflict, in which the Palestinians would be granted an independent state.

For More Information

BOOKS

Kahane, Meir. *Never Again! A Program for Survival.* New York: Pyramid Books, 1972.

———. *They Must Go.* New York: Grosset & Dunlap, 1981.

Simon, Thomas W. *Democracy and Social Injustice: Law, Politics, and Philosophy.* London: Rowman & Littlefield, 1995, p. 115.

PERIODICALS

Kifner, John. "Meir Kahane, 58, Israeli Militant and Founder of the Jewish Defense League." *New York Times* (November 6, 1990). Available online at http://www.nytimes.com/1990/11/06/obituaries/meir-kahane-58-israeli-militant-and-founder-of-the-jewish-defense-league.html?scp=3&sq=meir+kahane&st=nyt (accessed on November 30, 2011).

WEB SITES

Mizrahi, Ilan. "Israel: Rise of the Right." *Aljazeera* (June 29, 2009). http://english.aljazeera.net/programmes/general/2009/06/20096229244641270.html (accessed on November 30, 2011).

"The Rav's Writings." *Kahane Tzadak.* http://www.kahanetzadak.com/KT/Writings/Writings.html (accessed on November 30, 2011).

Shyovitz, David. "Rabbi Meir Kahane." *Jewish Virtual Library.* http://www.jewishvirtuallibrary.org/jsource/biography/kahane.html (accessed on November 30, 2011).

Ayatollah Ali Khamenei

BORN: July 17, 1939 • Mashhad, Razavi Khorasan,
Iran

Iranian religious leader, political leader, president

"What I firmly announce is that a new movement, with the
grace of God, has started in the region.... This widespread awakening of nations, which is directed towards Islamic goals, will definitely
become victorious."

Ayatollah Ali Khamenei.
© PERSIAN EYES/CORBIS.

Ayatollah Ali Khamenei (also spelled Khāmene'i) became the Supreme
Leader of Iran in 1989 after the death of **Ayatollah Ruhollah
Khomeini** (1900–1989; see entry). (An ayatollah is a high-ranking Shiite
religious leader.) Iran's constitution gives the Supreme Leader significant
political powers, more so than even the elected president, for the Supreme
Leader is deemed the guardian of principles enshrined by the 1979
Iranian Revolution (also known as the Islamic Revolution), which transformed Iran from a secular (nonreligious) nation to an Islamic state, based
on the belief that Islam should provide the basis for political, social, and
cultural life in Muslim nations. In a *Newsweek* article, journalist Maziar
Bahari explains that Khamenei "is the constitutionally designated leader of
a modern state ruled by religious laws devised 1,400 years ago. And he

must placate both the modern and the medieval sides of the schizoid [divided] Iranian state—a task that has grown increasingly complex."

Born into a family of clerics

Khamenei was born in 1939, in the city of Mashhad in Iran. One of eight children, he grew up in an Iranian-Azeri family. Azeris are a Turkish ethnic group that, for centuries, dominated parts of northern Iran, as well as present-day Azerbaijan and Armenia. The family extended to the ancient city of Tabriz, Iran, an Azeri stronghold, and to Najaf, a holy city in Iraq. The Khamenei family also claimed descent from the Muslim prophet Mohammed (c. 570–632), and this ancestry allowed them to use the title "Sayyid" (a noble and honorific title given to males accepted as descendants of Muhammad). Thus Khamenei is also known as Sayyid Ali Khamenei. His father, a cleric (ordained religious official) named Sayyid Jawad Husaini Khamenei, led morning and midday prayers at two mosques in Mashhad. (A mosque is a Muslim place of worship.) Two of Khamenei's grandfathers were clerics, and three of Khamenei's sons would also become clerics. The family was poor but devout and lived in a one-room building.

Two years after Khamenei's birth, British and Russian troops invaded Iran as World War II (1939–45; a war in which the Allies [Great Britain, France, the Soviet Union, the United States, and China] defeated the Axis Powers [Germany, Italy, and Japan]) spread to the Middle East. Reza Shah (1878–1944), was removed from power and his twenty-one-year-son, **Mohammad Reza Pahlavi** (1919–1980; see entry), was installed as the shah of Iran in an effort to keep the vital pipelines of the Anglo-Iranian Oil Company from falling under the control of Nazi Germany. "Although Mashhad was outside the battle zone and most goods were by comparison cheaper than other towns," Khamenei wrote in a biographical statement that appeared on his official Web site, *The Office of the Supreme Leader Ali Sayyid Khamenei.* "[B]ecause of our family's material want, we could not afford to eat wheat bread. We usually ate barley bread, and at times a mixture of both. I can recall that sometimes we had nothing to eat. At dinner time, my mother used to take the money which my grandmother gave me and my brothers and sisters, to buy milk and raisins for us to eat with bread."

Sweeping changes came to Iran in the years following World War II. Pahlavi barely kept his throne after an uprising in 1953; once again, foreign powers intervened and Pahlavi returned to power in 1954. Pahlavi maintained power with the help of a new secret-police agency known as SAVAK, which is an acronym for *Sazeman-e ettela'at va amniat-e keshvar* (National Intelligence and Security Organization).

During this time, Khamenei attended religious schools, and was on a career path to become one of the ulema, scholars who interpret sharia (Islamic religious law) and issue pronouncements on how to properly follow a devout path for Shiites, followers of the Shia branch of Islam. The ulema were the unofficial leaders of a swelling section of the Iranian populace who felt marginalized by and disenchanted with Pahlavi's rapid modernization of the country. These conservative Iranians were already insulted by the changes decreed by Pahlavi and his father before him, such as a ban on traditional dress and the introduction of movie theaters and other forms of entertainment that to them symbolized Western decadence. Pahlavi's father had discontinued many of the long-held powers of the Shiite clerics, and Pahlavi went even further in setting up a modern university system by which clerics were to be educated. Jurists (those who practiced the law) were to be educated in new secular universities, permanently removing the influence of judges who believed the law should be based on sharia.

Studies in Qom

One of the major opponents of these changes was a cleric named Ayatollah Ruhollah Khomeini. When Khamenei began his religious schooling, he started first at the theological seminary in Mashhad, then went to neighboring Iraq to enter a seminary in Najaf, a Shiite holy city. A year later, in 1958, he returned to Iran and began seminary studies in Qom, the major center of Shiite scholarship. He became a proégé of Khomeini, by then a respected lecturer and emerging theorist, while studying and supporting himself as a teacher of Islamic jurisprudence, called *Fiqh* in Arabic. This is the field of scholarship surrounding sharia (Islamic religious law). Khamenei gained some renown as an expert on one of the most important documents of Shia Islam, the *Nahj al-Balagah* (Peak of Eloquence), a collection of writings by Ali ibn Abi Talib (c. 596–661), who was the son-in-law of the prophet Muhammad. Khamenei was notably multilingual, fluent in Persian, the language of Iran, as well as in Arabic and Turkish.

From Qom in 1963 Khomeini organized opposition to Pahlavi's new program of reform, which bore the optimistic title of the White Revolution, in the hope that it would be bloodless. Pahlavi's plan included a land-redistribution deal that restricted the power of wealthy landowners; the nationalization (bringing under government ownership and control) of water resources, forests, and pasturelands; free university education for all; and women's rights. Khomeini and other Shiite clerics were vehemently opposed to these proposals and encouraged Iranians to boycott the referendum (a direct public vote on a single proposal). In a bold move Khomeini publicly denounced Pahlavi as a tyrant and warned that his policies would eventually lead to his removal.

Two days later, on June 5, 1963, the SAVAK seized Khomeini and imprisoned him. Massive protests erupted at this treatment of Iran's leading religious authority. Khamenei was arrested in Birjand later that year after delivering a public speech and was jailed for ten days. In 1964 he returned to Mashhad and worked for some years with other clerics organizing efforts to press for the end of the Pahlavi's rule. His translation of *Al-Mustaqbal li-hadha'l-Din* (The Future of this Religion), an influential book by Egyptian writer and radical Sayyid Qutb (1906–1966), from Arabic into Farsi landed him in another round of trouble with the SAVAK. This is because Qutb, who had studied in the United States, was a staunch opponent of Western influence in the Muslim world. Khomeini, meanwhile, was banished from Iran.

Ushers in revolution

In 1977 Khamenei was one of the founding members of the Society of Combatant Clergy, which worked to destabilize Pahlavi's regime. He organized demonstrations and strikes (work stoppages) throughout 1978 that called for an end to Pahlavi's rule. Ayatollah Khomeini's warnings about Pahlavi's eventual downfall proved prophetic. In January 1979 Pahlavi fled Iran. Khomeini returned to Iran on February 1 and appointed Khamenei to a seat on the Revolutionary Command Council, a powerful body that essentially controlled the country in the power vacuum caused by Pahlavi's departure. With other clerics, Khamenei founded the Islamic Republican Party in mid–February 1979. During these years, Khamenei bore the title Hojjat ol-Islam, which means an authority on Islam. He and other ulema were charged with implementing the principles of Khomeini's influential 1970 treatise, *Velayat-e faqih (Islamic Government: Governance of the Jurist)* which described an Islamic theocracy (a form of government in which the clergy exercise political power and religious law is dominant over civil law).

As Iran evolved into a genuine Islamic state, Khamenei held several key jobs, including leader of the Friday prayers at the main mosque in Iran's capital of Tehran. He sat on the Supreme Defense Council and played an important role in the decisions related to the Iran-Iraq War (1980–88), which erupted in September 1980. The new Islamic Republic of Iran held its first elections earlier that year, and Abul-Hassan Bani-Sadr (1933–), one of Khomeini's followers who had spent time in exile in France with him, was elected president. Bani-Sadr and Khomeini soon began to disagree on crucial matters, and Khomeini installed himself as commander in chief of the armed forces in early June 1981. Bani-Sadr then disappeared, and it was Khamenei who condemned Bani-Sadr on a radio broadcast on June 21, blaming him for "any shortcoming or back-wardness in the country," as quoted in the *New York Times* on June 20, 1981. He also denounced Bani-Sadr's claims that the new Revolutionary Guard, which served the same function as the former regime's widely loathed SAVAK, used torture. "Is it right that you as President go and spread such a big lie all over the world and disgrace the Islamic republic?," Khamenei said. "Are you interested in Islam? Did you love the revolution? By God, you are lying if you say you love it."

A week later, after impeachment proceedings (a formal process in which an official is accused of misconduct) against Bani-Sadr were success-ful, Khamenei was the target of an assassination attempt. A bomb inside a tape recorder went off during a press conference. Khamenei's right arm was injured and left permanently paralyzed. A day later, Ayatollah Mohammad Beheshti (1928–1981), one of the founders of the Islamic Republican Party, was killed by a bomb planted by members of the People's Mujahedin of Iran. They were also believed responsible for the assassi-nation of Bani-Sadr's successor, Mohammed Ali Rajai (1933–1981), who was killed when a briefcase bomb successfully detonated during a meeting of the Supreme Defense Council on August 30, 1981.

Condemns U.S. attack

Iranians went to the polls on October 2, 1981, and elected Khamenei president with 95 percent of the vote. Khamenei stated that the results served as an affirmation of "trust for the clergy, a vote for Islam, a vote for independence and a vote for stamping out deviation, liberalism and

American-influenced leftists," he asserted, as quoted by the *New York Times* in an October 14, 1981, article. Khamenei was sworn in as president of Iran on October 13, 1981. He was the first cleric to hold that office, even though Ayatollah Khomeini had initially been reluctant to permit members of the clergy from holding political office. His installation as president marked a turning point for Iran's mission to become the first modern Islamic theocratic country.

Khamenei was reelected president in 1985 as the Islamic Republican Party candidate, winning some 12 million votes. He continued to play a key role in the ongoing war with Iraq, harshly criticizing U.S. aid to the country. In September 1987 Khamenei made his first visit to the United States, where he addressed the opening of the United Nations General Assembly. (The United Nations is an international organization of countries founded in 1945 to promote international peace, security, and cooperation.) This was an especially tense period in the war with Iraq, and one of the items on the agenda of the UN Security Council was a motion for possible sanctions against Iran for its failure to participate in U.S.-brokered peace talks. (Sanctions are punitive measures adopted by the international community against a nation that has violated international law, usually in the form of diplomatic, economic, or social restrictions.) A month earlier, the United States had launched a program to protect crude-oil tankers in the Persian Gulf from Iranian air strikes during the war. A day before Khamenei arrived in the United States, U.S. military helicopters fired on an Iranian ship, the *Iran Ajr*, after surveillance measures determined it was a mine-laying merchant vessel, which Iran flatly denied. (A mine is a type of bomb placed on or just below the surface of the ground or in the water that explodes on contact.) Khamenei had planned for his UN speech to be a conciliatory measure, but he changed his mind and instead harshly condemned the United States. "The Islamic revolution in Iran was meant to be against a regime that had put all this at the service of the interests of the imperial-minded powers of the world and particularly the United States," he said, according to a *New York Times* September 23, 1987, article. "Our revolution proved that imperial-minded powers may be ignored."

Succeeds Khomeini

For years the cleric Hussein-Ali Montazeri (1922–2009) had been the designated successor to Ayatollah Khomeini as Supreme Leader, a position that is held for life. Montazeri was a loyal deputy for many years, but in 1987 he began speaking out about human-rights abuses in Iran, the lack of genuine political parties, and its mission to fund Islamic fundamentalist groups in other countries. Montazeri also commented unfavorably on Ayatollah Khomeini's *fatwa* calling for the death of author Salman Rushdie (1947–). (A fatwa is statement of religious law issued by an Islamic cleric and intended to instruct devout Muslims.) Rushdie was to live under police protection in the West for nearly a decade for what were considered blasphemous statements against the prophet Mohammed in his novel *The Satanic Verses*. Montazeri resigned as Khomeini's deputy in March 1989.

The eighty-six-year-old Ayatollah Khomeini's death on June 3, 1989, prompted a public outpouring of grief throughout Iran. A day later the Assembly of Experts, a council of eighty-six *mujtahids* (Islamic scholars), voted to install Khamenei in the office of Supreme Leader. There was some internal debate over his qualifications, for he did not hold the higher clerical rank of *marja*, the highest authority on sharia, as required by Iran's constitution. The constitution was amended to remove this requirement, and the Assembly of Experts approved Khamenei's new title as Grand Ayatollah and Supreme Leader of Iran.

The end of Khomeini's leadership marked a period of transition in Iran. The constitution was amended to give the elected president more executive powers, and the prime minister's job was eliminated. Khamenei supported Ali Akbar Hashemi Rafsanjani (1934–), a cleric like himself but also an advocate of free-market reforms, for president. Rafsanjani was elected in 1989, and reelected in 1993. In 1997 another cleric, Mohammad Khatami (1943–), became president. He also served two terms.

Khamenei's role as Supreme Leader of Iran gives him much more authority than that of the elected president. He is commander in chief of all the armed forces, including the elite Islamic Revolutionary Guard Corps, also known as Revolutionary Guards, which serve to quell dissent and punish acts or statements deemed heretical. (Heresy is a religious opinion that conflicts with accepted doctrines.) The guards oversee the Basij, volunteer militias which act as a strike force in the event of anti-government demonstrations and are known for rebuking women for public violations of the strict dress code.

The Supreme Leader also appoints the director of the national judiciary and the chairperson of the national media, who serves a five-year term as head of the Islamic Republic of Iran Broadcasting (IRIB), a government agency. Khamenei keeps a lower profile than his predecessor and is known for making provocative anti-American and anti-Israel statements. When Khatami's attempts to introduce some democratic reforms gathered popular support, Khamenei moved to revive the Basij in the summer of 1999, after the civilian militias had been dormant for several years when official support for them had cooled. Reenergized, the Basij broke up student demonstrations in Tehran while Khamenei moved to shut down certain newspapers. After the September 11, 2001, terrorist attacks on the United States, Khamenei spoke in characteristically vivid terms about U.S. president George W. Bush's (1946–) rallying cry for support, in which the American leader stated nations were either "with us or against us" in the fight against terrorism, according to R.W. Apple in the *New York Times*. "The behavior and remarks of the American government and officials concerning this incident were very arrogant and pretentious and continue to be so," Khamenei asserted in a speech commemorating the Iran-Iraq War, as quoted by Elaine Sciolino in the *New York Times*. "Of course, their dignity has been badly harmed, their security reputation has been badly dented, but those are not reasons for resorting to their arrogant image in order to compensate for their humiliation."

Warns 2009 protesters

Khamenei supported the candidacy of **Mahmoud Ahmadinejad** (1956–; see entry) in Iran's 2005 presidential race. Ahmadinejad won the 2005 election and was reelected in June 2009. Ahmadinejad won with 60 percent of the vote. However, there were accusations of election fraud and protests erupted in the streets when the results were announced. On June 19, after a week of street protests, which came to be known as the Green Movement, Khamenei called for a halt to the unrest, noting that a margin of eleven million votes, with an 85 percent voter turnout rate across Iran, would be impossible to invent. In a two-hour speech at Tehran University, he warned protest leaders that they would be morally responsible for any bloodshed. Over the next two days further protests erupted in mass defiance of Khamenei's warnings, and major clashes occurred between riot police and demonstrators.

Iranian judicial authorities carried out harsh reprisals on those involved in the protests and put dozens on trial in August 2009. That same month, a petition was circulated by former legislators that challenged the legitimacy of Khamenei's rule, and the Assembly of Experts convened in an emergency meeting to discuss the matter. "The verbal attacks illustrate the erosion of a

Iranians listen to Ayatollah Ali Khamenei at Friday prayers in Tehran, on June 19, 2009. Khamenei tried to calm unrest over the disputed presidential election results, assuring citizens that the election had not been rigged. © STRINGERT/EPA/.CORBIS.

powerful taboo," write Robert F. Worth and Nazila Fathi in the *New York Times*. "Long unquestioned, Ayatollah Khamenei's status as a neutral arbiter and Islamic figurehead have suffered." They explain, "The harsh crackdown on street protests that followed has only deepened public anger with him. In recent days the phrase 'death to Khamenei' has begun appearing in graffiti on Tehran walls, a phrase that would have been almost unimaginable not long ago."

In 2011 a series of prodemocarcy uprisings, called the Arab Spring, spread throughout the Middle East and North Africa. Several longtime leaders were ousted by their own people. It began in Tunisia, where increasingly violent demonstrations finally forced president Zine El Abidine Ben Ali (1936–) from power. Egypt's president, **Hosni Mubarak** (1928–; see entry), was next. In March 2011 Khamenei delivered an address on the occasion of Nowruz, the traditional Iranian New Year, in

The Basij

For ordinary Iranians, the Basij are among the most feared elements of a strict theocratic society. Loosely organized by cities and then neighborhoods, the Basij are thought to be controlled by local mosque leaders while also working under orders of the Revolutionary Guard. Some members are young men, others are veterans of the Iran-Iraq War (1980–88), and most are ardent supporters of Ayatollah Ali Khamenei. They make up part of a devoted core known as *zobeh dar velayat*, which is Farsi for "those who are melted in the leadership." Iran's president since 2005, **Mahmoud Ahmadinejad** (1956–; see entry), is often photographed wearing a plain beige windbreaker, which denotes his identification as one of the Basij in his earlier days as a university student and civil servant.

In times of political unrest the Basij are deployed to break up street protests, as they did with brutal force in the 2009 election protests. In calmer periods they are known to roam the streets of Tehran and other cities, searching for violations of sharia. These may include men and women talking in public spaces; women violating the code of dress mandated for their gender; houses with satellite television dishes; or even dogs being taken for a daily stroll. Islam considers dogs to be *haram* (unclean), and while keeping one for guard purposes or farm work is permissible, it is against the law to keep a dog for companionship.

which he praised the uprisings in Tunisia and Egypt, linking the unrest to Islamic fundamentalism. "What I firmly announce is that a new movement, with the grace of God, has started in the region.... This widespread awakening of nations, which is directed towards Islamic goals, will definitely become victorious."

For More Information

BOOKS

Sciolino, Elaine. *Persian Mirrors: The Elusive Face of Iran.* New York: Simon & Schuster, 2001.

Wright, Robin. *The Last Great Revolution: Turmoil and Transformation in Iran.* New York: Knopf, 2000.

PERIODICALS

Anderson, Jon Lee. "After the Crackdown." *New Yorker* (August 16, 2010). Available online at http://www.newyorker.com/reporting/2010/08/16/100816fa_fact_anderson?currentPage=all (accessed on November 30, 2011).

Apple, R.W. "After the Attacks: News Analysis; No Middle Ground." *New York Times* (September 14, 2001). Available online at http://www.nytimes.com/2001/09/14/us/after-the-attacks-news-analysis-no-middle-ground.html?scp=1&sq=george+bush+%22with+us+or+against+us%22&st=nyt (accessed on November 30, 2011).

Bahari, Maziar. "Reign of the 'Melted Ones.'" *Newsweek* (April 5, 2007). Available online at http://www.thedailybeast.com/newsweek/2007/04/05/reign-of-the-melted-ones.html (accessed on November 30, 2011).

"Cleric Sworn in as Iran's President amid Cries of 'Death to America!.'" *New York Times* (October 14, 1981). Available online at http://www.nytimes.com/1981/10/14/world/cleric-sworn-in-as-iran-s-president-amid-cries-of-death-to-america.html?scp=16&sq= %22ali+khamenei%22&st=nyt (accessed on November 30, 2011).

"Excerpts From the Address to the General Assembly by the President of Iran." *New York Times* (September 23, 1987). Available online at http://www.nytimes.com/1987/09/23/world/excerpts-from-the-address-to-the-general-assembly-by-the-president-of-iran.html?scp=145&sq=%22ali+khamenei%22&st=nyt (accessed on November 30, 2011).

Ibrahim, Youssef M. "A Star of Iran Finds Destiny Against Him." *New York Times* (September 23, 1987). Available online at http://www.nytimes.com/1987/09/23/world/a-star-of-iran-finds-destiny-against-him.html?scp=141&sq=%22ali+khamenei%22&st=nyt (accessed on November 30, 2011).

"Iranian Forces Hunt for Bani-Sadr as He Is Blamed for Country's Ills." *New York Times* (June 20, 1981). Available online at http://www.nytimes.com/1981/06/20/world/iranian-forces-hunt-for-bani-sadr-as-he-is-blamed-for-country-s-ills.html?scp=3&sq=khamenei&st=nyt (accessed on November 30, 2011).

Kifner, John. "400 Die as Iranian Marchers Battle Saudi Police in Mecca." *New York Times* (August 2, 1987). Available online at http://www.nytimes.com/1987/08/02/world/400-die-iranian-marchers-battle-saudi-police-mecca-embassies-smashed-teheran.html?scp=119&sq=&pagewanted=all (accessed on November 30, 2011).

Sciolino, Elaine. "Word for Word/Islam's Argument." *New York Times* (September 30., 2001). Available online at http://www.nytimes.com/2001/09/30/weekinreview/word-for-word-islam-s-argument-you-expect-us-help-you-iran-gets-its-two-cents.html?scp=1&sq=khamenei&st=nyt (accessed on November 30, 2011).

Worth, Robert F., and Nazila Fathi, "Clerics' Call for Removal Challenges Iran Leader." *New York Times* (August 17, 2009): A4. Available online at http://www.nytimes.com/2009/08/17/world/middleeast/17iran.html?_r=1&ref=middleeast (accessed on November 30, 2011).

WEB SITES

Agah, Farzad. "Iranian Republic Splintering?" *Al Jazeera* (June 23, 2009). http://english.aljazeera.net/focus/iranincrisis/2009/06/200962355233501334.html (accessed on November 30, 2011).

'Biography.' *The Office of the Supreme Leader Ali Sayyid Khamenei.* http://www.leader.ir/langs/en/index.php?p=bio. (accessed on November 30, 2011).

Nikou, Semira N. "Iran Backs Libyan Rebels, Chastises West Over Oil, Bahrain." *PBS Frontline* (April 6, 2011). http://www.pbs.org/wgbh/pages/frontline/tehranbureau/2011/04/iran-backs-libyan-rebels-chastises-west-over-oil-bahrain.html#ixzz1WYBnQysq (accessed on November 30, 2011).

Ayatollah Ruhollah Khomeini

BORN: September 24, 1902 • Khomein, Persia

DIED: June 3, 1989 • Tehran, Iran

Iranian religious leader, political leader

Ayatollah Ruhollah Khomeini.
GABRIEL DUVAL/AFP/GETTY
IMAGES.

"Their plan is to keep us backward, to keep us in our present miserable state so they can exploit our riches, our underground wealth, our lands, and our human resources."

Ayatollah Ruhollah Khomeini was a major figure in the 1979 Iranian Revolution (also known as the Islamic Revolution), which made Iran an Islamic nation, meaning that Islam provides the basis for its political, social, and cultural life. (An ayatollah is a high-ranking Shiite religious leader.) Khomeini had been a vocal critic of Iran's shah, **Mohammad Reza Pahlavi** (1919–1980; see entry), whose alliances with the West and modernization of Iran had prompted widespread dissatisfaction. Khomeini's condemnations of Pahlavi galvanized large segments of the population into action in the late 1970s, and those mass protests culminated in the removal of Pahlavi and the establishment of a new Islamic Republic of Iran. As Supreme Leader of Iran, Khomeini wielded enormous influence and became a revered, and sometimes feared, figure across the Middle East for his role in shaping Iran into the world's first modern theocracy, a form of government in which the clergy exercise political power and religious law is dominant over civil law. He also committed Iran's resources to aid Islamic fundamentalists in other countries. (Fundamentalists stress adherence to a strict or literal interpretation of religious principles.) Some of those fundamentalist groups evolved into political movements that shaped the landscape of the modern Middle East in the decades after Khomeini's death in 1989.

Early life

The youngest of six children, Khomeini was born in September 1902, in what was then known as Persia. His mother, Hajar, was the daughter of Ayatollah Mirza Ahmad, a famous Muslim religious scholar from Najaf, Iraq. His father was murdered when Khomeini was just six months old. His paternal grandfather was Seyyed Ahmad Moussavi, a prominent Shiite scholar. (Shiites are followers of the Shia branch of Islam.) Moussavi was a Twelver, a follower of the Twelver branch of Shia Islam. Twelvers believe in the eventual return of a vanished imam (Muslim leader) known as the Mahdi.

Khomeini entered a seminary in Arak, Iran. There he was influenced by a renowned teacher, Ayatollah Abdulkarim Haeri Yazdi (1859–1937), one of Islam's most important theologians (religious scholars) of the era. Khomeini followed Haeri to the holy city of Qom, where Haeri established a seminary around 1921. This school attracted prominent clerics (ordained religious officials) from the holy city of Najaf, in neighboring Iraq, who had been forced to flee after leading a revolt against British rule there.

Political agitation

Khomeini lived in a land that had been an Islamic Shiite state since the early 1500s. During Khomeini's youth, Persia was ruled by the Qajar family, but in the early 1920s Reza Khan (1878–1944) seized power during a time of political instability. Reza Khan crowned himself shah, in 1925 and became known as Reza Shah. He made his eldest son, Mohammed, the crown prince. He also changed Persia's name to Iran and began a modernization program closely modeled on that of nearby Turkey under President **Mustafa Kemal Atatürk** (c. 1881–1938; see entry). Like Atatürk, Reza Shah introduced sweeping reforms at all levels of Iranian society, replacing sharia (Islamic religious law) with a secular (nonreligious) system of law and banned traditional Islamic dress, like the chador, the head-to-toe covering worn by women in public. Iran's oil resources made it important during World War II (1939–45; a war in which the Allies [Great Britain, France, the Soviet Union, the United States, and China] defeated the Axis Powers [Germany, Italy, and Japan]), and fears over Reza Shah's allegiances forced Great Britain, a majority holder of the Anglo-Iranian Oil Company, to intervene. Reza Shah was removed from power in 1941, and his eldest son, twenty-one-year-old Mohammad Pahlavi, became the new ruler of Iran.

During these years, Khomeini taught at the Qom and Najaf seminaries, and rose to the rank of *mujtahid*, which denotes proficiency in sharia. He opposed some of the teachings of Seyyed Hossein Tabatabai Borujerdi (1875–1961), who succeeded Haeri as the leading religious figure of the Twelvers, and developed a deep interest in the mysticism of Sufism, another branch of Islam, and the Persian poets of the medieval era. In 1943 Khomeini published his first book, *Kashef al-Asrar* (Discovery of Secrets), arguing that Reza Shah's policies should be reversed and Iranian laws should more closely conform with sharia. But during this era, Iran's leading clerics mostly adhered to a collective policy of avoiding politics and political statements altogether.

Denouncing the shah

In the 1950s Khomeini served as an adviser to another leading cleric, the Ayatollah Seyyed Abol-Ghasem Mostafavi Kashani (1882–1962), who for a brief time served as chair of Iran's *majlis* (parliament). Khomeini rose to prominence after Borujerdi's death in 1961. Two years later, while living and teaching in Qom, Khomeini became the unofficial spokesperson against a wide-ranging series of reforms Pahlavi had unveiled under the optimistic banner of the White Revolution. Pahlavi's White Revolution, announced in early 1963, was designed to modernize Iran. It included a land-redistribution program that would curb some of the power of elite landowners; the nationalization (bringing under government ownership and control) of Iran's water resources, forests, and pasture lands; free university education; and finally, women's rights. This last item was vehemently opposed by Khomeini and other Shiite clerics, who abided by strict rules regarding the role of women in society, both at home and in public.

Khomeini became the most vocal opponent of the White Revolution. It was a daring stance in a country that was effectively a police state, where public dissent of any kind inevitably brought swift and brutal retribution from the SAVAK, the shah's internal police agency. Khomeini denounced the White Revolution from Qom and urged Iranians to boycott the referendum (a direct public vote on a single proposal). On June 3, 1963, Khomeini delivered a speech in which he declared Pahlavi's reforms as a barely disguised scheme to let the United States colonize the country. "You wretched, miserable man," he railed against Pahlavi, as quoted by Baqer Moin in *Khomeini: Life of the Ayatollah*. "Forty-five years of your life have passed. Isn't it time for you to think and reflect a little?" Khomeini warned Pahlavi about his allies in the West in the same speech: "You don't know whether the situation will change one day nor whether those who surround you will remain your friends. They are the friends of the dollar. They have no religion, no loyalty. They have hung all the responsibility around your neck."

Living in exile

In the hours following Khomeini's speech in Qom, antishah protests erupted in Tehran, Iran's capital city. Khomeini was arrested, and when news of this spread, riots broke out in his home city, then other major urban centers. Some government ministers called for Khomeini to be tried for treason and sentenced to death, but moderates in Pahlavi's government argued that this would turn him into a martyr and further inflame tensions. (A martyr is a person who dies for a cause, usually his or her religion.) Instead Khomeini was imprisoned until April 1964, then released. Later that year, after speaking out against a law that gave American military personnel in Iran immunity from prosecution, he was arrested again on November 4. This time, SAVAK drove Khomeini to the Tehran airport, where he was handed a passport and told he was being deported to Turkey, where his wife and children would be allowed to join him.

Khomeini was closely watched by the Turkish police and intelligence agents in Ankara, Turkey's capital, and the smaller city of Bursa, where he eventually settled. Turkey was a Muslim, but dramatically secular, country, and Khomeini was forbidden to appear in public in his traditional garb of a long black clerical robe and black turban denoting his status as an authority on sharia. Khomeini complied with the requirement to wear Western-style trousers and remove his turban if he left the house.

Khomeini spent his first year in exile writing *Tahrir al-Wasilah*, a theological treatise. In October 1965 he was allowed to settle in Najaf, Iraq, where he had once studied. Like Qom, Najaf was a center of Shia scholarship. Khomeini's support base inside Iran continued to grow, however, and cassette tapes of his speeches were made and smuggled across the border, where his followers secretly circulated them. One of his most influential works was a series of lectures delivered at the Najaf seminary in early 1970. Transcribed and collected as *Velayat-e faqih* (published in English as *Islamic Government: Governance of the Jurist*), it became his most famous work in its arguments in favor of an Islamic theocracy, with sharia specialists serving as guardians of society.

A nation in turmoil

Khomeini continued to serve as the main opponent of Pahlavi and his rule. Khomeini was especially critical of Pahlavi's October 1971 gala commemorating the twenty-five hundredth anniversary of the founding of the Persian Empire. The lavish festivities, held at the ancient city of Persepolis, became one of the twentieth century's most fabled and luxurious grand parties. Ordinary Iranians watched the pageantry on television, and apparently even Khomeini tuned in from Najaf. Khomeini was particularly forceful in his published denunciation of the spectacle. "It is the kings of Iran that have constantly ordered massacres of their own people and had pyramids built with their skulls," he asserted, according to Robin Wright in *The Last Great Revolution: Turmoil and Transformation in Iran*. "Anyone who studies the manner in which the Prophet established the government of Islam will realise that Islam came in order to destroy these palaces of tyranny."

Khomeini's criticism of Pahlavi amplified considerably in late 1977, when Khomeini's eldest son, Mustafa, died suddenly in Najaf. Khomeini believed that Mustafa had been murdered by SAVAK agents. Dissent in Iran grew louder and more visible in mid–1977, when several prominent figures signed an open letter stating their opposition to Pahlavi's rule and calling for democratic reform. That, in turn, led to open demonstrations in Tehran, Tabriz, and other cities in early 1978. Some of the unrest was instigated by a new group made up of Khomeini's former students in Qom and Najaf, which called itself the Society of Combatant Clergy. These demonstrations were also linked to an article that appeared in an Iranian newspaper that was an attempt to discredit Khomeini. It hinted that his family was of Indian, not Persian origin; that he was an agent of the British Secret Intelligence Service, and that he drank alcohol and was possibly gay.

The defamatory article aside, even less devout Muslims in Iran were weary of Pahlavi's corrupt regime and the pervasive presence of SAVAK. As millions turned out on the streets in open defiance of martial law, Pahlavi's army reacted with violence. Iran became increasingly unstable, and Pahlavi managed to persuade Iraqi leader **Saddam Hussein** (1937–2006; see entry) to expel Khomeini from Iraq. In October 1978 Khomeini arrived in France and settled in Neauphle-le-Château. Ironically communication between him and his followers inside Iran was now much easier, because state-of-the-art telecommunication equipment installed by Pahlavi's government ensured superb telephone connections between Iran and France.

Pahlavi faced increasing pressure to step down. On January 16, 1979, Pahlavi and his family fled Iran. Khomeini, meanwhile, was in steady contact with the Iranian revolutionaries. He returned to Iran on February 1, 1979, arriving at Tehran's airport to triumphant crowds.

Establishing the Islamic Republic of Iran

Khomeini installed Mehdi Bazargan (1907–1995), a seventy-two-year-old moderate, as prime minister. Bazargan only ruled for eight months, as differences of opinion between the secular and religious elements of the ruling elites became too difficult to manage. Khomeini proved a deft manager of the competing forces during this time of turmoil. "There was no one in Iran with sufficient authority to challenge the Ayatollah successfully," notes Raymond H. Anderson in the *New York Times*. "In the aftermath of the revolution, he moved relentlessly toward his theocratic goal, consolidating power and silencing the opposition. In a frenzy of political retribution and Islamic purification, thousands of people were executed in public, including torturers, criminals, homosexuals, prostitutes and the Shah's officials."

A national referendum was held in late March 1979, and twenty million Iranians voted in favor of the creation of the Islamic Republic of Iran. A new constitution was approved by referendum in October 1979 that gave Khomeini significant political powers as Supreme Leader, a title he assumed in December 1979. He wielded more power than any political figure, even the elected president. The position made him commander in

Ayatollah Khomeini during a speech to followers in Tehran after his return from exile in 1979. © CORBIS/BETTMANN.

chief of the armed forces and director of the national judiciary. He was also in control of the media. Almost overnight Iran became a strict Islamic theocracy, with all levels of political, social, and economic life overhauled to meet sharia guidelines. The official portrait of Pahlavi in his resplendent

The Hostage Crisis

When **Mohammad Reza Pahlavi** (1919–1980; see entry) and his family left Iran in January 1979, they went first to Egypt, where President **Anwar Sadat** (also spelled al-Sadat; 1918–1981; see entry) gave them a warm welcome. Then they went to Morocco, then the Bahamas, and finally Mexico. Already ill with non-Hodgkin's lymphoma, a type of cancer, when he left Iran, Pahlavi suffered other medical problems that prompted him to seek treatment in the United States. When word surfaced that he had been admitted to New York Hospital (present-day New York-Presbyterian Hospital) in late October 1979 under an assumed name, Iran erupted in anger. Ayatollah Khomeini and his newly installed government demanded the return of Pahlavi to Iran to face prosecution. They were particularly critical of U.S. president Jimmy Carter (1924–), who had allowed Pahlavi to enter the United States on humanitarian grounds.

Islamic militants had already carried out occasional attacks on Americans and Westerners in Iran, and Khomeini famously derided the United States as "the Great Satan" in his public pronouncements. Anger against the United States turned deadly on November 4, 1979, when a group of university students stormed the U.S. Embassy in Tehran and took more than fifty Americans hostage. They demanded that the United States send Pahlavi back to Iran, and Khomeini supported the students' actions. Iran's prime minister, Mehdi Bazargan (1907–1995), resigned in disapproval as panic spread over what action the U.S. government might take. The standoff lasted 444 days, with the students symbolically releasing the hostages just after Ronald Reagan (1911–2004) was sworn in as president of the United States in 1981. By then the extradition was no longer a diplomatic issue, for Pahlavi eventually returned to Egypt, where he died on July 27, 1980, at a military hospital outside Cairo.

military uniform that hung in every Iranian home, business, classroom, and government office was replaced by one with Khomeini's stern, turban-wearing image.

War with Iraq

After the stunning victory of Islamic fundamentalists in the 1979 revolution, and the sharp criticism Khomeini had of Western nations and Israel, Iran was perceived throughout the world as a threat to peace and stability. No country was more endangered by the rise of an Islamic fundamentalist government in Iran than neighboring Iraq. In September 1980 Saddam invaded Iran. The move received significant international support, and there was hope for an easy victory. But the Iran-Iraq War (1980–88) lasted much longer than anticipated. In the spring of 1982, Iranian forces pushed back the Iraqi army. Khomeini then surprised many when he issued orders for a retaliatory invasion of Iraq. The war continued for another six years and cost almost one million Iranian and Iraqi lives. It also nearly destroyed the Iranian economy. Finally Khomeini accepted a United Nations Security Council call for a cease-fire, and hostilities formally ended in August 1988. (The United Nations is an international organization of countries founded in 1945 to promote international peace, security, and cooperation.)

After ten years as Supreme Leader of Iran, Khomeini began to appear less frequently in public, giving rise to rumors of illness. He made one final, international-crisis causing decree on February 14, 1989, when he issued a *fatwa* calling for the death of author Salman Rushdie. (A fatwa is statement of religious law issued by an Islamic cleric and intended to instruct devout Muslims.) Rushdie's novel *The Satanic Verses* was considered blasphemous. The fatwa forced him into hiding and he lived under police guard in the West for nearly a decade.

After eleven days in the hospital, and after an operation to stop internal bleeding, Khomeini died on June 3, 1989. The news prompted a public outpouring of grief throughout Iran, with an estimated one million mourners turning out for his funeral and displaying such fervor to see the coffin that eight people died in a stampede. **Ayatollah Ali Khamenei** (also spelled Khāmene'i; 1939–; see entry), one of Khomeini's former students at the Qom seminary, became Iran's second Supreme Leader.

For More Information

BOOKS

Mílaní, Abbas. *Eminent Persians: The Men and Women Who Made Modern Iran, 1941–1979*, vol. 2. New York: Syracuse University Press, 2008.

Moin, Baqer. *Khomeini: Life of the Ayatollah*. New York: Macmillan, 1999, p. 104.

Sciolino, Elaine. *Persian Mirrors: The Elusive Face of Iran*. New York: Simon & Schuster, 2001.

Wright, Robin. *The Last Great Revolution: Turmoil and Transformation in Iran*. New York: Knopf, 2000.

PERIODICALS

Anderson, Raymond H. "Ayatollah Ruhollah Khomeini, 89, Relentless Founder of Iran's Islamic Republic." *New York Times* (June 5, 1989). Available online at http://www.nytimes.com/1989/06/05/world/ayatollah-ruhollah-khomeini-89-relentless-founder-of-iran-s-islamic-republic.html?scp=2&sq=%22white+revolution%22+iran&st=nyt&pagewanted=all (accessed on November 30, 2011).

Markham, James M. "Joy Explodes in Teheran Streets As Millions Welcome Ayatollah." *New York Times* (February 2, 1979): A1. Available online at http://select.nytimes.com/gst/abstract.html?res=F3091FF63B5D12728DD DAB0894DA405B898BF1D3 (accessed on November 30, 2011).

Sadjadpour, Karim. "Arabs Rise, Tehran Trembles." *New York Times* (March 5, 2011). Available online at http://www.nytimes.com/2011/03/06/opinion/ 06sadjapour.html?scp=9&sq=ruhollah+khomeini&st=nyt (accessed on November 30, 2011).

OTHER SOURCES

Imam Khomeini: The Man Who Changed the World. YouTube. http:// www.youtube.com/watch?v=FfrJ2rBobGs (accessed on November 30, 2011).

Tzipporah Livni

BORN: July 8, 1958 • Tel Aviv, Israel

Israeli politician, lawyer

Tzipporah Livni. AP PHOTO/
DAVID KARP.

"Today's Israel is not a safer place for Jews to live than other places in the world. Sometimes Israel is more dangerous."

Tzipporah Livni is one of the few women to wield genuine political power in the Middle East of the modern era. Often compared to **Golda Meir** (1898–1978; see entry), the first woman to serve as prime minister of Israel, Livni heads the Kadima Party in Israel and is widely predicted to succeed Meir one day as the country's next female prime minister. Livni's role as one of the founding members of Kadima marked a surprise shift in her political philosphy, for she was once allied with the country's hard-line conservatives. She then evolved into a supporter of the controversial two-state solution in the Israeli-Palestinian peace process, a solution that would grant Palestinians an independent state. (Palestinians are an Arab people whose ancestors lived in the historical region of Palestine, comprising parts of present-day Israel and Jordan, and who continue to lay claim to that land.)

Early life

Tzipporah Livni, whose given name means "bird" in Hebrew (the ancient language of the Jewish people and the official language of present-day Israel), was born in Tel Aviv, Israel, on July 8, 1958, a few months after the country celebrated its tenth anniversary as a nation. Both of her parents had been active in Irgun Zvai Leumi, militant underground group founded in 1931 that worked to secure Israeli independence by staging violent attacks on British and Arab targets. (Arabs are people of the Middle East and North Africa who speak the Arabic language or who live in countries in which Arabic is the dominant language.) Irgun's goal was to aid in the establishment of a Jewish homeland in Palestine, which at that time was a British mandate, or a territory entrusted to foreign administration.

Livni's father was a Polish Jew who came to Palestine as a child in the mid–1920s as part of a renewed push for Jewish settlement there, a movement called Zionism. The goal of Zionism was to create a national homeland for the world's Jews, who had faced much social, economic, and political discrimination throughout history. Fixing their sights on Palestine, land once controlled by the ancient Israelite kingdom of biblical times, Zionist groups began a long and intensive process to claim this region as theirs. The problem was that Arab Palestinians already lived there. These people were predominantly Muslims and their ancestors had lived there for centuries.

Livni's parents, Eitan and Sara, met as Irgun fighters and Eitan eventually served as head of Irgun operations. They both participated in a major sabotage of British railways in 1946 and were jailed for it, but escaped in a dramatic prison break in Acre, a city in northern Israel. Irgun's most notorious act was the bombing of the King David Hotel in Jerusalem, on July 22, 1946, which killed ninety-one people. The hotel housed the headquarters of British officials, and in the aftermath of the tragedy British public opinion came to favor a full-scale withdrawal from Palestine. Livni's father was chief of Irgun operations at the time of the bombing. Her parents are also believed to have participated in the Deir Yassin massacre of April 1948, when the Arab village of Deir Yassin was attacked. The number of Arab Palestinians killed is uncertain. Some sources say that around two hundred fifty men, women, and children were killed; other sources place the number closer to one hundred. That incident came just weeks before the final withdrawal of British troops. The State of Israel was declared on May 14, 1948. Livni's parents were the first couple to be married by the new civil authority.

The right-wing views of Livni's family shaped her formative years. Even before the creation of Israel, the population of Palestine was generally divided between "doves," those who supported more diplomatic efforts to deal with the Palestinians and hostile Arab neighbors, and "hawks," those who argued that a well-armed and offensive-ready army was the best solution to ensure Israel's safety. Livni's parents were among the hawks. They were close to **Menachem Begin** (1913–1992; see entry), the former head of Irgun who went on to found the Herut Party. As a child, Livni and her brother Eli spent weekends with Begin and his family. Livni's father was active in the Herut Party and was elected to the Knesset, Israel's parliament, in 1973. When Livni was twelve years old, her school contacted her parents because she disagreed with her teachers over some interpretations of Israel's recent history. Eitan and Sara supported their daughter by arguing with the teachers on her behalf. Livni was a member of the Betar scouts, a militant youth group founded by Vladimir Ze'v Jabotinsky (1880–1940), in the 1920s. Betar was active in Eastern Europe and the United States during World War II and later allied with the Herut Party.

Joins army, then Mossad

Two Arab-Israeli wars also influenced Livni's political education and the troubled status of her homeland. The first was the 1967 Arab-Israeli War (known in Israel as the Six-Day War), in which Israeli forces seized significant parcels of land from their Arab neighbors. They took the Sinai Peninsula and the Gaza Strip from Egypt, the West Bank and East Jerusalem from Jordan, and the Golan Heights from Syria. Six years later, Egypt and Syria combined forces to launch the 1973 Arab-Israeli War (known in Israel as the Yom Kippur War). That conflict was marked by major international involvement. The United States played a key role in the unfolding of the drama; they had already provided military aid to Israel and U.S. Secretary of State Henry Kissinger (1923–) had contacted Israel urging them not to launch a preemptive strike. The Soviet Union tactically aided Egypt by providing crucial intelligence data from Soviet satellites showing Israeli troop movements. The threat of a nuclear missile strike by Israel loomed, and the United States negotiated a deal

Mossad

Tzipporah Livni joined Mossad, Israel's intelligence service, in 1980. Mossad was quite active in Europe at that time. It gained a reputation for finding Nazi war criminals who had evaded prosecution for war crimes in the aftermath of World War II (1939–45). During that conflict, Nazi Germany carried out an extensive plan to annihilate the Jews of Europe. The mass murder of six million European Jews and other groups became known as the Holocaust. Mossad either kidnapped and transported the Nazi war criminals to Israel for trial or assassinated them.

Mossad operated with similar aims to extract revenge for the massacre of Israeli athletes at the 1972 Olympic Games in Munich, Germany. The athletes were taken hostage by members of Black September, a pro-Palestinian militant group, and the event was captured by the news media that was there to cover the games. The situation ended tragically with a failed rescue attempt at a Munich airfield in which the Black September militants killed the remaining Israeli hostages. Israel's first female prime minister, **Golda Meir**

(1898–1978; see entry), was in office at the time of the Munich Massacre and authorized Mossad to conduct a covert mission code-named Operation Wrath of God. Its mission was to search for and assassinate the Black September militants who had eluded death or capture at the Munich airfield, along with members of the Palestinian Liberation Organization (PLO), which had ties to Black September. (The PLO is a political and military organization formed to unite various Palestinian Arab groups with the goal of establishing an independent Palestinian state.) The mission lasted nearly two decades, and several of the assassinations were carried out on European soil. This Mossad operation is dramatized in the 2005 movie *Munich*.

It is not known what missions Livni participated in during her time with Mossad. She spoke fluent French and posed as a student at the Sorbonne, a university in Paris, France. She may have run safe houses (houses in a secret location, used as hiding places or a secure refuge) for other Mossad agents during her time in the French capital.

between Egypt and Israel known as the 1975 Sinai Interim Agreement. Livni was a teenager when she took to the streets of Tel Aviv to join protests against the terms of the agreement. The 1973 Arab-Israeli War spurred a dramatic political shift in Israel, with Begin's new party, the Likud Party, finally gaining a significant number of seats in the Knesset.

On her eighteenth birthday in July 1976, Livni became eligible for military service, which is required of Israeli Jews of both sexes upon reaching the age of eighteen; men serve three years while women are required to serve two years. Livni completed officer training school and rose to the rank of lieutenant in the Israel Defense Forces (IDF). Following her discharge, she worked in a café in the Sinai Peninsula and in a hotel in Tel Aviv.

A friend from her childhood recruited Livni for Mossad, Israel's intelligence service. She joined Mossad in 1980 at the age of twenty-two, undergoing rigorous training and then moving to Paris, France. "It was wonderful," was all Livni would say of her life in Mossad in an interview with Steven Erlanger of the *New York Times*.

Allies with Netanyahu

After leaving Mossad, Livni earned a law degree at Bar-Ilan University near Tel Aviv and went to work as a real estate attorney. She also married and had two sons. As Israel's political climate shifted in the 1990s, she became more interested in a political career. In the 1996 Knesset elections the Labor Party lost several seats and **Benjamin Netanyahu** (1949–; see entry), the new head of the Likud Party, became prime minister. Livni had run for a seat in that election but lost by slim margin. Netanyahu, impressed with her skills and her family's unwavering conservatism, hired her to run a privatization program called the Government Corporate Authority, which was set up to turn previously state-run government industries over to the private sector.

Livni was elected to the Knesset in 1999, and Labor Party chief Ehud Barak (1942–) became prime minister. After the failure of the 1993 Oslo Accords, an agreement between Israel and the Palestinian Liberation Organization (PLO) to establish a framework for peace, Arab leaders and their Israeli counterparts met once again, this time at Camp David, the U.S. presidential retreat in Maryland, in 2000, but they failed to come to an agreement. The stalled peace process wearied many Israelis, which helped Likud's **Ariel Sharon** (1928–; see entry) win the 2001 election for prime minister, and he named Livni to serve as his minister of regional cooperation. He then appointed her minister for agriculture in 2002. From 2003 to 2006 she headed the Ministry for Immigrant Absorption and also held the cabinet post for Housing and Construction. She served a as minister of justice, too, from 2004 to 2006.

Joining the Kadima Party

In 2005 Livni joined Sharon's new political party, the Kadima Party. It was formed in response to divisions in Likud and took a more moderate stance on the still heatedly debated Arab-Israeli peace process. This marked an important break in Livni's political life, for one of Kadima's crucial platforms was to support Prime Minister Sharon's implementation of the disengagement plan earlier that year. This plan announced the complete withdrawal is Israelis from settlements in the West Bank and partial withdrawal from the Gaza Strip. (The West Bank and the Gaza Strip are Arab regions occupied by Israel after the 1967 Arab-Israeli War.) Livni had even authored part of Kadima's mission statement, which included support for Palestinian statehood. "Just as Israel was established for the Jewish people and gave refuge to them from European and Arab states, so a Palestinian state is the homeland of the Palestinian people, those who live in the territories and those who left in 1948 and are being kept as political cards in refugee camps," she told *New York Times Magazine* writer Roger Cohen. "This is the national answer. The solution for Palestinians is the Palestinian state. Israel is not part of the solution."

Livni had also played a role in the 2004 creation of Sharon's disengagement plan, suggesting a compromise that helped win its final approval. She also met with U.S. secretary of state Condoleezza Rice (1954–) and then–U.S. president George W. Bush (1946–), who in April 2004 became first U.S. president to agree that Palestinians need to be settled in a separate and independent Palestinian state. But the disengagement plan was widely criticized by right-wing Israelis, for it involved the expulsion of West Bank and Gaza Strip settlers who had been encouraged to move to there as far back as the early 1980s. At that time, these were important new territories for Israel, and young Israeli families were urged to fulfill

Tzipporah Livni and Prime Minister Ariel Sharon attending a Knesset (parliament) session in 2005. That year Livni joined Sharon's new political party, Kadima, and authored part of the party's mission statement.
GALI TIBBON/AFP/GETTY IMAGES.

their patriotic duty and settle there. International law, however, deemed the region unlawfully occupied territories. The debate over the rightful ownership of the West Bank and the Gaza Strip was one of the reasons the Israeli-Palestinian peace process had been stalled for so many years.

Livni's new political affiliation marked a significant shift relevant to the history of her family. Hard-liners like her parents had been firmly committed to the idea of Eretz Israel ("Land of Israel" in Hebrew; the ancient kingdom of the Jews). According to Genesis, the first book of the Jewish and Christian Bible, God had promised this land to the prophet Abraham and his descendants. Right-wing Israelis believe that this so-called "promised land" includes the Sinai Peninsula and the West Bank. But Livni came to support Sharon's willingness to return to the country's pre–1967 borders for a two-state solution—with an independent state for Palestinians. "A few years ago, when I was interviewed on Israeli television, I said I support the idea of two nation-states. I was afraid that my mother was listening," Livni recalled in an interview with Deborah Solomon for the *New York Times Magazine* in 2010. "But then one day she called me and said, 'I hear you. It gives me pain. But you need to make decisions about the future of Israel. We didn't establish this state for having just old people living here.'"

Named foreign minister

Israel's dramatic shift in carrying out Prime Minister Sharon's disengagement plan was hampered by the loss of Sharon, who suffered a stroke in November 2005 not long after the founding of the Kadima Party. A second stroke, in early 2006, permanently incapacitated him and he remained in a coma. His deputy prime minister, Ehud Olmert (1945–), became acting prime minister, and in an emergency cabinet reorganization Livni became the new minister of foreign affairs. She was the first woman to serve in that job since Meir, who served from 1955 to 1966. In March 2006 Livni was reelected to her Knesset seat, and after another round of elections in April due to Sharon's inability to carry out his duties, Olmert won the permanent post of prime minister and named Livni deputy prime minister. She remained in that post, and as minister of foreign affairs, until the end of March 2009.

The most dramatic incident to hamper the Israeli-Palestinian peace process came in June 2006, when Israeli soldier Gilad Shalit (1986–) was abducted by Hamas, an Islamic militant organization, in the Gaza Strip.

(Shalit was released in October 2011 in exchange for 1,027 Palestinian prisoners.) Five months earlier, Palestinians had elected members of Hamas to a majority of seats in the Palestinian Legislative Council, the legislative authority of the Palestinian Authority, the recognized governing institution for Palestinians in the West Bank and the Gaza Strip, established in 1993 as part of the Oslo Accords. On July 12, two more Israeli soldiers were kidnapped by Hezbollah, another Islamic militant organization, based in Lebanon. (Hamas is affiliated with the Sunni branch of the religion of Islam, while Hezbollah is with the Shia branch). The two soldiers were killed in a raid near the border with Lebanon, which marked the start of the three-and-a-half-week-long Israel-Lebanon War of 2006. In that conflict, Israel carried out significant bomb attacks on its Arab neighbor and invaded southern Lebanon. As minister of foreign affairs, Livni's role in the start of the war was later revealed to have been hampered by Olmert's apparent mistrust of her; she was not informed about the start of air strikes, for example. She did play a vital role in negotiating elements of the pre-cease-fire terms, which included an United Nations Interim Force in Lebanon (UNIFIL) and the withdrawal of Israeli ground forces from Lebanon.

A month later, Israel launched an official inquiry into the its war with Lebanon. The preliminary report was released in April 2007, and it was critical of Olmert and his defense minister, Amir Peretz (1952–). Livni called for Olmert to resign as head of the Kadima Party, based on his conduct and other allegations involving corruption. The stalemate over Olmert's political future and the date of his resignation dragged on until September 17, 2008, when Livni won the Kadima leadership primary race. She beat out Transportation Minister Shaul Mofaz, an Iranian-born Jew, war veteran, and staunch hard-liner. Livni told her supporters, "We have proved that in tough times, even in times of despair, we can replace despair with hope, and we can also dream," according to Rory McCarthy in the *Guardian* newspaper. "We have proved that security does not belong only to the right and peace does not belong only to the left." That same year, Livni dismissed doubts about her becoming prime minister of Israel. "The fact that I'm a woman doesn't make me a weak leader," she told Gil Hoffman of the *Jerusalem Post*, adding that Hezbollah leader **Hassan Nasrallah** (1960–; see entry) "said after the war that had he known that Israel would have fought back the way we did, he wouldn't have started the war. I would like to think that generals also think twice when they make decisions, just like I do. It's not that generals pull the trigger and women don't. I have no problem pulling the trigger when necessary."

Distancing herself from Olmert

Livni was still serving as foreign minister when Israel used force to halt rocket attacks from the Gaza Strip by Hamas militants. This three-week conflict is known as the 2008–09 Gaza War, and it was part of Israel's larger plan to quash Hamas militants that included a blockade by the Israeli navy in place since 2007. Israel's belligerent actions in the Gaza Strip to eliminate the Hamas threat aroused serious concern, and even more moderate Jews were appalled at the death toll, which was estimated at one thousand civilians. International news media repeatedly showed images of Palestinian casualties, which prompted reactions ranging from dismay to anger at Israel's actions. In an interview with David Samuels for the online magazine *Tablet* in 2010, Livni explained that civilian deaths sometimes occur. "Even though [Jews elsewhere] feel uneasy when these pictures are coming, they need to understand that these things happen when you defend your own citizens."

Hamas was founded during the First Intifada, a Palestinian uprising against Israeli occupation in the West Bank and the Gaza Strip, in the late 1980s. Its leaders are Holocaust deniers, people who believe that the Holocaust, the mass murder of European Jews and other groups by the Nazis during World War II (1939–45), was an elaborate hoax and that it aided the formation of Israel. Hamas also advocates the destruction of Israel, the removal of Jews, and the establishment of an Islamic state in its place.

Livni was involved in peace talks in Paris at which the leaders of several European Union (EU; an economic and political association of European countries) nations negotiated a cease-fire for the 2008–09 Gaza War. As a way to evade the naval blockade, relief ships were stocked and sent by international humanitarian agencies, but IDF vessels intercepted them. Livni was widely condemned for asserting there was no humanitarian crisis in the Gaza Strip.

The 2008–09 Gaza War ended in mid–January, just a few weeks ahead of Knesset elections on February 10, 2009. Led by Livni, the Kadima Party won the most seats, but two other parties also polled high numbers, so **Shimon Peres** (1929–; see entry), now the president of Israel, asked Netanyahu and the Likud Party to form a coalition government, in which

An Israeli woman walks by an election poster for Tzipporah Livni in Tel Aviv, in 2009. © PAVEL WOLBERG/EPA/ CORBIS.

political parties cooperate with each other, because no party holds the majority. Livni resigned as deputy prime minister and as minister of foreign affairs on the last day of March 2009, becoming instead the official leader of the opposition in the Knesset. The next legislative election is scheduled for February 10, 2013. Livni is widely expected to become her party's frontrunner for the 2013 election.

For More Information

BOOKS

Harel, Amos, and Avi Issacharoff. *34 Days: Israel, Hezbollah, and the War in Lebanon.* Translated by Ora Cummings and Moshe Tlamin. New York: Macmillan, 2009.

PERIODICALS

Cohen, Roger. "Her Jewish State." *New York Times Magazine* (July 8, 2007).

Erlanger, Steven. "Israel's Top Envoy: Lawyer Who Evokes Meir." *New York Times* (February 5, 2006): A10. Available online at http://www.nytimes.com/2006/02/05/international/middleeast/05livni.html?scp=1&sq=livni+meir&st=nyt (accessed on November 30, 2011).

Goldberg, Michelle. "Interview: Tzipi Livni." *Newsweek* (June 6, 2011): 26.

Hider, James, Charles Bremner, and Fran Yeoman. "The Secret Life of Tzipi Livni." *Times* (London, England) (September 20, 2008). Available online at http://www.timesonline.co.uk/tol/news/world/middle_east/article4791158.ece (accessed on November 30, 2011).

Hoffman, Gil. "Politics: Primary Concerns." *Jerusalem Post* (September 11, 2008). Available online at http://www.jpost.com/Features/FrontLines/Article.aspx?id=114140 (accessed on November 30, 2011).

Joffe, Lawrence. "Looking at Livni." *The Middle East.* (November 2008): 18.

McCarthy, Rory. "Profile: Tzipi Livni." *Guardian* (London, England; September 17, 2008): 21.

Solomon, Deborah, "Leader of the Opposition." *New York Times Magazine* (June 24, 2010). Available online at http://www.nytimes.com/2010/06/27/magazine/27FOB-Q4-t.html?scp=1&sq=livni+Leader+of+the+Opposition&st=nyt (accessed on November 30, 2011).

WEB SITES

"Livni: No Crisis in Gaza Strip." *Aljazeera* (January 1, 2009). http://english.aljazeera.net/news/europe/2009/01/20091115532645312.html (accessed on November 30, 2011).

"Profile: Tzipi Livni." *BBC News* (February 3, 2009). http://news.bbc.co.uk/2/hi/7621536.stm (accessed on November 30, 2011).

Samuels, David. "Q&A: Tzipi Livni." *Tablet* (October 8, 2010). http://www.tabletmag.com/news-and-politics/46846/qa-tzipi-livni/ (accessed on November 30, 2011).

"Tzipi Livni, MK." *Israeli Ministry of Foreign Affairs.* http://www.mfa.gov.il/mfa/about%20the%20ministry/foreign%20minister%20livni/bio/ (accessed on November 30, 2011).

Golda Meir

BORN: May 3, 1898 • Kiev, Ukraine

DIED: December 8, 1978 • Jerusalem, Israel

Israeli prime minister, political activist

"We have always said that in our war with the Arabs we had a secret weapon—no alternative."

Golda Meir (pronounced may-EAR) became the first woman elected prime minister of Israel. Her dynamic, forceful presence both in the Knesset, the Israeli parliament, and on the world stage made her a heroic figure to a generation of Israelis and the symbolic leader of their Jewish nationalism. (Nationalism is devotion and loyalty to the nation and its culture.) Often described as the grandmother of Israel—she was seventy years old when she took office—Meir was active in Zionism, an international political movement that called for the creation of an independent Jewish state in Palestine, for years before Israel was founded in 1948. (Palestine is a historical region in the Middle East on the eastern shore of the Mediterranean Sea, comprising parts of present-day Israel and Jordan.) She spent a decade as foreign minister in the 1950s and 1960s, helping to arrange the foundation for Israel's nuclear program. Meir resigned as prime minister in 1974 after the 1973 Arab-Israeli War

Golda Meir. AP PHOTO.

generations, launched a military operation against Israel. The 1948 Arab-Israeli War (known in Israel as the War for Independence) ended with a decisive Israeli victory. However, the conflict between Israel and its Arab neighbors over who had rightful ownership of the region would remain unresolved well into the first decades of the twenty-first century.

The turmoil in her newly formed country did not deter Meir from continuing her efforts. She was elected into the first Knesset in 1949, as a candidate of the Mapai Party, the country's strongest political party. She remained in the government for the next twenty-five years. Israel's first prime minister, David Ben-Gurion, issued Meir the new country's first passport in 1949 and sent her to the Soviet Union as Israel's ambassador to that country. She served in that job for seven months, until Ben-Gurion appointed her to his cabinet as minister of labor and development, a position in which she remained until 1956. As minister of labor, Meir worked to improve the living conditions of Israel's tens of thousands of immigrants, many of whom were living in tents. She initiated Israel's first national insurance bill; oversaw the development of the Meyerson Plan (at the time Meir was still using her married name), which provided for the building of thirty thousand low-cost housing units; and created a public works program to create jobs for Israelis. During her tenure, Meir eliminated Jewish tent cities in Israel and built roads, dubbed "golden roads" in her honor.

Reaching the top levels of government

Ben-Gurion appointed Meir to be his foreign minister in 1956. The position is considered the second-most important role in the Israeli government. Showing his respect for the tough Meir, Ben-Gurion declared her "the only man" in his cabinet, according to author Robert Slater in *Golda, the Uncrowned Queen of Israel.* As foreign minister, Meir negotiated cooperative efforts between Israel, Great Britain, and France to aid Israel. For example, France provided scientific help to launch a nuclear-energy program that would help Israel be self-sufficient. She also began a series of trips to Africa in order to win support and allegiance from African nations for Israel. She noticed that the emerging African nations were going through the same growing pains that Israel had experienced. She sent Israeli doctors, teachers, and engineers to Africa in order to help these new nations, which had previously been managed by Western powers, such as France and Great Britain. She succeeded masterfully, although many

Golda Meir waves as she leaves the Tel Aviv Airport in 1948 to begin her appointment as the first Israeli ambassador to the Soviet Union. AP PHOTO/JIM PRINGLE.

African countries later switched their allegiance from Israel to Arab nations after Meir left her position.

In 1965 at age sixty-seven Meir retired from some of her government duties. She resigned her cabinet position but continued to serve in the Knesset and remained active on the executive board of the Mapai Party. She had been diagnosed with cancer two years earlier and suffered a variety of other health problems that required frequent medical care. Meir kept the true nature of her health problems secret from even her closest friends, and each of her trips to the hospital was dismissed as related to a minor problem, such as a cold or fatigue. Not until her death would the public learn the severity of Meir's health problems. With fewer government responsibilities, Meir enjoyed spending time with her grandchildren.

Although her health continued to limit her activities, Meir remained a strong force within the Mapai Party. Party members strongly disagreed with each other, and many feared the party would suffer from its internal power struggles. By 1966 it became clear to Meir that she must come out of her semiretirement to assume the leadership of the party as its secretary-general. She was considered by most Mapai supporters to be a force so powerful and trustworthy that only she possessed the ability to unite the warring factions. "I truly believed that the future of the labor movement was at stake," Meir explains in her autobiography. "And although I could hardly bear the idea of giving up the peace and quiet I had finally attained—even if only for a few months—I couldn't turn my back at this stage of my life either on my principles or on my colleagues. So I said yes and went back to work, to traveling, to incessant meetings and to the bondage of an appointment book."

Becoming prime minister

As secretary-general, Meir worked hard to unify her party. When Israeli prime minister Levi Eshkol (1895–1969), who had succeeded Ben-Gurion in 1963, died on February 26, 1969, his cabinet members selected Meir to be his successor. Meir stepped in as interim prime minister, and in October of that year she was elected to her own four-year term in office. Upon her election as the fourth prime minister of Israel, Meir became one of only a few women to lead a nation at that time. As prime minister, Meir spent a great deal of time trying to negotiate peace in the Middle East. Israel had captured territory during the 1967 Arab-Israeli War (known in Israel as the Six-Day War) that more than doubled its size and created thousands of Arab refugees. (Refugees are people who flee their country to escape violence or persecution.) Israel had hoped to use the territory as a bargaining tool in peace negotiations with neighboring Arab nations. No nation would negotiate, however, and Israel remained in a state of alert while fending off periodic attacks along its borders.

"No Such Thing as Palestinians"

During the 1948 and 1967 Arab-Israeli Wars, thousands of Palestinians became refugees, people who flee their country to escape violence or persecution. These predominantly Muslim Palestinians have been seeking recognition of their right to their own nation ever since.

When Meir assumed the position of Israeli prime minister in 1969, Palestinians were becoming more organized and vocal. In an attempt to stop the growing momentum of the Palestinian movement, Meir declared, as quoted in the *Sunday Times* newspaper of London:

> There was no such thing as Palestinians. When was there an independent Palestinian people with a Palestinian state? It was either southern Syria before the first world war [World War I] and then it was a Palestine including Jordan. It was not as though there was a Palestinian people in Palestine considering itself as a Palestinian people and we came and threw them out and took their country away from them. They did not exist.

Meir's words infuriated Palestinians and further ignited their desire for their own homeland.

Many of them had lived on the land that was now Israel for generations. Arab countries contended that Palestinians had been evicted from their homes and had an equal, if not greater, right to that land. One of the most powerful groups to emerge out of this conflict was the Palestine Liberation Organization (PLO), a political and military organization formed to unite various Palestinian Arab groups with the goal of establishing an independent Palestinian state. The PLO committed itself not only to the creation of a Palestinian state, but also to the destruction of Israel.

As tensions between Israelis and Palestinians grew, according to author Robert Slater in *Golda, the Uncrowned Queen of Israel*, Meir later tried to soften the meaning of her earlier statement, saying, "I am a Palestinian. From 1921 to 1948 I held a Palestinian passport. And I was aware that there were Arabs and Jews in Palestine and that all were Palestinians." Her words did little to lessen Arab outrage.

SLATER, ROBERT. *GOLDA, THE UNCROWNED QUEEN OF ISRAEL: A PICTORIAL BIOGRAPHY.* MIDDLE VILLAGE, NY: DAVID, 1981.

Meir kept in daily contact with her advisers and ministers. She often met with influential members of her political party around her kitchen table the Saturday night before official Sunday meetings of her cabinet members. Doing so kept her informed of all the issues facing her country.

Peace was the most pressing issue in Israel during Meir's tenure as prime minister. On October 6, 1973, Syria and Egypt launched the 1973 Arab-Israeli War (known in Israel as the Yom Kippur War) to win back some of the territories they lost to Israel during the 1967 Arab-Israeli War. Although Meir and other Israeli officials secured military aid from

Golda Meir leaves a closed meeting of the Labor Coalition in Jerusalem after announcing her intention to resign as prime minister. AP PHOTO/MAX NASH.

the United States, the war, which ended in late October, resulted in heavy losses of Israeli soldiers, although no loss of territory. Meir's popularity in Israel suffered. An investigation was conducted to discover who in the Israeli government was responsible for the country's lack of readiness at the onset of the war. As tensions within Israel rose, Meir declared her desire to retire, but members of her Labor Party convinced her to remain in office through the next elections.

Resignation

When Meir won reelection on December 31, 1973, she was unsure of her ability to continue in the role of prime minister. She was tired and uncertain of her ability to successfully govern. Although party members convinced her to stay in office for a while, Meir's feelings did not change. On April 10, 1974, Meir announced her final retirement, and as she writes in her autobiography, she told her colleagues, "Five years are sufficient. It is beyond my strength to continue carrying this burden.... I beg of you not to try to persuade me to change my mind for any reason at all. It will not help."

Meir lived quietly in Jerusalem for another four years. She died of cancer on December 8, 1978. Only upon her death did her closest friends learn of her struggle with the disease. Her funeral was attended by almost one hundred thousand mourners from around the world.

Meir's grandmotherly likeness is periodically resurrected on stage, in film, and on television, including Swedish actress Ingrid Bergman's (1915–1982) final film, *A Woman Called Golda,* in 1982. In 2003 *Golda's Balcony,* a one-woman play by American playwright and novelist William Gibson (1914–2008) that followed Meir's intriguing journey from a small Jewish town to Milwaukee to Jerusalem, opened on Broadway in New York City. Meir remains one of the most popular historical figures for successive generations of Israelis and Jews everywhere.

For More Information

BOOKS

Adler, David A. *Our Golda: The Story of Golda Meir.* New York: Viking, 1984.

Gelvin, James L. *The Israel-Palestine Conflict: One Hundred Years of War.* New York: Cambridge University Press, 2005, p. 92.

Hitzeroth, Deborah. *The Importance of Golda Meir.* San Diego, CA: Lucent Books, 1998.

McAuley, Karen. *Golda Meir.* New York: Chelsea House, 1985.

Meir, Golda. *A Land of Our Own.* New York: Putnam, 1973.

———. *My Life.* New York: Putnam, 1975.

Meir, Menahem. *My Mother, Golda Meir: A Son's Evocation of Life with Golda Meir.* New York: Arbor House, 1983.

Pasachoff, Naomi. *Links in the Chain.* New York: Oxford University Press, 1997.

Slater, Robert. *Golda, the Uncrowned Queen of Israel: A Pictorial Biography.* Middle Village, NY: David, 1981.

PERIODICALS

"Israel's Golda Meir." *Time* (September 19, 1969). Available online at http://www.time.com/time/magazine/article/0,9171,901451,00.html (accessed on November 30, 2011)

Stolley, Richard. "'We Won Our Wars—We Don't Need Victories." *Life* (October 3, 1969): 32–33.

WEB SITES

"Golda Meir." *Jewish Virtual Library.* http://www.jewishvirtuallibrary.org/jsource/biography/meir.html (accessed on November 30, 2011).

"Golda Meir." *BBC Online Network.* http://news.bbc.co.uk/1/hi/events/israel_at_50/profiles/81288.stm (accessed on November 30, 2005).

The Golda Meir Center for Political Leadership. http://www.goldameircenter.org (accessed on November 30, 2005).

OTHER SOURCES

The Spielberg Jewish Film Archive—Line of Life with Golda Meir. YouTube. http://www.youtube.com/watch?v=ghWwEuHIH8w 9 (accessed on November 30, 2011).

Hosni Mubarak

BORN: May 4, 1928 • Kafr El-Meselha, Monufia Governate, Egypt

Egyptian president, military leader

"This is my country. This is where I lived, I fought and defended its land, sovereignty and interests, and I will die on its soil."

Hosni Mubarak was one of Egypt's longest-ruling leaders. He became the president of Egypt after the assassination of President **Anwar Sadat** (also spelled al-Sadat; 1918–1981; see entry) in 1981, and he skillfully guided Egypt to a position of power in the Middle East while maintaining peace with Israel. He was also successful in discouraging the rising influence of Islamic fundamentalism in Egypt. (Fundamentalism is a movement stressing adherence to a strict or literal interpretation of religious principles.) As calls for democratic reforms intensified in the first years of the twenty-first century, however, Mubarak proved resistant to change, and ultimately it was mass protests by Egyptians in the city of Cairo in the early months of 2011 that resulted in the end of his presidency. The ousting of Mubarak was part of a series of prodemocracy uprisings across the Middle East and North Africa that became known as the Arab Spring.

Hosni Mubarak. KHALED DESOUKI/AFP/GETTY IMAGES.

Early life and military career

Born on May 4, 1928, Mubarak was one of five children in a family of modest means. They lived in Monufia Governate, a province in the Nile Delta region of Egypt. His father worked as an inspector for the Ministry of Justice and inspired his son to seek a government career himself. Mubarak chose military service and graduated from the elite Egyptian Military Academy in 1949. He then trained at the Egyptian Air Force Academy, graduating in 1952 and remaining there for several more years as a flight instructor.

Mubarak was twenty-four years old when a group of higher-ranking officers in the Egyptian military carried out a successful coup (overthrow of the government) in July 1952. They ousted King Farouk I (1920–1965) and the monarchy was formally abolished a year later. The higher-ranking officers were members of the Free Officers Organization led by **Gamal Abdel Nasser** (1918–1970; see entry), who eventually assumed the presidency. In 1956 Nasser stunned the world when he announced that he was nationalizing (bringing under government ownership and control) the strategic Suez Canal, a shipping canal that connects the Mediterranean Sea with the Red Sea. This action sparked an international incident in which France and Great Britain teamed with Israel for a brief war against Egypt, but Egypt prevailed, in part because of generous Soviet military aid.

In 1964 Mubarak was among a number of Egyptian Air Force officers selected for advanced training in the Soviet Union. He learned to fly the Soviet Tupolev TU-16 bomber jets and studied at Moscow's Frunze Military Academy, the top military school in the Soviet Union. "After we were nominated [to attend Frunze], Nasser called us in," one of Mubarak's colleagues recalled years later, as quoted by Mary Anne Weaver in her book, *A Portrait of Egypt: A Journey through the World of Militant Islam.* "And he told us that he had only one request: he wanted us to return home as anti-Communists." (Communism is a system of government in which the state plans and controls the economy and a single political party holds power. The Soviet Union was a Communist nation.)

Returning to Egypt in 1965, Mubarak began to rise through the ranks of the Egyptian Air Force. He became a wing commander, then base commander for the Cairo West Air Base in October 1966. He was on duty when the 1967 Arab-Israeli War erupted on June 5, 1967. There had been conflict between Israel and neighboring Arab nations since 1948, when the Jewish nation was established in Palestine (a historical region in the Middle East on the eastern shore of the Mediterranean Sea, comprising parts of present-day Israel and Jordan). Jews had worked to establish a homeland in Palestine, the site of the ancient Jewish kingdom, in order to escape the discrimination and violence they had long faced throughout the world. But the area was already populated by Arabs, who had lived there for hundreds of years. When the state of Israel was established, Arab nations believed that the Jews had taken over land that rightfully belonged to Arab Palestinians. This was a source of conflict that led to several Arab-Israeli Wars.

The 1967 Arab-Israeli War began when Israeli planes launched a surprise, devastating strike against Egypt's air force, disabling nearly five hundred planes and preventing air defense when Israeli ground troops invaded Egypt's Sinai Peninsula. Mubarak ordered the remaining Cairo West squadrons to head south to safety, to bases near the cities of Aswan and Luxor. When the war ended, Egypt had lost the Sinai Peninsula and the Gaza Strip to Israel. Israel had also captured the heavily populated West Bank from Jordan and the Golan Heights from Syria.

Mubarak was promoted to air force commander in November 1967 and became director of the Egyptian Air Force Academy. In June 1969 Nasser made him chief of staff for the air force. In 1970 Nasser died and was succeeded by his vice president, Anwar Sadat, who singled out Mubarak as a loyal and trusted part of his inner circle. In April 1972 Mubarak became commander in chief of the air force, and Sadat gave Mubarak added duties as deputy minister of military affairs. During this period, Mubarak played a key role in rebuilding Egypt's crippled air force.

War hero

Mubarak became a national hero on October 6, the first day of the 1973 Arab-Israeli War, when he led the first strike on Israeli targets in the Sinai Peninsula. He was in charge of a twenty-minute Egyptian air attack that destroyed nearly all of the intended targets, and that victory, in turn, allowed Egypt's ground forces to march across the Suez Canal and retake part of the Sinai Peninsula on October 7, in Operation Badr. The territory taken in the 1973 Arab-Israeli War marked the first significant victory of an Arab nation against Israel and renewed nationalist pride across the Middle East.

On April 15, 1975, President Sadat appointed Mubarak as vice president of Egypt. Mubarak quickly proved himself a skillful negotiator, leading several diplomatic missions to Arab nations, Europe, and, most importantly, Israel. As Sadat became increasingly interested in personally negotiating with Israel in the late 1970s, Mubarak began to assume more control over Egypt's internal affairs. Sadat authorized Mubarak to run weekly cabinet meetings as well as the country's intelligence services, to oversee the development of Egypt's nuclear energy program, and to undertake other duties of the president's office. By 1978 Mubarak had also become vice chair of the National Democratic Party (NDP), the party created by Sadat.

Becomes president

On October 6, 1981, at a military parade commemorating the victory of Operation Badr, Mubarak and Sadat, who were watching the parade from a raised viewing stand, were attacked. As fighter jets streaked through the sky in celebratory flyovers, soldiers emerged from a truck in the parade lineup and began throwing grenades and firing automatic weapons at the presidential viewing stand. Sadat was fatally wounded, and Mubarak was hit in the hand.

The assassination was carried out by Islamic fundamentalists who opposed Sadat's 1979 peace treaty with Israel. The treaty was the result of the 1978 Camp David Accords, a peace agreement reached by Sadat and Israeli prime minister **Menachem Begin** (1913–1992; see entry), and made Egypt the first Arab nation to sign a peace treaty with Israel. For this Sadat was vilified as a traitor to the Palestinian cause. Mubarak announced Sadat's death with an emotional tribute broadcast to the nation. "God's will wanted the leader [Sadat] to become a martyr [someone who dies for a cause] in the day which in itself was a symbol for him and among his soldiers, his heroes, and among the millions of his people who were celebrating gloriously the anniversary of the day in which the Arab nation restored its dignity and glory," he said, as quoted by the *New York Times* in an October 7, 1981, article. Mubarak also pledged that the nation remained "committed to all charters, treaties, and international obligations which Egypt has concluded, and that we would not stop pushing the peace wheel in compliance with the mission carried by the leader."

Fearful that the assassination might lead to political instability in the country, Mubarak and the NDP moved quickly to affirm their authority.

On October 7, 1981, the People's Assembly of Egypt, the lower house of the legislature, unanimously approved a motion that named Mubarak as Sadat's successor. On October 13, Egyptians went to the polls and affirmed Mubarak as Egypt's president with 98 percent of the vote. The country's Emergency Law, a form of martial law that gave the police and judicial authorities broad powers to detain citizens without trial, also went into effect on the day of Sadat's assassination and remained in place for thirty years. The Emergency Law allowed government censors to operate freely and forbid public gatherings of five or more people without a permit. Ignoring persistent calls for its repeal, Mubarak kept the Emergency Law in place as an effective tool to supress political opposition.

Restores ties to Arab nations

Mubarak spent much of the 1980s rebuilding Egypt's status as one of the major powers of the Middle East. While maintaining peace with Israel under the terms of the 1979 treaty, he also sought to repair Egypt's relations with other Arab nations. The 1979 Egypt-Israel Peace Treaty had prompted nearly every Arab country to condemn Egypt's formal recognition of Israel. After the Camp David Accords in 1978, the Arab League formally expelled Egypt. (The Arab League is a regional political alliance of Arab nations formed in 1945 to promote political, military, and economic cooperation within the Arab world.) This was an especially painful rebuke, for Egypt had been a founding member of the organization decades earlier and the league's headquarters were in Cairo. The league moved its headquarters to Tunisia, and trade between Egypt and other Arab nations was severely limited by the drastic sanctions league members imposed. (Sanctions are punitive measures adopted by the international community against a nation that has violated international law, usually in the form of diplomatic, economic, or social restrictions.)

Mubarak first reached out to Iraqi leader **Saddam Hussein** (1937–2006; see entry), who welcomed Egyptian military aid during the Iran-Iraq War (1980–88). After careful negotiations, Mubarak secured a trade agreement with Jordan in 1983 and pursued separate agreements with other Arab nations. Egypt was readmitted to the Arab League in 1989, and a year later the league's headquarters returned to Cairo. Egypt's relations with Israel were noticeably cool during this period; in September 1986 Mubarak met with Israeli prime minister **Shimon Peres**

(1923–; see entry), marking the first formal meeting between the two nations in five years.

On October 5, 1987, Mubarak was reelected to his second six-year term. He was the sole candidate on the ballot. Similarly arranged elections were carried out in 1993 and 1999, and the NDP retained a majority of seats in the People's Assembly, which routinely passed all of Mubarak's initiatives.

Targeted by fundamentalists

Mubarak was able to quash criticism over Egypt's lack of democracy and deal harshly with opponents using the Emergency Law. It was also a useful tool for dealing with complaints about Egypt's stagnant economy, high unemployment, lack of press freedom, and absence of legitimate political debate. The biggest threat to the president, however, was from Islamic fundamentalists. During Mubarak's first years in power, his government dealt harshly with members of the Egyptian Islamic Jihad (EIJ) and its various other fundamentalist groups. Among them was the Muslim Brotherhood, an Islamic fundamentalist group organized in opposition to Western influence and in support of Islamic principles. It had a solid support base among more devout Muslims in Egypt but was never able to secure legitimate political power, because Egyptian electoral law does not permit political parties based on religious views or affiliations. There was a small group of Muslim Brotherhood members who served in the People's Assembly by winning election as independent candidates.

Mubarak's foreign policy and tough stance on fundamentalist groups made him a target for assassination attempts. The most serious one occurred on June 26, 1995, as his presidential limousine was leaving the airport in Addis Ababa, Ethiopia, where Mubarak had attended a meeting of the Organization of African Unity (OAU), an association of African states founded in 1963 for mutual cooperation. The attack was particularly well coordinated and planned in part by Ayman al-Zawahiri (1951–), a prominent Egyptian physician who had been jailed in the early 1980s for his EIJ involvement. Mubarak's armor-plated presidential limousine saved him from the gunmen's bullets. Two members of Mubarak's security detail were killed in the shootout, and five EIJ commandos died. A panicked Mubarak gave the order for his driver to return to the airport, and a second carful of EIJ operatives waiting farther down the road with deadly rocket grenades were left stranded there, with no target in sight. Another ringleader of that 1995 attempt was Mustafa Ahmed

Hassan Hamza, a staunch enemy of Mubarak who commanded the Egyptian branch of al-Qaeda, a terrorist organization founded by Saudi-born **Osama bin Laden** (1957–2011; see entry). Al-Zawahiri would eventually succeed bin Laden as al-Qaeda's leader after bin Laden was killed by U.S. military forces in 2011.

Islamic fundamentalists carried out many attacks on Egyptian targets, including police officers, government officials, and even tourists. There was a November 1997 attack at the Luxor ruins site, a popular international tourist destination for Egypt, by members of the group al-Gama'a al-Islamiyya. Fifty-eight foreign nationals died, most of them from a Swiss tour group, along with British, German, Japanese, and Colombian travelers and four Egyptians. The attack prompted a massive crackdown on suspected members of al-Gama'a by Mubarak's government. These Islamic fundamentalist groups opposed Mubarak's regime; his alliances with Western governments, who provided generous foreign-aid dollars to help Egypt's counterterrorist efforts; and his involvement in the Arab-Israeli peace process. Mubarak was said to have been integral in convincing **Yasser Arafat** (1929–2004; see entry), longtime leader of the Palestine Liberation Organization (PLO; a political and military organization formed to unite various Palestinian Arab groups with the goal of establishing an independent Palestinian state), into finally agreeing to officially recognize the nation of Israel and its right to exist.

Ignores calls to retire

During his fourth term as president, which began in 1999, Mubarak condemned the terrorist attacks on the United States on September 11, 2001, that killed nearly three thousand people. He opposed the U.S.-led coalition to oust Saddam in 2003. Addressing Egyptian troops at a military event in Suez several days after the start of the Iraq War (2003–11), Mubarak criticized the decision to invade Iraq, which followed an offensive into Afghanistan to find bin Laden and destroy al-Qaeda. "When it is over, if it is over, this war will have horrible consequences," Mubarak said of the Iraq invasion, as quoted by Ian Black and Chris McGreal in an April 2003 article in the *Guardian*. "Instead of having one bin Laden, we will have 100."

Mubarak finally gave in to internal and external pressures in 2004 and eased up on rules preventing other political parties from fielding

Hosni Mubarak and French president Jacques Chirac at one of numerous political discussions on the future of Arab-Israeli peace talks. AP PHOTO/PHILIPPE WOJAZER, POOL.

candidates in the parliamentary and presidential elections scheduled for 2005. Mubarak's main challenger was Ayman Nour (1964–) of the El-Ghad Party (Tomorrow's Party), and few were surprised when Mubarak won a fifth term as president with 88 percent of the vote. Nour was soon arrested on charges of forging the petition documents needed to enter the election, and an Egyptian court sentenced him to five years in prison.

Civil unrest

Nearing his third decade in power, Mubarak had never appointed a vice president or indicated a potential successor. However, his son, Gamal

(1963–), a former investment banker in London, England, with a degree from the American University of Cairo, soon advanced to a leadership post within the NDP and his father put him in charge of a reform plan designed to stimulate Egypt's ailing economy. In May 2008 Mubarak celebrated his eightieth birthday, and it seemed likely that Gamal would become the NDP candidate in the next scheduled presidential elections in 2011, especially after Mubarak underwent surgery to remove his gallbladder. In October 2010, however, NDP officials indicated Mubarak would seek a sixth term in office.

A month later, Egypt's parliamentary elections were marred by government interference and allegations of fraud. Calls for Mubarak to retire or introduce significant constitutional reforms increased, but the catalyst that brought an end to his twenty-nine years in power was the ouster of another North African leader, Zine El Abidine Ben Ali (1936–) of Tunisia. Four weeks of street protests in the country's capital of Tunis and other cities forced Ben Ali and his family to flee to Saudi Arabia on January 14, 2011. Eleven days later a protest set to take place in front of Egypt's Ministry of the Interior spiraled into massive demonstrations against Mubarak in Cairo and several other cities. In Cairo the action was centered in the enormous plaza called Tahrir Square, and protesters returned day after day, defying the Emergency Law and a newly imposed curfew. Crowds chanted for Mubarak to step down.

After a week of growing civil unrest originating in Tahrir Square, with an estimated quarter million Egyptians gathered there and calling for him to step down, Mubarak appeared on a televised broadcast to Egypt's 85 million citizens on February 1, 2011. "The Hosni Mubarak who speaks to you today is proud of his achievements over the years in serving Egypt and its people," he said, as quoted by Anthony Shadid in the *New York Times*. "This is my country. This is where I lived, I fought and defended its land, sovereignty and interests, and I will die on its soil." Crowds in Tahrir Square jeered at this, and although clashes between police and demonstrators continued over the next several days, Egypt's army failed to take action against the protestors, which was a notable signal to outsiders that Mubarak had likely lost the support of his top generals, who command one of the most well-equipped and strike-ready forces in the Middle East.

Steps down

On February 10 Mubarak appeared again on television, asserting once more that he would not resign, but hinting that he might possibly delegate

Tahrir Square

Tahrir Square is an enormous plaza in the center of Cairo, Egypt. It became the epicenter of protest against Hosni Mubarak's regime in 2011. The square was part of an ambitious urban plan devised by Ottoman Turkish ruler Ismail Pasha (1830–1895), in the 1860s and 1870s, when Egypt was part of the vast Ottoman Empire that included southwest Asia, northeast Africa, and southeast Europe, and lasted from the thirteenth century to the early twentieth century. Ismail wanted to replicate the grand boulevards and large parks of European capitals, specifically those of Paris, France, on what had been Cairo's undeveloped west bank of the Nile River. The public space he created was known as Ismailia Square for decades and was mostly famous for having one of the world's most terrifying traffic intersections. A rotary (also called a roundabout; a junction at which traffic travels in a circle around a central island) was created at its southern edge to ease automobile congestion in the modern era.

The leader of Egypt's 1952 revolution, **Gamal Abdel Nasser** (1918–1970; see entry), was behind the renaming the square from Ismailia to Tahrir, an Arabic word meaning "liberation," to commemorate an earlier 1919 uprising against British colonial rule. In late September 1970 massive crowds turned out in Tahrir Square to mourn Nasser's sudden death from a heart attack.

Tahrir Square has been a site for protests for several generations of Egyptians. In early 1946 crowds gathered to voice their objections to continued British interference in their affairs. Six years later, demonstrators massed to show their opposition to King Farouk I (1920–1965), the grandson of Ismail Pasha, and torched nearby buildings, starting a fire that quickly spiraled into a major catastrophic event in Cairo. There were riots in January 1977 when the price of basic foodstuffs rose sharply. This disruption was known as the Egyptian Bread Riots, and the violence directed against the middle-class

his presidential duties to a recently appointed vice president, Omar Suleiman (1936–), until the September election. The Tahrir Square crowds, so large by now they could be seen from satellite-imaging equipment orbiting Earth, were stunned at his defiance, and even larger crowds turned out on the morning of February 11. Later that same day, Suleiman made a brief announcement on state-run media stating that Mubarak had handed over presidential powers to the Supreme Council of the Armed Forces for a temporary period. A grim-faced Suleiman also noted that Mubarak and his family had gone to the presidential villa at Sharm el-Sheikh, Egypt's popular Red Sea resort city.

The Mubaraks were barred from leaving the country and their assets in foreign banks were frozen, meaning that he would be unable to access

prompted Egyptian president **Anwar Sadat** (also spelled al-Sadat; 1918–1981; see entry) to quickly reverse policy and renew the price subsidies (money granted by the government to keep prices down) that had kept cooking oil, bread, and other staples artificially low.

Tahrir Square in Cairo, Egypt, filled with anti-Mubarak protestors in 2011. Tahrir Square has been a site of protest for several generations of Egyptians. © IDEALINK PHOTOGRAPHY/ALAMY.

his money. On April 13, 2011, Mubarak was formally detained along with his two sons, and there were rumors that he suffered a heart attack while in police custody. Prosecutors issued charges of corruption and premeditated murder against him on May 24, and the first day of the trial was August 3, 2011. By that date Mubarak's health had sharply declined, and he was wheeled into the courtroom on a hospital bed. The proceedings were broadcast live on television, and for a few hours Egypt came to a virtual standstill as citizens throughout the country stopped to watch. "The broadcast," noted David D. Kirkpatrick in the *New York Times* "served as a national catharsis [emotional release] for postrevolutionary Egypt and electrified the Arab world with the image of an autocrat brought down for the first time by his own people to the standing of an ordinary criminal."

For More Information

BOOKS

Weaver, Mary Anne. *A Portrait of Egypt: A Journey through the World of Militant Islam.* New York: Farrar Straus & Giroux, 1999, p. 72.

Wright, Robin. *Rock the Casbah: Rage and Rebellion across the Islamic World.* New York: Simon & Schuster, 2011.

PERIODICALS

Black, Ian, and Chris McGreal. "Conflict Will Create 100 Bin Ladens, Warns Egyptian President." *Guardian* (April 1, 2003). Available online at http://www.guardian.co.uk/world/2003/apr/01/alqaida.Iraq (accessed on November 30, 2011).

"Egypt's Cautious Man with a Mission." *U.S. News and World Report* (March 18, 1985): 15.

"Excerpts from the Vice President's Statement." *New York Times* (October 7, 1981). Available online at http://www.nytimes.com/1981/10/07/world/excerpts-from-the-vice-president-s-statement.html?scp=11&sq=%22Hosni+Mubarak%22&st=nyt (accessed on November 30, 2011).

Hammer, Joshua. "The Contenders." *New Yorker* (April 5, 2010). Available online at http://www.newyorker.com/reporting/2010/04/05/100405fa_fact_hammer#ixzz1VOFUvfZ6 (accessed on November 30, 2011).

Kirkpatrick, David D. "Mubarak Orders Crackdown, With Revolt Sweeping Egypt." *New York Times* (January 29, 2011). Available online at http://www.nytimes.com/2011/01/29/world/middleeast/29unrest.html?ref=hosnimubarak (accessed on November 309, 2011).

———— "Egypt Erupts in Jubilation as Mubarak Steps Down." *New York Times* (February 11, 2011). Available online at http://www.nytimes. com/2011/02/12/world/middleeast/12egypt.html?ref=hosnimubarak (accessed on November 30, 2011).

———— "Judge Orders Televising of Mubarak Trial to End." *New York Times* (August 15, 2011). Available online at http://www.nytimes.com/2011/08/16/world/middleeast/16egypt.html?scp=1&sq=%22electrified+the+Arab+world+with+the+image+of+an+autocrat%22&st=nyt (accessed on November 30, 2011).

Shadid, Anthony. "Obama Urges Faster Shift of Power in Egypt." *New York Times* (February 1, 2011). Available online at http://www.nytimes.com/2011/02/02/world/middleeast/02egypt.html?sq=&st=nyt&%2334;=&scp=1&%2334;I%20will%20die%20on%20its%20soil=&pagewanted=all (accessed on November 30, 2011).

Shadid, Anthony, and David D. Kirkpatrick. "Mubarak Refuses to Step Down, Stoking Revolt's Fury and Resolve." *New York Times* (February 10, 2011). Available online at http://www.nytimes.com/2011/02/11/world/middleeast/11egypt.html?ref=hosnimubarak (accessed on November 30, 2011).

"We'll Clap Our Hands." *Newsweek* (October 29, 2001): 52.

WEB SITES

"Profile: Hosni Mubarak." *Al Jazeera* (February 11, 2011). http://english.aljazeera.net/focus/2009/12/200912693048491779.html (accessed on November 30, 2011).

"Times Topics: Hosni Mubarak." *New York Times* (updated August 15, 2011). http://topics.nytimes.com/top/reference/timestopics/people/m/hosni_mubarak/index.html?scp=1-spot&sq=hosni%20mubarak&st=cse (accessed on November 30, 2011).

Hassan Nasrallah

BORN: August 31, 1960 • Qarantina, Lebanon

Lebanese militant group leader

"The Israeli Air Force could destroy the Lebanese army within hours, or within days, but it cannot do this with us [Hezbollah]. We exercise guerilla warfare.... Lebanon still needs the formula of popular resistance."

Hassan Nasrallah. © JAMAL SAIDI/REUTERS/CORBIS.

Since 1992 Hassan Nasrallah has been the secretary-general of Hezbollah, a militant group that has struggled against Israel and developed great military and political power in Lebanon. Under Nasrallah's leadership, Hezbollah has become a dominant force in elective politics in Lebanon, while still maintaining an independent military force and a radical image. In the early twenty-first century, Hezbollah was considered a terrorist organization by the United States and other Western nations, but in Lebanon, particularly in the Shiite community, Hezbollah was very popular. (Shiites are followers of the Shia branch of Islam. Shiites believe that only direct descendants of the prophet Muhammad [c. 570–632] are qualified to lead the Islamic faith.) Hezbollah's representatives won the majority of votes in many local and national elections.

Nasrallah's bold leadership kept political observers throughout the world guessing whether he would reestablish himself as one of Lebanon's leading politicians or continue to exercise control from behind the scenes as the outspoken leader of a militant resistance movement. Political analyst Michael Young reflects on the two sides of Nasrallah in the book *Dreams and Shadows: The Future of the Middle East* by Robin Wright: "Deep down Nasrallah thinks he is better than Lebanese politics.... To have to go into the pit with the rest of Lebanon's politicians is not something he relishes.... But more fundamentally, he has to figure out: Is he just a local leader, or is he a regional Che Guevara [an Argentinean revolutionary]?"

Early life

Hassan Nasrallah was born on August 31, 1960, in the tiny, impoverished village of Qarantina, near Burj Hammud, a suburb of Lebanon's capital city, Beirut. His father, Abd al-Karim Nasrallah, owned a small grocery store, and as a boy, Nasrallah helped out in the store in his spare time. He was also an excellent student. When Nasrallah was fifteen years old, a bloody civil war began in Lebanon. Qarantina was soon in the middle of the fighting, and the people of Lebanon began to divide into factions. To escape the violence of the civil war, which would continue for fifteen years, the family moved back to their former home, the village of al-Bazuriyya, near Tyre in southern Lebanon.

Although his father was not a deeply religious man, Nasrallah developed a strong interest in the Shia branch of Islam from an early age. In 1975 Shiites were not well represented in Lebanon's government. They tended to be poorer than other religious sects (groups) in Lebanon and were often treated as inferior.

Nasrallah's interest in the politics of Lebanon, particularly in the heroes who had given their lives for the country, was as deep as his interest in his religion. After moving to southern Lebanon, he joined the Amal Movement, which was founded in 1975 by Imam Musa al-Sadr (1928–?), an Iranian-born Shiite cleric. (A cleric is an ordained official of a religion.) Amal was the militia wing of the Movement of the Disinherited, a political movement of the Shiites.

In 1976 with the encouragement and support of a local cleric, Nasrallah set off for Iraq to attend the renowned Shiite seminary in Najaf. There he studied under al-Sadr and another prominent Shiite cleric, Abbas

The Government of Lebanon

After World War I (1914–18), the League of Nations (an organization of nations formed after the war with the mission of maintaining peace) awarded Lebanon to France as a mandate. (A mandate is a territory entrusted to foreign administration.) France manipulated the borders of Lebanon in such a way that Christians were a majority. The largest Christian group at the time was the Maronites, an Arabic-speaking group of Christians who are in communion (share essential doctrines) with the Roman Catholic Church. Due to their large numbers, Maronites held many positions of power within the Lebanese government in the 1930s and 1940s.

When the French mandate ended in 1943, French officials used their influence to establish a system of government that ensured the Maronites would retain their power. The National Pact of 1943 created a sectarian system, one that divided the people by their religious groups. It was based on the results of a 1932 census in which Christians outnumbered Muslims by a ratio of six to five. Thus, under the National Pact, the Lebanese government was to be made up of six Christians for every five Muslims. The Lebanese president had to be a Maronite and the prime minister a Sunni Muslim. The speaker of the

house was to be a Shiite Muslim and the chief of staff a Druze. The National Pact clearly favored the Maronites and the Sunni Muslims, who had the largest populations in 1932.

Over the years, the Lebanese government continued to be shaped by the same ratio set by the 1932 census. While the government stayed the same, however, the population changed. Shiite Muslims became the single largest sect in Lebanon, but their representation in government remained limited. Tensions between the growing Muslim population's desires for greater political representation and the Maronites' attempts to retain their political power were at the root of Lebanon's civil war (1975–90), one of the most enduring conflicts of its time.

In 1989 the Lebanese parliament debated the structure of the Lebanese government for three weeks at a conference in Taif, Saudi Arabia. The result was the Taif Accord, which maintained the sectarian system of dividing the government, but changed the ratio that had previously been based on the 1932 census. Under the Taif Accord, Christians and Muslims are equally represented in the Lebanese government.

al-Musawi (1952–1992). Al-Musawi had been deeply influenced by his association with the renowned Iranian cleric **Ayatollah Ruhollah Khomeini** (1902–1989; see entry), who would become Iran's Supreme Leader after the 1979 Iranian Revolution (also known as the Islamic Revolution). In 1978, after completing courses in Muslim theology, Nasrallah, who was eighteen years old, returned to Lebanon. He taught in a school established by al-Musawi in Baalbek, a town in the Bekaa Valley of eastern Lebanon. He also continued his religious education under al-Musawi, who recruited the charismatic young man into Amal's political wing. By the early 1980s Nasrallah had become the leader of Amal in the district.

*The logo of Hezbollah, founded
in 1985 by Hassan Nasrallah
and Abbas al-Musawi.*
BLINOW61/
SHUTTERSTOCK.COM.

In 1992 Nasrallah became the secretary-general of Hezbollah. From the start he planned to transform the group, reaching out to all of Lebanon and using democratic processes as well as force. He pledged that Hezbollah would never impose Islamic rule (in which religion and state are not separated and all aspects of life are governed by Islam) on Lebanon unless the majority chose it. Meanwhile, Hezbollah's struggle against Israel continued. Hezbollah, with help from Iran and neighboring Syria, developed a strong military force. Its attacks on Israeli troops in southern Lebanon employed suicide bombers and rocket launchers called "Katyushas" supplied by Iran. The organization took credit for the estimated sixteen hundred Israelis killed in Lebanon between 1982 and 2000.

Hezbollah's persistent attacks eventually led to the Israeli decision to withdraw from southern Lebanon. In May 2000 the Israeli occupation of Lebanon, which had lasted more than eighteen years, was over. Nasrallah was celebrated by both Christian and Muslim Lebanese, and by Muslims worldwide for this success against Israel.

Along with its show of military might, Hezbollah had become a potent political force under Nasrallah. He led massive efforts to provide aid to poor Shiite communities. Hezbollah built schools and health clinics, distributed fresh water, established garbage collection services, and instituted many other necessary programs that the Lebanese government lacked the resources to provide. By the early twenty-first century, Nasrallah had become so popular that his face was seen throughout Lebanon on billboards and computer screensavers; parts of his speeches were even used as ringtones for cell phones. By 2005 Hezbollah had representatives in thirteen seats in Lebanon's parliament and was aiding tens of thousands of needy Shiites.

Hezbollah went on to accomplish many other things, but its mission to attack Israel never halted. By October 2000 it was again employing its large military force of an estimated three hundred thousand trained fighters and its large arsenal of missiles to attack targets within Israel's borders. Hezbollah was also aiding Palestinians in terrorist activities and guerrilla warfare against Israel. Although Nasrallah's group was gaining in popularity as a Lebanese political group, it had not abandoned its earlier terrorist practices. In a 2006 interview with Wright for the *Washington Post* Nasrallah said, "As long as there are fighters who are ready for martyrdom, this country will remain safe."

The Cedar Revolution

By the twenty-first century, Lebanon's Shiite community, once a minority, had grown to make up about 50 percent of the Lebanese population. Nasrallah decided the most effective way for Hezbollah to take power in Lebanon was to get Hezbollah representatives elected by democratic means. Although some of Hezbollah's more militant leaders opposed working within the government, Nasrallah repositioned the organization, changing its image from a militant opposition group to a political party. Even so, he refused to give up his independent military forces, which were stronger than those of the Lebanese government. Many of Lebanon's leaders looked on with great concern that such a group could be voted into power.

Hezbollah had long received huge amounts of support from Iran and Syria. In 2005 the relationship between Hezbollah and Syria became a problem for Nasrallah as he struggled to gain the popular vote. Syria's troops had been stationed in Lebanon since 1985, and Syria had played a large role in Lebanon's day-to-day government. Nasrallah tried to use his own popularity to raise support in his country for Syria's presence there. But on February 14, 2005, Lebanon's president, Rafiq Hariri (1944–2005), was assassinated, and the Lebanese people suspected that Syria was responsible for the killing. A month after the assassination, on March 14, 2005, an estimated one million Lebanese citizens took to the streets in a demonstration that was later called the Cedar Revolution to protest the Syrian presence in Lebanon. The public pressure worked; within weeks, Syria withdrew its troops from Lebanon.

Shortly after Syria's withdrawal, Lebanon held its first elections free of Syrian control in decades. The election pitted Hezbollah's Shiite supporters against the March 14 coalition, which was comprised mainly of Lebanon's Sunni Muslims (followers of the Sunni branch of Islam, who believe that elected officials, regardless of their heritage, are qualified to lead the Islamic faith) and Druze (members of a small religious community that emerged in eleventh-century Egypt and spread to what is, in the early twenty-first century, Lebanon, Syria, and Israel). The March 14 coalition won the majority of the votes. After the votes were counted, Hezbollah representatives had gained two positions in the cabinet and several parliamentary seats. Temporarily defeated, Nasrallah quietly joined forces with the coalition government.

Hezbollah's 2006 war with Israel

On July 12, 2006, Hezbollah attacked a small force of Israeli troops that was patrolling Israel's border with Lebanon, killing eight Israelis and wounding several others. Hezbollah took two Israeli soldiers hostage. The skirmish was relatively small, but Hezbollah had made a grave error. Israel responded by launching all-out war. Nasrallah later admitted that he never expected a major retaliation from Israel. Initially, Israel's motive for attack was to recover the kidnapped soldiers. But as the battle escalated, Israeli prime minister Ehud Olmert (1945–) and some of his ministers decided to try to destroy Hezbollah. Israel launched air, naval, and ground attacks at Hezbollah targets across Lebanon. Hezbollah, in turn, fired about four thousand rockets into northern Israel, some reaching as far as the Israeli city of Haifa. Forced into hiding, Nasrallah broadcast speeches day and night throughout the war. His forces proved to be the toughest guerilla warriors in the world.

The war between Israel and Hezbollah lasted for thirty-three days, ending in what Israel viewed as a stalemate. Destruction to the Shiite communities, from the south to the suburbs of Beirut, was devastating. In one month of fighting, about 1,200 Lebanese and 159 Israelis were killed. Nearly one million Lebanese were displaced from their homes. Hezbollah's missiles were destroyed, and it lost a large number of its trained soldiers. But Hezbollah had also harmed Israel, forcing its civilians to experience warfare firsthand and causing thousands to flee their homes. Most importantly, Hezbollah survived the powerful nation's forceful attack. In his first public speech after the war, Nasrallah declared the war to be, as quoted by Hirst, a "great, strategic, historic and divine" victory, and many people in the Middle East agreed.

Takeover of Beirut

The peaceful coexistence of Hezbollah and other government sectors of Lebanon did not last long. In November 2006 the Hezbollah ministers resigned their posts to protest what they viewed as the inequality of Shiite representation in the government. The majority of the ministers had refused to accommodate Hezbollah's demands for equal representation for fear of giving the militant group veto power in the coalition government. In 2007, when the president's term was over, the government stalemate caused by Hezbollah's protest prevented a presidential election. Suddenly Lebanon was without a president. As Hezbollah plotted against its rivals within the government, those rivals took actions against Hezbollah, firing at least one top official with known associations to the group and closing down Hezbollah's communication network.

Nasrallah struck back with force. On May 8, 2008, Hezbollah members swarmed areas of Beirut, taking over the party headquarters and communications networks of their rivals and even burning down the offices of the newspaper run by the powerful Hariri family. Two days later, they quietly withdrew, but a great deal of damage had been done. Clashes between people backing Hezbollah and those backing the

A poster of Hassan Nasrallah, damaged during Hezbollah's war with Israel, stands at the entrance of the devastated town of Bint Jbeil, Lebanon, in October 2006. RAMZI HAIDAR/AFP/GETTY IMAGES.

majority government had killed eighty-one people and brought fear of a second civil war to the Lebanese people.

On May 21, 2008, all the rival factions of the Lebanese government met in Doha, Qatar, and hammered out a resolution in which Hezbollah received veto power in the government. The Doha agreement paved the way for new presidential elections. By 2009 a unity government was again in place. Most of Nasrallah's demands had been met, and Hezbollah had become the most powerful force in Lebanon. Lebanon's new government functioned for more than a year.

More breakdowns

In 2011 the Hezbollah officials in Lebanon's cabinet once again resigned in protest. This time they were protesting a United Nations-sponsored tribunal investigating the 2005 assassination of President Hariri. (The

United Nations is an international organization of countries founded in 1945 to promote international peace, security, and cooperation.) The tribunal was expected to charge several Hezbollah members with the murder. Nasrallah demanded that Lebanon's prime minister, Saad Hariri (1971–), the son of the slain president, denounce the tribunal and end Lebanon's participation. Hariri refused and Lebanon's government was thrown once again into a stalemate.

Thomas P.M. Barrett, contributing editor of *Esquire* magazine, assessed Nasrallah's hold on Lebanon's government in a 2008 article for the magazine. He writes:

> Most terrorist movements go one of two ways: They either fall apart after the top leaders are captured or killed, or they are successfully drawn into the political process and ultimately assimilated by the ruling political forces. Hezbollah's rise within Lebanon increasingly looks like the latter, except it is Lebanon's splintered political system that is being assimilated into Hezbollah's radical Islamic agenda rather than the other way around. Through a variety of means, by 2011 Nasrallah was considered by most observers to be the most powerful person in the troubled nation of Lebanon.

For More Information

BOOKS

Hirst, David. *Beware of Small States: Lebanon, Battleground of the Middle East.* New York: Nation Books, 2010, p. 187.

Wright, Robin. *Dreams and Shadows: The Future of the Middle East.* New York: Penguin, 2008, p. 173, 211.

PERIODICALS

Barnett, Thomas P.M. "Hassan Nasrallah: Meet the Head of Hezbollah." *Esquire* (December 28, 2008). Available online at http://www.esquire.com/features/75-most-influential/hassan-nasrallah-1008 (accessed on November 30, 2011).

Wright, Robin. "Inside the Mind of Hezbollah." *Washington Post* (July 16, 2006). Available online at http://www.washingtonpost.com/wp-dyn/content/article/2006/07/14/AR2006071401401.html (accessed on November 30, 2011).

WEB SITES

"Hezbollah (a.k.a. Hizbollah, Hizbu'llah)." *Council on Foreign Relations* (July 15, 2010). http://www.cfr.org/lebanon/hezbollah-k-hizbollah-hizbullah/p9155 (accessed on November 30, 2011).

"Profile: Sheikh Hassan Nasrallah." *BBC News* (July 13, 2006). http://news.bbc.co.uk/2/hi/5176612.stm (accessed on November 30, 2011).

Gamal Abdel Nasser

BORN: January 15, 1918 • Alexandria, Egypt

DIED: September 28, 1970 • Cairo, Egypt

Egyptian president, military leader

"We have lived here for more than 7,000 years— old Egyptian civilization. It has withstood many invaders. . . . The endurance of this country, this people is very great."

G amal Abdel Nasser is one of the pivotal figures in the political development of the modern Middle East. As president of Egypt, he marshaled forces to drive the British out of Egypt after a seventy-two-year occupation. Nasser presided over Egypt's cultural, military, political, and economic rebirth in the twentieth century, and his bold move to nationalize the strategic Suez Canal in 1956 was a significant turning point in the Arab world's relations with the West. (Nationalization is the practice of bringing private industry under the ownership and control of the government.) Nasser promoted the ideals of Pan-Arabism, a movement for the unification of Arab peoples and the political alliance of Arab states, and became one of the most revered and charismatic Arab personalities of his generation for urging others to resist Western control and influence.

Gamal Abdel Nasser.
HOWARD SOCHUREK/TIME
LIFE PICTURES/GETTY
IMAGES.

301

Childhood and early military career

Nasser was born on January 15, 1918, in Alexandria, Egypt. His father, Abdel Nasser, was an inspector in the postal service, and the family moved frequently, including one move to Asyut, where his father's family still lived. His mother, Fahima Hamad, died in childbirth when Nasser was eight. By then Nasser was living with an uncle in Cairo, Egypt, in order to attend school there. Over the next decade he would change schools several more times, living with various family members. As a teenager, he was drawn into the growing Egyptian nationalist movement and participated in street demonstrations. (Nationalism is the belief that a people with shared ethnic, cultural, and/or religious identities have the right to form their own nation. In established nations nationalism is devotion and loyalty to the nation and its culture.) Much of the movement's focus was on the British occupation of Egypt, in place since 1882.

In 1937 Nasser entered the Egyptian Military Academy. There he met fellow cadet **Anwar Sadat** (also spelled al-Sadat; 1918–1981; see entry), the future president of Egypt, whose own rise to power would parallel Nasser's. Nasser graduated with the rank of second lieutenant and was posted to an army unit near his father's ancestral home, the village of Beni Mur, in southern Egypt. During this period of his life, Nasser also met Zakaria Mohieddin (1918–c. 2009), another military officer who would aid his career immensely in the coming years of turmoil.

British colonial officials held power, with the help of King Farouk I (1920–1965), over a territory that encompassed Egypt and its neighbor to the south, Sudan. British policy goals there included the training of a highly skilled Egyptian army so that the civil unrest could be more easily quelled by a home army, not a foreign one. Corruption during the colonial era was widespread, and the gap between Egypt's increasingly marginalized poor and an elite who lived in luxury was widening. A group of young army officers joined forces to fight against this corruption, against the occupation, and toward building Egypt's economic and political infrastructure. Nasser knew these young men and was impressed by their nationalism but was disappointed with their lack of organization.

The creation of the country of Israel in 1948 had marked a turning point for the Arab world. Many Arab nations did not recognize Israel as an independent state, believing that the Jews had taken land from Palestinians (an Arab people whose ancestors lived in the historical region of Palestine, comprising parts of present-day Israel and Jordan, and who continue to lay claim to that land) when they formed their state. Palestine had been a British mandate (a territory entrusted to foreign administration), but the British withdrew from the area just before the state of Israel was declared. King Farouk was therefore free join several other Arab nations, who to deployed army units to attack Israel in an attempt to retake Palestinian land. Israel emerged as the victor in the 1948 Arab-Israeli War. Nasser's Sixth Infantry Battalion was among the Egyptian army units involved in the war. This marked Nasser's first real combat experience, and it whetted his appetite for revolutionary armed struggle. He emerged from the failed effort a minor hero for successfully challenging the Israeli military while wounded and with no backup troops.

In 1949 Nasser became one of the founding members of the Free Officers Organization, a group formed for the purpose of expelling the British government from Egypt. The members considered themselves free from the influence of either the king or British officials. Initially it was a secretive underground organization, and the king's internal police made several attempts to infiltrate and quash it, but membership grew after the charismatic Nasser became the organization's president in 1950. The core leadership group also included Sadat, Mohieddin, and Muhammad Naguib (1901–1984), a high-ranking Egyptian army general.

Overthrowing the king

The Free Officers Organization published its manifesto and pushed it under the doors of thousands of homes across Egypt. It demanded that the Egyptian army be strengthened and run by Egyptians alone so that the country could defend itself and not rely on Western powers. The manifesto demanded that the price of bread, which was state regulated, be reduced so that more people could afford to buy it. It also demanded an end to corruption within the Egyptian government. King Farouk tried to appease the Egyptian people by lowering the prices of necessary food items and working to make the country more independent from the British, but it was too late.

Despite knowing who most of the members of the Free Officers Organization were, the king's men could not locate them to arrest them. A week before July 22, 1952, members huddled in their secret meeting place and planned to overthrow the king. The plan was that on the evening of July 22 they would storm the main army stations and take control of the army units. Then they would be able to take control of the whole army. Once this was achieved, Nasser thought, the king would have no way to defend himself. The next stage of the plan involved controlling the country's communication systems so that the king could not appeal to foreign powers for help. They would do this by storming the airport, train stations, and radio stations and by taking control of the telephone system.

If the Free Officers Organization could manage all of this, it could trick the palace into believing that nothing was happening. A week later, these plans were successfully carried out. By the morning of July 23, Sadat triumphantly declared to the Egyptian public over the radio that the revolution had begun and that Egypt had entered a new phase of development and modernization. Corruption and excess, he promised, were in the past. The Free Officers Organization exiled Farouk, allowing him to leave the country with only a few possessions. A year later a new constitution was drawn up, and Egypt was declared a republic, a state in which power is held by the people and their elected representatives. The monarchy was officially abolished, and the republic was established with a prime minister and a council. The British were duly informed that their presence was unnecessary, though they did not withdraw from Egypt until 1958. The British managed to retain control of the Suez Canal, a waterway connecting the Red Sea to the Mediterranean Sea. Naguib became the first prime minister, and Nasser was in control of the Revolutionary Command Council (RCC), the body established to supervise Egypt and which consisted mainly of members of the Free Officers Organization. Even though the prime minister was to work with the council to make new policies, it was the RCC that held most of the power in the government.

In time Nasser grew increasingly dissatisfied with Naguib's administration, for Naguib began to publicly side against many of the council's proposals. Nasser attempted to seize power in early 1954, but his efforts were thwarted. In July 1954 Nasser successfully negotiated an agreement with Great Britain over the withdrawal of British troops from the Suez Canal zone, a strategic strip of land in Egypt's Sinai peninsula which contained the Suez Canal. The agreement also allowed the Sudan provinces the right of self-determination, another point of contention among the new leadership. The Muslim Brotherhood, an Islamic fundamentalist group organized in opposition to Western influence and in support of Islamic principles, also played a role in the events of this period, as they battled for a share of power in Egypt. On October 26, 1954, a member of the Muslim Brotherhood attempted to assassinate Nasser as he was giving a speech before a large crowd in Alexandria. Believing the prime minister, who feared Nasser's support among the army, was behind the attempt, Nasser had Naguib arrested and proclaimed himself prime minister of Egypt without a public vote. Two years later nationwide elections were held, although the only candidates were from the newly created National Union Party. Nasser was sworn in as president on June 23, 1956.

Leading the republic

Nasser believed in socialism, a system in which the government owns the means of production and controls the distribution of goods and services, and he set out to establish socialism in Egypt. Egyptian landowners, who had prospered greatly under King Farouk, were vehemently opposed to land reform, a process by which their vast estates were confiscated and distributed equally to ordinary Egyptians. Nasser also began a program of nationalization. His efforts created an entirely new political system in Egypt based on Arab socialism. Islam also became the official religion of the country.

Accomplishments of the Nasser regime, such as land reform, industrialization, social welfare, and job creation, were carried out despite internal opposition from Muslims, supports of the king, and external opposition from the West. Nations of the West, including the United States and those in Europe, worried that the revolution had jeopardized their economic interests in the region, because the Suez Canal was vital to international shipping. Within Egypt Nasser's one-party system, in which all opposition parties were outlawed, created resentment. Those on the left of the political spectrum were readily integrated into the regime, while more conservative groups, especially the Muslim Brotherhood, were marginalized. But Nasser had made several attempts to create a political party that would represent the Egyptian masses. The Liberation Rally existed from 1953 to 1956; the National Union operated from 1958 to 1962; and the Socialist Union was created in 1962. Nasser's tight control on politics and the Egyptian economy provoked more than one attempt on his life, including one embarrassingly inept 1958 plot by the king of Saudi Arabia, Saud ibn Abd al-Aziz (known as Saud; 1902–1969), which ultimately forced Saud to cede the throne to his brother **Faisal ibn Abd al Aziz ibn Saud** (1906–1975; see entry).

Nasserism

Gamal Abdel Nasser's political ideas came to be known as Nasserism. At the center of his philosophy was Pan-Arabism, the movement for the unification of Arab peoples and the political alliance of Arab states. It is an Arab nationalist movement, based on the belief that Arabs (people who speak the Arabic language) are united by a shared history, culture, and language, and Pan-Arabism has been promoted at various times in the Middle East as a way of uniting Arab countries against Israel and the West. Also central to Nasserism was the modernization and economic development of Egypt, to be carried out by a highly centralized government and a strong army. Whenever there is a significant crisis in the Middle East, support for Pan-Arabism receives much more support by the people in the region than at other times.

The Suez Crisis

Completed in 1869, the Suez Canal is an artificial waterway that connects the Red Sea to the Mediterranean Sea, allowing for easier trade and travel between Europe and the Middle East. Previously, mariners had to sail around the entire African continent in order to reach the countries along the Persian Gulf, India, and Asia. The 100-mile-long (161-kilometer) Suez Canal was constructed by a French company and was owned and controlled by the French and the British for decades. It was the Suez Canal that led the British to occupy Egypt in the late 1800s and early 1900s in order to protect this strategic waterway, as well as the trade and profit it brought to Great Britain and its allies.

In July 1956, shortly after Great Britain pulled out of Egypt (although retaining control of the Canal Zone), Nasser announced on public radio that he was nationalizing the Suez Canal and setting up a company called the Egyptian Canal Authority to manage it, and Egyptian troops moved to take the Canal Zone from the British. This act marked the start of the Suez Crisis. No sooner had Nasser announced the canal's nationalization than he received congratulatory phone calls from most of the leaders of Middle East, who were overjoyed that Western control of this important gateway had ceased. To them it was the symbol of a new era and an end to foreign domination. But Great Britain and the United States were furious and cut off promised foreign aid to Egypt.

The Suez Canal had provided important access to the sea for Israel, and Egyptian control of the canal would limit Israel's use of the waterway. Israel, along with Great Britain and France, responded to the Egyptian nationalization of the Suez Canal by invading the Sinai Peninsula. Nasser sank forty ships in the canal to block passage in November 1956, and the canal was closed for four months. In 1956 Israeli soldiers crossed over into the Egyptian-controlled Gaza Strip and took control of the land. Although Egyptian soldiers fought bravely, they were not as well trained as the Israelis and lost most of the battles. Pressure from the United

Gamal Abdel Nasser is carried through the streets of Port Said after the British evacuation from Egypt, marking the end of British occupation there. Shortly after, Nasser announced that he was nationalizing the Suez Canal. ROLLS PRESS/POPPERFOTO/GETTY IMAGES.

Nations and the United States brought an end to the fighting, and Egypt retained full control of the Suez Canal. (The United Nations is an international organization of countries founded in 1945 to promote international peace, security, and cooperation.) The United States was worried about Egypt turning to the Soviet Union for support, and helped Egypt repair the damage from the war. The canal reopened in March 1957, and was guarded until 1967 by a United Nations Emergency Force to ensure peaceful operations.

Controlling the canal infused the Egyptian economy with a steady flow of revenue from tariffs (taxes) the ships paid to use the waterway. Nasser also accepted foreign aid from the Soviet Union, which was delighted to have such an ally in the Middle East during the Cold War, period of intense political and economic rivalry between the United States and the Soviet

Union that lasted from 1945 to 1991. Due to Nasser's seizure of the Suez Canal, Egypt was transformed from a poor country into a prosperous one.

Humiliated in the 1967 Arab-Israeli War

Nasser's vision for Pan-Arabism took a step forward in 1958, when Egypt united with Syria to become the United Arab Republic (UAR). Nasser served as president of the new country, and the move excited those interested in integrating Arab nations into one Arab state. Yemen joined the union later in 1958. The vision of one Arab state was dashed in 1961, however, when Syria pulled out of the union after a military coup (overthrow of the government). Yemen soon followed, uneasy with a potentially risky alliance. The dissolution of the union hurt Nasser's political standing.

By 1967 the relationship between the Arabs and Israelis had severely disintegrated. As tensions mounted, Israel believed that its Arab neighbors were planning for war. Israel decided to strike first, and Israeli ships entered the Gulf of Aqaba, a body of water shared by Israel, Jordan, and Egypt, ready for a war. Facing them were hundreds of Egyptian guns onshore. Israel attacked Egypt and occupied the entire Sinai Peninsula, right up to the Suez Canal. Despite the small numbers of Israeli troops and the large numbers of Arab soldiers, the Israelis were victorious, especially when their air strikes on Egyptian air force bases eliminated Nasser's ability to retaliate. The 1967 Arab-Israeli War was viewed by many as a significantly hostile move on Israel's part and did much to dampen support for its status as the world's first Jewish state. Nasser, who felt responsible for the humiliating and devastating blow, resigned but was so highly regarded by his people that they took to the streets demanding that he stay in office, and he did.

Although he turned his attentions to modernizing the country and building relationships with foreign powers, especially the rest of the Arab world, Nasser never recovered from the humiliation of Egypt's defeat in the 1967 Arab-Israeli War. He launched the War of Attrition in 1969, a series of attacks on Israel designed to win back Egyptian honor, if not its lost land, which included the Gaza Strip. A cease-fire agreement between the countries was signed in 1970, with Egypt having regained neither its honor nor its land.

Despite his military defeat, Nasser's era ended with what many Egyptians consider his second greatest accomplishment after the Suez stand-off, the construction of the Aswan Dam in the south of Egypt. Completed in 1970, the dam provided water to previously non-irrigated land and vastly improved the fortunes of the struggling farmers in the region. Egypt also retained control of the Suez Canal, and in the 1973 Arab-Israeli War it was the site of the stunning Operation Badr, in which Egyptian forces crossed the canal to retake the Sinai Peninsula.

A sudden death

On September 28, 1970, Nasser suffered a heart attack and died at the age of fifty-two. The unexpected loss sent shock waves through the Arab world. Egypt went into a prolonged period of national mourning, and an estimated five million people followed his funeral procession in Cairo on October 1.

Decades later, many Arabs continued to revere Nasser as the man who challenged the West and freed his country from Western control and influence. Despite criticism for creating a state with repressive control and censoring the media, Nasser is remembered as a brilliant politician and patriot and for bringing Egypt into the twentieth century as a prosperous nation with an emerging middle class. "He will enter history as representative of Egypt, the same as [Emperor] Napoleon [Bonaparte] of France," declared the French writer André Malraux, as quoted in the book *Nasser: The Last Arab* written by Saïd K. Aburish.

For More Information

BOOKS

Aburish, Saïd K. *Nasser: The Last Arab*. New York: St. Martin's, 2004.

Mansfield, Peter. *Nasser's Egypt*. New York: Penguin, 1969.

Nutting, Anthony. *Nasser*. New York: Dutton, 1972.

Paparchontis, Kathleen. *100 Leaders Who Changed the World*. Milwaukee, WI: World Almanac, 2003.

Stephens, Robert Henry. *Nasser*. New York: Simon and Schuster, 1972.

PERIODICALS

Black, Ian. "The Suez War." *Guardian* (October 30, 1986).

Cambanis, Thanassis. "For Egypt's Revolutionaries, History Offers Discouraging Lessons." *The Atlantic* (June 14, 2011). Available online at http://www.theatlantic.com/international/archive/2011/06/for-egypts-revolutionaries-history-offers-discouraging-lessons/240401/ (accessed on November 30, 2011).

Doran, Michael Scott. "The Heirs of Nasser: Who Will Benefit from the Second Arab Revolution?" *Foreign Affairs* (May–June 2011).

"Egypt's Crisis, America's Dilemma." *Foreign Affairs* (Summer 1986): 960.

Reston, James. "Excerpts from Interview with President Gamal Abdel Nasser of the U.A.R." *New York Times* (February 15, 1970).

Benjamin Netanyahu

BORN: October 21, 1949 • Tel Aviv, Israel

Israeli prime minister, politician

"The founding of Israel did not stop the attacks on the Jews. It merely gave the Jews the power to defend themselves against those attacks."

Benjamin Netanyahu.
MANAHEM KAHANA/AFP/
GETTY IMAGES.

Benjamin Netanyahu served as Israel's prime minister twice in two decades. A well-known hawk (someone who advocates using military force or warlike action in order to carry out foreign policy), Netanyahu contends that his main political goals over the years have been prosperity through freedom and peace through security. He has promoted new high-tech industries, a free market economy, and democracy as the means to a prosperous Israel, and he has been outspoken regarding Israel's foreign policy for decades. In a 2009 speech to the United Nations, he signaled his willingness to move forward in the ongoing peace processes between Israel and the Palestinians (an Arab people whose ancestors lived in the historical region of Palestine and who continue to lay claim to that land) by saying, "All of Israel wants peace. . . . And if the Palestinians truly want peace, I and my government, and the people of Israel, will make peace. But we want a genuine peace, a defensible peace, a permanent peace."

Netanyahu does not believe that Palestinians accept Israel as a state. He remains firm in his belief that certain conditions must be met by the Palestinians to ensure Israel's safety before Israel will agree to a self-governed Palestinian state in the West Bank and the Gaza Strip, Arab regions occupied by Israel after the 1967 Arab-Israeli War (known as the Six-Day War in Israel). His conditions have been unacceptable to the majority of Palestinians. The prime minister, who began his second term in 2009, has many supporters in Israel and the United States who view his hard-line approach as a necessity for Israel, but he has also drawn international criticism for standing in the way of the peace process.

Growing up in two cultures

Benjamin (nicknamed "Bibi") Netanyahu was born on October 21, 1949, in Tel Aviv, Israel, just over a year after the state of Israel was established. He was the second of the three sons of Benzion Netanyahu, a noted professor of Jewish history and editor of the *Hebrew Encyclopedia*, and Tsilla (also spelled Cela) Netanyahu. Netanyahu's father was a prominent activist in Revisionist Zionism. (Zionism was an international political movement originating in the late nineteenth century that called for the creation of an independent Jewish state in Palestine.) Before the establishment of the state of Israel, the Revisionist Zionists fought for the Jewish right to sovereignty over *Eretz Yisrael* ("Land of Israel" in Hebrew; the ancient kingdom of the Jews). This region had come to be known as Palestine, and comprised parts of present-day Israel and Jordan. Netanyahu's father held very rigid ideas about Zionism. Even some of his contemporaries in the Zionist movement considered his views to be extreme.

Before Netanyahu was born, his parents worked in the New Zionist Organization in New York City. They moved to Israel soon after its founding in 1948 and the subsequent 1948 Arab-Israeli War (known as the War for Independence in Israel). During that war, hundreds of thousands of Arabs who had lived in Palestine became refugees, people who flee their country to escape violence or persecution. The conflict between Israel and the Palestinians would absorb Netanyahu for decades to come.

As a boy, Netanyahu lived with his family in the city of Jerusalem. In 1963, when Netanyahu was fourteen years old, the family moved to Philadelphia, Pennsylvania, where he attended high school.

In 1967 the neighboring Arab nations of Egypt, Syria, and Jordan began preparing to attack Israel with the goal of taking back Palestinian land. But Israeli forces attacked first, and after six days of fighting, Israel had conquered East Jerusalem, the Golan Heights, the West Bank, the Gaza Strip, and the Sinai Peninsula, nearly tripling its size. This short war, the 1967 Arab-Israeli War, would profoundly affect the Middle East and Netanyahu's life. Netanyahu, eighteen years old at the time, returned to Israel to serve in the Israeli Defense Forces (IDF) in the elite commando unit called the Sayeret Matkal. His older brother Jonathan (also spelled Yonatan, nicknamed "Yoni") served in the same unit. In 1972 Netanyahu was a member of a sixteen-person Sayeret Matkal rescue team, led by another future prime minister, Ehud Barak (1942–). The team rescued the passengers of a Sabena Boeing aircraft that had been hijacked by members of the Black September Organization, a Palestinian terrorist group. Netanyahu served in the IDF with distinction, and by 1972, when he was discharged from service, he had reached the rank of captain.

After military service, Netanyahu returned to the United States to attend the Massachusetts Institute of Technology (MIT) in Cambridge, Massachusetts, where he earned a master's degree in business. He interrupted his studies to return to Israel to fight in the 1973 Arab-Israeli War (known as the Yom Kippur War in Israel), in which Israel fought a coalition of Arab states led by Egypt and Syria. In 1976 Netanyahu's brother Jonathan took part in an IDF mission to free one hundred kidnapped passengers of an Air France flight that had been taken to Entebbe, Uganda, by its hijackers. Jonathan was killed in the operation, a painful event that influenced Netanyahu to become active in anti-terrorism efforts.

Political career begins

When Netanyahu returned to Israel in 1978 after completing his education, he went to work as a marketing manager for a large furniture company. When he was not at work, he spent a great deal of time commemorating his brother through antiterrorist seminars and writings, and by founding the Jonathan Netanyahu Anti-terror Institute. He organized two international conferences about combating international terrorism in 1979 and in 1984, drawing the attention of some major political figures. One of the people he impressed was Israel's ambassador to the United States, Moshe Arens (1925–).

In 1981 Arens offered Netanyahu the position of deputy chief of mission (the second-highest ranking diplomat in an embassy) at the Israeli embassy in the United States, which he accepted. In 1984 Netanyahu became Israel's ambassador to the United Nations, an international organization of countries founded in 1945 to promote international peace, security, and cooperation. Because Netanyahu spoke perfect English and was an outstanding public speaker, he became a familiar spokesperson in the United States, where he was often seen on television explaining Israeli policy. By the 1980s, the Palestinians had organized to fight Israel using whatever means they could against the more powerful nation, including guerrilla warfare (combat tactics used by a smaller, less equipped fighting force against a more powerful foe), such as launching small rockets at Israeli targets, and terrorist acts, such as hijacking planes and kidnapping people. While in Washington D.C., Netanyahu connected with conservative American Jews who pledged to support Israel in taking a very strict approach with the Palestinian Liberation Organization (PLO), a political and military organization formed to unite various Palestinian Arab groups with the goal of establishing an independent Palestinian state.

Rising in the ranks of Likud

In 1988 Netanyahu was elected to the Knesset, the Israeli parliament, as a member of the Likud Party. Likud is a large, conservative political party in Israel that takes some of its basic ideas from Revisionist Zionism, the branch of Zionism to which Netanyahu's father belonged. In the 1990s Likud stood for Israel's right to control the lands of Eretz Yisrael and opposed the formation of a Palestinian state. Netanyahu was named foreign minister, and in 1992 he became a deputy minister in the prime minister's office.

In 1992 Labor Party leader **Yitzhak Rabin** (1922–1995; see entry) was elected prime minister after pledging to strive for peace with the Palestinians. By 1993 he and PLO leader **Yasser Arafat** (1929–2004; see entry) had forged the historic peace agreement known as the Oslo Accords. The accords embraced a two-state solution to the Israeli-Palestinian conflict, paving the way for an independent nation called Palestine to exist alongside Israel. The agreement called for the withdrawal of Israeli troops from the Gaza Strip and some of the West Bank, and upheld the Palestinians' right to rule themselves in those territories. The accords were hailed worldwide as a path to peace in the Middle East. Netanyahu, who had been elected the party chairman of Likud in March of that year, was outspoken in his opposition to the Oslo Accords.

On November 4, 1995, a twenty-five-year-old Israeli student assassinated Rabin. The student believed that making peace with the Palestinians violated divine Jewish law. Israelis were shocked by the murder, and some blamed Netanyahu, whose fervent opposition to the prime minister's policies, they said, may have played a part in inflaming extremists like Rabin's murderer.

First term as prime minister

Netanyahu campaigned in the prime minister elections of 1996, promising to fight terrorism and to provide peace for Israel through strengthened security measures. Few expected him to win the election, but early in 1996 there were four suicide bombings in Israel, assumed to be the acts of Palestinian terrorists, that frightened many Israelis. Netanyahu's tough stance on terrorism gained appeal for some, and he was elected with a slight majority.

Within Israel and in the international community, many feared that Netanyahu would become an obstacle to the peace process begun with the Oslo Accords, and his term as prime minister was, indeed, tumultuous. Within months of taking office, he authorized the opening of the northern end of the Western Wall Tunnel in Jerusalem. The Western Wall (also known as the Wailing Wall) is a portion of the ancient wall that surrounded the Jewish Temple (also called the Second Temple), and is a sacred place for Jews. But the Al-Aqsa Mosque, a sacred Muslim shrine, sits above the Western Wall on the Temple Mount. Israeli security experts had warned Netanyahu against this project, because opening the tunnel was likely to be seen by Palestinians as an attempt by the Israeli authorities to stake a claim to ownership of part of the Muslim Quarter of Jerusalem. Netanyahu went forward despite the warnings. The project quickly sparked rioting and violent clashes between Israeli and Palestinian security forces. At least eighty people were killed.

With Israel deeply divided about the terms of the Oslo Accords, Netanyahu was in a difficult position. In 1997 he complied with the agreement by ceding control of the city of Hebron in the West Bank to the Palestinian Authority (PA), the new body of Palestinian government in the West Bank and the Gaza Strip that had been authorized by the Oslo

*Benjamin Netanyahu
acknowledges supporters at
Likud party headquarters in
Tel Aviv as he awaits results of
the 1996 election. Netanyahu
was elected prime minister with
a slight majority.* AP PHOTO/
NATI HARNIK.

Accords. The Israeli right wing (the conservative faction) was irate that
the prime minister had given up what many viewed as Israeli territory. In
1998 Netanyahu participated in negotiations with Arafat in the United
States, which resulted in both leaders signing the Wye River Memoran-
dum. Under this agreement, Israel was to withdraw its security forces
from 13 percent of the West Bank, thus allowing the Palestinian Authority control of approximately 40 percent of the area. In return, Arafat
agreed to help locate and arrest Palestinian agents of terror and violence

against Israel. Once again, the right-wing factions in Israel were outraged that Netanyahu had given up land to the PA. In the months that followed, however, Netanyahu failed to withdraw Israeli forces as promised, claiming that the PA had failed to live up to the terms of the agreement. He was then criticized sharply by supporters of the earlier peace agreements for freezing the peace process.

In addition to alienating both sides of the peace process debate, Netanyahu became the object of a police investigation into possible corrupt practices in his hiring of an attorney general. The case was dropped, but later that year another investigation into possible corrupt use of government funds was underway. No charges were ever filed against the prime minister. It was mainly dissatisfaction with his handling of the peace process that led the Knesset to grant a vote of no confidence in his government, pushing up the date of elections for prime minister. In the subsequent 1999 prime minister elections, Netanyahu lost to Labor Party leader Ehud Barak. Upon his defeat, Netanyahu resigned all political positions and announced that he would take a break from politics.

Netanyahu's return

When Netanyahu stepped down as the chairperson of the Likud Party, his rival, **Ariel Sharon** (1928–; see entry), took his place. In 2002 Sharon became Israel's prime minister and asked Netanyahu to serve as foreign minister. Netanyahu, who had spent several years as a business consultant to high-tech companies and giving speeches about Israel throughout the world, returned to full-time politics, serving in top positions in Sharon's government until 2005. He quit in August of that year in protest of Sharon's historic disengagement plan, in which the Israeli government evacuated (removed) all Jewish settlers from their communities in the Gaza Strip and withdrew its forces; it also evacuated some communities in the West Bank. This region had been occupied by Israel since the 1967 Arab-Israeli War and Israeli civilians had been settling there for many years. Netanyahu's anger at the idea of Israel ceding territory gained him favor among the country's right wing. Because of the deep divisions in the Likud Party, Sharon decided to form the more progressive Kadima Party. Netanyahu resumed his role as chair of Likud.

Later in 2006 Sharon suffered a stroke that left him in a permanent coma. Sharon's successor, Ehud Olmert (1945–) was accused of several counts of corruption and resigned in 2008. The Kadima Party was thrown into turmoil. In an election in 2009, the Kadima Party got the most votes and gained the most Knesset seats, but it was not enough to outweigh the combined seats of the right-wing parties, primarily Likud and the far-right party Yisrael Beiteinu. To avoid a stalemate, Israel's president asked Netanyahu to form a coalition government, in which political parties cooperate with each other, because no party holds the majority. In March 2009 Netanyahu was once again prime minister of Israel.

The situation in the Israeli-Palestinian conflict had changed since the last time Netanyahu was prime minister. Arafat had died in 2004. **Mahmoud Abbas** (1935–see entry), one of the cofounders of the Fatah Party, a Palestinian militant group and political party dedicated to the establishment of an independent Palestinian state, became the elected president of the PA. In the 2006 legislative elections, Hamas, the Islamist organization that had long refused to recognize Israel or renounce violence against it, won an overwhelming majority of the PA's parliamentary seats, giving it the right to form the next cabinet under Abbas. For a time, Fatah and Hamas attempted to work together in one government, but less than a year after the election fighting broke out between the two groups. After a violent split, Hamas took over the government of the Gaza Strip and Fatah, under Abbas, ruled the West Bank for the next four years. Hamas had been proclaimed a terrorist organization by the United States in 1993, and Netanyahu refused to engage in any dialogue with the group.

Netanyahu's primary concern in 2009 continued to be the security of Israel, and the increasingly powerful government of Iran was at the top of his worries. He feared that Iran was providing Hamas with military training and funding in order to destroy Israel. In neighboring Lebanon, the militant anti-Israeli group and political party Hezbollah was gaining control, not only through its large military forces, but also by democratic vote. Hezbollah, which had been placed on the U.S. list of foreign terrorist organizations in 1999, had long received support from Iran. Soon after his election, Netanyahu stated, "Iran is developing nuclear weapons and poses the greatest threat to our existence since the war of independence. Iran's terror wings surround us from the north and south," as quoted in the *Times* (London, England) newspaper.

Drawing fire from the international community

As prime minister of a large government coalition, Netanyahu was answering to powerful ministers who were even farther to the political right than he was. Many Western leaders and analysts feared that he would not seriously work toward the establishment of a Palestinian state, at least partly because it would result in the wrath of the right, whose support was essential to him. Of utmost concern to the international community in 2009 was the issue of Jewish settlements in the West Bank and East Jerusalem.

In 2009, as part of an attempt to restart the Middle East peace process, U.S. president Barack Obama (1961–) asked Israel to commit to a ten-month freeze on building new housing units in Jewish settlement communities in the West Bank and East Jerusalem. Netanyahu agreed to the moratorium in the West Bank, but he refused to restrict Jewish settlements in East Jerusalem. He also continued to allow the construction of schools, synagogues, and other buildings in the West Bank. The PA, in turn, refused to enter into negotiations to advance peace.

The settlement issue culminated in March 2010, when U.S. vice president Joe Biden (1942–) made a state visit to assure the Israeli people of the United States's steadfast commitment to their country. Hours after he arrived, Israel announced a plan to build sixteen hundred housing units for Jews in East Jerusalem. The announcement's timing embarrassed and infuriated the United States and cooled relations with the prime minister. Tensions increased when it became evident that even with the partial moratorium in place, Israel had found enough loopholes to continue building in the West Bank at a rapid pace. According to most authorities, the settlements violated the Geneva Conventions, international law which, among other things, prohibits an occupying power from settling its own civilians on militarily controlled land.

In 2010 Netanyahu drew more international criticism over an incident in which Israeli troops boarded a Turkish flotilla (fleet of ships) carrying aid to the Gaza Strip. Since Hamas had taken control of Gaza in 2007, the territory had been isolated by a blockade enforced by Israel on one side and Egypt on the other, preventing most shipments of supplies into the territory. Observers, including the United Nations, claimed that the blockade had caused a humanitarian crisis, a situation in which the safety, health, and well-being of a group of people are threatened. Pro-Palestinian activists decided to take action. They organized six ships, called the Free Gaza Flotilla, in Turkey, which were to carry supplies and more than six hundred activists to Gaza. On May 31, 2010, the ships attempted to break the blockade and were intercepted by Israeli navy

Jewish Settlements in the West Bank and the Gaza Strip

Jewish settlements are Israeli civilian communities established in the territories that were occupied by the Israeli army after the 1967 Arab-Israeli War. The settlements were established by Israeli policy, and the government invested heavily in their construction, maintenance, and military protection. They were meant to boost security in Israel by making its borders more defensible. They also increased the amount of land controlled by Israel, and many of their inhabitants were motivated to settle by religious zeal. Jewish religious groups such as Gush Emunim and others encouraged Jewish settlements throughout Palestine, because they believed that God have given this land to the Jewish people. Some believed that the resettling of the Jewish people in its homeland would lead to the coming of the Messiah, the anticipated savior of the Jews. But these settlements are located on land where the Palestinians intend to establish a self-governed nation. With their rapidly growing populations, the Jewish communities threaten Palestinian hopes for self-rule. They have been a constant obstacle in peace negotiations.

Article 49 of the Geneva Conventions (international laws regarding the treatment of prisoners of war and of civilians in wartime) prohibits an occupying power from moving its own civilian population onto occupied lands as permanent residents. In 2004 the International Court of Justice ruled that Israeli settlements in the occupied Palestinian territory violated the Geneva Conventions. The United Nations General Assembly stated in a 1997 resolution that "Israeli settlements in the Palestinian territory, including Jerusalem, and in the occupied Syrian Golan are illegal and an obstacle to peace and economic and social development."

Israel dismantled 18 settlements in the Sinai Peninsula in 1982, and in 2005 it evacuated all of its 21 settlements in the Gaza Strip and 4 in the West Bank. However, the remaining settlements in the West Bank and Jerusalem continued to grow at a rapid pace. In 2010

commandos. According to Israel's report, as the commandos boarded the ships, they were attacked by passengers and used their weapons only after being attacked. The activists, however, reported that the Israeli commandos fired first. Nine activists were killed, and many more were wounded. Netanyahu defended the commandos' action, stating that they had acted in accordance with international law. He denied that the blockade had caused a humanitarian crisis and accused Hamas and the international community of creating the illusion of a crisis as a pretext for breaking the blockade. Netanyahu refused to participate in a United Nations investigation of the incident, threatening to withdraw from the organization if Israeli commandos were questioned.

there were approximately 223 Israeli settlements in the West Bank and East Jerusalem. The settlements were inhabited by a population of nearly 500,000 Israeli settlers, with about 200,000 Israelis in settlements around Jerusalem and 300,000 in various regions of the West Bank. The population of Palestinians in the West Bank and Jerusalem is about 2.5 million.

An Israeli bulldozer breaks ground on new Jewish settlements in the West Bank city of Ramallah in 2010. © FADI AROURI/XINHUA PRESS/CORBIS

Uncertain times in the Middle East

In 2011 a rapid series of prodemocracy uprisings in countries such as Tunisia, Egypt, Libya, Syria, Yemen, and Bahrain shook the Middle East. The democratic movement, which came to be known as the Arab Spring, brought new challenges to Israel. For instance, it could no longer rely on Egypt, Israel's long-time ally, for support, after Egypt overthrew its president, **Hosni Mubarak** (1928–; see entry), who had upheld a strong alliance with Israel. New democracies in the Middle East could potentially elect militant Islamist groups (those who believe that Islam should provide the basis for political, social, and cultural life in Muslim nations) that were frequently anti-Western and anti-Israel. Although

Protestors in London, England, demonstrate against Israel after Israeli troops boarded a Turkish flotilla carrying aid to the Gaza Strip, killing nine activists and wounding others. Prime Minister Benjamin Netanyahu drew international criticism over the incident. FRANTZESCO KANGARIS/AFP/GETTY IMAGES.

Netanyahu strongly supported democracy, he feared that in the short run the Arab Spring might result in aggression toward Israel from its neighbors. Thus he advocated tightening Israeli security measures.

In April 2011, after four years of division, Hamas and Fatah reconciled and formed a unity government for the Gaza Strip and the West Bank. Soon after the PA announced this reconciliation, Netanyahu released a videotaped response in which he stated, as quoted on the *Ynetnews* Web site, "Palestinian Authority needs to choose between peace with the people of Israel and peace with Hamas. You cannot have peace with both, because Hamas aspires to destroy the State of Israel, and it says so openly."

A month later Obama once again urged Israel to take steps to start a new peace process. He said that Israel must begin by withdrawing to the borders it had prior to the 1967 Arab-Israeli War, using land swaps, or trading parcels of land, to make the new borders more acceptable to both parties. Netanyahu quickly rejected the president's request, claiming that the 1967 borders were indefensible for Israel. He affirmed his long-held position: Israel would not consider allowing the return of the millions of Palestinian refugees, and it would never allow Jerusalem to be divided.

Although Netanyahu repeatedly stated that Israel would make painful concessions to the Palestinians in the quest for peace, he refused to consider any arrangement that involved Hamas. Although he received a great deal of support in Israel and the United States for his tough stance, many analysts contend that he actually conceded nothing to the Palestinians and provided no route for a peace process. Daniel Levy, co-director of the Middle East Task Force at the New America Foundation, summed up this point of view, as quoted by James Kirkland in the *The Atlantic*, "I think Netanyahu knows a real peace deal will require compromises he is not willing to make, which has left him absolutely bereft of any viable vision for peace."

Still, when he spoke to the U.S. Congress on May 24, 2011, contesting Obama's position on Israel's borders, Netanyahu received multiple standing ovations. At one point in the speech Netanyahu stated, as quoted in the *Atlanta Journal-Constitution*, "We must take calls for our destruction seriously. When we say never again, we mean never again." In September 2011 Abbas appeared before the United Nations Security Council to request recognition of a Palestinian state with pre–1967 borders. Netanyahu's response stated that the core of the Israeli Palestinian conflict was Palestine's refusal to recognize the state of Israel, and called for Palestinians to first make peace with Israel.

For More Information

BOOKS

Netanyahu, Benjamin. *A Durable Peace: Israel and Its Place among the Nations.* New York: Grand Central Publishing, 1999.

Tessler, Mark. *A History of the Israeli-Palestinian Conflict*, 2nd ed. Bloomington: Indiana University Press, 2009.

PERIODICALS

Hider, James. "Binyamin Netanyahu Warns of Iranian Nuclear Threat." *The Times* (London, England; February 21, 2009). Available online at http://www.timesonline.co. uk/tol/news/world/middle_east/article5776460.ece (accessed on November 30, 2010).

Kitfield, James. "Netanyahu's 'Unvarnished Truth' Tour." *The Atlantic* (May 25, 2010). Available online at http://www.theatlantic.com/international/archive/2011/05/netanyahus-unvarnished-truth-tour/239443/ (accessed on November 30, 2010).

Remnick, David. "A Man, A Plan." *New Yorker* (March 21, 2011). Available online at http://www.newyorker.com/talk/comment/2011/03/21/110321taco_talk_remnick (accessed on November 30, 2011).

WEB SITES

"Benjamin Netanyahu." *New York Times* (May 24, 2011). http://topics.nytimes.com/top/reference/timestopics/people/n/benjamin_netanyahu/index.html (accessed May on 19, 2011).

"Benjamin Netanyahu's [2009] Speech at the UN." *Jerusalem Post.* http://www.jewishpost.com/news/Benjamin-Netanyahu-Speech-at-the-UN.html (accessed November 30, 2011).

"Fatah, Hamas Sign Reconciliation Agreement." *Ynetnews.com* (April 27, 2011). http://www.ynetnews.com/articles/0,7340,L-4061418,00.html (accessed on November 30, 2011).

"General Assembly Resolution 51/133." *United Nations* (February 20, 1997). http://www.un.org/documents/ga/res/51/ares51-133.htm (accessed on November 30, 2010).

"Prime Minister Benjamin Netanyahu." *Ynetnews.com* (May 4, 2009). http://www.ynetnews.com/articles/0,7340,L-3482383,00.html (accessed on November 30, 2010).

"Prime Minister Benjamin Netanyahu's Speech to AIPAC Conference." *Haaretz.com* (March 23, 2010). http://www.haaretz.com/news/prime-minister-benjamin-netanyahu-s-speech-to-aipac-conference-1.265227 (accessed on November 30, 2010.)

Teibel, Amy. "Netanyahu: Israel Ready for Painful Compromises." *ABC News, U.S* (May 24, 2011). http://abcnews.go.com/US/wireStory?id=13676143 (accessed on November 30, 2010.)

Mohammad Reza Pahlavi

BORN: October 26, 1919 • Tehran, Persia

DIED: July 27, 1980 • Cairo, Egypt

Iranian emperor

"A sovereign may not save his throne by shedding his countryman's blood."

Mohammad Reza Pahlavi was the shah of Iran from 1941 to 1979, and he is widely credited with bringing Iran into the modern age. Pahlavi was the last royal figure to lead Iran, and his autocratic leadership style, bolstered by a seemingly endless supply of oil revenue and strong alliances with the United States and other Western powers, eventually lead the country into the 1979 Iranian Revolution (also known as the Islamic Revolution). Pahlavi was overthrown and Iran emerged as one of the Middle East's mostly deeply entrenched theocracies, or a government based on religious principles.

Becomes crown prince of Persia

Pahlavi was born in Tehran, Persia (present-day Iran), on October 26, 1919, arriving before his twin sister, Ashraf. His father, Reza Khan (1878–1944), was a military officer serving with the Persian Cossack

Mohammad Reza Pahlavi.
BACHRACH/GETTY IMAGES.

325

Brigade, an elite guard unit. His mother was Nimtaj Ayromlou, a descendant of a family of Caucas roots that had risen to military prominence in Persia in the nineteenth century. In early 1921 Reza Khan, by then leader of the Cossack Brigade, capitalized on fears that the Russian Civil War (1917–23) would spill across Persia's northern borders and seized power in Persia. Four years later he crowned himself shah and Mohammad, his eldest son, became the new crown prince.

Pahlavi's father had ousted the ruling Qajar dynasty, which had held power in Persia since the 1790s. (A dynasty is a series of rulers from the same family.) Reza Shah was determined to modernize the kingdom. The land had a long history dating back to ancient times and was one of the first places on Earth with permanent human agricultural settlements. In the third century CE the Persians began expanding into neighboring territories by force, creating the immense Parthian and Sassanid empires, which endured for more than four centuries. Persia lost territory and a significant chunk of its population during the Mongol invasions of the early Middle Ages (c. 500–c. 1500). It became a Shiite state in 1501, ruled by various royal clans who successfully resisted foreign dominance. (Shiites are followers of the Shia branch of the religion of Islam.)

Reza Shah began a modernization program modeled on that of neighboring Turkey under President **Mustafa Kemal Atatürk** (1881–1938; see entry). He replaced sharia, Islamic religious law, with a secular (non-religious) legal code in 1926. He banned traditional dress in 1928, and outlawed the chador, the head-to-toe covering worn by Muslim women in public in 1934. Pahlavi's mother, now known as Tadj ol-Molouk, which roughly translates as "crown of the king," supported this effort by appearing in public with her daughters in Western dress. Pahlavi's father also undertook a concerted effort to curtail the power of the Shiite clerics (ordained religious leaders), who were based in the ancient religious city of Qom.

Oil was discovered in southern Persia in the years just before World War I (1914–18). The Anglo-Persian Oil Company was established to drill, extract, refine, and export this valuable commodity, but the British government owned 51 percent of the company and paid Iran just 16 percent of the profits; the foreign deal was necessary because a less-developed nation like Iran lacked the technical resources to extract, refine, and ship crude oil on the export market. The battle over ownership of this resource would drag on for decades and play a significant role in Iran's political atmosphere during the modern era, with Iranians believing the set-up was simply a modernized, legally sanctioned form of colonial exploitation. In 1935, Reza Shah resurrected an ancient name for the kingdom, and the country became known as Iran.

Educated in Switzerland

While his father worked to modernize the nation, Pahlavi attended a military school in Tehran until 1931, then enrolled at Le Rosey, an elite boarding school in Switzerland. His classmates there included princes from the royal houses of Europe as well as young men of newer American fortunes. Pahlavi's entourage included a chauffeur, valet, footman, and diplomatic attaché. He excelled both academically and on the playing fields, and even captained the soccer team before graduating in 1936. Returning to Iran, he completed his studies at the Tehran Military College in 1938.

On March 16, 1939, Pahlavi married the spectacularly glamorous Princess Fawzia bint Fuad, sister of Egypt's King Farouk I (1920–1965). Their marriage produced a daughter, Shahnaz, born in 1940, but no male heirs, and the couple divorced in 1948. In 1951 Pahlavi wed Soraya Esfandiari Bakhtiari, the daughter of an Iranian diplomat. Their marriage produced no children, and this was worrisome for Pahlavi and his circle. It was feared that one of his half brothers, or a child born to Shahnaz, would be able seize the throne. Soraya refused to let him take a second wife, as Muslim law permitted, and they divorced in 1958. Pahlavi then searched for eligible brides among Europe's aristocracy, including princesses of the British and Italian royal families, but if he married a non-Muslim he would have risked losing the support of Iranians, who were predominantly Shiite. On December 21, 1959, he married Farah Diba, the daughter of an Iranian bureaucrat whom he had met while she was studying architecture in Paris, France. A long-awaited son, Reza, was born in October 1960. The couple had three more children: Farahnaz, born in 1963; Ali Reza, born in 1966; and Leila, born in 1970.

Assuming the throne

The two full decades between Pahlavi's first and third marriages had been tumultuous ones for the nation. Iran's oil fields in the south were vital to the Allies (Great Britain, France, the Soviet Union, the United States, and China) in World War II (1939–45) as they fought the Axis Powers (Germany, Italy, and Japan). Yet the oil fields' strategic location made them vulnerable to a preemptive move by the Soviet Union to seize them. His father had long battled with the Anglo-Persian Oil Company, now renamed the Anglo-Iranian Oil Company (AIOC), for an increased share of revenues and won international support for his mission. Despite the presence of a majlis (parliament), Reza Shah ran the country like a personal fiefdom, or a piece of property wholly controlled by a single family, who exploit its resources for their own personal gain. Iran's royal family grew immensely wealthy, which prompted resentment inside Iran. On August 25, 1941, Iran was invaded by a combined force of British and Russian troops, who deposed Reza Shah. Pahlavi, now twenty-one years old and considered far more progressive than his father, was installed in his place as few weeks later. "If he continues in that modest strain—giving the people a share in the government and more liberty than they have known for the past 20 years—then there is no reason to believe that he will not reign happily for a long time," asserted the *Times* of London on September 18, 1941.

Pahlavi's father was sent into exile, expelled first to the British-controlled Indian Ocean island of Mauritius, then to South Africa, where he died in July 1944. The Persian Corridor, a supply route through Iran which supplied the Soviets with U.S. and British armaments and aided in the fight against the Axis Powers, remained a vital element in the ultimate success of the war, ferrying trucks, munitions, and even bomber planes via the Persian Gulf. Pahlavi even hosted a top-secret meeting in November 1943, known as the Tehran Conference, attended by British prime minister Winston Churchill (1874–1965), U.S. president Franklin D. Roosevelt (1882–1945), and Soviet premier Joseph Stalin (1879–1953).

On February 4, 1949, Pahlavi stepped out of his black Rolls-Royce limousine for an event at Tehran University. A young man posing as a photographer pulled out a pistol and fired; one of the bullets grazed Pahlavi on his cheek. The assassin turned out to be an Islamic radical, who tried to flee but was quickly felled by bullets from the Shah's security detail. Pahlavi's government used the incident as a convenient justification for cracking down on the Communist Tudeh Party, which had been created earlier in the 1940s and was gaining some significant support. A new Constitutional Assembly convened a few months later. The assembly delegates gathered to draft a new constitution, and gave the shah the power to dissolve the majlis if he so desired.

Reza Shah's deal with the AIOC still rankled many Iranians, especially when Saudi Arabia cut a generous fifty-fifty deal with Standard Oil of

California for access to its kingdom's even larger oil fields after the Saudi king threatened to nationalize them entirely in 1950. (Nationalization is the practice of bringing private industry under the ownership and control of the government.) In March of 1951 the majlis voted in favor of taking control of Iran's oil fields. On May 1, 1951, Pahlavi announced that the AIOC and its holdings in Iran would be nationalized, voiding the contract that gave the company control of the oil fields until 1993.

Strikes fatal deal with CIA

In the 1951 election a new National Front coalition won a majority of majlis seats. The leader of the National Front was Mohammed Mossadegh (1882–1967), a popular Iranian politician. Because Iran used a parliamentary system of government, in the general election the head of the party that received the most votes won the right to form a government. This meant that the head of the party became prime minister. Mossadegh became prime minister, and Pahlavi appointed him to serve as premier, as well. Pahlavi and Mossadegh began a power struggle that dragged on for more than two years; Mossadegh enjoyed immense popular support, while the Shah was viewed as the figurehead of an increasingly outdated regime. The U.S. and British governments feared Mossadegh, whose popularity inside Iran seemed a sign that the Iranians were determined to rule themselves, free from any foreign interference. The U.S. and British began to provoke internal discord, using Pahlavi as their ally. In October 1952 Mossadegh broke all diplomatic ties with Great Britain, and even exiled Princess Ashraf, the shah's twin sister, who had spent time in Western Europe and come under the influence of Western intelligence agents. Finally in August 1953 Pahlavi dismissed Mossadegh, but the prime minister refused to step down. Widespread protests erupted in Tehran and other cities in support of the ousted Mossadegh. In the early morning hours of August 16, when it appeared that Pahlavi had lost the support of a key Iranian army general, he fled the country with his family. They flew first to Baghdad, Iraq, and then on to Rome, Italy, where they were besieged by international media outside the Hotel Excelsior.

He would not remain in exile for long. The plan to oust Mossadegh was a carefully planned covert operation conducted by agents of Great Britain's Secret Intelligence Service and the U.S. Central Intelligence Agency (CIA). Known by its code name Operation Ajax, it was devised in part by Kermit Roosevelt Jr. (1916–2000), grandson of former U.S.

president Theodore Roosevelt (1858–1919) and chief of the CIA's Middle East section at the time. Demonstrations in support of Pahlavi and against Mossadegh and the National Front were organized while Pahlavi met with U.S. officials in Italy. On August 19, he received word that royalist (supporters of the monarchy) mobs and a few tanks had attacked the prime minister's office, and Mossadegh had fled. The prime minister was placed in military custody, convicted of treason by judges allied with Pahlavi, and sentenced to death. The sentence was commuted (reduced) by Pahlavi, and Mossadegh spent the rest of his life under house arrest. He died in 1967.

The events of August 1953 played a pivotal role in Pahlavi's regime and eventual downfall. "The Shah's legitimacy was irreparably compromised by owing his throne to Washington [the U.S. government]," argues Mostafa T. Zabrani, a United Nations official, in a 2002 article titled "The Coup That Changed the Middle East: Mossadeq v. the CIA in

Shah Reza Pahlavi saluting Iranian troops upon his return from exile in 1953. CARL MYDANS/TIME LIFE PICTURES/GETTY IMAGES.

Retrospect" in the *World Policy Journal*. "It is a reasonable argument that but for the coup [overthrow of the government] Iran now would be a mature democracy." The new prime minister, Fazlollah Zahedi (1897–1963), restored AIOC rights to Iran's oil fields but cut a new, much more favorable deal for the Iranian treasury.

Establishes an internal police force

Pahlavi remained on the throne for another twenty-six years. In 1957 a team of U.S. Army officers helped him establish a tough, new secret-police agency known as SAVAK, which is an acronym for *Sazeman-e ettela'at va amniat-e keshvar* (National Intelligence and Security Organization). SAVAK was a widely feared tool of Pahlavi's regime. The agency had wide powers to question and detain those deemed a threat to the throne or the country's stability. It was particularly skilled in some of the more heinous methods of torture, which were a blight on Pahlavi's regime and widely denounced by international human-rights agencies.

In 1963 Pahlavi announced Iran's new White Revolution, named for what he believed would be a significant but bloodless reform. At the center of the program was a massive land-redistribution deal that restricted the power of wealthy landowners. Other elements of his program included the nationalization of Iran's water resources, forests, and pasturelands; free university education; and a literacy corps. Women's rights was the most controversial part of the White Revolution, and it included reform of divorce and family law. Iranian women benefited greatly from these measures, which were vehemently opposed by Shiite clerics. Government price controls imposed under the economic modernization also served to alienate the *bazaari*, Iran's traditional merchant class. Riots erupted in Tehran and several other cities in early June 1963 after Shiite leader **Ayatollah Ruhollah Khomeini** (1900–1989; see entry) was jailed for publicly criticizing Pahlavi and the White Revolution.

On the day of his forty-eighth birthday, October 26, 1967, Pahlavi crowned himself emperor of Iran in a magnificent coronation ceremony that included opulent horse-drawn carriages. He made Farah Diba the first empress of Iran, and she wore a couture gown from the House of Dior and a 3.5-pound (1.6-kilogram) diadem (crown) featuring 1,646 diamonds.

Party in Persepolis

Pahlavi's most decadent display of wealth and power came at the twenty-five-hundredth anniversary celebration to commemorate the founding of the Persian Empire by Cyrus the Great (c. 600–530 BCE) in 530 BCE. Held over four days in October 1971 after a decade of preparation, the party was held under tight security in the ancient city of Persepolis. The cost of the party was estimated at two hundred million dollars. There was a fleet of new, red, Mercedes-Benz limousines to transport international heads of state and celebrities, who were housed in fifty tents outfitted to serve as five-star hotels. The royal entourage's tents included marble bathrooms. Pahlavi's elite Household Guard sported new uniforms made by a Paris designer. The event included a lavish five-and-a-half hour banquet at which the attendees dined on porcelain dinnerware and drank champagne, followed by a fireworks display. **Ayatollah Ruhollah Khomeini** (1900–1989; see entry), then living in exile in Iraq, denounced the festivities. "It is the kings of Iran that have constantly ordered massacres of their own people and had pyramids built with their skulls," he said, according to Elaine Sciolino in *Persian Mirrors: The Elusive Face of Iran*. "Islam came in order to destroy these palaces of tyranny. Monarchy is one of the most shameful and disgraceful reactionary manifestations."

SCIOLINO, ELAINE. *PERSIAN MIRRORS: THE ELUSIVE FACE OF IRAN*. NEW YORK: SIMON & SCHUSTER, 2001, PP. 162–163.

Faces growing unrest

Pahlavi grew increasingly autocratic, ruling with absolute authority as challenges arose to his power. Even the SAVAK, which closely watched the members of the extended Pahlavi family and reported on their misdeeds, became a threat. In 1975 Pahlavi created a new single political party, Hizb-i Rastakhiz (Resurgence Party). With membership compulsory for any professional advancement the new party only increased domestic opposition to Pahlavi's regime. There were also signals that leaders of Western nations were losing faith in the shah, particularly after the 1976 election of U.S. president Jimmy Carter (1924–), due to Iran's long record of human-rights abuses and anti-democracy measures. Carter was an avowed supporter of human rights worldwide and had taken office with a pledge that the United States would not support reactionary regimes. The signs of discontent and enmity toward SAVAK in Iran, were, as Western nations realized, a threat to the stability of the region, and Western leaders came to believe that Pahlavi should be persuaded to either enact genuine political reforms or step down.

Pahlavi did not agree with either option, and Iran grew increasingly restless, a situation accidentally reinforced by its excellent educational system. Young Iranians were frustrated by the lack of a political voice in their country, while devout Muslims supported Khomeini, who continued to rail against Pahlavi's regime from exile. Others were aghast at Iran's relations with Israel, the world's first Jewish state and a sworn enemy to nearly all Arab (Arabic-speaking) countries. Under Pahlavi, Iran became the first nation in the Middle East with a Muslim-majority population to establish formal diplomatic ties with Israel.

Iran's writers, poets, lawyers, and other members of the intellectual elite first took up the daring act of publicly stating their opposition to the Pahlavi autocracy in the spring and summer of 1977. This dissent turned into demonstrations in Tehran, Tabriz, and other cities by early 1978. Pahlavi claimed the unrest was a plot by the United States and its allies, working with the Soviet Union, to oust him from power because they were displeased over his influence as a key member of the Organization of Petroleum Exporting Countries (OPEC), and organization formed in 1960 by the world's major oil-producing nations to coordinate policies and ensure stable oil prices in world markets. He warned Iranians that they were being exploited by foreign elements who wanted to see him removed from power. With civil war seemingly imminent, U.S. and British authorities considered coming to Pahlavi's aid but decided against it because the Pahlavi regime had so clearly lost the support of the clerics, the middle-class, and even the military.

Loses access to credit

Iran was destabilized by growing civil unrest throughout the summer of 1978. Historians cite August 19, 1978, as the beginning of the end of Pahlavi's rein. On that date more than three hundred people died in a fire in a movie house in the city of Abadan. The doors of the Cinema Rex were locked by a mob from the outside during a showing of *Gavaznha* (The Deer), and theatergoers burned to death inside after a fire was set. It was one of the worst disasters to befall modern Iran, and word quickly spread that the incident was the work of SAVAK agents. Later revelations cast the blame for the act on Islamic revolutionaries, who considered movies a particularly revolting symbol of Western decadence. The tragedy galvanized otherwise indifferent Iranians into choosing sides in the growing movement to oust Pahlavi.

Martial law (the imposition of military rule on an emergency basis) was declared in Tehran on September 7, 1978, with little effect on the unrest. In October a general strike (work stoppage) was declared by leaders of the movement to oust the shah, and the country's economy shuddered to a halt within days. Even oil workers went on strike. When oil production halted, so did Pahlavi's access to international credit and he was unable to keep his government running.

In early November Pahlavi installed a military government, and there were several attempts to devise a plan for Pahlavi to step down from office that would satisfy everyone, including the National Front and the Islamic revolutionaries. One issue was whether or not he could remain in the country. He sent his valet to Switzerland with a planeload of personal items, then on January 16, 1979, he departed for what the press and diplomatic advisers termed "a vacation." Images from this day at Tehran airport show Pahlavi's supporters clad in Western-style suits bidding emotional farewells to Pahlavi and his wife, who wore a fur hat and high-heeled leather boots. Their private plane flew first to Aswan, Egypt, where Pahlavi met with the last major world leader who offered him support, President **Anwar Sadat** (also spelled al-Sadat; 1918–1981; see entry). The Pahlavis stayed in Egypt for a week before departing for Morocco, where King Hassan II (1929–1999) had offered shelter. Then the Moroccan monarch, pressured by internal and external forces, asked the Pahlavis to leave. Only the Caribbean island nation of the Bahamas would grant them a tourist visa. Pahlavi had hoped to settle in England, but two successive British governments rejected his request. U.S. officials persuaded Mexico to give the Pahlavis an entry visa, and the Pahlavis settled in Cuernavaca, near Mexico City.

Endures exile

Pahlavi had secretly been suffering from non-Hodgkin's lymphoma, a type of cancer, since 1973. His judgment in the crisis that precipitated his ouster was said to have been compromised by side effects from the strong chemotherapy drugs he was taking, according to those who were close to the shah during the crisis, who would later say that his mental acuity appeared to have declined. His health worsened considerably with the stress of exile, and physicians in Mexico City advised him to seek treatment in the United States. After receiving permission to enter the United States, he arrived at New York's LaGuardia Airport on October 22, 1979, and checked into New York Hospital (present-day New York-Presbyterian Hospital) under a false name. The *New York Times* discovered the ruse, and Pahlavi's plight became a major international news story. Back in Tehran, a group of university students plotted to force the United States into a situation where the U.S. would be forced to send the shah back to Iran. On November 4, 1979, they stormed the U.S. embassy in Tehran and took several Americans hostage. The standoff lasted 444 days, with a total of fifty-two hostages held for that duration. The new Islamic government, with Khomeini as its head, symbolically released the hostages on the day Carter left the White House and Ronald Reagan (1911–2004) was sworn in as president of the United States. The Islamic militants remained angry that Carter had refused to extradite the shah and had allowed him to enter the United States for medical treatment.

Surgeons in New York removed Pahlavi's gallbladder, and he flew to Lackland Air Force Base in Texas for a few weeks to recover while U.S. officials arranged his next journey. Finally Panama offered to accept the Pahlavis, and they stayed at a luxury resort on a private island called Contadora. Their stay was a short one, for Panama was informed of an arrest warrant for Pahlavi and a request for his extradition to Iran. Pahlavi was forced to return to Cairo in March 1980. The plane stopped in the Azores Islands to refuel, where he feared the U.S. government had tricked him and was indeed planning to deliver him to Iran in exchange for the release of the American hostages once his plane was airborne. But the plane landed in Cairo and Pahlavi spent the final months of his life under heavy guard at Koubbeh Palace, working on his memoir with a pair of journalists. Egypt had no plans to honor Iran's extradition order and hand over the ex-shah. He was under guard because of credible threats on his life; pro-Islamic militants might have carried out a kidnapping or assassination attempt if he had not been under Egyptian military protection. He died on July 27, 1980, at Maadi military hospital outside Cairo from complications of non-Hodgkin's lymphoma.

Khomeini returned to Iran two weeks after Pahlavi left. He became Supreme Leader of Iran and the guiding force behind the Islamic Revolution, which restored sharia law to Iran, removed all Western influences, and broke ties with Israel. The new regime went on to provide training, funds, and arms to scores of Islamic militant movements throughout the Middle East.

For More Information

BOOKS

Afkhami, Gholam Reza. *The Life and Times of the Shah*. Berkeley: University of California Press, 2009.

Kamrava, Mehran. *The Modern Middle East: A Political History since the First World War*. Berkeley: University of California Press, 2011.

Mílaní, Abbas. *The Shah*. New York: Palgrave Macmillan, 2011.

Sciolino, Elaine. *Persian Mirrors: The Elusive Face of Iran*. New York: Simon & Schuster, 2001, pp. 162–163.

PERIODICALS

"Deposed Shah Dies in Egypt at 60." *New York Times* (July 28, 1980).

"Good Start by New Shah." *Times* (London, England; September 18, 1941).

"Iran: The Military Is in Charge." *Time* (November 27, 1978).

MacFarquhar, Neil. "Persepolis Journal; Shah's Tent City, Fit for Kings, May Lodge Tourists." *New York Times* (September 7, 2001).

Pace, Eric. "Iran's Shah Crowns Himself and Queen." *New York Times* (October 27, 1967).

Solomon, Deborah. "The Exile: Questions for Reza Pahlavi." *New York Times* (June 28, 2009).

Zahrani, Mostafa T. "The Coup That Changed the Middle East: Mossadeq v. the CIA in Retrospect." *World Policy Journal* (Summer 2002): 93.

Shimon Peres

BORN: August 1923 • Wiszniewo, Poland

Israeli president, prime minister, cabinet official

"Peace reflects the most fundamental right and human desire—the right to life. Peace is the right of a parent to protect a child from poverty and conflict, and peace is the profound social diktat [decree] that a man must put down his gun."

Shimon Peres has spent the majority of his life working to ensure Israel's independence and security. A political veteran who served almost fifty years in the Knesset, Israel's parliament (legislature), Peres helped build the nation's armed forces as minister for defense and went on to serve multiple times as foreign affairs minister. He served as prime minster from 1984 to 1985, and again in 1995. In 1994 he won the Nobel Peace Prize, an honor he shared with fellow Israeli **Yitzhak Rabin** (1922–1995; see entry) and the Palestine Liberation Organization (PLO) leader **Yasser Arafat** (1929–2004; see entry). (The PLO is a political and military organization formed to unite various Palestinian Arab groups with the goal of establishing an independent Palestinian state.) In 2007 Peres was elected to serve as Israel's ninth president, a position with a seven-year

Shimon Peres. ALEX WONG/ GETTY IMAGES.

term of office. In a 2007 article for *Haaretz*, a newspaper in Israel, Amiram Barkat writes, "What is unusual about Peres' biography is not just his accomplishments to date, but the fact that Peres, who has written 11 books and has promoted the development of Israel's security industry, never attended university or served in the army."

Early life

Shimon Peres was born Szymon Perski in Wiszniewo, Poland (present-day Vishneva, Belarus), in August 1923. His father, Yitzhak (1749–1821), was a well-to-do merchant, and his mother, Sara, was descended from Chaim Volozhin, a prominent rabbi (a Jewish scholar, teacher, and religious leader). Peres's grandfather was a rabbi, too, and gave him his first religious training. As a youth, Peres was active in two youth groups, Hashomer Hatzair and the Betar scouts. These were Zionist groups, supporting the international political movement that called for the creation of an independent Jewish state in Palestine. (Palestine is a historical region in the Middle East on the eastern shore of the Mediterranean Sea, comprising parts of present-day Israel and Jordan.)

Poland's high taxes on Jewish citizens and Jewish-owned businesses compelled Peres's father to follow some of his relatives who had immigrated to Palestine. Yitzhak left Poland in 1932, and he sent for his wife and two sons in 1934 after he had established himself in the city of Tel Aviv. They arrived in 1935, and the transition was not a difficult one, as Peres recalls in his autobiography, *Battling for Peace: A Memoir*. "We had not merely come to a new place but had become new and different people," he writes. Instead of a brutal Polish winter and the isolation of the Baltic forestlands, Peres found himself living in a bustling, cosmopolitan city with movie theaters, beachfront cafés, and abundant good weather.

Peres eagerly embraced Zionism, joining Hanoar Haoved (Working Youth), an organization that prepared youngsters for eventual membership in the Haganah, the underground defense force of Zionists in Palestine from 1920 to 1948. It became the basis for the Israeli army. He moved to Hanoar Haoved's kibbutz (a Jewish communal farming settlement in Israel, where settlers share all property and work collaboratively together) and was especially attracted to the group's socialist ideals, although he would later disavow socialism. (Socialism is a system in which the government owns the means of production and controls the distribution of goods and services.) At age fifteen, he moved to Ben-Shemen Agricultural School, where students grew their own food, ran the school, and completed their formal education. There he also began weapons training and worked as a night guard for the school, which experienced regular attacks by hostile neighbors. When Jews began immigrating to Palestine, the area was already populated by Arabs who had lived there for hundreds of years. Conflict between the two groups, who both had historic claims to the land, was unavoidable. (Arabs are people who speak the Arabic-language or who live in countries in which Arabic is the dominant language.)

Devotes years to kibbutz

In the early 1940s Peres became an officer of Hanoar Haoved and lived for a few years on Kibbutz Alumot, where he raised crops, tended cattle, and even worked as a shepherd. In 1945 he married Sonia Gelman, with whom he would have three children. That year also marked the end of World War II (1939–45; a war in which the Allies [Great Britain, France, the Soviet Union, the United States, and China] defeated the Axis Powers [Germany, Italy, and Japan]). The Perskis were devastated to learn that every member of their family back in Wiszniewo had perished after Germany invaded Poland. Peres's grandfather and most of Wiszniewo's Jews had been locked inside the town's synagogue, which was then set on fire.

As a recruiter for and officer of Hanoar Haoved, Peres demonstrated a talent for public speaking. He visited existing Hanoar Haoved branches and established new ones, and that role prepared him for a life in politics. Showing his commitment to his adopted homeland, he changed his first and last names to Hebrew versions, becoming Shimon Peres. (Hebrew is the ancient language of the Jewish people and the official language of present-day Israel.)

Peres was a devoted follower of **David Ben-Gurion** (1886–1973; see entry), the early Zionist pioneer who would become Israel's first prime minister. He joined Ben-Gurion's Mapai Party; wrote a daily column for the party newspaper, *Yediot Hadashot*; and edited the newspaper of the youth branch of the party. In 1946, at age twenty-three, Ben-Gurion appointed Peres as a delegate to the World Zionist Congress in Basel, Switzerland. A year later, he was posted to the high command of the Haganah and was put in charge of obtaining weapons, a job in which he excelled. After the Jewish nation of Israel was established in 1948, Peres remained in the Haganah leadership ranks as it evolved into the new country's military, the Israel Defense Forces (IDF). Levi Eshkol (1895–1969), then director general of the ministry of defense, noticed Peres's abilities, and when he needed an IDF representative to acquire weapons in the United States, he chose Peres, even though Peres did not speak English and had relatively little experience with Americans.

After becoming deputy head of the defense ministry's mission in New York City, Peres moved with his wife and daughter to the United States in 1949. He quickly learned English, and began recruiting supporters and obtaining equipment for the Israeli military. Building relationships with wealthy Americans and Canadians who were eager to support Israel, he helped persuade a Jewish-American aerospace engineer, Al Schwimmer (1917–2011), to move to Israel and establish Israel's aircraft industry. He also continued his own education, enrolling in courses at the New School for Social Research in New York City and taking courses in management at Harvard University in Cambridge, Massachusetts.

Holds top defense positions

Upon his return to Israel in 1952, Peres became deputy director general of the ministry of defense. By 1953 he became director general, a position he held until 1959. During this period, he was a key figure in establishing Israel's nuclear weapons program, which started with the top-secret Dimona reactor, built with French assistance and located in the Negev desert. Peres viewed nuclear weapons as essential to Israel's security because the country largely lacked conventional natural barriers, such as large rivers or mountain ranges, and was surrounded by hostile Arab nations who believed that Israel had established itself on land that rightfully belonged to Arab Palestinians. Several Arab nations had even gone to war against Israel in 1948, after the new Jewish nation was created. This was the 1948 Arab-Israeli War (known in Israel as the War for Independence). "Israel never said that we were introducing nuclear bombs," he told Adrian Blomfield, a journalist with Great Britain's *Daily Telegraph*, years later. "We don't mind the suspicion because we think it is a deterrent [something that discourages enemy attack]. That's what we wanted to achieve, a deterrent. Our policy is to have a deterrent because we are being threatened."

In 1959 Peres was elected to the Knesset on the Mapai Party ticket and promoted to deputy minister of defense in Ben-Gurion's cabinet. He remained in that post until 1965, when he resigned in order to join Ben-Gurion in the formation of a new political party, called Rafi, with several other former Mapai members of the Knesset. Rafi failed to win enough seats in the 1965 election, however, and three years later would merge into the newly formed Labor Party.

Israel's conflict with its Arab neighbors had remained unresolved, and the plight of the Palestinians, thousands of whom had become refugees (people who flee their country to escape violence or persecution) after the 1948 Arab-Israeli War, aroused international sympathy. Hostilities between Israel and its Arab neighbors intensified in late May and early June 1967. Israel claimed to have learned of large troop movements at its north and south borders and its well equipped air force attacked first, destroying the Egyptian air force in a matter of hours. Thus began the 1967 Arab-Israeli War (known in Israel as the Six-Day War), fought against Egypt, Jordan, and Syria. The conflict was a pivotal moment in the history of modern Israel. In less than a week's time, Israel tripled in size, seizing the entire Sinai Peninsula and the Gaza Strip from Egypt, the heavily populated West Bank from Jordan, and the Golan Heights from Syria.

Cabinet posts

After the war, Peres served in various cabinet posts under successive Alignment governments. The Alignment was initially an alliance of the Labor and Ahdut HaAvoda parties that joined forces in 1965 and lasted for three years; in 1969 a new Alignment emerged between the Labor Party and the Mapam Party, an offshoot of Mapai. In 1969 **Golda Meir** (1898–1978; see entry) became Israel's first female prime minister and Peres was named minister of immigrant absorption. He was next named minister of information. In 1973, on the Jewish holiday of Yom Kippur, Egypt and Syria attacked Israel. Israel successfully defended itself in the 1973 Arab-Israeli War (known in Israel as the Yom Kippur War). But the nation had been unprepared, and this lack of preparedness caused widespread public and legislative rancor against Prime Minister Meir's government, which eventually dissolved. Inside the Labor Party ranks, Peres challenged defense minister Yitzhak Rabin for the party leadership, as well as the job of prime minister, but lost that 1974 contest. Rabin

Operation Moses

As prime minister, Peres was particularly proud of Operation Moses, a secret airlift of Jews out of Ethiopia between late 1984 and early 1985. Ethiopian Jews, thought to have been practicing their religion in this forgotten part of the Horn of Africa since at least the fourth century, had been harassed by a new military regime that came to power in Ethiopia in 1974. Persecuted, and also victims of a widespread famine that swept through Ethiopia from 1983 to 1984, thousands of Ethiopian Jews trekked hundreds of miles to neighboring Sudan, where they gathered in camps to await transport to Israel. The Israel government secretly flew small groups from the camps into Israel. But by late 1984, so many starving refugees filled the camps that Israel appealed to the United States for help. Coordinating with an Israeli aid organization, the U.S. Air Force flew approximately eight thousand Ethiopian Jews to Israel.

Peres and other dignitaries greeted some of the arrivals. Peres remembered the moment well, writing in his autobiography, *Battling for Peace: A Memoir*:

> I will never forget the night they arrived. I stood there with other officials, speechless with emotion, as the doors of these huge

planes opened and the elders of the community, gaunt but stately in their robes, came down the steps and kneeled to kiss the soil of the Holy Land [Israel]. After them came mothers with wide-eyed, handsome children and then the rest of the families. Six planes landed, one after the other, and soon the terminal was full of these new arrivals. Yet not a sound of distress or complaint was to be heard. All of them, old and young alike, maintained this dignified, emotion-laden silence. . . . I felt as though history had awarded me a precious ringside seat at a unique presentation.

Although viewed as a success, Operation Moses was not a complete victory. An estimated fifteen thousand Jews were still in Ethiopia, mainly those too old, weak, or sick to make the journey to Sudan. Arab nations pressured Sudan to close its borders to Jews wishing to travel to Israel, leaving Ethiopian Jews utterly stranded. A secret follow-up mission led by the United States rescued another eight hundred Ethiopian Jews, but thousands more remained.

PERES, SHIMON. *BATTLING FOR PEACE: A MEMOIR.* NEW YORK: RANDOM HOUSE, 1995, P. IX.

formed a new government under the Alignment banner and appointed Peres to serve as defense minister.

After just two years as Israel's minister of defense, Peres helped devise a plan to rescue Israeli hostages from a particularly grim situation at the airport in Entebbe, Uganda. The crisis began on June 27, 1976, when an Air France flight, en route from Tel Aviv, Israel, to Paris, France, via Athens, Greece, was hijacked by a combined team of Palestinian militants and West German radicals. It was one of a long string of hijackings that occurred during this period by similar pro-Palestinian groups, and the militants were usually successful in achieving the release of fellow militants from Israeli and/or European detention. The hijackers landed the plane in Entebbe and over the next few days released all but the Jewish passengers and crew members. Late on the night of July 3, Israeli special-forces commandos stormed the plane, freeing 102 hostages and killing seven of the ten hijackers. Peres was said to have played a key role in convincing his Knesset colleagues and senior officials to authorize the bold mission. "The picture of a German lady and man again threatening with pistols the lives of innocent people whose only crime is that they are Jewish is something that Israel cannot stand for," he said at a news conference after the rescue, as quoted by Terence Smith in the *New York Times*.

The Labor Party lost the elections in 1977 to a relatively new right-wing party, the Likud Party. Peres spent the next several years rebuilding his party's power base. In 1984 he was involved once again in the creation of a government of national unity, this time between the Labor and Likud parties. One political compromise the new government made was to alternate the prime minister's position from one party to the other. Peres served as prime minister for the first twenty-five months of the new government and then Yitzhak Shamir (1915–) of the Likud Party assumed the position.

Nobel Peace Prize

Peres served in another unity government from 1988 to 1990, as minister of finance and vice premier. The Labor Party returned to power in the 1992 election, and Rabin became prime minister. He appointed Peres as his foreign minister. In this capacity Peres worked with Rabin and U.S. president Bill Clinton (1946–) to revive the Arab-Israeli peace process. Those efforts bore dramatic fruit in the 1993 announcement of a peace agreement called the Oslo Accords. The terms included recognition of Israel's right to exist as a nation by Yasser Arafat, and a commitment by Israel to withdraw its settlements and armies from the West Bank and the Gaza Strip, which had been under Israeli occupation (the physical and political control of an area seized by a foreign military force) since the 1967 Arab-Israeli War. The Oslo Accords also included a framework for the establishment of the Palestinian Authority, the recognized governing institution for Palestinians in the West Bank and the Gaza Strip. For their

Shimon Peres accepting the Nobel Peace Prize with Yasser Arafat (left) and Yitzhak Rabin (right) after the Oslo Peace talks which brokered a tentative peace between Israel and Palestine. GOVERNMENT PRESS OFFICE OF ISRAEL.

efforts, Peres, Rabin, and Arafat were awarded the Nobel Peace Prize in 1994.

The Oslo Accords divided Israelis. Many were aghast at the prospect of retreating from territory held for more than a quarter century. Moderates and liberals, on the other hand, viewed the accords as a significant step toward resolving a conflict that had erupted in violence many times. Those who were upset about the Oslo Accords were also upset with those who negotiated it. On November 4, 1995, Rabin was assassinated in front of Tel Aviv's city hall. Peres took over the duties of prime minister, and then campaigned in the spring of 1996 to keep the job. He lost to a staunch right-winger, Likud's **Benjamin Netanyahu** (1949–; see entry), whose older brother was the lone Israeli commando to have lost his life during the hostage crisis in Entebbe, Uganda.

Peres stayed on as leader of the Labor Party until 1997 and served as a member of the Knesset foreign affairs and defense committee from 1996 to 1999. During this period, he also established the Peres Center for Peace, an organization with a mission to bring positive change in the Middle East. The center sponsored agricultural and economic projects to benefit both Israeli and Palestinian communities. From 1999 to 2001 Peres served as Israel's minister of regional cooperation, then became deputy prime minister and minister of foreign affairs under Likud prime minister **Ariel Sharon** (1928–; see entry), positions he held until November 2002. In 2003 Peres was elected once again to lead the Labor Party, and worked with Sharon to form a national unity government in 2004.

Becomes president

At age eighty-one, Peres was appointed to the post of vice premier on January 11, 2005. Later that year he followed Sharon into the newly formed Kadima Party, created to rally support around Sharon's controversial disengagement plan, which would the evacuate Jewish settlers from the Gaza Strip and parts of the West Bank. It was another source of great internal tension. In early 2006 Sharon was incapacitated by a stroke, which left him in a permanent coma, and he was succeeded by Ehud Olmert (1945–), his deputy prime minister. Olmert created a new ministry for the development of the Negev and the Galilee and installed Peres as its first minister. Peres remained in that position, as well as that of vice premier, until June 2007, when the Knesset elected him president of Israel. He was the first former prime minister to become president, and he resigned from his Knesset seat, which he had held since 1959 except for a three-month period in 2006.

The Israeli presidency is a seven-year term, and candidates are not eligible for reelection. A few weeks after Peres was sworn into office, he celebrated his eighty-fourth birthday, but nevertheless proved himself capable of carrying out the job's travel-heavy demands. He traveled to Ankara, Turkey, in November 2007, becoming the first president of Israel to speak before the legislature of a Muslim nation. Closer to home, he welcomed heads of state and other leaders to Jerusalem. Although the president of Israel is a largely ceremonial title, its holder does have the power to formally invite prime ministers to form a government. Peres did this after the February 2009 Knesset elections, requesting

Likud's Netanyahu to form a new government, despite the fact that the Kadima Party had barely edged out the Likud Party in the election.

As president, Peres spearheaded a Valley of Peace initiative to develop the economy of a zone along the border with Jordan, which would create jobs for Palestinians in the region. In 2008 Peres also launched the Israeli Presidential Conference, a meeting of world leaders, business leaders, and even the occasional entertainment celebrity. Peres penned the foreword to a 2008 book, *Peace First: A New Model to End War*, written by Uri Savir, that reflects his goals for the future of Israel. "While the champions and beneficiaries of globalization continue to accumulate wealth, know-how, and power; to reach unparalleled levels of education, communication, and quality of life; and to create a megaculture as a byproduct, the other half still lives differently," he notes. "The developing world remains impoverished and disease-stricken, and many of these countries exist to sustain conflict. . . . The union of poverty, fundamentalist ideologies, and weapons of mass destruction is a devastating hybrid that has planted its roots in the fertile lands of frustrated and estranged constituencies."

For More Information

BOOKS

Bar-Zohar, Michael. *Shimon Peres: The Biography*. New York: Random House, 2007.

Peres, Shimon. *Battling for Peace: A Memoir*. New York: Random House, 1995.

Savir, Uri. *Peace First: A New Model to End War*. Foreword by Shimon Peres. San Francisco, CA: Berrett-Koehler, 2008, p. ix.

PERIODICALS

Barkat, Amiram. "Presidency Rounds off 66-Year Career." *Haaretz* (June 14, 2007). Available online at http://www.haaretz.com/print-edition/news/presidency-rounds-off-66-year-career-1.223139 (accessed on November 30, 2011).

Blomfield, Adrian. "Interview with Israeli President Shimon Peres." *Daily Telegraph* (October 16, 2009). Available online at http://www.telegraph.co.uk/news/worldnews/middleeast/israel/6340953/Interview-with-Israeli-President-Shimon-Peres.html (accessed on November 30, 2011).

Farrell, Stephen, and Heba Afify. "Egypt and Israel Move to Halt Growth of Crisis." *New York Times* (August 21, 2011). Available online at http://www.nytimes.com/2011/08/22/world/middleeast/22egypt.html (accessed on November 30, 2011).

Smith, Terence. "Israelis Return with 103 Rescued in Uganda Raid." *New York Times* (July 5, 1976): 1. Available online at http://select.nytimes.com/gst/abstract.html?res=F3081FFF3C55157A93C7A9178CD85F428785F9& scp=1&sq=shimon+peres+AND+entebbe&st=p (accessed on November 30, 2011).

WEB SITES

"Middle East: Israel's Shimon Peres Speaks to RFE/RL." *Radio Free Europe.* http://www.rferl.org/featuresarticle/2005/01/4ce608a9-0553-4c10-9757-6695b60acbeb.html (accessed on November 30, 2011).

"Shimon Peres." *Peres Center for Peace.* http://www.peres-center.org/ShimonPeres.html (accessed on November 30, 2011).

"Shimon Peres." *Jewish Virtual Library.* http://www.jewishvirtuallibrary.org/jsource/biography/peres.html (accessed on November 30, 2011).

Mu'ammar al-Qaddafi

BORN: June 7, 1942 • Sirte, Libya

DIED: October 20, 2011 • Sirte, Libya

Libyan president, army colonel

"There is a conspiracy to control Libyan oil and to control Libyan land, to colonize Libya once again. This is impossible.... We will fight until the last man and last woman to defend Libya from east to west, north to south."

Mu'ammar al-Qaddafi. ©
SABRI ELMHEDWI/EPA/
CORBIS.

Libya's Mu'ammar al-Qaddafi (also spelled Moammar al-Gaddafi) marked his forty-second year as head of the Socialist People's Libyan Arab Jamahiriya, the official name of Libya, on September 1, 2011, at an unknown location amidst the turbulence of a civil war. Seven weeks later, he was captured and killed by rebel forces. The eigth-month-long Libyan uprising was one of the most dramatic turnabouts in the Arab Spring, a series of prodemocracy uprisings that spread throughout the Middle East and North Africa. Rebel forces took control Tripoli and much of this immense North African nation with the help of aerial strikes conducted by American and British military forces. Al-Qaddafi held a first-place spot for longevity among rulers of the Arab world and Middle East. Only three other non-royal rulers bested al-Qaddafi's forty-two-year rule: Cuba's Fidel Castro (1926–), China's Chiang Kai-shek (1887–1975), and Kim Il-sung (1912–1994) of North Korea.

Descended from Berbers

Al-Qaddafi was born on June 7, 1942, in what was then known as Italian Libya. Italy had taken control of Libya in 1934 after more than two decades of Libyan resistance. Libyans were aghast at the plan to turn the North African nation's Mediterranean coastline into Italy's Quarta Sponda (Fourth Shore). Once control was firmly established, the Italians imposed a repressive program to stamp out challenges to their authority throughout its four newly created administrative provinces.

Al-Qaddafi and his family lived in the province of Tripolitania, located along the western half of Libya's border with Algeria and Tunisia. Tripolitania was home to the capital of Italian Libya, Tripoli, and also to Sirte, the coastal city that al-Qaddafi's family called home. The family was Arabized Berbers, indigenous people of North Africa who speak Arabic. They were descendants of the original inhabitants of the Maghreb, a region of northwest Africa that stretches from Morocco and Mauritania eastward to Algeria, Tunisia, and finally Libya, and included an enormous part of the Sahara. The Berbers were "Arabized" after conquests by Muslims that began in the seventh, and they gradually adopted Arabic as their language and Islam as their religion.

Al-Qaddafi 's surname shows his family's affiliation with the Qadhadhfa clan in the Sirte region. His forebears were cattle tenders, who operated out of the Hun Oasis in the Sahara. Al-Qaddafi's first home was a tent, and his earliest education was at a local religious school. In 1943, a year after his birth, Italy lost control of its colonial holdings in Africa, with the British taking over most of the area. The French occupied Libya's southern province of Fezzan, where the al-Qaddafi family moved in the mid–1950s. By that point, Libya had gained its independence and was a constitutional and hereditary monarchy under King Idris I (1889–1983).

Emerges as opposition leader

In his teens al-Qaddafi spent five years at the Sabha Preparatory School before completing high school in the city of Misratah. From there he entered the military academy at Benghazi, another coastal city, where he spent the first half of the 1960s. Inspired by the antimonarchist revolt in neighboring Egypt led by **Gamal Abdel Nasser** (1918–1970; see entry) a decade earlier, al-Qaddafi cofounded a secret group at the academy, called the Free Officers Movement, whose goal was to oust Idris and other Libyan elites viewed as overly accommodating to Western powers. They were also supporters of Pan-Arabism (a movement for the unification of Arab peoples and the political alliance of Arab states), as well as Nasser's pan-Arab theory that a united Arab world could best repel foreign intervention in the Middle East. One major source of controversy for Libyans was the presence of Wheelus Air Base, a U.S. Air Force installation near Tripoli, originally built during the Italian occupation. It housed a few thousand U.S. military and civilian personnel and was home to a huge fleet of fighter jets and planes that practiced regular surface-to-surface air missile tests in the Sahara.

Al-Qaddafi and other young Libyans were emboldened in part by the discovery of vast crude-oil deposits in the 1950s. This brought an influx of foreign companies into Libya who were friendly to the Idris regime, and although the country's economy began to grow exponentially after it began exporting oil in 1959, the majority of ordinary Libyans failed to benefit from the oil boom. Under these conditions the country ripened for a potential coup (overthrow of the government). Al-Qaddafi, after graduating from the academy at Benghazi in 1965, traveled to England for a six-month English-language course at the Royal Army Education Corps Centre at Wilton Park, a picturesque corner of Buckinghamshire. When he returned to Libya, he was posted to the Signal Corps of the Royal Libyan Army in Benghazi and also enrolled at the University of Benghazi to study history. He continued his underground political-organizing activities, even setting up rudimentary radio and crypto-graphic (secret code) communications systems to enable him to keep in contact with other members of the Free Officers Movement.

On June 5, 1967, Israel attacked Egypt, Jordan, and Syria in what came to be known as the 1967 Arab-Israeli War. Al-Qaddafi and other officers were angered that Idris had provided only small military support to neighboring Egypt, a fellow Arab nation, when it was assaulted. Egypt lost its entire Sinai Peninsula and the Gaza Strip to Israel. Israel also seized the West Bank from Jordan and the Golan Heights from Syria. With popular support against his regime rising, the eighty-year-old Idris agreed to step down in favor of his son, Crown Prince Hasan as-Senussi (1928–1992), effective September 2, 1969, and he flew to Turkey for medical treatment. On September 1, al-Qaddafi led a bloodless coup

with other officers of the Signal Corps. He became head of the Revolutionary Command Council (RCC), which abolished the monarchy and proclaimed the new Libyan Arab Republic. Idris never returned to Libya, and his nephew was placed under house arrest, then later tried and convicted on treason and corruption charges. After his release from prison in the mid–1970s, as-Senussi and his family lived in a humble beachfront cottage near Tripoli.

Becoming a regional power

Al-Qaddafi was just twenty-seven years old when he became the new leader of Libya as president of the RCC. His government moved swiftly to remake Libyan society. Scores of former government ministers were arrested, tried, and convicted of treason and corruption; the military also moved to oust senior officers they accused of cooperating with the West. Al-Qaddafi ordered U.S. officials to shut down operations at Wheelus Air Base, and they complied. There was also a significant number of Italians in Libya, descendants of the colonial settlement program of decades earlier, and al-Qaddafi ordered the expulsion of these twenty thousand Italian Libyans; a Jewish colony was also forced out.

In the early 1970s al-Qaddafi unsuccessfully tried to unite his nation first with Sudan, then Egypt. Libya emerged as a key player in the Organization of Petroleum Exporting Countries (OPEC), an organization formed in 1960 by the world's major oil-producing nations to coordinate policies and ensure stable oil prices in world markets. Al-Qaddafi urged fellow Arab nations to vote in favor of an oil embargo after the 1973 Arab-Israeli War in order to demonstrate their collective strength to the West and voice their objections to military aid that the United States and other nations gave to Israel. This embargo (a halt on oil exports to the United States and other nations that provided military aid to Israel) prompted an energy crisis in the United States and elsewhere. In 1974 there was a brief possibility of a merger with Tunisia, but Tunisian leader Habib Bourguiba (1903–2000) reassessed this idea and canceled a scheduled referendum, a direct public vote on a single proposal.

During this period, al-Qaddafi turned to the Soviet Union as an ally. The Soviets provided generous military aid, and al-Qaddafi abandoned his hopes for a Middle East united under Pan-Arabism. The Free Officers Movement evolved into a political party, the Arab Socialist Union, which became the only legal party in Libya. Al-Qaddafi laid out his ambitious reform plan in a document published in multiple volumes in the 1970s, called *Third International Theory*, also known as the *Green Book*. "Loosely combining elements of socialism and Islam, along with his own erratic ideas, he abolished private enterprise, expropriated [seized] foreign-owned property, and renamed the country the Great Socialist People's Libyan Arab Jamahiriyah—the State of the Masses, in which he was not the President but the Brother Leader," writes Jon Lee Anderson in *New Yorker*.

Proclaims new "Jamahiriya"

In March 1977 the Socialist People's Libyan Arab Jamahiriya was proclaimed. *Jamahiriya* is Arabic for "state of the masses," and al-Qaddafi asserted the country would be run by Libyans for Libyans through the Basic People's Congresses, which were local deliberative bodies that met every few months. Anyone over age eighteen could participate, and the congresses grew to number nearly five hundred over the next quarter century.

Al-Qaddafi dealt harshly with threats to his authority. A movement by university students who objected to Libya's new military conscription (required enlistment) laws, a consequence of its war with neighboring Chad, was brutally suppressed. Islamic fundamentalists (people who stress adherence to a strict or literal interpretation of religious principles) were also targeted, and a campaign of terror ensued in the late 1970s, with public hangings that were broadcast on state-run television. Dissidents fled the country in droves, and al-Qaddafi famously ordered them to return or face a life on the run from the death squads he sent out to assassinate them. One of those victims was Mohammed Ramadan, a journalist active in Hizb-ut Tahrir (Party of Liberation), a pan-Arab group. After leaving Libya, Ramadan went to work for the British Broadcasting Corporation's Arabic-language section in London, England, and was shot to death outside of the Regent's Park Mosque in April 1980.

Al-Qaddafi openly provoked Western nations with such acts, while secretly his regime was giving aid to various militant groups, like the Irish Republican Army, which worked to end British rule in Northern Ireland through a campaign of terror. This prompted significant hostility with Great Britain under Prime Minister Margaret Thatcher (1925–). Al-Qaddafi even made enemies of Shiites, followers of the Shia branch of Islam. In August 1978 a prominent Shiite cleric in Lebanon named Musa al-Sadr (1928–?) went to Libya to meet with officials of al-Qaddafi's government. Neither al-Sadr nor his two traveling companions were ever seen again, although al-Qaddafi steadfastly maintained the trio had arrived in Libya as planned, then went on to Italy. Al-Qaddafi provoked the United States multiple times. The first was in the summer of 1981, after a dispute over new international boundary waters in the Mediterranean Sea. The U.S. Navy sent aircraft carriers to patrol the zone, but Libyan fighter planes flew near as the Americans conducted routine flight exercises in the Gulf of Sidra, prompting the U.S. Navy to shoot down a pair of Libyan Air Force jets.

Linked to deadly attacks

In April 1984 protests erupted outside the Libyan Embassy in London, which had been taken over by pro-al-Qaddafi activists. When exiled Libyan dissidents planned a protest there, a detachment of Metropolitan Police was assigned to patrol St. James Square, where the embassy is located. The demonstration grew violent, and shots rang out from the embassy, killing Yvonne Fletcher, a twenty-five-year-old unarmed policewoman. After that event, Prime Minister Thatcher broke all diplomatic ties with Libya. In late 1985 both the Rome, Italy, and Vienna, Austria, airports were the scenes of massacres carried out by the Abu Nidal Organization, a terrorist group, and Libya was linked to the attacks. In March

1986, after the United States imposed economic sanctions on Libya, Libyan forces fired two surface-to-air missiles at U.S. military planes, but missed their targets. (Sanctions are punitive measures adopted by the international community against a nation that has violated international law, usually in the form of diplomatic, economic, or social restrictions.) A month later, a discotheque in West Berlin, Germany, that was frequented by U.S. military personnel was bombed. Two Americans and a Turk were killed. This provoked U.S. president Ronald Reagan (1911–2004) to condemn al-Qaddafi as the "mad dog of the Middle East," according to transcripts of Reagan's April 9 press conference that appeared in the next day's *New York Times*. Thatcher agreed to let U.S. planes use British bases to carry out an aerial attack on several Libyan targets on April 15, 1986. Among the targets were al-Qaddafi's compound in Tripoli, the former Wheelus Air Base now used by the Libyan Air Force, and the military barracks in Benghazi from which the 1969 coup had been launched.

In December 1988 Pan Am Flight 103 exploded over Lockerbie, Scotland. The flight was en route from London to New York City, and all 259 passengers and crew, plus eleven Lockerbie residents on the ground were killed. Investigators linked two Libyans to the crime, but the legal case against them took years to process. Al-Qaddafi refused to obey a United Nations (UN) order to extradite (hand over to the authorities of another country) the men, and that resulted in further sanctions imposed by the UN Security Council. The Libyan economy suffered.

As internal opposition to al-Qaddafi's rule increased, he began reaching out to the West. South African president Nelson Mandela (1918–) reportedly convinced him to allow the extradition of the two Pan Am bombing suspects, and in 2001 al-Qaddafi condemned the September 11, 2001, terrorist attacks on the United States, even cooperating with U.S. intelligence to provide information. By 2006 sanctions against Libya had been lifted, and both the United States and Great Britain resumed diplomatic relations.

In 2008 U.S. secretary of state Condoleezza Rice (1954–), who is African American, visited al-Qaddafi in Tripoli, after he had spoken glowingly about her a year earlier in an interview with the news network Al Jazeera. "I support my darling black African woman," he said of the secretary of state, as quoted by Glenn Kessler in the the *Washington Post*. "I admire and am very proud of the way she leans back and gives orders to the

A billboard of Mu'ammar al-Qaddafi in Tripoli, Libya. Over the years al-Qaddafi built a cult of personality, placing his image on billboards across the country. REZA/GETTY IMAGES.

Arab leaders. . . . I love her very much. I admire her, and I'm proud of her, because she's a black woman of African origin." Similarly bizarre pronouncements and stunts became increasingly frequent for al-Qaddafi, who famously created an elite all-female, personal-protection detail, with the belief that an Arab man would hesitate before firing a weapon at a woman during an assassination attempt. Over the years he also created a cult of personality, with his image staring forth from billboards across Tripoli and other cities.

Refuses to cede power

In early 2011 a series of prodemocracy uprisings known as the Arab Spring spread across the Middle East and North Africa. Demonstrations began in Tunisia in December 2010, and on January 14, 2011, Tunisia's Zine El Abidine Ben Ali (1936–), who had been president since 1987, fled to Saudi

Arabia. Days later, Egyptian protesters gathered in Tahrir Square, in Egypt's capital city of Cairo, and those protests forced longtime Egyptian president **Hosni Mubarak** (1928–; see entry) out of office on February 11. Protests began in Libya on February 15. Al-Qaddafi ordered a full assault on demonstrators, but army units were forced to retreat from Benghazi after suffering heavy losses to armed rebels in that city. The Benghazi group proclaimed its independence from Al-Qaddafi's regime and formed a National Transitional Council. In early March the disruptions spilled into Port Brega and other cities in eastern Libya that are home to major oil refineries and export centers. Libyan army units battled waves of *shabab*, civilians who took up arms against the regime.

Al-Qaddafi gave a series of increasingly bizarre interviews, claiming that the rebellion had been instigated by members of the terrorist group al-Qaeda who had been released from U.S.-run detention camps in Iraq, Afghanistan, and Cuba, and that the shabab were being fed hallucinogenic drugs to maintain their stamina. He also claimed that he could not step down as leader, because back in 1979 he had handed over all authority to the People's Congresses, and that he was a mere figurehead leader, similar to the position of Great Britain's queen. In one televised address in early March 2011 he warned that foreign intervention would not force regime change in Libya. "Do they want us to become slaves once again like we were slaves to the Italians?" he said, as quoted by Raja Abdulrahim and David Zucchino in the *Los Angeles Times*. "We will never accept it. We will enter a bloody war, and thousands and thousands of Libyans will die if the United States enters or NATO enters." (NATO is the North Atlantic Treaty Organization, an international organization created in 1949 for purposes of collective security.)

The UN Security Council passed a resolution in mid–March authorizing a no-fly zone over Benghazi to protect civilians, along with air strikes on sites thought to be held by pro-Qaddafi forces. The airstrikes were carried out British and American planes under the command of the North Atlantic Treaty Organization (NATO). Al-Qaddafi's heavily secured compound in Tripoli was bombed several times, and some of his grandchildren were reported to have been killed in one April raid. Senior government officials began surrendering to the Transitional National Council, an interim (temporary) government that operated out of Benghazi, and Tripoli fell to rebel forces on August 28. Al-Qaddafi, meanwhile, had disappeared

Al-Qaddafi's Children

In April 1986 reports surfaced that the death toll from U.S. air strikes on Libya included Mu'ammar al-Qaddafi's fifteen-month-old adopted daughter, Hana. Al-Qaddafi publicly condemned U.S. president Ronald Reagan (1911–2004) as a child killer. Bab al-Aziziya, the same heavily fortified compound in Tripoli that was home to the al-Qaddafi family, was targeted again during NATO air strikes in the spring and summer of 2011.

Al-Qaddafi had one son from a short-lived marriage, Muhammad, who was born in 1970. Muhammad went on to hold key positions in his father's regime as an adult. He ran Libya's Internet service provider and initially surrendered to rebels during the civil war in 2011, then disappeared. Al-Qaddafi's first child from his 1971 marriage to Safia el-Brasai produced several more children. Seif el-Islam (1972–), al-Qaddafi's second son, studied architecture before beginning graduate studies in political philosophy at the London School of Economics. Al-Saadi (1973–), al-Qaddafi's third son, played soccer at the professional level in Italy. Hannibal, born in 1975, held a top position in the Libyan oil export agency. He and his wife spent time in Europe and had run-ins with authorities there related to domestic-violence incidents. Hannibal and Muhammad were believed to have fled Libya with their mother and respective families as rebel forces closed in on Tripoli in the spring of 2011. At Hannibal's seaside villa, rebel troops found a badly burned Ethiopian woman, the nanny for al-Qaddafi's grandchildren, among the household staffers who had remained behind. She said that Hannibal's wife had poured boiling water on her for disobeying orders.

Al-Qaddafi's fifth son, Moatassem-Billah (1977–2011), served as his father's national security adviser and commanded Libyan army

and was thought to be hiding in Bani Walid, a desert outpost southeast of Tripoli, or perhaps in Sirte, his birthplace, which he proclaimed as the new capital of the Great Socialist People's Libyan Arab Jamahiriyah on September 1, the forty-second anniversary of his 1969 coup. That same day, an audio message aired on Al Rai TV, a Kuwaiti satellite television channel, from a man claiming to be al-Qaddafi. "Let there be a long fight and let Libya be engulfed in flames," the voice said, as quoted by J. David Goodman in the *New York Times*. "We're not going to give way.... Yes, people will die. All the traitors, they will go back where they came from."

By September 2011, Sirte was one of the last strongholds for al-Qaddafi supporters. A month-long battle here led to the end of the al-Qaddafi regime. On October 20, 2011, al-Qaddafi was captured and killed by rebel forces. Reports of his capture and death vary, and the public was allowed to view his body for confirmation. He was buried at an undisclosed location.

units in the Port Brega battles during the 2011 civil war. A few months later he appeared to have vanished. In October he was captured at Sirte, along with his father, and later killed. Seif al-Arab (1982–2011), al-Qaddafi's sixth son, also commanded units in the conflict but was said to have died on April 30, when NATO bombs hit Bab al-Aziziya. Al-Qaddafi's youngest son, Khamis, was born in 1983. He was put in charge of defending Bani Walid, but he later disappeared and was presumed dead.

Al-Qaddafi's only biological daughter, Ayesha, was born in 1986 and went on to become an attorney and minor celebrity in the Arab world. She was part of the defense team for ousted Iraqi president **Saddam Hussein** (1937–2006; see entry). In April 2011, after two months of civil unrest in Libya, Ayesha appeared before a crowd of al-Qaddafi loyalists in Tripoli's Green Square. "Talk about al-Qaddafi stepping down is an insult to all Libyans because al-Qaddafi is not in Libya, but in the hearts of all Libyans," she asserted, as quoted by Harriet Sherwood in the *Guardian*. Ayesha was married to an officer in the Libyan army who was killed in battle in July 2011. At the end of August, a pregnant Ayesha fled to Algeria with her mother and brothers, Muhammad and Hannibal. She gave birth a day later.

Whether or not al-Qaddafi's infant daughter died in the 1986 raid remains a mystery. The infant was said to be named Hana, but photographs found after rebel forces broached the security of the al-Qaddafi family compounds in 2011 showed a young woman with that same name as a teen and young adult. She apparently became a physician and was on staff at a Tripoli hospital when the civil war erupted.

SHERWOOD, HARRIET. "GADDAFI'S DAUGHTER WHIPS CROWD INTO FRENZY OF LOYALTY." *GUARDIAN* (APRIL 16, 2011). HTTP://WWW.GUARDIAN.CO.UK/WORLD/2011/APR/15/GADDAFI-DAUGHTER-SUPPORTERS-TRIPOLI (ACCESSED ON NOVEMBER, 2011).

For More Information

BOOKS

Martínez, Luis. *The Libyan Paradox.* New York: Columbia University Press, 2007.

Simons, Geoffrey Leslie. *Libya: The Struggle for Survival.* New York: Palgrave Macmillan, 1993.

PERIODICALS

Abdulrahim, Raja, and David Zucchino. "Rebels Repel Kadafi's Forces in Port Brega." *Los Angeles Times* (March 3, 2011). Available online at http://articles.latimes.com/2011/mar/03/world/la-fg-libya-fighting-20110303 (accessed on November 30, 2011).

Anderson, Jon Lee. "Sons of the Revolution." *New Yorker* (May 9, 2011). Available online at http://www.newyorker.com/reporting/2011/05/09/110509fa_fact_anderson?currentPage=all (accessed on September November 30, 2011).

Kessler, Glenn. "Rice and Gaddafi Hammer at Wall Built by Decades of Animosity." *Washington Post* (September 6, 2008). Available online at http://www.washingtonpost.com/wp-dyn/content/article/2008/09/05/AR2008090501149.html (accessed on November 30, 2011).

"President's News Conference on Foreign and Domestic Issues." *New York Times* (April 10, 1986). Available online at http://www.nytimes.com/1986/04/10/us/president-s-news-conference-on-foreign-and-domestic-issues.html?scp=1&sq=%22mad+dog+of+the+Middle+East%22&st=nyt (accessed on September November 30, 2011).

Sherwood, Harriet. "Gaddafi's Daughter Whips Crowd into Frenzy of Loyalty." *Guardian* (April 16, 2011): 18. Available online at http://www.guardian.co.uk/world/2011/apr/15/gaddafi-daughter-supporters-tripoli (accessed on November 30, 2011).

Solomon, Andrew. "Circle of Fire." *New Yorker* (May 8, 2006): 44. Available online at http://www.newyorker.com/archive/2006/05/08/060508fa_fact_solomon?currentPage=all (accessed on November 30, 2011).

WEB SITES

Goodman, J. David. "Qaddafi Vows Resistance in Audio Message." *New York Times* (September 1, 2011). http://thelede.blogs.nytimes.com/2011/09/01/qaddafi-vows-resistance-in-audio-message/?scp=48&sq=muammar+el-qaddafi&st=nyt (accessed on November 30, 2011).

Mekay, Emad. "Gaddafi Hits with Deadly Force." *Al Jazeera* (February 21, 2011). http://english.aljazeera.net/indepth/features/2011/02/2011221133437954477.html (accessed on November 30, 2011).

Yitzhak Rabin

BORN: March 1, 1922 • Jerusalem, Palestine

DIED: November 4, 1995 • Tel Aviv, Israel

Israeli prime minister

"Walls of enmity [hatred] have fallen. No longer are we necessarily a people that dwells alone, and no longer is it true that the whole world is against us."

Yitzhak Rabin is one of the heroes of Israel. As a young man, he participated in decisive battles that helped Israel become a country in the 1940s, then rose to become a commander in Israel's military, the Israel Defense Forces (IDF). He also played a key role in the 1967 Arab-Israeli War (known in Israel as the Six-Day War). After a period as Israel's ambassador to the United States, became his nation's first native-born prime minister in 1974. During Rabin's second term as prime minister in the early 1990s, he, along with his foreign minister, **Shimon Peres** (1923–; see entry), forged the Oslo Accords peace agreement with Palestine Liberation Organization (PLO) leader **Yasser Arafat** (1929–2004; see entry), for which they were all awarded the Nobel Peace Prize in 1994. (The PLO is a political and military organization formed to unite various Palestinian Arab groups with the goal of establishing an independent

Yitzhak Rabin. GOVERNMENT PRESS OFFICE OF ISRAEL.

Palestinian state.) The accords, unfortunately, also cost Rabin his life. He was assassinated on November 4, 1995, in front of the city hall in Tel Aviv, Israel, by an extremist who opposed the peace agreement.

Early life

Rabin was born in Palestine in March 1922. (Palestine is a historical region in the Middle East on the eastern shore of the Mediterranean Sea, comprising parts of present-day Israel and Jordan.) He was the first of two children born to Nehemiah and Rosa Rabin, both émigrés from lands under Russian control. His parents had met in Palestine in 1920 while defending a Jewish section of the city of Jerusalem against an Arab attack, and they later settled in Tel Aviv. (Arabs are people who speak the Arabic language or who live in countries in which Arabic is the dominant language.) Rabin's father worked for the area's first telephone and electric utilities, while his mother was a construction-company accountant. She later worked at a bank. Rabin's parents both felt strongly about the importance of community service and volunteered their time to a variety of Zionist causes. (Zionism is an international political movement originating in the late nineteenth century that called for the creation of an independent Jewish state in Palestine.) Rabin's mother was active in the executive ranks of Haganah, the underground defense force of Zionists in Palestine that later evolved into the IDF.

Youths like Rabin were raised with the belief that communal farming settlements known as kibbutzim were essential to the goal of securing a homeland for Jews, both as a way to bond them physically to a foreign land and to help the growing Zionist community become self-sufficient. Although Rabin had grown up in a city, he decided to study agriculture and planned to become an irrigation engineer. He entered the Kadoori Agricultural High School in 1937, where he learned farming techniques and graduated with distinction in 1940. He also learned how to use weapons, because Jewish settlements and schools sometimes came under attack by hostile Arab neighbors. These neighbors were predominantly Muslim and had inhabited the region for centuries. They were not happy about the increasing numbers of Jews immigrating to Palestine and, since both groups had historic ties to the region, conflicts frequently erupted between them. Palestine had been under Muslim rule since 638 CE, except for a brief period of Christian conquest during the Crusades, a series of military campaigns ordered by the Roman Catholic

Church between 1095 and 1291 with the main goal of taking the Holy Land from the Muslims. After World War I (1914–18; a global war between the Allies [Great Britain, France, and Russia, joined later by the United States] and the Central Powers [Germany, Austria-Hungary, and their allies]) the region came under British mandate (administrative authority). The British continued to allow Zionist settlers to arrive in the 1920s and 1930s, which exacerbated tensions between Arabs and Jews.

Continued fighting between Arabs and Jews, and then the start of World War II (1939–45; a war in which the Allies [Great Britain, France, the Soviet Union, the United States, and China] defeated the Axis Powers [Germany, Italy, and Japan]), interrupted Rabin's education. While still at Kadoori, he won a coveted scholarship to study at the University of California at Berkeley in the United States, but turned down the opportunity because, as he writes in *The Rabin Memoirs*, "I was simply incapable of leaving the country, and my friends, during wartime." This decision changed the course of his life.

Defending Israel

During World War II, Rabin lived on a kibbutz, where he worked as a police officer. He became especially skilled at setting ambushes to stop Arab attacks on his community. In 1941, when Haganah established a mobilized force named the Palmach, a Hebrew alphabet acronym for *plugot machatz* (strike force). Rabin was among the first to be invited to join. He rose quickly from foot soldier to battalion leader, to chief of operations in October 1947.

Although Palmach had coordinated some of its missions with the British army during the war, British authorities outlawed the organization in 1942. Palmach became an underground organization, and began a systematic effort to defend Jews from Arab attacks and aid a new group of settlers: Jewish refugees in British-run holding camps. (Refugees are people who flee their country to escape violence or persecution.) During World War II, the Germans had operated concentration camps, complexes built for the confinement and extermination of political opponents and ethnic minorities, especially Jews. Jews who had made it to Palestine were denied entrance by British officials, who had paid heed to the concerns of Arabs about increased immigration. Rabin assisted in operations that freed hundreds of Jews from British holding camps before they could be sent back to Europe.

At the end of the war the fate of Palestine rested in the hands of the United Nations, an international organization of countries founded in 1945 to promote international peace, security, and cooperation. On November 29, 1947, the United Nations voted to divide Palestine into two separate nations: one Jewish and the other Arab. This triggered a six-month period of violent conflicts between Jews and Arabs. In April 1948 Rabin was made commander of the Harel Brigades, a reserve unit of the IDF, and charged with the task of guarding the route from Tel Aviv to Jerusalem. Part of this included Operation Nachshon, which destroyed Arab villages along the route that had served as bases for attacks against Jews. The British failed to evacuate Jewish residents from the Old City of Jerusalem, and Rabin and his men arrived there to find it "almost a ghost town," he writes in his memoir. "Its ninety thousand Jewish inhabitants [were] totally isolated. At night they would lock themselves in their homes, and during the day they dodged about the streets terrified of snipers." Rabin and the Harel Brigades worked to capture other vital slices of territory around the city, and on May 14, 1948, Israel declared its independence as a nation. The next day, the 1948 Arab-Israeli War began, with neighboring Arab nations attempting to take back the land that they believed belonged to Arab Palestinians. Battalions from Egypt, Jordan, Syria, and Lebanon massed to attack the newly created Jewish state. Rabin participated in all of the most decisive battles of the war and gained renown for one campaign that drove a well-trained Egyptian force out of the Negev desert. He was also present in cease-fire negotiations between Israel and Egypt that led to the war's end in 1949.

With the establishment of the state of Israel in 1948, the Palmach was absorbed into the IDF. Rabin steadily rose through the ranks of the newly established military, and by 1959 he was appointed as chief of operations, the second-highest post in the IDF, and achieved the top position of chief of staff in 1964.

Leads a major offensive

Rabin had just reorganized the IDF when Israel became enmeshed in the 1967 Arab-Israeli War. With new weapons from the United States and newly organized defensive and offensive sections, the IDF had become a formidable force. When Israel learned of troop movements near its borders that suggested a coming attack from Egypt, Jordan, and Syria, the Jewish nation decided to strike first. On June 5, 1967, the Israeli Air

Force launched a massive air strike on the Egyptian Air Force, destroying almost five hundred fighter planes on the ground. Ground troops then moved in to seize the Sinai Peninsula and the Gaza Strip from Egypt, the West Bank from Jordan, and the Golan Heights from Syria. When the war ended one week later, Israel had nearly tripled its original size. Rabin's role in planning the operation gave him, according to Israeli military tradition, the postevent honor of naming the conflict, and he chose the "Six-Day War" because of its biblical connotations. According to the Book of Genesis, God created the world in six days. Outside of Israel the conflict is known as the 1967 Arab-Israeli War.

The 1967 Arab-Israeli War was a critical event that significantly shifted the balance of power in the Middle East to Israel's favor. It also gave Israel access to the Western Wall, also known as the Wailing Wall, a monument in Jerusalem that Jews had lost during the 1948 Arab-Israeli War. In his memoir Rabin writes:

> The Wall was and is our national memento of the glories of Jewish independence in ancient times. Its stones have a power to speak to the hearts of Jews the world over.... For years I secretly harbored the dream that I might play a part not only in gaining Israel's independence but in restoring the Western Wall to the Jewish people, making it the focal point of our hard-won independence. Now that dream had come true, and suddenly I wondered why I, of all men, should be so privileged. I knew that never again in my life would I experience quite the same peak of elation.

Secures F-4 Phantom IIs

After the decisive success of the 1967 Arab-Israeli War, Rabin retired from the IDF and was appointed Israel's ambassador to the United States. He brought along his wife, Leah, and a son, Yuval. His daughter, Dalia, remained in Israel to complete high school. American Jews considered him a hero, as he was in Israel. An excited crowd at New York City's Yeshiva University greeted him with the roar "Am Yisroel Chai!" (The Jewish people shall live!) when he appeared as a speaker at the school's June 1968 commencement ceremony. Rabin spent five years in Washington, D.C. finding support for Israel and defending its actions in the 1967 Arab-Israeli War. He asserted that the seizure of territories, which displaced or placed under Israeli occupation (political and military control) around one million former citizens of Jordan, Syria, and Egypt, was a necessary diplomatic move, giving Israel something to bargain with in future peace talks. Arab countries demanded immediate withdrawal from the occupied territories as a precondition to any talks, but Rabin explained Israel's position. "If you are not ready to abandon your policy of seeking Israel's destruction, why then do we have to withdraw even one in inch?" he said, as quoted in a March 1968 the *New York Times* article.

During Rabin's tenure as ambassador, Egypt waged the War of Attrition against Israel in an attempt to win back land lost during the 1967 Arab-Israeli War, and Israel needed outside military aid and international backing to defend its new borders. Speaking with U.S. president Richard Nixon (1913–1994) in 1970, Rabin described Israel's position in blunt terms. He recalls his words in his memoir: "Whenever the U.S. is believed to be reducing her support for Israel, the Arabs revive their old hope of overcoming us by force. . . . Once again, Mr. President, I appeal to you as the only man in whose sympathy and understanding we have trust: Give us the arms we need!" Rabin was said to have been vital in persuading key decision makers to lift the embargo (ban) on Israel's purchase of state-of-the-art F-4 Phantom II fighter jets, developed by the American aerospace industry and deployed with notable success by the United States in the Vietnam War (1954–75).

While working to secure a close relationship between Israel and the United States, Rabin became close friends with Nixon. After Rabin's last meeting with the president, Nixon told Israeli prime minister **Golda Meir** (1898–1978; see entry), "If you don't need him in Israel, you're welcome to leave him here! I'll be glad to have him!" according to Rabin's memoirs. The relationship Rabin built with the United States would serve his country well in the coming years. He also enjoyed a close working relationship with U.S. national security adviser Henry Kissinger (1923–), who played a key role in Middle East diplomacy during this period.

Becomes prime minister

In March 1973 Rabin returned to Israel. Later that year he was elected to a seat in the Knesset, Israel's legislature, on a new leftist party ticket known as the Alignment that eventually merged into the Labor Party. Rabin rose to a cabinet post in March 1974 with his appointment as minister of labor by Meir. At the time of his appointment, Israel was in the middle of the 1973 Arab-Israeli War (known in Israel as the Yom Kippur War), a conflict initiated by a surprise attack from Egypt and

Syria on Yom Kippur, a Jewish holy day. Israel suffered military failures and devastating loss of life at the beginning of the war, prompting Meir to resign. Rabin successfully challenged a political veteran, Shimon Peres, for the post of prime minister and was sworn into office on June 3, 1974. He was the first prime minister in Israeli history to have been born inside the boundaries of the future nation.

While he was prime minister, from 1974 to 1977, Rabin worked to revamp the country's tax code, to develop the economy in order to increase job opportunities for the waves of immigrants moving into the country, and to deal with dramatically amplified attacks on Israeli targets from the PLO and groups sympathetic to Palestinians. He also tried to secure peace with Egypt, and by 1975 Israel and Egypt had reached an interim (temporary) agreement for peace. Rabin left office in the spring of 1977 after a scandal about his American bank account. In November 1977, seven months after Rabin stepped down as prime minister, Egyptian president **Anwar Sadat** (also spelled al-Sadat; 1918–1981; see entry) became the first head of state from the Arab world to formally visit Israel.

The Dollar Account Affair

In 1977, just months before national elections in Egypt, an investigative report in *Haaretz*, a newspaper in Israel, revealed that Yitzhak Rabin and his wife, Leah, had not closed their American bank account when they returned to Israel after Rabin's job as Israeli ambassador to the United States was over. At the time, Israeli law forbade citizens from holding foreign bank accounts without official approval from the Treasury Department. The offense was viewed as a technicality by Rabin's supporters, for the account reportedly contained just a few thousand dollars and was only used by Leah. Prosecutors announced they would file charges against Leah when it was discovered the account, in fact, had a large balance. The Dollar Account Affair, as it became known, was viewed as a significant moral breach by Rabin's political foes, who exploited the scandal. Rabin publicly apologized, took a leave of absence from the office of prime minister, and announced his decision not to seek reelection that year. Leah was ordered to pay a fine of twenty-seven thousand dollars.

The First Intifada

Rabin resigned as head of the Alignment on April 8, 1977, and Peres succeeded him. In Knesset elections on May 17 the Likud Party won by a solid margin, marking the first time a right-wing party had gained control of the legislature and installed its own prime minister. The Likud Party would remain in power for the next seven years. When Peres became Israel's eighth prime minister in 1984 in a Labor Party victory, he appointed Rabin to serve as minister of defense, a job he would hold until 1990. Called "Mr. Security" for his tough stance on safeguarding Israel, Rabin dealt firmly with the Intifada, a Palestinian uprising against Israeli occupation in the West Bank and the Gaza Strip that began in 1987 and continued for the next six years. IDF soldiers fired rubber bullets at Palestinians, whose weapons were mostly rocks, and Rabin issued orders to use force, but not lethal force. As casualties mounted, however, there were increasing calls for him to step down by early 1989. In one Knesset session he asserted, "As long as they say, 'We will continue with violence,' their violence will be met with force," as quoted by the *New York Times* on January 19, 1989.

Rabin stayed on as minister of defense until March 1990. In 1992 he led the Labor Party to victory in Knesset elections and was sworn in for his second term as prime minister on July 13. He made international headlines the next day for his inaugural speech. Directing his remarks to Palestinians, he said, as quoted by Sarah Helm in the *Independent*, "You will not get everything you want. Neither will we. So once and for all, take your destiny in your hands. Don't lose this opportunity that may never return." Then he addressed the war-weary Israeli populace: "No longer are we necessarily a people that dwells alone.... We must join the international movement towards peace, reconciliation and co-operation that is spreading over the entire globe these days—lest we be the last to remain, all alone, in the station."

The Nobel Peace Prize

In the first year of Rabin's second term, fighting between Israelis and Palestinians increased. Official negotiations held in the United States stalled, but secret talks between Israeli and Palestinian officials in Oslo, Norway, were a success. In September 1993 Israel formally recognized the PLO, and Rabin shook Arafat's hand on the White House lawn in Washington, D.C., on September 13. The Oslo Accords agreement granted Palestinians limited self-rule in the Gaza Strip and the West Bank under the governance of the newly created Palestinian Authority. For their historic efforts, Rabin, Arafat, and Peres (Israel's foreign minister at the time) were awarded the Nobel Peace Prize in 1994.

Support for peace in the Middle East continued. On October 26, 1994, Rabin signed a peace treaty with Jordan, ending forty-six years of conflict between the two nations. It was Israel's second peace treaty with an Arab country.

At a peace rally on November 4, 1995, one hundred thousand Israelis gathered in support of Israel's Land for Peace Plan, which called for Israel

Yitzhak Rabin and King Hussein of Jordan discussing the recently signed peace treaty between Jordan and Israel in 1994, ending years of war between the two countries. GOVERNMENT PRESS OFFICE OF ISRAEL.

to withdraw from some of the lands it had seized during the 1967 Arab-Israeli War and allow Palestinians to govern themselves. Rabin spoke to the crowd, saying, as quoted on the *Yitzhak Rabin Center* Web site, that "violence is eating away at the foundations of Israeli democracy. It must be condemned, denounced, and isolated. It is not the way of the state of Israel.... This rally must send a message to the Israeli public, to the Jewish people throughout the world, and to many, many in the Arab world and the world at large, that the people of Israel want peace."

As Rabin made his way from the podium to his waiting car, a twenty-five-year-old Israeli law student named Yigal Amir (1970–) stepped from the crowd and shot him. Rabin slumped in the back seat of his car as his driver sped to the hospital, but doctors were unable to revive him. Amir later admitted that he killed Rabin because he felt that the peace that Rabin was creating in the Middle East would eventually result in the creation of an independent Palestinian nation that would one day threaten the existence of Israel. Rabin was the first Israeli prime minister to be assassinated. His death prompted a grievous period of mourning and self-examination in Israel. Several months later **Benjamin Netanyahu** (1949–; see entry) and the Likud Party won the Knesset elections, and as party chief Netanyahu became prime minister.

Hawks versus Doves

In times of conflict, and especially in war, politicians are often described as either hawks or doves. Hawks take aggressive approaches to conflicts, advocating for war. Doves generally oppose war in favor of negotiations and compromise. During the First Intifada of the late 1980s, Yitzhak Rabin instituted what he called the iron fist policy to quash the uprisings. Rabin's reputation as a hawk dated back far beyond his role in the 1967 Arab-Israeli War, all the way to his Palmach years, and that helped him win the election as prime minister in 1992. While Labor Party governments were generally viewed as soft on defense, Rabin's tough stance was viewed as a counterweight to other dominant members of the party who were more willing to try diplomacy first.

Rabin proved to be both a hawk and a dove. He worked to secure Israel's security using both military force and political diplomacy. Rabin explained to a crowd on the day of his death, as quoted by the *Yitzhak Rabin Center* Web site, that he "waged war as long as there was no chance for peace." But on that November day in 1995, Rabin said, "Today I believe that there are prospects for peace, great prospects. We must take advantage of this for the sake of those standing here, and for the sake of those who do not stand here. And they are many among our people."

THE YITZHAK RABIN CENTER. HTTP://
WWW.RABINCENTER.ORG.IL/ENGLISH/
ARCHIVES/DOCUMENTS/RABIN%20
ADDRESS%20AT%20A%20PEACE%20
RALLY%20-%20NOVEMBER%
204%201995.PDF (ACCESSED ON
NOVEMBER 30, 2011).

For More Information

BOOKS

Horovitz, David Phillip, ed. *Shalom, Friend: The Life and Legacy of Yitzhak Rabin.* New York: Newmarket Press, 1996.

Inbar, Ephraim. *Rabin and Israel's National Security.* Woodrow Wilson Center Press, 1999.

Pasachoff, Naomi. *Links in the Chain: Shapers of the Jewish Tradition.* New York: Oxford University Press, 1997.

Rabin, Yitzhak. *The Rabin Memoirs.* Berkeley: University of California, 1996, pp. 111–112.

PERIODICALS

Helm, Sarah. "Rabin Brandishes an Olive Branch." *Independent* (London, England; July 14, 1992). Available online at http://www.independent.co.uk/news/world/rabin-brandishes-an-olive-branch-1533127.html (accessed on November 30, 2011).

"Rabin at Center of Israeli Storm." *New York Times* (January 19, 1989). Available online at http://www.nytimes.com/1989/01/19/world/rabin-at-center-of-israeli-storm.html?scp=8&sq=intifada+rabin &st=nyt (accessed on November 30, 2011).

"Rabin Restates Policy." *New York Times* (March 7, 1968). Available online at http://select.nytimes.com/gst/abstract.html?res=FA0D14FB3A5C 147493C 5A91788D85F4C8685F9&scp=5& sq=rabin+ambassador&st=p (accessed on November 30, 2011).

WEB SITES

"The Assassination and Funeral of Yitzhak Rabin." *CNN.* http://www.cnn.com/WORLD/9511/rabin/umbrella/ (accessed on November 30, 2011).

The Yitzhak Rabin Center. http://www.rabincenter.org.il/English/Archives/Documents/Rabin%20Address%20at%20a%20peace%20rally%20-%20 November%204%201995.pdf (accessed on November 30, 2011).

"Yitzhak Rabin." *Nobelprize.org.* http://nobelprize.org/peace/laureates/1994/rabin-bio.html (accessed on November 30, 2011).

Anwar Sadat

BORN: December 25, 1918 • Mit Abul al-Kum, Egypt

DIED: October 6, 1981 • Cairo, Egypt

Egyptian president, military leader

"The people of Egypt have embarked upon a major effort to achieve peace in the Middle East. . . . We will spare no effort, we will not tire or despair, we will not lose faith, and we are confident that, in the end, our aim will be achieved."

Egyptian president Anwar Sadat (also spelled al-Sadat) rose from relative obscurity to become one of the most powerful and controversial leaders in the modern history of the Middle East. Taking over in 1970 after the unexpected death of President **Gamal Abdel Nasser** (1918–1970; see entry), Sadat introduced a series of reforms that proved popular with the public, then attained hero status when he coordinated with Syria to attack Israel in the 1973 Arab-Israeli War. In 1978 Sadat made history as the first Arab (Arabic-speaking) leader to be awarded the Nobel Peace Prize, sharing the honor with Israeli prime minister **Menachem Begin** (1913–1992; see entry) for their historic Camp David Accords, a peace agreement that made Egypt the first Arab nation to formally acknowledge Israel's right to exist. But other Arabs reviled Sadat for this, and it cost

Anwar Sadat. AP PHOTO.

371

him his life. In October 1981 he was assassinated by members of the fundamentalist group Egyptian Islamic Jihad.

Early life and military career

Sadat was born on December 25, 1918, in the small Egyptian village of Mit Abul al-Kum, located in the fertile Nile Delta. His father, Mohamed, was a military hospital clerk. His mother, Sitt al-Barrein, was one of his father's multiple wives, and Sadat's siblings and half siblings totaled thirteen in all. He spent some of his early years in the care of his grandmother in a sun-dried brick and straw-roofed house in Mit Abul al-Kum, where he loved the village's variety of orchards and many festivals. His grandmother regaled him with stories of Egyptian heroes who had fought British aggression. At the time, Egypt was a colony of the British Empire, as was neighboring Sudan, where Sadat's mother had roots.

Young Sadat attended classes at the village *kuttab*, or elementary school, where he learned the Koran (also spelled Qur'an or Quran; the holy book of Islam). In 1924 he returned to live with his father, who had settled in Cairo, Egypt's capital. Sadat was fortunate that his older brother had no interest in education, for their father's meager salary could not have paid for both sons to attend school at the same time. Sadat gladly completed both his primary and secondary education and then attended the Royal Military Academy, which had recently relaxed its entrance requirements to allow students from less-affluent backgrounds like Sadat's to enroll. Upon graduation in February 1938 he became a second lieutenant in the Egyptian army and was assigned to the military station in Manqabad, in southern Egypt. Among the other young Egyptian officers at the academy also posted to Manqabad was Nasser, a native of Alexandria, Egypt, whose father was also a civil servant. Both became part of a core group of nationalists (people who advocate political independence for a country) inside the army, committed to the idea of a free and independent Egypt. They were also critical of King Farouk I (1920–1962), who was considered by many Egyptians to be little more than a puppet of the British.

When World War II (1939–45; a war in which the Allies [Great Britain, France, the Soviet Union, the United States, and China] defeated the Axis Powers [Germany, Italy, and Japan]) began, many Egyptian military personal resented having to fight on the war's African front, when

Germany's ally, Italy, invaded Libya, and Egyptian troops were deployed to defend the western border of British territory. In 1940 Sadat was transferred to a military station near Cairo, where he secretly participated in the Free Officers Movement. He and a few others planned an uprising with the assistance of Nazi agents. When the British discovered this, Sadat was stripped of his military rank, arrested, and sent to prison for two years before he escaped in 1944. He spent several months living under a fake name and working menial jobs but resumed plotting against British rule after the war's end.

In January 1946 a fellow revolutionary managed to fatally wound a pro-British official. The perpetrator was taken into custody and implicated Sadat in the plot. Jailed again for two more years before trial, Sadat was finally acquitted and released. Both periods in jail further deepened his loathing of British rule and the Wafd Party, which had once taken up Egypt's independence cause back in the 1920s but was corrupted into a cooperative relationship with the British.

Sadat's acquittal allowed him to rejoin the military, and he reentered with the rank of captain in January 1950. In the interim years, the Free Officers group had continued to grow with Nasser as its charismatic leader. One of the most significant factors that aided its cause—to remove the British from Egypt—was the humiliating defeat of Egyptian forces in the 1948 Arab-Israeli War. The movement to create a Jewish homeland in Palestine had been underway for some years by then, but the region was already populated by Arabs, who had lived there for hundreds of years. Clashes between Jews and Arab Palestinians intensified and, when Israel declared its sovereignty on May 14, 1948, several thousand troops from neighboring Arab nations rushed to aid the Palestinians. Egypt had a fairly well-equipped and well-trained army, but Farouk I's distrust of other Arab leaders meant that a larger, more coordinated effort was impossible. Egypt was the first among the war's Arab participants to be forced to sign a cease-fire agreement, which it did in February 1949.

Voice of revolution

Sadat advanced to a seat on the governing council of the Free Officers group, while social unrest erupted in several Egyptian cities in late 1951 and early 1952. Nasser finally decided to strike and carried out a military coup (overthrow of the government) on July 22 and 23. Sadat read the Free Officers' official announcement of the coup and its aims over Egyptian radio. Nasser became chair of the new Revolutionary Command Council (RCC) and in the next few years moved to marginalize his main rival for power, Muhammad Naguib (1901–1984), a war hero and fellow Free Officer who had become Egypt's first president. Nasser forced Naguib to resign in late 1954 and placed the respected military general under house arrest, where he would remain for the next eighteen years until Sadat lifted the order.

During this period, Egyptian and British diplomats fought bitterly over the future of the strategically situated Suez Canal, a shipping canal that connects the Mediterranean Sea with the Red Sea. The canal was built by a French company and was owned and controlled by the French and the British. The canal became an important issue after the 1948 Arab-Israeli War, with British troops maintaining a large garrison in the Canal Zone to protect international shipping interests. The zone lay between Egypt and its mighty Sinai Peninsula. In July 1956 Nasser announced plans to nationalize (bring under government ownership and control) the canal, prompting the Suez Crisis, in which Great Britain, France, and Israel invaded Egypt in an attempt to regain control of the canal. Egypt prevailed, and full control of canal brought much-needed revenue, in the form of usage fees, to the country.

During these years, Sadat was a trusted adviser to Nasser, serving as minister of state between 1954 and 1956. He also wrote books about recent events and served as editor in chief of the *al-Gumhurriyah* (The Republic), a newspaper which looked at issues from an Arab point of view and was sharply critical of the West and its attempt to influence Middle East politics.

Nasser was an ardent proponent of Pan-Arabism, movement for the unification of Arab peoples and the political alliance of Arab states. This resulted only in a short-lived union with Syria from 1958 to 1961. For a time Sadat served as secretary-general of the National Union, a powerful new political party that united both nations.

The 1967 Arab-Israeli War

Tensions between Egypt and Israel amplified in the 1960s and finally culminated in the 1967 Arab-Israeli War. Military maneuvers had escalated that spring on all sides, and Israel struck first to prevent a combined offensive that it believed was coming from Egypt, Jordan, and Syria. The now-formidable Israel Defense Forces (IDF), Israel's military, launched a massive air strike on the Egyptian Air Force, wiping out the majority of its fighter planes in a matter of hours on June 5, then moved to seize Egypt's Sinai Peninsula and the Gaza Strip. Israel also invaded and seized Jordan's West Bank and Syria's Golan Heights. By the end of the week Israel had nearly tripled its original size. After the cease-fire, Israel refused to return any of these lands, which included Egypt's vital Suez Canal, but Egyptian forces managed to impose a blockade and shut down the canal.

The 1967 Arab-Israeli War ruined the confidence of the Egyptian government and military, and swift internal reprisals followed. Nasser initiated the War of Attrition to try to win back Egypt's lost land, but he had only limited success. In 1969 Nasser appointed Sadat as his vice president. Nasser died of a heart attack on September 28, 1970, and Sadat became acting president. His permanent presidency was confirmed by national referendum a little over two weeks later. (A referendum is a direct public vote on a single proposal.)

Assuming leadership

Sadat proved himself unexpectedly adept at leading Egypt while it was on the brink of political chaos after Nasser's death. While paying homage to the founder of modern Egypt, Sadat also began to dismantle some of the tools Nasser had used to wield control, such as the wiretapping of officials' telephone conversations. Nasser had also periodically cracked down on newspapers and other media outlets that voiced criticism of the policies of the Arab Socialist Union, the ruling political party, and Sadat loosened some of these rules. In the spring of 1971 Sadat began to fire members of cabinet ministries, the military, and the civil service who had been loyal to Nasser, while dismantling the socialist-driven economic programs of the past fifteen years. (Socialism is a system in which the government owns the means of production and controls the distribution of goods and services.) He ordered the denationalization of some industries and returned property and assets that Egypt had seized years earlier from private individuals and companies. Foreign investors were courted, especially those from wealthy Arab countries located along the Persian Gulf.

Sadat's boldest move came as a shock even to Israel. On October 6, 1973, Egypt attacked Israel in a surprise move on Yom Kippur, a Jewish holy day. The offensive was carried out by Egyptian and Syrian forces. This time, the Egyptian air force struck Israeli targets in the Sinai Peninsula, which allowed ground troops to cross the Suez Canal and into Israeli territory, where they held firm; the Syrians, meanwhile, entered the Golan Heights. The situation quickly descended into a stalemate (a situation in which no progress can be made) on all sides, with Israel requesting and receiving military aid from the United States and Sadat, in turn, making an overture to the Soviet Union.

Egypt's Arab allies willingly sent troops and armaments, but more importantly the Organization of Arab Petroleum Exporting Countries (OAPEC; an organization formed in 1968 by the world's major oil-producing nations to coordinate energy policies among Arab nations and whose main purpose is developmental) imposed an oil embargo (ban) on all of Israel's allies. This prompted crude-oil prices on the world market to spike sharply, and gas prices in Western nations, especially in the automobile-dependent United States, skyrocketed. U.S. secretary of state Henry Kissinger (1923–) worked to hammer out a cease-fire and withdrawal deal to be supervised by the United Nations, an international organization of countries founded in 1945 to promote international peace, security, and cooperation. The 1973 oil embargo was a turning point for international relations, proving just how economically dependent the West was on oil extracted from the Middle East and displaying for the first time the power wielded by oil-rich nations like Saudi Arabia to influence foreign affairs. In the end, the 1973 Arab-Israeli War was declared a success, for although no land was gained or lost, Israel had been caught unprepared for the first time. Sadat was lauded as a visionary Egyptian hero of the modern age.

Reopens Suez Canal

Throughout these events, the Suez Canal issue remained unresolved. It had been closed since the 1967 Arab-Israeli War, when Israel took control of the canal and Egypt blockaded it. Sadat worked with the United States to negotiate a new agreement with Israel in which Israel returned land on the east bank of the canal and the oil fields in the Sinai Peninsula, and Egypt allowed Israel access to the Gulf of Aqaba so that its ships could reach the Red Sea and the canal. The canal reopened in June 1975.

Elections in Egypt had often been conducted under questionable democratic rules since the 1952 revolution. Nasser had banned independent political parties, and those that were allowed on the ballot were actually closely monitored by the government. Certain parties, like the Communist and Wafd parties, had been shut down altogether, and members of the powerful Muslim Brotherhood, an Islamist group founded in Egypt back in the 1920s that had supported Nasser and the 1952 revolution, were banned from running for political office. In 1976 Sadat was reelected via another yes-no referendum, winning 99 percent of the vote.

Egypt and Israel had signed a cease-fire after the 1973 Arab-Israeli War, but there was no formal resolution yet. Sadat began making overtures to the West for help in arranging a peace treaty, knowing that because Egypt was the sole nation ever to have achieved even a small military victory over Israel, he possessed an excellent negotiating advantage. When he announced that he would be willing to go anywhere in the world, including Israel, to secure peace, Israeli prime minister Menachem Begin invited Sadat to Israel. In November 1977 Sadat became the first leader of an Arab nation to visit Israel. He spoke before the Knesset (the Israeli legislature) on the issue of peace between the two countries.

Loses alliance with Arab nations

Although several Arab countries, including Syria, Libya, and Saudi Arabia, voiced their disagreement with Sadat's peace plans, he pushed forward, pledging to use the opportunity to help Palestinians in their quest for their own country. On September 5, 1978, Sadat and Begin met at Camp David, the U.S. presidential retreat in Maryland, in the United States, to begin talks. The wording of the agreement, announced thirteen days later, largely concerned the borders of Israel and Egypt, leaving the issue of a future Palestinian state unresolved.

For their efforts, Sadat and Begin were awarded the Nobel Peace Prize in 1978, a few short weeks after the Camp David Accords, the peace agreement they had reached at Camp David, were announced. It was thought that a resulting peace treaty would have been signed by then, but the process had been delayed by unresolved issues over the final wording. Sadat chose not to attend the Nobel Peace Prize ceremony in Oslo, Norway. Instead Sadat sent an emissary to deliver his Nobel lecture, which states, according to *Nobelprize.org*, "I am convinced that we owe it to this generation and the generations to come, not to leave a stone unturned in our pursuit of peace. The ideal is the greatest one in the history of man, and we have accepted the challenge to translate it from a cherished hope into a living reality."

The Camp David Accords finally led to the historic Egypt-Israel Peace Treaty, signed in March 1979. With that, Egypt became the first Arab state to affirm Israel's right to exist; since 1948 all other Arab nations and the Palestinians had openly called for the destruction of Israel. Both the Camp David Accords and the resulting treaty prompted angry debate

U.S. president Jimmy Carter watches as Israeli prime minister Menachem Begin and Egyptian president Anwar Sadat shake hands at Camp David in 1978. This historic meeting resulted in the Camp David Accords peace treaty. © CORBIS.

across the Middle East, with many Arab leaders criticizing Sadat. The leaders of the Arab League met in Baghdad, Iraq, in late 1978 and voted to expel Egypt, a founding member of the organization, from the league. (The Arab League is a regional political alliance of Arab nations formed in 1945 to promote political, military, and economic cooperation within the Arab world.) The Arab League even moved its headquarters from Cairo to Tunis, the capital of Tunisia. Seventeen Arab countries imposed economic sanctions against Egypt. (Sanctions are measures adopted by the international community against a nation that has violated international law, usually in the form of diplomatic, economic, or social restrictions.) Closer to home, the Islamic fundamentalist groups, whose support Sadat

Anwar Sadat was assassinated in 1981. This photo shows one of the gunmen involved in the attack, which took place during a military parade in Cairo.
AP PHOTO.

had courted over the years, were even more upset at the prospect of a peace with Israel. (Fundamentalists stress adherence to a strict or literal interpretation of religious principles.) In retaliation Palestinian militants launched deadly attacks on Egyptian and Israeli targets.

Assassination

On October 6, 1981, Sadat sat in full military dress on a viewing stand, watching the annual festivities commemorating the day Egypt won back the Suez Canal and parts of the Sinai Peninsula in the 1973 Arab-Israeli

War. While Mirage E-5 fighter jets performed stunts in the sky, a truck pulled up in front of the president's viewing stand. Four attackers jumped out of the vehicle; one threw a grenade and the others fired Kalashnikov automatic weapons at the stand. Sadat was gravely wounded and died shortly afterward. His vice president, **Hosni Mubarak** (1928–; see entry), was also wounded, although less severely. The attack was carried out by the Egyptian Islamic Jihad, a fundamentalist group whose goal was to turn Egypt into an Islamic state (in which Islam provides the basis for political, social, and cultural life), similar to that established in Iran after the 1979 Iranian Revolution (also known as the Islamic Revolution).

Thousands of Muslims turned out in Arab-world capitals, including Beirut, Lebanon, and Damascus, Syria, that night to celebrate Sadat's death. Three former U.S. presidents attended Sadat's funeral, but the president of neighboring Sudan was the sole head of state from the Arab world to pay his respects. Mubarak assumed the presidency and the Emergency Law that was enacted on the day of Sadat's assassination to quell political opposition remained in place for thirty years.

For More Information

BOOKS

Aburish, Saïd K. *Nasser: The Last Arab.* New York: St. Martin's, 2004.

Al-Sadat, Anwar. *In Search of Identity.* New York: Harper & Row, 1977.

Sadat, Jehan. *My Hope for Peace.* New York: Simon & Schuster, 2009.

PERIODICALS

MacManus, James. "President Sadat Assassinated at Army Parade." *Guardian* (October 7, 1981). Available online at http://www.guardian.co.uk/theguardian/2010/oct/07/archive-president-sadat-assassinated?INTCMP=SRCH (accessed on November 30, 2011).

Pace, Eric. "Anwar El-Sadat, the Daring Arab Pioneer of Peace with Israel." *New York Times* (October 7, 1981). Available online at http://www.nytimes.com/1981/10/07/obituaries/anwar-el-sadat-daring-arab-pioneer-peace-with-israel-sadat-s-innovations-sprang.html?scp=268&sq=anwar+sadat&st=nyt&pagewanted=all (accessed on November 30, 2011).

WEB SITES

Abdelhadi, Magdi. "Sadat's Legacy of Peace and Conflict." *BBC News* (October 6, 2006). http://news.bbc.co.uk/2/hi/middle_east/5412590.stm (accessed on November 30, 2011).

"Anwar al-Sadat." *Jewish Virtual Library.* http://www.jewishvirtuallibrary.org/jsource/biography/sadat.html (accessed on November 30, 2011).

"President Anwar Sadat's Address to the Israeli Knesset." *Jewish Virtual Library* (November 20, 1977). http://www.jewishvirtuallibrary.org/jsource/Peace/sadat_speech.html (accessed on November 30, 2011).

Al-Sadat, Anwar. "Nobel Lecture." *Nobelprize.org* (December 10, 1978). http://www.nobelprize.org/nobel_prizes/peace/laureates/1978/al-sadat-lecture.html (accessed on November 30, 2011).

Herbert Louis Samuel

BORN: November 6, 1870 • Liverpool, England

DIED: February 5, 1963 • London, England

British diplomat, politician

Herbert Louis Samuel.
© HULTON-DEUTSCH
COLLECTION/CORBIS.

"Let a Jewish centre be established in Palestine; let it achieve, as I believe it would achieve, a spiritual and intellectual greatness; and insensibly, but inevitably, the character of the individual Jew, wherever he might be, would be ennobled."

Herbert Samuel was a British diplomat appointed to serve as the first high commissioner for Palestine, which at the time was under British administration. (Palestine is a historical region in the Middle East on the eastern shore of the Mediterranean Sea, comprising parts of present-day Israel and Jordan). Samuel held this post for five crucial and challenging years from 1920 to 1925. His role required him to appease three disparate groups: the Zionists, who wanted him to support a Jewish homeland in Palestine; the Arabs (Arabic-speaking people), who insisted that he protect their historic claims to Palestine; and the British, who asked that he reconcile these conflicting demands in order to provide a politically stable country that the British could help move toward independence. Samuel satisfied none of the parties involved, and the

383

decisions he and other diplomats made in that era continued to resonate into the twenty-first century.

Samuel not only played a central role in the development of Palestine in the twentieth century, but he also had a distinguished career in British politics. First elected to the British parliament (legislature) in 1900, he was a faithful member of the Liberal Party his entire life. (The Liberal Party was a political party that focused on the rights and privileges of the British people over the rights of the government.) Over the years Samuel served as a cabinet member for several prime ministers, crafted key legislation relating to the juvenile court system, reorganized the postal service and the national telephone company, and led the Liberal Party for many years. Samuel also wrote several books on politics and philosophy, including *Liberalism: An Attempt to State the Principles and Proposal of Contemporary Liberalism in England* (1902), *Practical Ethics* (1935), and *Belief and Action: An Everyday Philosophy* (1937).

Growing up in the Cousinhood

Samuel grew up among a group of people who enjoyed extreme wealth and advantage, yet because of their Jewish religion were never fully accepted as part of the British aristocracy (members of the highest social class). His father, Edwin Samuel, and his uncle, Samuel Montagu (he switched the order of his name), managed one of the largest banks in Great Britain, and another relative, the Baron de Rothschild, was the head of the large Rothschild banking corporation. The family's great wealth gave it enormous influence in politics, but their Jewish religion made them outsiders in a British society that was predominantly Protestant. These elite British Jews often socialized and married only with other British Jews, creating a group jokingly referred to as the Cousinhood. Samuel was born into this society on November 6, 1870, in Liverpool, England.

The Samuel family, with their five children, soon moved to London, England, where Samuel attended school. His father died when he was seven years old, and he was raised primarily by his mother, Clara, whose orthodox (traditional) religious faith was very restrictive. His uncle, Montagu, was the dominant male influence in his life both religiously and politically. In 1893 Samuel graduated from Oxford University, one of Great Britain's top universities, with little interest in his religion and with the goal of becoming a politician. According to biographer Bernard

Wasserstein, author of *Herbert Samuel: A Political Life*, the future diplomat "left university a self-confident junior politician, able to hold his own in any setting."

Even though Samuel was knowledgeable about politics and came from a moderately well-connected family, he faced difficulties in getting elected early in his career. He announced his candidacy for a seat in the House of Commons from the riding (electoral district) of South Oxfordshire and actively campaigned, but he lost the election, first in 1895 and again in 1900. The intelligence and determination he showed during his campaigning were noticed by the Liberal Party, and his status with the party improved in 1902 when he wrote *Liberalism: An Attempt to State the Principles and Proposal of Contemporary Liberalism in England*, which expresses the party's main ideas. Samuel writes in the book that, "It is the duty of the State to secure to all its members, and all others whom it can influence, the fullest possible opportunity to lead the best life." This idea, which guided Samuel as a politician within Great Britain, proved far more troubling when applied to Palestine.

Although Samuel spent much of the 1890s immersed in politics, in 1897 he found time to marry Beatrice Franklin, a member of the small British Jewish community. The pair enjoyed a happy marriage and eventually had five children.

Elected to British government

In 1902 Samuel was elected to the House of Commons (the lower branch of the British parliament) as a representative of the Liberal Party for the constituency of Cleveland, an area home to many working-class miners and laborers who supported Samuel's political ideas. In Parliament Samuel soon gained a reputation as a gifted orator. Although not fiery or passionate as a speaker, he had a way of convincing others with his reasonable manner and his skillful understanding of details. These qualities aided in his reelection campaigns and eventually led to administrative positions within the Liberal Party.

Samuel was made undersecretary at the Home Office (the British government department in charge of domestic affairs) in 1905, and he helped create legislation that provided care for the poor, especially children; protected the rights of workers; regulated immigration to Great Britain; and reformed the juvenile-justice system. In 1909 Samuel was named chancellor of the Duchy of Lancaster, a position that made him a junior member of the cabinet to Prime Minister Herbert Henry Asquith (1852–1928). With this promotion, Samuel became the first Jew to ever hold a cabinet-rank position in Great Britain. (Jewish-born Benjamin Disraeli [1804–1881] had served as prime minister in the 1870s, but he was baptized into the Church of England as an infant.) Next Samuel took charge of the Royal Mail (the government-owned postal service), then the largest employer in Great Britain and one of the largest businesses in the world in that era. Samuel ran the Royal Mail from 1910 to 1914, transforming it into a more modern and efficient business. He also oversaw the introduction of air mail to Great Britain in 1911 and orchestrated the government takeover of the National Telephone Company.

In 1914 Samuel was appointed secretary of the Local Government Board, a government agency in charge of government services on the local level, including taxes, poor laws (statutes governing the poor and relief-aid efforts), and public health. It was in this position that Samuel served during World War I (1914–18; a global war between the Allies [Great Britain, France, and Russia, joined later by the United States] and the Central Powers [Germany, Austria-Hungary, and their allies]). He contributed to his country's war effort by easing the effects of the war on working-class families and creating a system to process war refugees, people who flee their country to escape violence or persecution. He left the position when the Liberal Party was forced into a coalition government in 1915 as a result of several wartime-related crises. (A coalition government is one in which political parties cooperate with each other, because no party holds the majority.)

Throughout his career as a member of Parliament, a high-level government administrator, and a cabinet member, Samuel earned a reputation for accomplishing difficult tasks and for his attention to detail. He was admired and respected for these skills but never personally well liked, even by those within his party. Observing his work at the Royal Mail, future prime minister Winston Churchill (1874–1965) compared him to a machine. Even Wasserstein, who admired Samuel, wrote that "Samuel seemed at times inhuman and priggish [excessively devoted to proper speech and manner]." Samuel never expressed passion for any of his duties, except for one: Zionism, which he embraced around 1913. (Zionism is an international political movement originating in the late nineteenth century that called for the creation of an independent Jewish state in Palestine.)

Support for Zionists

In Europe and parts of Russia, Jews had been subjected to discrimination for hundreds of years. In underdeveloped rural areas in eastern Europe, they were even the targets of pogroms that persisted well into the early twentieth century. (A pogrom is a racially-motivated riot in which mobs, usually organized and sanctioned by the state, attack a minority group, most often Jews.) Because they were a minority, Jews were an easy target for those looking to cast blame for poorly performing economies and other domestic troubles. Beginning in the late nineteenth century, persecuted Jews fled Russia and formed settlements in Palestine, a region in the Middle East that was home to early Jewish holy sites, including the city of Jerusalem. In 1896 **Theodor Herzl** (1860–1904; see entry) published *The Jewish State* and helped turn Zionism into a credible political movement. By the early part of the twentieth century, many Jewish settlements had been created in Palestine, although they struggled without official support from any world power. Samuel proved the unlikely force that brought international recognition to the Zionist movement.

Even though Samuel did not practice the religious rituals of his faith, he knew firsthand the discrimination experienced by Jews, even wealthy, powerful Jews living in tolerant countries, like Great Britain. Furthermore, he had seen during his travels that impoverished Jews lived in dire conditions in less tolerant places, such as Russia. And he came to believe strongly that people deserve the chance to govern themselves. So Samuel pushed for British recognition of the idea of a Jewish homeland in Palestine, even though many British Jews did not support Zionism, because they feared it would indicate a lack of loyalty to Great Britain. For Samuel, however, Zionism became what Wasserstein calls "the one political passion of a singularly passionless career."

In 1914 Great Britain became involved in World War I. As a result of the complicated political alliances that developed during the war, Great Britain placed troops in Palestine to fight against the Ottoman Empire, the vast empire of the Ottoman Turks which included southwest Asia, northeast Africa, and southeast Europe, and lasted from the thirteenth century to the early twentieth century. As an Allied victory neared, members of the British and French governments, including Samuel, wanted to establish governments in the region that were friendly to Europe. Yet Samuel was even more ambitious. He petitioned British politicians on behalf of the Zionist movement, circulating a draft document called

The Balfour Declaration

The Balfour Declaration is one of the single most important documents in the history of the conflict between Jews and Arab Palestinians. Issued during World War I by British foreign secretary Arthur Balfour, the declaration committed Great Britain to supporting Jewish interests in creating an independent nation in Palestine, but it also pledged that such support would not come at a cost to the Arab communities that had existed in Palestine for centuries. The declaration itself is very brief, reading:

> "His Majesty's Government view with favour the establishment in Palestine of a national home for the Jewish people, and will use their best endeavours to facilitate the achievement of this object, it being understood that nothing shall be done which may prejudice the civil and religious rights of the existing non-Jewish communities in Palestine, or the rights and political status enjoyed by Jews in any other country."

Over the years, maintaining these dual commitments proved impossible. Arab Palestinians and Jews fought frequently and violently over conflicting claims to land and access to holy sites. Neighboring Arab nations became involved, and British officials in Palestine were unable to help the two sides reach a compromise.

One of the main problems with the Balfour Declaration was that it failed to define exact boundaries of where the Jews' future "national home" would be located. However, the phrase "in Palestine of a national home for the Jewish people" indelibly enshrined the right of a Jewish homeland as a core principle of international law regarding the region. Thus, when Great Britain withdrew from Palestine in 1948 and Jews in Palestine declared the existence of the state of Israel, the international community granted official recognition to the new Jewish nation. Neighboring Arab nations, however, did not recognize Israel as a legitimate state. Thus the Arab-Israeli conflict began, with the 1948 Arab-Israeli War (known in Israel as the War for Independence). Several other wars followed, as well as attempts to negotiate peace. The Balfour Declaration and its terms would resonate in the Arab-Israeli conflict well into the twenty-first century.

"THE BALFOUR DECLARATION.' *ISRAEL MINISTRY OF FOREIGN AFFAIRS.* HTTP://WWW.MFA.GOV.IL/MFA/PEACE%20 PROCESS/GUIDE%20TO%20THE%20 PEACE%20PROCESS/THE%20BALFOUR% 20DECLARATION (ACCESSED ON NOVEMBER 30, 2011).

"The Future of Palestine" that outlined the benefits that would result if Great Britain recognized the existence of a Jewish homeland in the region. Finally, on November 2, 1917, British foreign secretary Arthur Balfour (1848–1930) released a statement, written by Samuel and other prominent Zionists, that promised British support for the Zionist cause. The Balfour Declaration forever changed the shape of the Middle East.

Appointed high commissioner

Gaining British support for a Jewish homeland in Palestine was seen as a great triumph by Zionists, but it did not ensure peace in the Middle East. After the war, several Middle Eastern regions fell under the mandate, or administrative authority, of Western nations. Palestine was a British mandate. British mandate officials soon discovered that disputes among native Arabs and Jewish immigrants eager to create settlements in the region would be a major problem. They needed to appoint a governor, called a high commissioner, skilled at seeking compromise between opposing sides.

Samuel was appointed high commissioner of Palestine in May 1920, and in many ways he was a perfect choice for the position. He was supported by Zionists in Palestine and around the world and was a close associate of Chaim Weizmann (1874–1952), a leading Zionist. But Samuel had

Herbert Louis Samuel arriving in Jerusalem to govern Palestine as high commissioner in 1920, followed by religious leaders and soldiers. © CORBIS.

no intention of using British power to push aside Arab interests in Palestine and did not support the use of violence against Arab resistance. He was convinced that he could use diplomacy to promote peaceful coexistence between Arabs and Jews in Palestine. With this goal in mind, he arrived in Palestine on June 30, 1920.

Samuel immediately demonstrated his negotiating skills, settling border conflicts with the Lebanese and Syrians to the north and using his office to help establish stable rule in Transjordan (present-day Jordan) and Iraq. He met frequently with representatives of both Jewish and Arab interests in the region, establishing strong relations with both. Yet these early successes would not continue throughout his term. Financial support for Jewish immigration and settlement building was never sufficient, and Samuel proved unable to convince wealthy European Jews to significantly donate to the cause. But the lack of funding was a minor issue compared to the determined resistance to Jewish settlements in the area that came from the Arab inhabitants, who were predominantly Muslim. Their resistance was demonstrated very clearly in May 1921, when anti-Jewish riots broke out in the Palestinian city of Jaffa and surrounding villages, leaving forty-seven Jews and forty-eight Arab Palestinians dead. Authorities in Great Britain quickly placed limits on Jewish immigration, which angered Zionists. These riots were the start of an armed conflict between the Jews and the Arab Palestinians that would continue well into the twenty-first century.

Samuel began his term as high commissioner hopeful that he would be able to work with both sides to draft a constitution that would allow self-rule in Palestine; however, the deep hostility between the Jews and Arabs made this a difficult task. Samuel may have contributed to conflict when he supported religious leader **Amin al-Husayni** (also spelled Haj Āmin al-Husayni; 1893–1974; see entry) as the leader of Arab Palestinians in Jerusalem. Al-Husayni led determined Arab resistance to Zionism, including riots, and repeatedly damaged Samuel's plans to reduce conflict. Samuel also lost support from Zionists when he agreed to place limits on the number of Jews who could immigrate to Palestine each year. When Samuel left office at the end of his term in 1925, one of his few major accomplishments was that there was no open fighting between the two sides. Even though Samuel did deal with riots during his term as high commissioner, Palestine was relatively peaceful while Samuel was in control, and this most likely allowed the Zionist cause to grow in size and strength, ensuring its future in the region.

Herbert Louis Samuel posing with delegates from both the Arabic and Jewish religious sects that resided in Palestine. Samuel was constantly trying to keep the peace between the Jewish and Arabic people who lived in the region. © BETTMANN/CORBIS.

Finishes career as liberal mediator

Samuel returned to Great Britain determined to find time to write and reflect but circumstances denied him this period of rest. The coal industry in Britain was in crisis, and a mediator was needed to settle differences between workers, mine owners, and the government. Hence, Samuel reentered politics and continued to serve in various public-service posts for many years. He was drawn back into Liberal Party politics in the late 1920s and again won election to the House of Commons in 1929. He struggled to unite the party during the difficult years of the Great Depression (1929–41; a period of depressed world economies and high unemployment), holding various cabinet positions over the years. In 1937 he was named a viscount (a British honorary title), which gave him a permanent seat in the House of Lords (the upper chamber of the British parliament).

From 1944 until 1955 he was the leader of the Liberal Party in the House of Lords, using his dispassionate approach to urge compromise between competing factions. Samuel also found time to write several books of practical philosophy.

Samuel did not forget the Zionist cause once he left Palestine. Over the years he used his influence in Parliament to influence British policy toward Jews and toward Palestine. He urged that Great Britain increase immigration limits of Jews wishing to escape Germany in the 1930s, where they were suffering extreme discrimination. He opposed efforts to divide Palestine into Jewish and Arab territories in the late 1930s. Although he supported Zionism, Samuel was sympathetic to Arab Palestinians, who made up a majority of the population in the region. His ability to see both sides of the issue made him a popular radio commentator in the 1940s and 1950s, but kept him from ever being a true part of the Zionist community. Samuel died on February 5, 1963, at the age of ninety-two.

For More Information

BOOKS

Bowle, John. *Viscount Samuel: A Biography*. London: Gollancz, 1957.

Hunedi, Sahar. *A Broken Trust: Herbert Samuel, Zionism and the Palestinians, 1920–1925*. New York: Tauris, 2001.

McTague, John J. *British Policy in Palestine, 1917–1922*. Lanham, MD: University Press of America, 1983.

Samuel, Herbert. *Liberalism: An Attempt to State the Principles and Proposal of Contemporary Liberalism in England*. London: Grant Richards, 1902.

Schneer, Jonathan. *The Balfour Declaration: The Origins of the Arab-Israeli Conflict*. New York: Random House, 2010: 341.

Wasserstein, Bernard. *Herbert Samuel: A Political Life*. Oxford: Clarendon Press, 1992.

PERIODICALS

Oren, Michael B. "An End to Israel's Invisibility." *New York Times* (October 13, 2010). Available online at http://www.nytimes.com/2010/10/14/opinion/14oren.html?scp=1&sq=%22Balfour+Declaration%22&st=nyt (accessed on November 30, 2011).

Segev, Tom. "'View With Favor.'" *New York Times* (August 20, 2010). Available online at http://www.nytimes.com/2010/08/22/books/review/Segev-t.html?scp=1&sq=it%20is%20considered%20the%20original%20sin%20by%20 Israel%27s%20opponents&st=cse (accessed on November 30, 2011).

WEB SITES

"The Balfour Declaration.' *Israel Ministry of Foreign Affairs.* http://www.mfa.gov.il/MFA/Peace%20Process/Guide%20to%20the%20Peace%20Process/The%20Balfour%20Declaration (accessed on November 30, 2011).

"Herbert Louis Samuel." *Jewish Virtual Library.* http://www.jewishvirtuallibrary.org/jsource/biography/samuel.html (accessed on November 30, 2011).

Ariel Sharon

BORN: February 26, 1928 • Kfar Malal, Palestine

Israeli prime minister, military leader

"It is necessary to see things in a very realistic way: in the end, there will be a Palestinian state. . . . I don't think that we need to rule over another people and run its life. I don't think that we have the strength for that."

A riel Sharon was the prime minister of Israel from 2001 to 2005. Known for decades as an uncompromising patriot and staunch defender of Israel's aggressive military policies and actions, Sharon rose to the rank of major-general in Israel's military, the Israel Defense Forces (IDF), and served a controversial eighteen months as defense minister in the early 1980s. As head of the Likud Party, he became prime minister of Israel in 2001 but left the party in November 2005 to form the Kadima Party. In one of the Middle East's most famous reversals of opinion, Sharon had come to endorse a plan that included a retreat from the occupied territories (lands under the political and military control of Israel, especially the West Bank and the Gaza Strip) that Israel had held since the 1967 Arab-Israeli War (known in Israel as the Six-Day War). Two

Ariel Sharon. EITAN ABRAMOVICH/AFP/GETTY IMAGES.

months after forming the Kadima Party, Sharon was incapacitated by a stroke.

Early life

Sharon was born Ariel Scheinerman on February 27, 1928, to Shmuel and Vera Scheinerman. The Scheinermans were Russian Jews who moved to Palestine in 1922. (Palestine is a historical region in the Middle East on the eastern shore of the Mediterranean Sea, comprising parts of present-day Israel and Jordan.) They established a farm in Kfar Malal, a Jewish settlement in the Sharon Valley, about 10 miles (16 kilometers) from the city of Tel Aviv, and both Sharon and his older sister grew up farming the land.

Sharon joined Haganah, the underground defense force in Palestine, when he was fourteen years old. At the time Palestine was under British mandate (administrative authority). At first the British seemed sympathetic to the Zionist cause, which sought to create a Jewish homeland in Palestine, the site of the ancient Jewish kingdom. However, the British began limiting the number of Jews who were allowed to immigrate to Palestine, due to pressure from local Arab rulers, who were unsettled by an influx of newcomers to a land already scarce in resources. (Arabs are people who speak the Arabic language or who live in countries in which Arabic is the dominant language.) Zionists were taking over lands that had been home to predominantly Muslim Arabs for centuries. Both groups had historic claims to the region, and this led to conflicts between Arabs and Jews.

During World War II, Germany and was conducting an extensive campaign to eliminate the Jewish population of Europe. Many Jews attempted to escape this fate and immigrate to Palestine, but the British either sent them back or detained them in holding camps. Haganah worked to help the Jews by force. Its members attacked British administration buildings and smuggled Jewish immigrants into Palestine illegally. Sharon supported these efforts and eagerly pursued his military training.

Fierce fighter for independence

By 1947 Great Britain was planning to give up its control over Palestine, and the United Nations voted in favor of a plan to divide Palestine into separate Arab and Jewish states. (The United Nations is an international organization of countries founded in 1945 to promote international peace, security, and cooperation.) While the Jews accepted this proposal, the Arabs did not, and fighting between the two groups increased considerably. During these conflicts, Sharon proved himself to be a skillful fighter with Haganah, and he soon commanded a platoon in attacks against Arab positions.

Israel declared its independence on May 14, 1948, and the 1948 Arab-Israeli War (known in Israel as the War for Independence) officially began a day later. This war pitted Israel against Arab neighbors who believed that the region rightfully belonged to Arab Palestinians, including Egypt, Syria, Jordan, Iraq, Saudi Arabia, and Lebanon. Haganah became a part of the country's newly formed IDF. As a member of the IDF, Sharon participated in key battles, was wounded in one, and was eventually elevated to the rank of company commander. It was during this period that he changed his surname from Scheinerman to Sharon, the name of his valley birthplace. Many of the Jewish leaders changed their names as a show of pride for their newly created homeland.

Sharon achieved some notoriety for his bold military actions, but he saw limits to his ability to advance in the IDF because he often chafed at the hierarchy of rank and obedience the institution demanded. For a time, he left the army, marrying Margalit Zimmerman, a woman he had known since her teenage years, and enrolling at Hebrew University to study Middle Eastern history. Before Sharon could begin his civilian career, however, Arab attacks on Israeli civilians grew increasingly frequent, and Sharon returned to active duty in the IDF. Several years later he would return to school and earn a bachelor of law degree.

Commando Unit 101

By the summer of 1953 Sharon was back on the battlefield, leading a group into an Arab village in the dark of night in search of a Jordanian operative. The mission did not go well due to his troops' lack of preparation and training. Sharon made his concerns known about this to the highest military officials. He wrote a report outlining the skills and training such Israeli commando units needed. His report impressed IDF officials, and Sharon was put in charge of training a group he named Commando Unit 101. He devised a vigorous program to perfect his men's physical condition, stealth, hand-to-hand fighting, and navigational skills. Once operational, Commando Unit 101 quickly gained notoriety when it attacked the Arab village of Qibya in the West Bank, in October 1953. Known as the Qibya massacre, the event brought strong international

Ariel Sharon addresses the famous Commando Unit 101 before an attack on Arab targets in 1955. MINISTRY OF DEFENSE VIA GETTY IMAGES.

condemnation, for a majority of the sixty-nine Arab casualties were women and children.

In 1956 Egyptian president **Gamal Abdel Nasser** (1918–1970; see entry) nationalized (brought under government ownership and control) the Suez Canal, a shipping canal that connects the Mediterranean Sea with the Red Sea. The canal was built by a French company and, until Nasser nationalized it, was owned and controlled by the French and the British. Great Britain, France, and Israel responded by sending troops to Egypt in an attempt to regain control of the canal. Sharon disobeyed orders to march his troops across the Sinai Desert and avoid the Mitla Pass, although he did secure permission to send a patrol out. The patrol was fired upon by the Egyptians who had taken positions in the surrounding cliffs, and that attack brought in the rest of Sharon's forces into the fray. His troops eventually won the battle but suffered heavy casualties as a result, and Sharon's disobedience angered his superiors.

As a result of his actions in Egypt, Sharon was sent to England for training at the Camberley Staff College, and on his return in 1958 he was demoted to head of an infantry training school, a noncombat post. For the next four years, Sharon administered the school and earned a law degree. The time away from the battlefield helped restore Sharon's reputation, and he received several promotions in the early 1960s, becoming chief of staff of the Northern Command (the portion of the Israeli army defending Israel's border with Syria) in 1963 and a major general in 1965.

Urges war against Egypt

As tensions grew between Israel and its Arab neighbors, Sharon became an outspoken supporter of an Israeli strike against Egypt, the leading opponent in the ongoing conflicts. When Israel finally did attack Egypt and other Arab countries by launching the 1967 Arab-Israeli War, Sharon himself led one of the strikes against Egyptian positions in the Sinai Peninsula. When the war ended, Israel had more than tripled the size of the territory under its control, taking the entire Sinai Peninsula and the Gaza Strip from Egypt, plus the West Bank from Jordan and the Golan Heights from Syria. Sharon became a national hero along with a few other notable IDF commanders and was promoted to lead all IDF military training.

In 1969 Egypt waged the War of Attrition in an attempt to regain the territory it lost during the 1967 war. That year Sharon had taken charge of the Southern Command, which oversaw Israel's borders with Egypt and Jordan. Sharon disagreed with the IDF chief of staff's plan to set up a line of Israeli defenses along the Suez Canal. He spoke out publicly against the plan and again angered many in the army. However, many still supported Sharon due to several strikes that he led, which destroyed Palestine Liberation Organization (PLO) hideouts in the Gaza Strip in the early 1970s. (The PLO is a political and military organization formed to unite various Palestinian Arab groups with the goal of establishing an independent Palestinian state.)

A Tragic Family Life

Ariel Sharon suffered more than his share of personal tragedy. His wife, Margalit, died in 1962 in a car accident. Unable to care for their young son, Gur, alone, he came to rely on his wife's sister, Lily. The two developed a close relationship and married in 1963. The couple had two children together. In 1967 ten-year-old Gur fatally shot himself in the head while playing with a rifle. In 2000, after consistently supporting Sharon's career, Lily died of cancer. Sharon would later say that his two surviving sons, Omri and Gilad, and their beliefs about the future of Israel played a decisive role in the shifting of his own attitudes toward a reconciliation with the Palestinian people.

The Likud Party

Feeling that his attitude toward authority would keep him from reaching top positions in the army, Sharon looked for other career opportunities. In 1973 he again retired from the IDF and became a farmer in the Negev desert. He soon gained political contacts and developed a plan to build a new political party. Along with **Menachem Begin** (1913–1992; see entry), the former head of Irgun Zvai Leumi, the militant underground group founded in 1931 that worked to secure Israeli independence by staging violent attacks on British and Arab targets, Sharon created the Likud Party. Sharon envisioned the new conservative party as a supporter of a strong military policy that would disrupt the power of the Labor Party, the political party whose more liberal views had dominated Israel since its independence in 1948.

In 1973 Sharon was called back to duty as a member of the army reserves, due to threats of an attack from the Egypt. When Egyptian forces struck on October 6, 1973, the Jewish holy day of Yom Kippur, the defensive line Israel had built along the Suez Canal was broken by the massive attack. Sharon fought difficult battles against the advancing Egyptian army, while other Israeli troops pushed back the Syrian armies advancing from the north in alliance with Egypt. The conflict became known as the 1973 Arab-Israeli War (known in Israel as the Yom Kippur War).

His reputation was bolstered by victories in the 1973 Arab-Israeli War, and Sharon won a seat in the Knesset, Israel's parliament, on the Likud Party ticket in the elections of 1973. A cease-fire agreement between Israel and Egypt in 1974 forced Israeli troops to pull back to a position that put the Suez Canal back under Egypt's control. Sharon spoke out against this agreement and criticized the IDF commanders' decisions during the war. When **Yitzhak Rabin** (1922–1995; see entry) was elected as Israel's prime minister in 1974 in the wake of investigations into the Israeli government's failures during the 1973 Arab-Israeli War, he requested that his friend Sharon return to the army. Sharon had served under Rabin in the army during the 1960s, and the two had developed a mutual respect for each other's abilities. Sharon agreed to Rabin's request, giving up his seat in the Knesset. He became a special adviser on defense issues to Rabin in 1975.

Cabinet positions

In 1976 Sharon planned his return to politics. He challenged Begin for leadership of the Likud Party but lost, and in the 1977 Knesset elections

Begin became prime minister. Begin appointed Sharon to his cabinet as minister of agriculture. In this position, Sharon oversaw the development of Jewish settlements in the occupied territories, the lands under the political and military control of Israel since the 1967 Arab-Israeli War. Sharon considered these communities to be essential to Israel's defense, because they established a claim on the land and served as a buffer zone (a neutral area separating two hostile countries) between Israel and its Arab neighbors. Sharon concentrated on building settlements in the West Bank and the Gaza Strip, an extremely controversial move, because the status of the territories had not yet been resolved in any treaty agreement. The United Nations deemed them to have been illegally taken by Israel in the 1967 war, and therefore Sharon's settlement program was roundly condemned. Furthermore, international law established by the Geneva Conventions prohibited an occupying force from establishing civilian settlements on occupied land. (The Geneva Conventions are a series of international agreements that establish how prisoners of war and civilians in wartime are to be treated.)

In 1981 Begin appointed Sharon as defense minister, and in 1982 Sharon led an invasion of southern Lebanon. The goal was to drive the PLO out of Lebanon, because the neighboring country served as an ideal base for the PLO to launch attacks on Israel. The 1982 Lebanon War successfully forced the PLO out of Lebanon, but there were heavy civilian casualties. Of a particularly troubling nature were the attacks by Lebanese forces on Shatila and Sabra, two Palestinian refugee camps in the Lebanese capital of Beirut, in the hours following the assassination of Lebanon's president-elect Bashir Gemayel (1947–1982) in September 1982. The IDF assisted in the incident, which remains so dramatic an event that neither side can come to an agreement on the exact number of Palestinians and Lebanese who died; most sources place it around two thousand.

For the Shatila and Sabra massacres Sharon earned the nickname "the Butcher of Beirut" and was branded a war criminal by his enemies. He was forced to resign his post as defense minister after an investigative commission judged Israel to be indirectly responsible for deaths at Shatila and Sabra, and Sharon himself personally responsible as defense minister. He sued *Time* magazine for libel (a published false statement that is damaging to a person's reputation) in U.S. federal court for one article on the commission's verdict that ran in early 1983, but the lawsuit was unsuccessful.

In the mid–1980s, the Likud Party and the Labor Party formed a joint government and each party assigned people to high-ranking positions.

Sharon, as a representative of the Likud Party, served as minister of trade and industry from 1984 to 1990 and as minister of housing from 1990 to 1992. These years were difficult for Sharon, because the Labor Party members he worked with had very different opinions about how to lead Israel. Of paramount importance was the status of the occupied territories, an issue that continued to divide the Knesset and the nation. Sharon felt strongly that Israel should hold onto the territory it had won in battle and continue to build settlements to strengthen Israel's claim to the land. When Palestinians in the occupied territories mobilized in 1987 into an uprising known as the First Intifada, Sharon also opposed any talk of removing Jewish settlements from the Gaza Strip, where most of the rioting was occurring. Sharon felt that giving in to Palestinian violence would lead to more violent uprisings and might also draw other Arab countries into the conflict if they thought that Israel was weakening.

Opposes the Oslo Accords

In 1992 the Labor Party, now headed by Rabin, returned to power. In 1993 Rabin and other members of the Labor Party attended secret peace negotiations between Israel and the PLO that resulted in the Oslo Accords. The terms of this historic peace agreement included the PLO's formal recognition of Israel's right to exist and Israel's pledge to withdraw its settlements and armies from parts of the West Bank and the Gaza Strip. Sharon publicly criticized the Israeli government for signing the Oslo Accords and giving up land that he felt was vital to the protection of Israel. However, since the Likud Party was not in control of the government, there was little that Sharon could do to influence policy in the occupied territories.

This changed after Rabin was assassinated. He was shot by a right-wing extremist in November 1995, and a new Likud Party leader named **Benjamin Netanyahu** (1949–; see entry) became prime minister in 1996. In a bold move, Netanyahu appointed Sharon as his minister of national infrastructure, a position that again put Sharon in charge of Jewish settlements in the occupied territories. Ignoring the Oslo Accords, Sharon oversaw the creation of new Jewish settlements in both the Gaza Strip and the West Bank. Palestinian attacks intensified, and many Israelis began to push for a peace agreement. Netanyahu lost his bid for reelection in 1999 and Labor Party chief Ehud Barak became prime minister.

Becomes prime minister

Israel and the PLO were unable to negotiate peace by 2000, despite the agreements made in the Oslo Accords. Instead, tensions rose. In late 2000 a new Palestinian uprising, called the Second Intifada, erupted. In contrast to the First Intifada, when the main weapons used against Israeli targets were rocks, this time suicide bombers and rockets were deployed. (A suicide bombing is an attack intended to kill others and cause widespread damage, carried about by someone who does not hope to survive the attack.) Within three months this uprising had killed more than two hundred and wounded many more, and the violence between the IDF and the Palestinians continued. Barak swiftly lost control, and in the February 2001 elections Sharon became the eleventh prime minister of Israel.

Sharon surprised many by announcing his willingness to negotiate an end the violence, yet there were doubts in the Arab world about his sincerity. As the Second Intifada continued, he ordered increased Israeli defensive measures. The IDF dug deep trenches around Palestinian towns where violence originated in order to isolate them. It conducted targeted missile attacks on the buildings owned by the Palestinian Authority, the recognized governing institution for Palestinians in the West Bank and the Gaza Strip, and invaded the Gaza Strip in search of Palestinians who were considered terrorists by the Israelis. Even when the United States

Ariel Sharon prays at the Western Wall (also known as the Wailing Wall) in Jerusalem after his election as prime minister in 2001. AP PHOTO/ DAVID GUTTENFELDER.

pressured Sharon to stop building Jewish settlements in 2001 and honor the Oslo Accords, Sharon refused. Over the next three years, Palestinians and Israelis would continue to fight over the occupied territories.

Disengagement plan

In 2003 the Likud Party won another victory in the government elections and Sharon won another term as prime minister. As the Second Intifada continued, Sharon began to seek solutions to end the violence. The man who had spent more than six decades of his life in battle against the Palestinians seemed to have had a genuine change of heart as he neared his seventy-fifth birthday. He embraced the idea of creating separate Palestinian and Jewish nations.

Deploying his customary bluntness, Sharon managed to push the Knesset to enact his disengagement plan in late 2004. Under this plan, Israel would withdraw entirely from its settlements in the Gaza Strip, and close four settlements in the West Bank. Israeli settlers who did not willingly vacate their homes and accept government compensation packages would be evicted. Evictions from the West Bank and the Gaza Strip began in 2005 and were met with fierce resistance in some quarters. "Thirty-eight years of Israeli occupation of Gaza came to an end with televised scenes of Israeli soldiers dragging Israeli settlers from their homes and synagogues, and of bulldozers leveling Israeli buildings," writes Ari Shavit in the *New Yorker*. "And it was Sharon—the man who himself was known as 'the bulldozer' for both his desire to build new outposts and his brutal means—who had done it."

In early 2005 the Palestinian Authority had elected **Mahmoud Abbas** (1935–; see entry) as its president. The change in leadership made many hopeful that a long-standing peace might be reached between Israel and the Palestinians, and Sharon even sat down for talks with Abbas. Battling significant opposition within his own party, Sharon broke away with other moderates to form the Kadima Party in November 2005. Less than a month later, on December 18, he suffered a stroke. Sharon suffered a second, much more debilitating stroke on January 4, 2006, and as of late 2011 remained in a coma. His deputy prime minister, Ehud Olmert, took over leadership duties, but Israeli law decrees that a new election must be held in the event a prime minister is incapacitated for more than one hundred days. Olmert won that new election, and in the 2009 elections Netanyahu became prime minister.

For More Information

BOOKS

Dan, Uri. *Ariel Sharon: An Intimate Portrait*. London: Palgrave Macmillan, 2006.

Miller, Anita, Jordan Miller, and Sigalit Zetouni. *Sharon: Israel's Warrior Politician*. Chicago, IL: Academy Chicago Publishers and Olive Publishing, 2002.

Sharon, Ariel, and David Chanoff. *Warrior: The Autobiography of Ariel Sharon*. New York: Simon & Schuster, 2001.

PERIODICALS

Shavit, Ari. "The General." *New Yorker* (January 23, 2006). Available online at http://www.newyorker.com/archive/2006/01/23/060123fa_fact_shavit (accessed on November 30, 2011).

Weymouth, Lally. "No Guts, No Glory, No Peace." *Newsweek* (December 6, 2004): 32.

WEB SITES

"Ariel Sharon." *Israel Ministry of Foreign Affairs*. http://www.mfa.gov.il/MFA/MFAArchive/2000_2009/2003/2/Ariel+Sharon.htm (accessed on November 30, 2011).

Jeffay, Nathan. "Ariel Sharon's Shadow Still Looms Large over Political Landscape." *Forward* (February 4, 2009). http://www.forward.com/articles/15103/ (accessed on November 30, 2011).

Where to Learn More

Books

Al Aswany, Alaa. *On the State of Egypt: What Made the Revolution Inevitable.* New York: Vintage Books, 2011.

Anderson, Sean, and Stephen Sloan. *Historical Dictionary of Terrorism.* Lanham, MD: Scarecrow Press, 2002.

Barr, James. *A Line in the Sand: Anglo-French Struggle for the Middle East.* New York: W.W. Norton and Co., 2012.

Brown, Nathan J. *Palestinian Politics after the Oslo Accords: Resuming Arab Palestine.* Berkeley: University of California Press, 2003.

Carew-Miller, Anna. *Palestinians.* Philadelphia: Mason Crest, 2010.

Cleveland, William L. *A History of the Modern Middle East.* Boulder, CO: Westview Press, 2004.

Council on Foreign Relations/Foreign Affairs. *New Arab Revolt: What Happened, What It Means, and What Comes Next* . New York: Council on Foreign Relations, 2011.

Currie, Stephen. *Terrorists and Terrorist Groups.* San Diego, CA: Lucent Books, 2002.

DeFronzo, James. *The Iraq War: Origins and Consequences.* Boulder, CO: Westview Press, 2009.

Drummond, Dorothy. *Holy Land Whose Land: Modern Dilemma Ancient Roots.* Seattle, WA: Educare Press, 2002.

Encyclopedia of the Modern Middle East and North Africa. 4 vols. New York: Macmillan Reference USA, 2004.

Engel, David. *Zionism.* Harlow: Pearson/Longman, 2009.

Etheredge, Laura S., ed. *Persian Gulf States: Kuwait, Qatar, Bahrain, Oman, and the United Arab Emirates.* New York: Rosen/Britannica Educational Publishing, 2011.

Farsoun, Samih K., with Christina E. Zacharia. *Palestine and the Palestinians*. Boulder, CO: Westview Press, 1997.

Finkel, Caroline. *Osman's Dream: The History of the Ottoman Empire*. New York: Basic Books, 2007.

Gelvin, James L. *The Modern Middle East: A History*, 3rd ed. New York: Oxford University Press, 2011.

Gunderson, Cory Gideon. *The Israeli-Palestinian Conflict*. Edina, MN: Abdo, 2004.

Hirst, David. *Beware of Small States: Lebanon, Battleground of the Middle East*. New York: Nation Books, 2010.

Hourani, Albert. *A History of the Arab Peoples*. Cambridge, MA: Belknap, 1991.

Kalin, Ibrahim. "Roots of Misconception: Euro-American Perceptions of Islam before and after September 11." In *Islam, Fundamentalism, and the Betrayal of Tradition: Essays by Western Muslim Scholars*. Edited by Joseph E.B. Lumbard. Bloomington, IN: World Wisdom, 2004, pp. 144–187. Available online at http://www.worldwisdom.com/uploads/pdfs/58.pdf (accessed on November 30, 2011).

Karsh, Efraim. *The Arab-Israeli Conflict: The 1948 War*. New York: Rosen Publishing, 2008.

———. *The Iran-Iraq War: 1980–1988*. Oxford, UK: Osprey, 2002.

Kennedy, Hugh. *The Great Arab Conquests: How the Spread of Islam Changed the World We Live In*. Cambridge, MA: Da Capo Press, 2008.

Khalidi, Rashid. *The Iron Cage: The Story of the Palestinian Struggle for Statehood*. Boston, MA: Beacon, 2006.

Kherdian, David. *The Road from Home: The Story of an Armenian Girl*. New York: Greenwillow Books, 1979.

Kinross, Lord. *The Ottoman Centuries: The Rise and Fall of the Turkish Empire*. New York: Morrow Quill Paperbacks, 1979.

Kort, Michael. *The Handbook of the Middle East*. Brookfield, CT: Twenty-First Century Books, 2002.

Lewis, Bernard. *The Middle East: A Brief History of the Last 2,000 Years*. New York: Scribner, 1995.

Mackey, Sandra. *Mirror of the Arab World: Lebanon in Conflict*. New York: W.W. Norton, 2009.

Miller, Debra A. *The Arab-Israeli Conflict*. San Diego, CA: Lucent Books, 2005.

Milton-Edwards, Beverly, and Stephen Farrell. *Hamas: The Islamic Resistance Movement*. Cambridge, England: Polity Press, 2010.

Myre, Greg, and Jennifer Griffin. *This Burning Land: Lessons from the Front Lines of the Transformed Israeli-Palestinian Conflict*. Hoboken, NJ: Wiley, 2010.

Nardo, Don. *The Islamic Empire*. Detroit, MI: Lucent Books, 2011.

Polk, William R. *Understanding Iran: Everything You Need to Know, from Persia to the Islamic Republic, from Cyrus to Ahmadinejad.* Basingstoke, United Kingdom: Palgrave Macmillan, 2011.

Ra'ad, Basem L. *Hidden Histories: Palestine and the Eastern Mediterranean.* London: Pluto Press, 2010.

Rabinovich, Itamar. *The Lingering Conflict: Israel, Arabs, and the Middle East, 1948–2011.* Washington, DC: Brookings Institution Press, 2011.

Rapoport, David C. "Terrorism." In *Encyclopedia of Violence, Peace, & Conflict.* Vol. 3. 2nd ed. Edited by Lester Kurtz. San Diego, CA: Academic Press, 2008.

Shindler, Colin. *A History of Modern Israel.* Cambridge: Cambridge University Press, 2008.

Schneer, Jonathan. *The Balfour Declaration: The Origins of the Arab-Israeli Conflict.* New York: Random House, 2010.

Shlaim, Avi. *Israel and Palestine: Reappraisals, Revisions, Refutations.* London and New York: Verso, 2010.

Slavicek, Louise Chipley. *Israel.* New York: Chelsea House, 2008.

Smith, Charles D., ed. *Palestine and the Arab-Israeli Conflict: A History with Documents,* 7th ed. Boston MA: Bedford/St. Martin's, 2009.

Taheri, Amir. *The Persian Night: Iran Under the Khomeinist Revolution.* New York: Encounter Books, 2010.

Wingate, Katherine. *The Intifadas.* New York: Rosen, 2004.

Wright, Robin. *Dreams and Shadows: The Future of the Middle East.* New York: Penguin, 2008.

Young, Michael. *The Ghosts of Martyrs Square: An Eyewitness Account of Lebanon's Life Struggle.* New York: Simon and Schuster, 2010.

Periodicals

Anderson, Jon Lee. "Who Are the Rebels?" *New Yorker* (April 4, 2011). Available online at http://www.newyorker.com/talk/comment/2011/04/04/110404taco_talk_anderson (accessed on November 30, 2011).

Beinin, Joel. "Is Terrorism a Useful Term in Understanding the Middle East and the Palestinian-Israeli Conflict?" *Radical History Review* no. 85 (Winter 2003): 12–23. Available online at http://www.why-war.com/files/85.1beinin.pdf (accessed on November 30, 2011).

"A Bitter Stalemate." *Economist* (September 24, 2011): 58.

Diamond, Larry. "Why Are There No Arab Democracies?" *Journal of Democracy* 21, no. 1 (January 2010).

"Gaza Strip," *New York Times* (August 11, 2011). Available online at http://topics.nytimes.com/top/news/international/countriesandterritories/gaza_strip/index.html (accessed on November 30, 2011).

Ghosh, Bobby. "Islamophobia: Does America Have a Muslim Problem?" *Time* (August 19, 2010). Available online at http://www.time.com/time/print out/0,8816,2011936,00.html (accessed on November 30, 2011).

Hogan, Matthew."The 1948 Massacre at Deir Yassin Revisited." *Historian* 63, no. 2 (Winter 2001).

Huntington, Samuel P. "The Clash of Civilizations?" *Foreign Affairs* 72, no. 3 (Summer 1993). Available online at http://www.polsci.wvu.edu/faculty/ hauser/PS103/Readings/HuntingtonClashOfCivilizationsForAffSummer 93.pdf (accessed on November 30, 2011).

Khouri, Rami G. "Drop the Orientalist Term 'Arab Spring.'" *Daily Star* (August 17, 2011). Available online at http://www.dailystar.com.lb/Opinion/ Columnist/2011/Aug-17/Drop-the-Orientalist-term-Arab-Spring.ashx#axzz 1ZMX0FZfe (accessed on November 30, 2011).

Lebanon: The Israel-Hamas-Hezbollah Conflict. CRS Report for Congress. U.S. Library of Congress, Congressional Research Service (September 15, 2006). Available online at http://www.fas.org/sgp/crs/mideast/RL33566.pdf (accessed on November 30, 2011).

Masoud, Tarek. "The Upheavals in Egypt and Tunisia: The Road to (and from) Liberation Square." *Journal of Democracy* Vol. 22, No. 3 (July 2011). Available online at http://www.journalofdemocracy.org/articles/gratis/ Masoud-22-3.pdf (accessed on November 30, 2011.

Shapiro, Samantha. "Revolution, Facebook Style." *New York Times* (January 22, 2009). Available online at http://www.nytimes.com/2009/01/25/magazine/ 25bloggers-t.html (accessed on November 30, 2011).

Steavenson, Wendell. "Roads to Freedom: The View from within the Syrian Crackdown." *New Yorker* (August 29, 2011): 26–32.

Web Sites

"Al-Qaeda (a.k.a. al-Qaida, al-Qa'ida)." *Council on Foreign Relations* (June 17, 2011). http://www.cfr.org/terrorist-organizations/al-qaeda-k-al-qaida-al-qaida/p9126 (accessed on November 30, 2011).

Asser, Martin. "The Muammar Gaddafi Story." *BBC News* (October 21, 2011). http://www.bbc.co.uk/news/world-africa-12688033 (accessed on November 30, 2011).

"Background Note: Lebanon." *U.S. Department of State* (May 23, 2011). http:// www.state.gov/r/pa/ei/bgn/35833.htm#history (accessed on November 30, 2011).

"Bahrain News: The Protests (2011)." *New York Times* (September 26, 2011). http://topics.nytimes.com/top/news/international/countriesandterritories/ bahrain/index.html (accessed on November 30, 2011).

"The Battle for Libya: Killings, Disappearances, and Torture." *Amnesty International* (September 2011). http://www.amnesty.org/en/library/asset/ MDE19/025/2011/en/8f2e1c49-8f43-46d3-917d-383c17d36377/mde 190252011en.pdf (accessed on November 30, 2011).

Beinin, Joel, and Lisa Jajjar. "Palestine, Israel and the Arab-Israeli Conflict: A Primer." *Middle East Research and Information Project.* http://www.merip.org/palestine-israel_primer/intro-pal-isr-primer.html (accessed on November 30, 2011).

Brown, Nathan J. "U.S. Policy and the Muslim Brotherhood." *Carnegie Endowment for International Peace* (April 13, 2011). http://carnegieendowment.org/2011/04/13/u.s.-policy-and-muslim-brotherhood/i6 (accessed on November 30, 2011).

"Bullets to Ballet Box: A History of Hezbollah." *Frontline World.* www.pbs.org/frontlineworld/stories/lebanon/history.html (accessed on November 30, 2011).

Collelo, Thomas, ed. "Syria." *Country Studies.* (1987). http://countrystudies.us/syria/ (accessed on November 30, 2011).

El Mansour, Mohammed. "The U.S.-Middle East Connection: Interests, Attitudes, and Images." *Teach Mideast* (2004). http://teachmideast.org/essays/28-history/110-the-us-middle-east-connectioninterests-attitudes-and-images (accessed on November 30, 2011).

"Foreign Terrorist Organizations." *U.S. Department of State.* (May 19, 2011). http://www.state.gov/s/ct/rls/other/des/123085.htm (accessed on November 30, 2011).

Grace, Francie. "Munich Massacre Remembered." *CBS News.* (February 11, 2009). http://www.cbsnews.com/stories/2002/09/05/world/main520865.shtml (accessed on November 30, 2011).

"The Gulf War." *Harper's Magazine.* http://www.harpers.org/GulfWar.html (accessed on November 30, 2011).

"The Gulf War: an In-Depth Examination of the 1990-1991 Persian Gulf Crisis." *PBS Frontline.* http://www.pbs.org/wgbh/pages/frontline/gulf/ (accessed on November 30, 2011).

"A History of Conflict—Israel and the Palestinians: A Timeline." *BBC News.* http://news.bbc.co.uk/2/shared/spl/hi/middle_east/03/v3_ip_timeline/html/ (accessed on November 30, 2011).

"Hunting Bin Laden." *PBS Frontline..* http://www.pbs.org/wgbh/pages/frontline/shows/binladen/ (accessed on November 30, 2011).

Internet Islamic History Sourcebook. Fordham University, http://www.fordham.edu/halsall/islam/islamsbook.html#Islamic%20Nationalism (accessed on November 30, 2011).

"Iran: A Brief History." *MidEast Web..* http://www.mideastweb.org/iranhistory.htm (accessed on November 30, 2011).

"Guide to the Middle East Peace Process." *Israeli Ministry of Foreign Affairs.* http://www.mfa.gov.il/MFA/Peace+Process/Guide+to+the+Peace+Process/ (accessed on November 30, 2011).

The Islamic World to 1600. Applied History Research Group, University of Calgary. http://www.ucalgary.ca/applied_history/tutor/islam/ (accessed on November 30, 2011).

"Islamophobia." *Council on American-Islamic Relations (CAIR)*. http://www.cair.com/Issues/Islamophobia/Islamophobia.aspx (accessed on November 30, 2011).

The Ottomans.org. http://www.theottomans.org/english/history/index.asp (accessed on November 30, 2011).

"Profile: Egypt's Muslim Brotherhood." *BBC News Middle East.* http://www.bbc.co.uk/news/world-middle-east-12313405 (accessed on November 2, 2011).

The Question of Palestine and the United Nations. United Nations Department of Public Information (March 2003). http://www.un.org/Depts/dpi/palestine/ (accessed on September 16, 2011).

Slim, Randa. "Hezbollah's Most Serious Challenge." *Foreign Policy* (August 5, 2011). http://mideast.foreignpolicy.com/posts/2011/05/03/hezbollah_s_most_serious_challenge (accessed on November 30, 2011).

"The Suez Crisis: An Affair to Remember." *Economist* (July 27, 2006). http://www.economist.com/node/7218678 (accessed on November 30, 2011).

"Zionism and the Creation of Israel." *MidEast Web.* http://www.mideastweb.org/zionism.htm (accessed November 3, 2011).

Index

Bold type indicates major entries. Illustrations are marked by (ill.).

Q

R

Middle East Conflict: Biographies, 2nd Edition

225